"In the psychoanalytic literature, there are many
the communicative function and power of silence, yet there is no major comprehensive monographic treatment of silence. This book closes that gap. After an overview of culturally determined forms of silence, the two main sections focus on its significance in psychoanalytic treatments. The clinical perspective is complemented – and this is the special feature of this volume – by empirical studies using the method of conversation analysis, which provides results that will be inspiring for clinicians. The editors have succeeded in creating a book that shows silence as a fundamental human phenomenon, a tremendously important element of talk and interaction, and an inevitable part of psychoanalytic treatments."

Werner Bohleber, PhD, former editor-in-chief of the German psychoanalytic journal *Psyche*

"This impressive edited volume significantly contributes to our knowledge of an under-investigated aspect of the talking cure. Silence, as readers will come to learn from a large cast of international experts, is not a mere absence of talk, but a resource that serves crucial interactional, therapeutic, and cultural functions. This book will become essential reading for anyone wanting to know more about the importance of silence and silencing."

Peter Muntigl, Simon Fraser University

"This book contains a wealth of information about silence and silencing. It examines how psychoanalysts and psychotherapists understand their patients' and their own silences during therapy sessions, but also the influence of culture, religion, history, and music on human behaviour and communication patterns, as well as the research on short and long silences in the psychotherapeutic treatment room. I consider this publication to be a monumental textbook that increases the reader's knowledge of human nature and our awareness of therapeutic approaches to silence and silencing."

Vamik D. Volkan, MD, emeritus professor of psychiatry, University of Virginia, and the author of *Psychoanalytic Technique Expanded: A Textbook on Psychoanalytic Treatment*

Silence and Silencing in Psychoanalysis

This book is the first comprehensive treatment in recent decades of silence and silencing in psychoanalysis from clinical and research perspectives, as well as in philosophy, theology, linguistics, and musicology.

The book approaches silence and silencing on three levels. First, it provides context for psychoanalytic approaches to silence through chapters about silence in phenomenology, theology, linguistics, musicology, and contemporary Western society. Its central part is devoted to the position of silence in psychoanalysis: its types and possible meanings (a form of resistance, in countertransference, the foundation for listening and further growth), based on both the work of the pioneers of psychoanalysis and on clinical case presentations. Finally, the book includes reports of conversation analytic research of silence in psychotherapeutic sessions and everyday communication. Not only are original techniques reported here for the first time, but research and clinical approaches fit together in significant ways.

This book will be of interest to all psychologists, psychoanalysts, and social scientists, as well as applied researchers, program designers and evaluators, educators, leaders, and students. It will also provide valuable insight to anyone interested in the social practices of silence and silencing, and the roles these play in everyday social interactions.

Michael B. Buchholz is professor of social psychology at the International Psychoanalytic University (IPU), Berlin, Germany. He is a psychologist and social scientist and a fully trained psychoanalyst. He is head of the Doctorate Program at IPU and chair of the social psychological department. He has published more than 20 books and more than 350 scientific papers on topics like analysis of therapeutic metaphors and therapeutic conversation, including the supervisory process, and he has contributed to psychoanalytic treatment technique, theory, and history. Michael has conducted conversation analytic studies on group therapy with sexual offenders about therapeutic "contact scenarios," as well as on therapeutic empathy. His current interest is the study of therapeutic talk-in-interaction using Conversation Analysis.

Aleksandar Dimitrijević, PhD, is a clinical psychologist and psychoanalyst. He works as a lecturer at the International Psychoanalytic University and in private practice in Berlin. He has given lectures, seminars, university courses, and conference presentations throughout Europe and in the United States of America. He is author of many conceptual and empirical papers about attachment theory and research, psychoanalytic education, and psychoanalysis and the arts, some of which were translated into German, Hungarian, Italian, Slovenian, Spanish, and Turkish. He has also edited or co-edited ten other books or special journal issues, the most recent of which is *Ferenczi's Influence on Contemporary Psychoanalytic Traditions* (with Gabriele Cassullo and Jay Frankel, 2018).

RELATIONAL PERSPECTIVES BOOK SERIES

ADRIENNE HARRIS,
STEVEN KUCHUCK & EYAL ROZMARIN
Series Editors

STEPHEN MITCHELL
Founding Editor

LEWIS ARON
Editor Emeritus

The Relational Perspectives Book Series (RPBS) publishes books that grow out of or contribute to the relational tradition in contemporary psychoanalysis. The term *relational psychoanalysis* was first used by Greenberg and Mitchell[1] to bridge the traditions of interpersonal relations, as developed within interpersonal psychoanalysis and object relations, as developed within contemporary British theory. But, under the seminal work of the late Stephen A. Mitchell, the term *relational psychoanalysis* grew and began to accrue to itself many other influences and developments. Various tributaries—interpersonal psychoanalysis, object relations theory, self psychology, empirical infancy research, feminism, queer theory, sociocultural studies, and elements of contemporary Freudian and Kleinian thought—flow into this tradition, which understands relational configurations between self and others, both real and fantasied, as the primary subject of psychoanalytic investigation.

We refer to the relational tradition, rather than to a relational school, to highlight that we are identifying a trend, a tendency within contemporary psychoanalysis, not a more formally organized or coherent school or system of beliefs. Our use of the term *relational* signifies a dimension of theory and practice that has become salient across the wide spectrum of contemporary psychoanalysis. Now under the editorial supervision of Adrienne Harris, Steven Kuchuck and Eyal Rozmarin, the Relational Perspectives Book Series originated in 1990 under the editorial eye of the late Stephen A. Mitchell. Mitchell was the most prolific and influential of the originators of the relational tradition. Committed to dialogue among psychoanalysts, he abhorred the authoritarianism that dictated adherence to a rigid set of beliefs or technical restrictions. He championed open discussion, comparative and integrative approaches, and promoted new voices across the generations. Mitchell was later joined by the late Lewis Aron, also a visionary and influential writer, teacher and leading thinker in relational psychoanalysis.

Included in the Relational Perspectives Book Series are authors and works that come from within the relational tradition, those that extend and develop that tradition, and works that critique relational approaches or compare and contrast them with alternative points of view. The series includes our most distinguished senior psychoanalysts, along with younger contributors who bring fresh vision. Our aim is to enable a deepening of relational thinking while reaching across disciplinary and social boundaries in order to foster an inclusive and international literature.

A full list of titles in this series is available at https://www.routledge.com/mentalhealth/series/LEARPBS.

Note

1 Greenberg, J. & Mitchell, S. (1983). *Object Relations in Psychoanalytic Theory.* Cambridge, MA: Harvard University Press.

Silence and Silencing in Psychoanalysis

Cultural, Clinical, and Research Perspectives

Edited by Aleksandar Dimitrijević and Michael B. Buchholz

LONDON AND NEW YORK

First published 2021
by Routledge
2 Park Square, Milton Park, Abingdon, Oxon OX14 4RN

and by Routledge
52 Vanderbilt Avenue, New York, NY 10017

Routledge is an imprint of the Taylor & Francis Group, an informa business

© 2021 selection and editorial matter, Aleksandar Dimitrijević and Michael B. Buchholz; individual chapters, the contributors

The right of Aleksandar Dimitrijević and Michael B. Buchholz to be identified as the authors of the editorial material, and of the authors for their individual chapters, has been asserted in accordance with sections 77 and 78 of the Copyright, Designs and Patents Act 1988.

All rights reserved. No part of this book may be reprinted or reproduced or utilised in any form or by any electronic, mechanical, or other means, now known or hereafter invented, including photocopying and recording, or in any information storage or retrieval system, without permission in writing from the publishers.

Trademark notice: Product or corporate names may be trademarks or registered trademarks, and are used only for identification and explanation without intent to infringe.

British Library Cataloguing-in-Publication Data
A catalogue record for this book is available from the British Library

Library of Congress Cataloging-in-Publication Data
Names: Dimitrijević, Aleksandar, editor. | Buchholz, Michael B., editor.
Title: Silence and silencing in psychoanalysis: cultural, clinical, and research aspects/edited by Alexsander Dimitrijević and Michael B. Buchholz.
Description: Abingdon, Oxon; New York, NY: Routledge, 2021. | Series: Relational perspectives book series | Includes bibliographical references and index. |
Identifiers: LCCN 2020024060 (print) | LCCN 2020024061 (ebook) | ISBN 9780367367046 (hbk) | ISBN 9780367367053 (pbk) | ISBN 9780429350900 (ebk)
Subjects: LCSH: Psychoanalysis and philosophy. | Silence–Psychological aspects. | Psychoanalytic interpretation. | Psychotherapy.
Classification: LCC BF175.4.P45 S54 2021 (print) | LCC BF175.4.P45 (ebook) | DDC 150.19/5–dc23
LC record available at https://lccn.loc.gov/2020024060
LC ebook record available at https://lccn.loc.gov/2020024061

ISBN: 978-0-367-36704-6 (hbk)
ISBN: 978-0-367-36705-3 (pbk)
ISBN: 978-0-429-35090-0 (ebk)

Typeset in Times
by Deanta Global Publishing Services, Chennai, India

Contents

List of figures	xiv
List of contributors	xv
Editors' introduction	xxi
Acknowledgements	xxvii

PART I
Cultural 1
Introduction to Part I 3

1 Silence in phenomenology: Dream or nightmare? 7
   DONNA ORANGE

2 Encountering religious and spiritual silences 26
   COLUM KENNY

3 Forms and functions of silence and silencing: An approach from linguistics and conversation analysis with reference to psychotherapy 41
   SILVIA BONACCHI

4 The many forms of silence in music 62
   HELGA DE LA MOTTE-HABER

5 Silence in an age of distraction 87
   PATRICK SHEN

PART II
Clinical   99
Introduction to Part II   101

6   Cultural function and psychological transformation of silence in psychoanalysis and psychoanalytic psychotherapy   105
ELSA RONNINGSTAM

7   Varieties of silence in the analytic setting   128
SALMAN AKHTAR

8   Silence as a manifestation of resistance   142
ALEKSANDAR DIMITRIJEVIĆ

9   Silence is golden (usually)   157
JAY FRANKEL

10   Winnicott's capacity for silence in understanding and healing human nature   171
MARGARET BOYLE SPELMAN

11   Silence as a condition for analytic listening: Site, situation and process   187
HOWARD B. LEVINE

12   Silence and silencing of the traumatized   198
ALEKSANDAR DIMITRIJEVIĆ

PART III
Research   217
Introduction to Part III: Researching silence in (therapeutic) conversation   219

13   Measuring silence: The pausing inventory categorization system and a review of findings   233
HEIDI M. LEVITT AND ZENOBIA MORRILL

14   Pauses are conversations: What they tell us when we listen   251
MICHAEL B. BUCHHOLZ

15 **How to move on after silences: Addressing thought processes to restart conversation** 275
FLORIAN DREYER AND MICHAEL M. FRANZEN

16 **The interaction order of silent moments in everyday life: Lapses as joint embodied achievements** 307
ANNA VATANEN

17 **Speaking that silences: A single case multi-method analysis of a couple's interview** 333
MICHAEL B. BUCHHOLZ, OLIVER EHMER, CHRISTOPHER MAHLSTEDT, STEFAN PFÄNDER, AND ELKE SCHUMANN

Index 371

Figures

15.1	RLRI model	278
16.1	Frames of Example 1	309
16.2	Frames of Example 2	315
16.3	Frames of Example 3	317
16.4	Frames of Example 4	319
16.5	Frames of Example 5	321
16.6	Frames of Example 6	322
16.7	Frames of Example 7	324
17.1	"Yes, but Felix"	341
17.2	The brooding thinker	345
17.3	Start of the gesture, hands on the left knee, gaze into emptiness, strike of a gesture uprising and outside	346
17.4	The apex of the gesture, hands open, head bowed, and gaze downwards. Depressed face	347
17.5	The refraction phase of the gesture: return to start	348
17.6	Musicalization of Mary's complaint: "and that is hurting me"	350
17.7	The pause before Mary's saying "the lemon pie is so:: sour"	356
17.8	Mary fighting with her tears, Peter tackling with fingers	357
17.9	Mary: "The lemon pie is so:: sour" – her face lightened and fresh	357
17.10	Mary surprised by her own discovering how sour the lemon pie is, face in hands, feet in tension upwards, Peter having stopped tackling his fingers, looking down bored	358

Contributors

Salman Akhtar is professor of psychiatry at Jefferson Medical College, and a training and supervizing analyst at the Psychoanalytic Center of Philadelphia. He is an internationally sought speaker and teacher, who has given plenary addresses at the meetings of both the International Psychoanalytic Association and American Psychoanalytic Association. His more than 400 publications include 100 authored and edited books. He has received the prestigious Sigourney Award in 2012. He has also published nine collections of poetry.

Silvia Bonacchi is professor of German studies and Intercultural Communication at the University of Warsaw, Faculty of Applied Linguistics, Institute of Specialised and Intercultural Communication (ISIC), deputy director for Science and Organisation. Her research interests cover pragmalinguistics, intercultural communication studies, multimodal communication, conversational and discourse analysis; her main research fields are (im)politeness and verbal aggression, multilingualism and multiculturalism, history of thought, and Gestalt Theory in language.

Margaret Boyle Spelman is a chartered clinical and counselling psychologist, a psychoanalytic psychotherapist, and an organizational psychologist in private practice in Dublin, Ireland. She worked for more than three decades as a clinical psychologist in the Irish health services. Margaret is a former Board Member and Director of Clinical Training at the Irish Institute of Psychoanalytic Psychotherapy and past member of the executive council of the Psychological Society of Ireland and has been a director on the boards of the Irish Forum for

Psychoanalytic Psychotherapy, the Irish Council for Psychotherapy and its Psychoanalytic Section.

Florian Dreyer is a PhD candidate in Linguistics at the Albert-Ludwigs University in Freiburg and lecturer at the International Psychoanalytic University (IPU) in Berlin. Using Multimodal transcripts and Motion Tracking algorithms, he analyzes how patterns of embodied interaction evolve over the course of video-taped psychotherapy sessions. He has published on formulations and empathy in psychotherapy, as well as on Conversation Analysis of child psychotherapy.

Oliver Ehmer is an assistant professor of linguistics at the University of Freiburg (Germany). He studied speech science and received his PhD and Habilitation in Romance Linguistics. His research is informed by interactional, cognitive, and usage-based linguistic approaches. He investigates the grammatical and embodied resources through which people construct meaning and organize interaction. In his current work he focuses on knowledge transmission in instructional interaction, imagination, and remembering in conversation, and the emergence and sedimentation of linguistic structures.

Jay Frankel is an adjunct clinical associate professor, and clinical consultant in the New York University Postdoctoral Program in Psychotherapy and Psychoanalysis; associate editor, and previously executive editor, of the journal *Psychoanalytic Dialogues,* and author of three dozen journal articles and book chapters, and numerous conference presentations, on topics including the work of Sándor Ferenczi, trauma, identification with the aggressor, authoritarianism and mass submission to authority, the analytic relationship, play as inherent to the therapy process, child psychotherapy, relational psychoanalysis, and others.

Michael M. Franzen is a university lecturer and research associate for Social Psychology at the International Psychoanalytic University (IPU) Berlin (Germany); current research projects: recurrent practices in therapeutic interactions (PhD student in Linguistics at Institute of German Language (IDS) Mannheim).

Colum Kenny is Professor Emeritus of Communications at Dublin City University. A lawyer and journalist, he has been chair of the Masters in

Journalism programme at DCU, where he developed original courses including a module on 'Belief & Communication'. A founding and council member of the Irish Legal History Society, he has served on the Broadcasting Authority of Ireland.

Howard B. Levine, is a member of APSA, PINE, the Contemporary Freudian Society, on the faculty of the NYU post-doc Contemporary Freudian track, on the editorial board of the *IJP* and *Psychoanalytic Inquiry*, editor-in-chief of the *Routledge Wilfred Bion Studies Book Series*, and in private practice in Brookline, Massachusetts. He has authored many articles, book chapters, and reviews on psychoanalytic process and technique, intersubjectivity, and the treatment of primitive personality disorders.

Heidi M. Levitt is a professor in the Clinical Psychology program within the Department of Psychology at The University of Massachusetts Boston. Using mixed-method and qualitative approaches, she has studied common factors such as significant moments, emotion, narrative, and silence within psychotherapy. In her psychotherapy research, she develops principles for clinical practice that focus on critical decisions within the moment-to-moment process of facilitating change in therapy. In another line of research, she studies LGBTQ gender communities and the process of healing from and resolving sexual minority stressors. She has been awarded Fellow status by the American Psychological Association via Division 5 [Quantitative and Qualitative Methods], Division 29 [Psychotherapy], Division 32 [Society of Humanistic Psychology], and Division 44 [Society for the Psychology of Sexual Orientation and Gender Diversity].

Christopher Mahlstedt was born in 1985 in Delmenhorst. After spending most of his youth at the local music school, he decided to study jazz saxophone at the *Hochschule für Musik Franz Liszt Weimar* in 2006. He finished his BA in 2012 at the *Jazz-Institut Berlin*, which belongs to the *Universität der Künste* and *Hochschule für Musik Hanns Eisler*. In his master studies he focused on the musical dimensions of a couples' interaction. In the field of music-psychology Christopher Mahlstedt researched on the topic "Comparing perceived emotions while playing and listening to music". As a member of the *Deutsche Gesellschaft für Psychoanalyse and Musik e.V.* he gave workshops and a lecture at the symposia in 2017, 2018 and 2019. From 2019 on he has been working as a psychologist with people with disabilities e-entering the general labour market.

Zenobia Morrill is a doctoral candidate at the University of Massachusetts Boston where she studies Counseling Psychology. Her research is broadly focused on conceptual and ethical issues related to pursuing a social justice mission in psychology including topics such as psychotherapy, qualitative inquiry, and global mental health. Her dissertation explores the intersection of humanistic and feminist multicultural theoretical approaches and navigating expert and cultural power dynamics within the psychotherapy process.

Helga de la Motte-Haber, taught for eight years at the Department of Musicology at the Technical University in Berlin. She went on to hold a Professorship at the Pädagogische Hochschule in Köln. In 2002, she was awarded the Glaskasten Marl for the Mediation of Sound Art, and in 2015 was awarded an honorary doctorate by the Hochschule für Musik und Darstellenden Kunst, Hannover. Helga is an Honorary member of the Deutsche Gesellschaft für Musikpsychologie and Gesellschaft für Musikforschung. She has published research on the psychology of music, sound art, and music of the twentieth century.

Donna Orange is educated in philosophy, clinical psychology, and psychoanalysis. She teaches at NYU Postdoc (New York) and at IPSS (Institute for the Psychoanalytic Study of Subjectivity, New York), and in private study groups.

Stefan Pfänder, Prof. Dr., is an interactional linguist and full professor (Chair) at Freiburg University, Germany and Co-Director of the Hermann Paul School of Linguistics Freiburg-Basel. One of his main research areas is Collaborative Storytelling in multimodal talk-in-interaction. This research focus has been developed out of an interdisciplinary research project with social psychology, funded by the Fritz Thyssen Foundation. Narrative research within the Thyssen project was followed up during a FRIAS senior fellowship and the successful co-acquisition of a research training group funded by the German Research Foundation, a lead agency project funded by the German

Science Foundation and the SNF on "Emergent Remembering" and a cooperative project with cultural anthropology and psychosomatics/body psychotherapy which investigates and models the synchronization of interactants in everyday and clinical interaction and is co-funded by the Freiburg Institute for Advanced Studies (FRIAS) and the European Union (Marie-Curie Fellowships).

Elsa Ronningstam is an associate professor of Clinical Psychology in the Department of Psychiatry at Harvard Medical School, and a clinical psychologist and psychotherapist in the Gunderson Outpatient Clinic at McLean Hospital. She is also a psychoanalyst, and a member of the Faculty of Boston Psychoanalytic Society and Institute, where she has been teaching since 2006.

Elke Schumann graduated in German and Slavic Studies at the University of Freiburg and in 2007 received her doctorate in the field of neuro-linguistics. Since 2009, she has been working at the Department of Romance Languages of the University of Freiburg, in the field of conversation analysis and multimodal interaction analysis—for example in projects on autobiographical narration (retelling, collaborative remembering) and on synchronization in embodied interaction. She also works as a lecturer for communication and conversation in nursing and medical contexts.

Patrick Shen is a filmmaker and the founder of Transcendental Media. Patrick's cinematic works include the award-winning films *Flight from Death: The Quest for Immortality*, *The Philosopher Kings*, *La Source*, and the SXSW 2016 film, *In Pursuit of Silence*. His films have received 24 awards and 11 nominations, and have been featured on the TED blog, CNN, *Huffington Post*, *NY Times*, *LA Times*, *Boston Globe*, and the *Washington Post*. In 2009, Patrick was the recipient of the *Emerging Cinematic Vision Award* from Camden International Film. In 1999, Patrick was invited to the White House to meet with President Clinton in recognition of his work on the Emmy-nominated documentary *We Served With Pride*. Since 2012, Patrick has been lecturing and teaching filmmaking workshops all over the globe as a film envoy for the U.S. State Department and the USC School of Cinematic Arts for their American Film Showcase. Patrick is currently at work on a new slate of films which include *Day of a Stranger*, *In Praise of Shadows*, and *Four Minutes*.

Anna Vatanen, works currently as a postdoctoral research fellow at the Research Unit for Languages and Literature at the University of Oulu, Finland. She has also worked at the Centre of Excellence on Intersubjectivity in Interaction at the University of Helsinki. Vatanen is an interactional linguist and conversation analyst who works on video-recorded Finnish and Estonian conversational data. Her research has been published, for instance in *Research on Language and Social Interaction*, *Journal of Pragmatics*, and several edited volumes. The phenomena she has studied include silent moments in interaction, units of language, various social actions, turn-taking organization, and multiactivity.

Editors' introduction

Silence seems to be, at the same time, omnipresent and extremely difficult to grasp. From Zen Buddhism to twentieth-century (post)classical music, silence is central to so many traditions around the globe. From Hamlet to Heidegger, everyone has contemplated it at least once. Nevertheless, who can claim to have understood its meaning and importance, given that it disappears as soon as you try to put it into words? It is not more accessible even when we learn that fMRI scanning shows that (1) brains of people who practice silent meditation work more efficiently (Prochnik, 2010, pp. 13–14); (2) during listening to symphonic music, it is the silent intervals that produce the most intense, positive brain activity (ibid, p. 14); and (3) as many as 45,000 fatal heart attacks per year can be attributed to noise-related cardiovascular strain (Prochnik, 2010, p. 15). How are we supposed to understand this? Lovers cherish silent understanding; true friends can be of help to one another without words; many people cannot achieve concentration without silence. Why is silence this important for humans?

When we first stumbled upon the idea of a book about silence in psychoanalysis, we were instantly sure that there had to be at least a shelf full of such volumes. We have seen and heard silence mentioned as a symbol of psychoanalytic practice so many times that, once we started talking about the silence, it seemed to us it had always been at the core of our professional lives. We were not able, however, to come up with a familiar title in that initial conversation, and, worse still, subsequent literature searches led nowhere. To our utmost surprise, we had to conclude that not a single book of this kind had been published in the last several decades.[1]

It then turned out that it was different in the history of psychoanalysis, though only for a time. It seems that Theodore Reik, the pioneer of psychoanalytic research of both silence and music, was right when he wrote "we shall take a lonely path, scarcely trod upon, for we shall talk about the silence of the psychoanalyst" (1948, p. 124). In the first half-century of the development of psychoanalysis, silence was quite an obscure topic, uncontested in its particular position at the centre of the analytic attitude. To quote from Reik again: "In psychoanalysis, too, what is spoken is not the important thing. It appears to us more important to recognize what speech conceals and what silence reveals" (ibid., p. 127). As many other traditions recognized before or simultaneously, a voice from the depths, from the unconscious, can hardly be heard, if we do not clear the more superficial layers for it to start appearing.

In the 1950s and 1960s, tides turned, probably because of the appearance of new psychoanalytic paradigms, and silence became a prominent topic. A brief search of PEP-Web leads to papers, panel reports, book reviews. Suddenly, everyone grew talkative about silence, mostly in terms of psychoanalytic technique (resistance and how to overcome it), but for the first time also in terms of silence as a possible precondition for therapeutic growth and maturation.

Since 1980, the number of psychoanalytic papers on silence has steadily risen. We believe that this is a consequence of the proliferation of publications, and not so much of new conceptualizations or research. There seem to have been only a few important papers about silence in recent decades, and there are two basic approaches to it. First, there are case presentations, about patients who are silent for long periods of time, or of different diagnostic categories, going even to the level of pathologizing the phenomenon with expressions like "the silent patient" (Ferber, 2004; Fuller & Crowther, 1998; Hadda, 1991; Leira, 1995). Second, some papers offer connections between psychoanalysis (usually Bion or Lacan) and artistic, mystic, or spiritualistic approaches (like Götzmann, 2011; Leky, 2012). And finally, more and more authors approach silence in the therapeutic space from the intersubjective perspective (Bravesmith, 2012; Knutson & Kristiansen, 2015; Little, 2015).

Opposite to this situation in the world of psychoanalysis, we discovered a plethora of research about silence in many other traditions. It even has a historiography of its own (Corbin, 2018), it is deemed "one of the least understood elements of our lives" (Brox, 2019), and many people publish memoirs of what they have discovered thanks to long periods of silence (see, for instance, LeClaire, 2010; Maitland, 2009). However, silence turns out to be, first of all, a central topic of mysticism, spirituality, and theology (see, for instance, Hanh, 2015). There are possibly more books in this domain than one can read in a lifetime, yet it seems safe to claim without fear of simplification, that silence is a rare, if not unique, factor that can unite all religious traditions: numerous teachers, not to say prophets, from different epochs and regions, ascribe a precious role in their "enlightenment" to silence. It is always a necessary method of self-exploration, and some consider it the cardinal trait of a god, the being, or the non-being.[2] Many find its vanishing from contemporary Western world to be a sign of the societal spiritual and ethical decadence, and its focus on material and ephemeral values.

It is almost the same when it comes to the importance of silence in music. Although we may be focused on sound, i.e. tones, during a concert we hear an equal amount of silence before, in-between, and after the tones. This turns silence into a matter of great attention for both composers and performers.[3] One need not look for examples further than the despair expressed in the *morrendi* of Shostakovich's late string quartets, his most intimate compositions,[4] or deliberate experiments with protracted silences in the middle of a concert performance by Jim Morrison of "The Doors". And then there is language and the puzzle of its relationship to silence: are they opposite to one another, necessary for one another, and how are they understood and dealt with by two or more interlocutors?

That is also precisely how this book opens. The first section of this collection consists of five essays that help position psychoanalytic approaches inside a broader cultural and societal context. Precisely because psychoanalysts have long thought and written as if history began with Sigmund Freud, this book provides insight into the centuries, or even millennia, of human curiosity about the phenomenon of silence. The space allotted to this, only one book section, cannot do justice to numerous prolific traditions of mystics, philosophers, poets, and all inquisitive minds, who found silence important, if not central, for their quests.

The second and most extensive section of the book is, and understandably so, devoted to psychoanalysis. Psychoanalysis is often ridiculed, in films, novels, and caricatures, for notoriously long silences that can happen in sessions and which are almost impossible to imagine in everyday conversations. Psychoanalysts believe that these silences are necessary and have a specific meaning depending on the phase and moment of "the dialogue of two unconsciouses". When clients are silent, psychoanalysts try to understand the affective tone and possible meanings of this form of expression, so that "talking cure" sometimes turns into "being-silent-together cure". Also, those who perform the talking cure are seldom talkative: even if a psychoanalyst were confident that s/he had understood something important about a patient's inner life, s/he would speak only scarcely and briefly. We hope that the seven chapters of this section provide enough insight into these processes. This is of the utmost importance because, although not always recognized, silence has a central place in psychoanalysis:

- as a part of the analytic attitude, where it is considered a necessary element without which the psychoanalytic process would never develop;
- in the domain of psychoanalytic technique, where skills of working with silence as a manifestation of resistance, and with one's own contribution to it, are what distinguishes a master clinician;
- because joint patient–analyst silence can sometimes be a sign that a phase of inner growth, the objective and purpose of the treatment, and fundamental change on psychic levels where words cannot reach, is taking place.

Furthermore, we hope to elucidate a need to listen to psychoanalytic silences in two different registers. Beside the perspective of clinical psychoanalysis (and the three types of papers mentioned earlier), the second approach is based on the findings of psychotherapy process research, where silence as one of the elements of psychotherapeutic conversations and its relations with other elements can be studied with various qualitative and quantitative techniques for data analysis. Strangely, this opportunity has never been used thus far, and this book offers unique and primary insights into silence in psychoanalysis obtained by the method of conversation analysis. The overlaps are inspiring, as when, for instance, researchers and clinicians agree that there are different types of silence in psychotherapy. As editors, we also hope that these types are all well described in this book, so that practitioners will find this helpful in everyday work with patients and researchers will find it inspirational for future studies.

Just as psychoanalysis must find its place in the broader context of various approaches to the human condition and to human existence, it also must remain open to the feedback that comes from empirical research. If nothing more, research methodology teaches us that it is impossible to take several steps at a time, which, in our enthusiasm for psychoanalysis, we tend to do, and thus create prematurely closed and overdeveloped systems. Furthermore, research presented in this volume shows where our weaknesses and blind spots are, as well as how to study them in order to become capable of overcoming them.

We cannot, of course, make an objective assessment or prediction of the possible contributions of, and reception to, this book. And, possibly, we cannot hope for much more than to turn the attention of the psychoanalytic community to the phenomenon of silence in the consulting room, and beyond, and thus save silence from the fate of being merely the "empty time" of psychoanalytic treatment.

Notes

1 That is, not in English and German, because we did discover one in French, albeit it consisted mostly of the reprints of classical papers (Nasio, 1998). Also, the collection of German translations of papers from the *International Journal of Psychoanalysis* was published under the title "Silence" (Junkers, 2007). However, none of the chapter titles included the words "silent" or "silence" with the exception of Elsa Ronningstam's contribution (also included in this book). The other ones mention that silent episodes happen in psychoanalytic treatments, but they do not focus on this topic. We think that this indicates how deeply the need for a monographic treatment of the topic is felt, but how little was said about.
2 This can give silence an ontological status at a transcendental level, higher than that of natural phenomena.
3 The same is also true of theatre performances, where suspended silence can be the most exciting part of the evening.
4 Probably the most widely known example of this, John Cage's *4'33"*, seems to suffer from the plague that has corrupted most contemporary artworks. In essence, they are merely illustrations of societal, philosophical, ideological, or religious principles, with very little artistic creativity to them.

References

Bravesmith, A. (2012). Silence lends integrity to speech: Transcending the opposites of speech and silence in the analytic dialogue. *British Journal of Psychotherapy*, *28*(1), 21–34.

Brox, J. (2019). *Silence. A Social History of One of the Least Understood Elements of Our Lives*. Boston, MA: Houghton Mifflin Harcourt.

Corbin, A. (2018). *A History of Silence. From the Renaissance to the Present Day* (J. Birrell, Trans.). London: Polity. (Original work published in 2016).

Ferber, S. G. (2004). Some developmental facets of silence: A case study of a struggle to have a proximity figure. *British Journal of Psychotherapy*, *20*(3), 315–332.

Fuller, V. G., & Crowther, C. (1998). A dark talent: Silence in analysis. *Journal of Analytical Psychology*, *43*(4), 523–543.
Goetzmann, L. (2011). "The sound of silence" — O in der modernen Malerei. *Psyche*, *65*(12), 1139–1155.
Hadda, J. (1991). The ontogeny of silence in an analytic case. *International Journal of Psycho-Analysis*, *72*(1), 117–130.
Hanh, T. N. (2015). *Silence. The Power of Quiet in a World Full of Noise*. San Francisco, CA: Harper One.
Junkers, G. (Ed.) (2007). *Ausgewählte Beiträge aus dem "International Journal of Psychoanalysis"*. Tübingen: Ed. Diskord.
Knutson, H. V., & Kristiansen, A. (2015). Varieties of silence: Understanding different forms and functions of silence in a psychotherapeutic setting. *Contemporary Psychoanalysis*, *51*(1), 1–30.
Leclaire, A. D. (2010). *Listening Below the Noise: The Transformative Power of Silence*. New York: Harper Perennial.
Leira, T. (1995). Silence and communication: Nonverbal dialogue and therapeutic action. *The Scandinavian Psychoanalytic Review*, *18*(1), 41–65.
Leky, L. G. (2012). For ever silent?. *Dialog zwischen Psychoanalyse und Zen? Psyche*, *66*(12), 1139–1160.
Little, S. (2015). Between silence and words: The therapeutic dimension of quiet. *Contemporary Psychoanalysis*, *51*(1), 31–50.
Maitland, S. (2009). *A Book of Silence. A Journey in Search of the Pleasures and Powers of Silence*. London: Granta Books.
Nasio, J.-D. (1998). *Le silence en psychanalyse*. Second printing. Paris: Payot & Rivages.
Prochnik, G. (2010). *In Pursuit of Silence. Listening for Meaning in a World of Noise*. New York: Doubleday.
Reik, T. (1948). *Listening with the Third Ear*. New York: Pyramid Books.

Acknowledgements

We would like to thank all the contributors whose work has made this book possible and whose patience has made the lengthy editing process bearable.

We were, from the start of our planning this volume, greatly encouraged by Lewis Aron, PhD, who accepted this project a mere 45 minutes after we had sent him the first description, called it a "no-brainer", and initially agreed to write a concluding chapter for it. Overcoming his untimely death may be an unsurmountable task for relational psychoanalysis as a school of thought and a community, and we miss his clear insight and profound thought in this book, too.

Michael B. Buchholz wants to express thanks to have been invited as senior research fellow to the FRIAS (Freiburg Institute of Advanced Studies) in 2018. This institution grants an atmosphere of lively studying and communicating only topped by the cooperation with Professor Stefan Pfänder, who organized his stay in Freiburg, Christopher Mahlstedt, Elke Schumann, and Oliver Ehmer.

Further, Michael wants to express a deep "thank you!" to Professor Dr. Dorothea Huber (Munich and IPU Berlin), who granted access to the audio tapes of the "Munich Psychotherapy Study". My collaborators, especially Marie-Luise Alder, Florian Dreyer, and Michael Franzen (formerly Dittmann), carefully transcribed 45 of these sessions and created the basis for a comparison between psychoanalysis, cognitive-behavioral therapy, and psychodynamic conversation in our CEMPP-Project (Conversation analysis of Empathy-Psychotherapy Process). This project, then, was part of our PICOR-Network (Psychoanalytic Interdisciplinary Network for Conversation Research) where Prof. Dr. Gabriele Brandstetter, Prof. Dr. Christoph Wulf (both from Freie Universität, Berlin), and Prof. Dr. Andreas Hamburger, our colleague from IPU, continuously cooperated for more than five years in a qualitative multi-method project of analysing interviews with holocaust survivors, school disputes, dance projects by Pina Bausch, a video-taped child therapy, and other audio- or video-taped material. Jasmine Bleimling, Veronika Heller, and Ingrid Kellermann contributed with wonderful ideas for the analyses of balance, rhythm, and resonance. Sometimes we were full of enthusiasm about the richness and detailed micro-perspectives of e.g. analyses of movement, as they were developed in the science of dance and nobody in psychotherapy process research had ever heard of it. However, sometimes the psychotherapists in our sessions, and conversation analysts, were not lazy in contributing their views. It was a new multi-method experience of an excellent quality. We were able to present results of this singular cooperation over many years and in two PICOR-conferences in 2015 and 2016. A German publication followed in *Paragrana*, 2018.

We are grateful to Jay Frankel, PhD, for being always available for advice and feedback, and to our former students Shira Dushy and Julianne Walther, who saved us much time by performing thorough literature searches and unifying references lists.

Many thanks also to the Routledge editorial team, especially Kate Hawes and Hannah Wright, for their guidance and patience.

We also thank Taylor & Francis for their permissions to reprint the following:

Salman Akhtar's chapter "Listening to silence" from his book "*Psychoanalytic Listening. Methods, Limits, and Innovations*," published by Karnac in 2012.

Donna Orange's chapter "Silence in phenomenology: Dream or nightmare?" from her book "*Psychoanalysis, History, and Radical Ethics. Learning to Hear*", published by Routledge in 2019.

Elsa Roningstam paper "Cultural function and psychological transformation in psychoanalysis and psychoanalytic psychotherapy," published in *The International Journal of Psychoanalysis*, 2006, 87(5), 1277–1295.

Part I

Cultural

Part I

Introduction to Part I

When a patient is silent, we do not think about the nature of the phenomenon of silence. Preoccupied with the psychological meaning of that person's silence at that specific moment, we tend to overlook the fundamental questions about it. Silence, for instance, certainly exists in nature, but is it a natural phenomenon? Is silence in nature a mere absence of sound or a phenomenon with foundation and purpose of its own? Is it integral to beauty and communication? Should it be a part of our value system? These questions transcend the domains of psychology and psychoanalysis, but they are integral to many individuals and traditions in theology, philosophy, aesthetics, or linguistics. This book opens with essays about these fundamental questions related to silence as human experience and as a (super)natural phenomenon.

In the first chapter, Donna Orange utilizes her double identity of a philosopher and a psychoanalyst to review various phenomenological approaches to silence ("pregnant silence," "threatening silence," "trauma-frozen silence," and "silence as complicity") mostly dwelling on Merleau-Ponty and Levinas. She also connects her intense sense of social responsibility with her profound clinical experience and shows that silence can also be full of violence, traumatizing, especially when it becomes active silencing. There is, however, also hope in the form of "unfrozen silence" and of personal statements like "no one in our generation ever beat their children."

Colum Kenny then enriches this volume by a silence-walk through the history of religions from Egypt and ancient Greek culture to Christianity, balanced by reporting on silence in India and other Eastern traditions, as well as in Judaism and Buddhism. Kenny masterfully weaves the story about facets of all these traditions that claim one and the same thing—"God is silence." He also sets the experience of deep silence in meditation in relation to religious experience—and separates one from the other in order to open this experience for people who do not want to join any kind of religious group thinking.

A prominent linguist, Silvia Bonacchi from Warsaw, delivers an insight into how silence and silencing are understood in her field. The linguistic approach has been to set silence in relation to speech, and silence has been viewed as the absence of speech. Bonacchi only refers to these starting points in order to step over to relevant contemporary authors who have written about the rhetoric of silence. She describes the role and function of silencing with distinctions like endo- and exophasia, which are sometimes followed by esophasia; sometimes we use words for thinking, sometimes for speaking, and sometimes both modes are responded to by respecting the deep need for silence. Sometimes we regain our sense of being within a conversational flow from which we emerge with better cognitive and emotional elaboration. This is an important dimension of therapeutic talk. Interestingly, this same dimension is found in the conversation analytic study by Dreyer and Franzen (Chapter 15). Silence is endowed with a quality to restore human resonance, as Bonacchi describes with reference to many psychoanalytic authors, such as Michael Balint. She also gives rich hints as to the communicative power of the silencing process.

Helga de la Motte-Haber's chapter graces this volume with an extremely knowledgeable contribution about silence in music. She starts by considering whether to speak of silence in music could be thought of as a joke. Along the way, we learn that it is not, that it is more a paradox, a paradox of humanity, which she spells out with great precision. As music has deep origins in religious rituals of all kinds, it is no wonder that this dimension is again touched upon. De la Motte-Haber analyses the role of silence in the creations of many composers, from Händel, Haydn, and Mozart, to Debussy and Ravel, to Xenakis, Nono, Feldman, and John Cage.

When Patrick Shen, a prominent film-maker and author of *In pursuit of Silence*, quotes the words of the ancient wise man Chuang Tzu, who wishes to talk to a man who has forgotten all words, he illuminates the same paradox that was tackled in de la Motte-Haber's chapter. To talk to someone who has lost all words seems impossible, but we are led to understand that in studying silence sometimes talking is the more serious problem. Shen gives a critique of a culture which has lost a deeper sense of how this paradox can be balanced. Culture, in this view, is a human achievement to teach its members how to handle times of talk and to profoundly value times of silence. Losing touch with this issue equals losing depth. And this sounds like a very precise description of contemporary Western culture, where Shen hopes "we may devise methods to restore and protect that silence for future generations."

We believe that the position and role of silence in psychoanalysis cannot be fully grasped without being contextualized by the five essays in the first part and hope that the direct link will be obvious to readers too.

Chapter 1

Silence in phenomenology
Dream or nightmare?

Donna Orange

Silence, at best, is ambiguous. It may protect, attack, or give consent. One may be reduced to silence either by humiliation, or out of failure to find the right word. One may be struck silent by art, by holiness, by outrageousness. Persons or groups may find themselves silenced through acts of familial, cultural or political domination, even by violence. Probably every human being has some experiences with silence, with silencing others, or having been silenced. David Kleinberg-Levin provides an evocative list, challenging all explanations:

> What comes to mind are these: the heavy silence of one going deep into her grief; the silence of one whom unspeakable horror has rendered speechless; the awkward silence of shame or embarrassment; the aggressive silence of one who is hiding his guilt; the benumbed silence of a deep depression; the silence of an anger which accuses and causes hurt by using silence as a weapon; withholding the kindness of speech; the heroic silence of the political prisoner, who refuses to surrender the names of his comrades even under extremes of torture; the guarded silence of citizens who must endure constant surveillance under the rule of a police state; the silence of timidity; the silence of shyness; the silence of rapt attention; the silence of prayer; the silence of spellbound anticipation; the silence of a joy that needs to be deeply felt.
>
> (p. 100)

No phenomenological account of silence can fail to address this array, if only indirectly.

But what is silence itself? Phenomenology, of course, ever allergic to universalizing definitions and mindful of Wittgenstein's family resemblances, will look to descriptions and contexts. Let us first trace a meandering path through silence in the company of phenomenologists Jean-Paul Sartre, Maurice Merleau-Ponty, and Emmanuel Levinas. Finally, we return to the everyday silences of clinical work, to see what phenomenologists might teach working psychoanalysts, and vice versa.

Pregnant silence

Sartre, writing after the war about the resistance, saw silence as a heroic act of freedom. Kleinberg-Levin's list surely has Sartre's "republic of silence" in mind:

> We were never more free than during the German occupation. We had lost all our rights, beginning with the right to talk. Every day we were insulted to our faces and had to take it in silence. Under one pretext or another, as workers, Jews, or political prisoners, we were deported EN MASSE. Everywhere, on billboards, in the newspapers, on the screen, we encountered the revolting and insipid picture of ourselves that our oppressors wanted us to accept. And, because of all this, we were free. Because the Nazi venom seeped even into our thoughts, every accurate thought was a conquest. Because an all-powerful police tried to force us to hold our tongues, every word took on the value of a declaration of principles…
>
> (In Liebling, 1947, pp. 498–500)

Thus Sartre teaches us first about the effects of violent silencing. He continues, indicating that keeping silence may also be heroic:

> All those among us – and what Frenchman was not at one time or another in this situation who knew any details concerning the Resistance--asked themselves anxiously, "If they torture me, shall I be able to keep silent?" Thus the basic question of liberty itself was posed, and we were brought to the verge of the deepest knowledge that man can have of himself.… It was completely forlorn and unbefriended that they held out against torture, alone and naked in the presence of torturers, clean-shaven, well-fed, and well-clothed, who

laughed at their cringing flesh, and to whom an untroubled conscience and a boundless sense of social strength gave every appearance of being in the right. Alone. Without a friendly hand or a word of encouragement. Yet, in the depth of their solitude, it was the others that they were protecting, all the others, all their comrades in the Resistance. Total responsibility in total solitude – is this not the very definition of our liberty?

(In Liebling, 1947, pp. 498–500)

Merleau-Ponty, explicitly addressing Sartre but implicitly speaking to all who have considered silence a mere lack of noise or the opposite of speech, provides another surprising account in his 1952 "Indirect Language and the Voices of Silence". Silence speaks, in particular through the work of Cezanne or Klee.[1] From depths before, after, under, and between words or music, but intricately involved in them and providing to them layers of meaning, silence can be full, generous, and generative. "We should consider speech before it has been pronounced," Merleau-Ponty later wrote, "against the ground of silence which precedes it, and without which it would say nothing" (1973, pp. 45–46). When the conductor raises her baton to evoke a "Kyrie" or the expected notes of Beethoven's Fifth Symphony, when a pause follows an unexpected question, silence creates the breath or ground for music, for painting, or for language. At the end of a talk, a story, or a concert, a moment of silence, unpremeditated, may testify to the depth of feeling produced in the audience. When someone has revealed something shockingly painful, perhaps the loss of a child or a terminal prognosis, a reverent, receptive, compassionate silence must often precede any few words that may be possible. "Oh, oh, oh," may be all we can say. Silence may accompany and witness.

Merleau-Ponty, however, meant to speak a silence even more inclusive and originary than what his earlier words have suggested to me. As in Schelling before him, he came in his last years to identify silence with nature itself,[2] not contrasted with language—"language lives only from silence"[3]—but as its very underpinning. A language, he wrote, "sometimes remains a long time pregnant with transformations which are to come… even if only in the form of a gap, a need, or a tendency" (1964, p. 41). In its indirectness, all language is silence (1964, p. 43). In his recent *Merleau-Ponty and the Face of the World: Silence, Ethics, Imagination, and Poetic Ontology* (2016), Glen Mazis places silence at the center of

Merleau-Ponty's early account of perception as well as of his mature work on chiasm and intertwining. Silence becomes the invisible source of the visible. Not a literal silence, it occurs in painting, in music, in poetry. Expressive and lyrical, it gives sense to the sensible.

But this silence can be stumped. We can avoid it, but only at our peril. Long before computers and the internet dominated our daily lives, Merleau-Ponty warned of reducing thinking to data-collecting. In the name of science we then test, operate, and transform the data. In this way, he wrote, "we enter into a cultural regimen in which there is neither truth nor falsehood concerning humanity and history, into a sleep or nightmare from which there is no awakening" (1964, p. 122). Like Hegel's night in which all cows are black, we have entered the postmodern era Merleau-Ponty did not live to see, but which he surely described. Our headlong rush into the big-data world comes with a loss of connection to what Merleau-Ponty in his 1952 essay would have called the "voices of silence," as Mazis repeatedly points out.

Of course, such concern about the deadening effects of technical rationality has been common among phenomenologists, especially Heidegger, whose critique in its original form unfortunately included a far-too-casual reference to the production of corpses in concentration camps, as if nothing more had been at stake: "Farming is now a motorized food industry, in essence the same as the fabrication of corpses in gas chambers and extermination camps, the same as the blockade and starving of the peasantry, the same as the fabrication of the hydrogen bomb" (1994, p. 27). Merleau-Ponty takes a very different path, linking cybernetics to a loss of the world's silent and speaking wholeness, but likewise worried that reductive data-focus would lead to disastrous consequences. He might not be surprised by our climate catastrophe. When we lose the sense of shuddering and shivering as silence comes to speech, we may also lose reverence for our world, for the nature that we are.[4]

Phenomenologist Bernard Dauenhauer has considered silence as a phenomenon. He first described two types: intervening silence that punctuates speech, and second, anticipatory and afterwards silences, expectant and haunting. His third type, deep silence, links him to Merleau-Ponty, though he means perhaps something more recognizable, as he speaks of the silence of intimate contact, of liturgical silence, and of the silence-of-the-to-be-said. This last transcends all saying, but he relates it, with Gadamer, to tact and inexpressibility. Dauenhauer provides such examples as Shakespeare's Richard the Third's refusal to answer his victims before their execution (1980, p. 22).

Threatening silences

Phenomenologists have spent less time describing silences that menace, but the disadvantaged of the world know them well. No less pregnant than those Merleau-Ponty described in his many writings about painting, or that Wittgenstein might have included in his "showing" as contrasted with "saying," these have quite another feel. In the natural world, we speak of "the calm before the storm." Patients tell their analysts of parents whose silences were worse than beatings or tirades. Border agents refuse to tell children what has happened to the parents from whom they have been violently separated. People historically excluded from being counted as human—whether from skin color, gender, sexual orientation, religion, or whatever—know that silence concerning their stories wipes out their history and threatens their further significance. "Black Lives Matter" protests such menacing silence. Naming can murder, but so can refusal to name.

Frantz Fanon (1961/2004, 1967/2008), psychiatrist and phenomenologist, described in detail the ways that speaking out of silent assumptions shaped the experience of blacks and of those suffering under colonial regimes. He had sat in Merleau-Ponty's courses, but for him the silence was dangerous. The view or "gaze" that whites directed toward blacks and Arabs, he understood, infected their experience of themselves. Only by recontextualizing their experience, a revolutionary idea, could colonized or enslaved people gain any ground of their own. Diagnosing them as insane, or as inherently defective, silenced their own voices and made them invisible. Fanon's psychiatric work (Gibson, 2014; Gibson & Beneduce, 2017) challenged the colonialist thinking and practice behind the psychiatric hospital and gave voices to the silenced.

Trauma-frozen silences

Another step distant from Merleau-Ponty's silence of "mute radiance" (1964, p. 98), we find the silences involved in traumatic experience. We can distinguish, perhaps, the silence of anticipation, that of abandonment, and the failure of witness, where silence itself becomes trauma *nachträglich*. Assuming an understanding of psychological trauma as shockingly disorganizing experience that leaves a person disoriented in time and distrustful of self and others, we may be tempted to think of noisy violence, of school shootings, of atomic bombs, of rape. Even though these images are too often accurate, the silence before, during, and after them rarely receives its phenomenological due. If phenomenologist Emmanuel Levinas could write that his entire life had been shaped by the anticipation and memory of the Nazi horror, no wonder he wrote in the postwar years of insomnia, of the noisy and ominous silence of the *il y a*, always portending violence. Like single-sided deaf people who suffer from tinnitus, the traumatized hear rumbling noises reminding them that the worst *can* ever happen and that all *can* be lost. Many, of course, scream into the night, at the all-too-present realities in their nightmares. In the daytime they may be mute.

So we should not expect that Levinas would endorse either Sartre's heroic postwar conception of silence, or Merleau-Ponty's mystical, quasi-romantic Schellingian idea. For him, silence gives consent to violence and refuses responsibility.

Trauma therapists and students of extreme dissociative conditions have, I believe, provided important questions to phenomenology, about which philosophers have until now been all too willing to keep silent. What kind of silence fails to speak of climate catastrophe, threatening to make further speech on this subject degenerate into a hopeless wail? What kind of silence keeps me from greeting the miserable homeless person on the street asking me for a euro or a dollar? What kind of silence keeps me from asking what part my own ancestors had in supporting slavery, or in the colonizing of the so-called Terra Nullius, so that indigenous peoples were slaughtered or disastrously reduced? How did these people become nobody for me, so that I cannot even speak their names or their languages?[5] How does a person or a group become "reduced to silence"?

And what about silence as the refusal, out of fear or out of cowardice, to witness to injustice and atrocity? *Shoah* producer Claude Lanzmann speaks of a "conspiracy of silence": "There are many ways of being silent. There are some good ways, and there are very bad ways as well. To talk too much about the Holocaust is a way of being silent, and a bad way of being silent" (Caruth, 2014, p. 208). He does not explain, but clearly he sides with Merleau-Ponty in refusing to oppose speech and silence. Apparently, speech itself can obfuscate historical realities, can minimize, can silence the sufferer of atrocity.

Silence in the phenomenology of Emmanuel Levinas

Like Sartre and Merleau-Ponty, Levinas (1905–1995) lived before and after the occupation in Paris, but unlike them, spent the five war years in captivity in a labor camp near Hannover, where, as a French officer, he survived, but where the Jewish captives were segregated and much more harshly treated. Not for them was the genial "university in the camp" described by fellow phenomenologist Paul Ricoeur a reality. Levinas wrote:

> There were seventy of us in a forestry commando unit for Jewish prisoners of war in Nazi Germany... but the other men, called free, who had dealings with us or gave us work or orders or even a smile—and the children and women who passed by and sometimes raised their eyes—stripped us of our human skin. We were subhuman, a gang of apes. A small inner murmur, the strength and wretchedness of persecuted people, reminded us of our essence as thinking creatures, but we were no longer part of the world. Our comings and goings, our sorrow and laughter, illnesses and distractions, the work of our hands and anguish of our eyes, the letters we received from France and those accepted for our families—all that passed in parenthesis. We were beings entrapped in their species; despite all their vocabulary, beings without language. Racism is not a biological concept; anti-Semitism is the archetype of all internment... It shuts people away in a class, deprives them of expression and condemns them to being 'signifiers without a signified'... How can we deliver a message about our humanity which, from behind the bars of quotation marks, will come across as anything other than monkey talk?
>
> And then, about halfway through our long captivity, for a few short weeks, before the sentinels chased him away, a wandering dog entered our lives. One day he came to meet this rabble as we returned under guard from work. He survived in some wild patch in the region of the camp. But we called him Bobby, an exotic name, as one does with a cherished dog. He would appear at morning assembly and was waiting for us as we returned, jumping up and down and barking in delight. For him, there was no doubt that we were men... This dog was the last Kantian in Nazi Germany, without the brain needed to universalize maxims and drives
>
> (Levinas, 1990, pp. 152–153)

Many have written about this passage, but here I want to ask what it tells the phenomenologist about silence and affirming or negating human dignity. To speak means more than to bark out words ("*Hier ist kein Warum!*" from the guard to desperately thirsty Primo Levi who asks why his small icicle has been swatted away). To speak to the other may mean a joyful greeting from a pet, or from someone who cannot speak my language. It may mean recognizing without words that a sufferer is a fellow human who should never be so mistreated. Colleagues who work daily with victims of torture must listen and listen and listen to the unspeakable, bearing witness to the humanity of the other. Ironically our silent horror at what has been done to these fellow humans begins to undo their tortured silencing, if only a little. This silence trembles, on both sides.

Silence unfrozen

To unfreeze traumatic silences, speaking becomes necessary. Whatever the exact text, "Black lives matter," "Me too," or "Never again," among many, this ethical speaking insists that the silenced and persecuted and murdered ones are human, and that injustice to them requires active response. Indifference by us who profit from the continued silence—we who live in the houses stolen from the deported and murdered Jews of Europe, for example, or on land stolen from indigenous peoples—deepens the trauma and further isolates those traumatized.

Psychoanalysis, the "talking cure," has long known that speaking the unspeakable in the right context can restore, if not cure, traumatized people.[6] Voices from the classical tradition, even after the shameful banishment of Sándor Ferenczi (Dimitrijević, Cassullo, & Frankel, 2018), have spoken for the "soul murdered" and for those nearly destroyed by historical atrocity. Relational psychoanalysis has begun to consider relational trauma, and especially the "self states" it may lead us to disavow (Bromberg, 1994; Bromberg, 1998). Intersubjective systems theorists (Atwood, 2013; Stolorow, 1995) have brought trauma—in development and adulthood—into the center of their phenomenological account of pathogenesis and psychoanalytic process. The shattered experiential world of the traumatized becomes a psychotic state to find connection and understanding by a therapist or analyst who is a brother or sister in the worlds of trauma. Often, as Davoine and Gaudillière (2004) write from a European perspective, the patient's madness finds the analyst's history, and connects so as to undo the wretched silencing.

Attempting to undo silencing psychoanalytically often runs directly into shame. Shame, built into most traumatic experience with its inherent degrading and dehumanizing qualities, does not add to trauma or constitute a defense against awareness of it. Instead, it pre-reflectively disempowers and disentitles the potential speaker. What right have I, so much below any ladder or scale, to speak of mistreatment or injustice done to me? The traumatized person, humiliated in many ways not always evident, has been preemptively silenced by the resulting shame. Why did I not fight off my rapist? Why did I not work harder in the face of the school's rejection of me? Why could I not keep silent after days or weeks of torture? All these questions, and more, disqualify the traumatized from speaking, and from being heard and re-included in human community.

Shamed silence may also result from the community's refusal of witness to massive injustice. Consider, for example, the desperate plight of those psychoanalysts who fled Germany and Austria in the 1930s only to find that many of their colleagues did not want them, either because they feared competition or because of anti-Semitism. Already terrified and alone, often without the language skills they needed, and without the medical credentials to practice in the US, they and their families faced rejection in Britain and the US, as well as terrible losses in Europe. Their traumatic experience has shaped the learning of those of us who have been their students, but has almost never been spoken or written about until recently. We have inherited the fruits of bystandership, reminding me of the words of Emmanuel Levinas, "as if consenting to horror."

Silence as complicity

As usual, Philip Cushman has written the work on ethics, psychology, and torture that I would have wanted to write, with a thoroughness that never masks his commanding prophetic voice. Reminding me of those originals who made me shudder and cower in shame reading Abraham Heschel's *The Prophets*, calling us psychologists to account for our semi-deliberate moral unconsciousness, Cushman holds us responsible—rightly, in my view—for the evils our neglect of ethical education, as well as our thoughtless "individualism, consumer capitalism, neoliberalism, scientism," (2018a, p. 1) have wrought in our name. I have shared his trenchant critiques of these ideologies and attitudes precisely, and thus will not repeat them, but restrict myself to a few related reflections, leaning toward the psychoanalytic, since he has chosen to publish this work in a psychoanalytic journal. Though greatly honored to respond to any work from Cushman, I realize that this piece indicts me along with all our colleagues, that the deep and thick ethical failures he explains in the torture context are running, as he says, like a fault line below our professional communities, preventing us from responding adequately to current crises, leaving us befuddled and confused in just the ways he describes, polluting the work we pursue with good intentions. His prophetic warning is more than urgent.

Like Cushman's, my concerns intersect at the crossroads of philosophy (especially phenomenology, philosophical hermeneutics, and ethics), history (including psychoanalytic history, and the histories of settler colonialism and chattel slavery), climate science, and psychoanalysis. Not for a moment to minimize the importance of all humanistic psychotherapies, it seems important to notice the ways in which psychoanalytic theories may have obfuscated ethical concerns, just as Cushman illuminates in psychology and the "psy disciplines" generally. Though I particularly want to honor those psychologist/psychoanalysts who have led the fight to expose and to end the involvement of psychologists in the US torture program, we must grant that most of us were silent, and even now inadequately horrified by the acts done in our name. I am reminded of the infamous Göring Institute of psychoanalysis in Berlin during the Third Reich, as well as of the doctors I met in Heidelberg, who no longer even call themselves psychiatrists (now it is the faculty of psychosomatics) because of the atrocities their profession had committed "in those years." (The work of Robert Jay Lifton should surely be background reading here). Freud's concern with unconscious motivation has not helped enough, in his time or ours, to challenge organized crimes against humanity.

Where is our commensurate shame? Perhaps the same moral fault lines, made up of individualism, scientism, and Irwin Hoffman's (2009) masterfully described "doublethinking", leading us to moral fog and evasion, now keep us underreacting to the support that organized psychology gave the Bush torture program, which now threatens to resume. All that is needed for evil to prevail is for good people to do nothing, according to an idea often attributed to Edmund Burke.[7] Cushman explains how the deep structure of the psychological professions, almost never examined and brought into dialogue, make it almost impossible to generate the kind of ethical deliberation that might have put on the brakes, or activated the "good people." But given that our deep assumptive structures continue unquestioned by most, what other horrors may we be supporting or overlooking? Our colleagues of color could tell us the answer if we would give them five minutes. So could the millions of climate refugees. So Cushman's prophetic demand to consider our sins of individualistic and consumerist mindlessness—Warren Poland likes to define the unconscious as what we do not want to know about ourselves—also constitutes a call to psychoanalysis, to meaning-and-dialogue-oriented psychotherapy, to a kind of human and ethical work never to be doublethought into a STEM (science, technology, engineering, math) discipline.

Unfortunately, just as Cushman suggests, we contemporary psychoanalysts—like our grandparents who excluded humanistic and ethical voices like Erich Fromm, Erik Erikson, and John Bowlby—lean, perhaps unintentionally, toward ethical ambiguity. Some advocates of multiple self-states,[8] asked who is responsible for voting in their name in elections, fall silent. No one is responsible when everyone is standing in the spaces.[9] (I do it myself, living intricately implicated in an extreme capitalist system that systemically destroys millions of innocent human lives, and the planet that could support them.) The autonomous ego of ego psychology was, of course, too simple to describe complex relationally emergent self-experience, but the developmentally and relationally described ego of Hans Loewald, for example, appropriated from the parents its moral responsibilities. Without a theory and practice of ethical selfhood,[10] I believe, we cannot expect psychoanalysis to lead the "psy disciplines" in creating moral dialogues, even protests, to resist ethical fogs and ambiguities like those that permitted us to stand by while psychologists participated in torture in our names. If we theorize away the possibility of integrity and responsibility, we are lost.

Pretending to be a hard science will not solve our problem. In a STEM discipline, as in our omnipresent devices, everything functions by rules. If the rules are properly formulated, everything runs just fine. Bending the rules will cause crashes. Even malware runs by the rules, showing us that the rules are indeed value-free.[11] In our human sciences trying to be STEM sciences, though, we tend to ignore those ethical problems that cause crashes in human relationships, that reduce human beings to things, in Cushman's elegant and horrifying language:

How did we allow this series of betrayals, humiliations, and sadistic acts to be thought of as a subject of legal debate, instead of recognizing it as an ethical scandal? Torture is an utterly reprehensible act, unjustifiable both ethically and practically. It is a betrayal that wounds the very soul of the prisoner (Apuzzo, Fink, & Risen, 2016), degrades the perpetrator, and undermines the moral integrity of the society that is responsible for it. It starkly illuminates what must be considered the most egregious of human mistakes: treating fellow humans as things to be used, not precious lives to be cherished and honored. It…is the graphic and perhaps most extreme enactment of an instrumental relationship, one that strikes at the very core of human social existence by its objectification of the other and its denial of the limits of one's own understandings. It is in part what the Hebrew prophets meant by idolatry (see Fromm, 1955, 1966): the process by which humans first uncritically admire and worship inanimate and human-made creations such as wealth, automobiles, social status, national emblems, revanchist fantasies, or demagogic behavior, and by so doing are themselves turned into things.

(2018a, p. 10)

No one who remembers Jean Améry's description of the first time he was tortured could claim that Cushman exaggerates. But Améry preceded his story with a quotation from British novelist Graham Greene who commented on photographs of Vietcong torture emerging in the American and British press at the time:

The strange new feature about the photographs of torture now appearing in the British and American press is that they have been taken with the approval of the torturers and are published over captions that contain no hint of condemnation. They might have come out of a book on insect life… Does this mean that the American authorities sanction torture as a means of interrogation? The photographs certainly are a mark of honesty, a sign that the authorities do not shut their eyes to what is going on, but I wonder if this kind of honesty without conscience is really to be preferred over… the old hypocrisy.

(Quoted in Améry, 1980, p. 23)

Améry commented: "The admission of torture, the boldness—but is it still that?—of coming forward with such photos is explicable only if it is assumed that a revolt of public conscience is no longer to be feared" (1980, p. 23). So these questions, possible and actual long before the Bush administration, make it clear that the climate for shoulder-shrugging in the US, and in psychology cultures, was fertile soil, with little opposition to be expected, after 9/11. And psychoanalysis, with a stronger intellectual tradition, could do no better?

But ethical scandals tend not to be the topics of our training, conferences, or journals. Not only do we fail to learn the hermeneutic dialogue necessary to consider ethical questions in depth and to confront their meanings, but when breaches of this magnitude do "occur" (note my minimizing, anonymizing language), we do not immediately devote our next national or international conference to them. A few concerned souls may offer one panel, probably not even a plenary. We do not, for the most part, engage in collective soul-searching, asking how we could have been complicit in so much evil, or even what exactly is wrong with torture.

And yet, why should we be surprised? When famous psychoanalysts have committed egregious sexual boundary violations, sometimes even leading to loss of professional licenses, institutions have protected them despite widespread knowledge, as if the offender's privacy were more important than our duty to protect patients and trainees. Sometimes senior colleagues even invite the offender to social gatherings and continue to teach his papers and books, as if to say to trainees that respecting and protecting patients does not matter. Wink, wink, nod, nod. He or she is one of us. "Could shoot someone on Fifth Avenue and no one would object." Or senior colleagues may blame the patient, to training committees or licensing boards. Of course, the offender cannot then explain to self or others *why* the transgression was wrong, or *why* the boundary is a boundary. Not to mention the confusion of tongues, and debilitating shame, resulting for the patient or trainee. Our collective failure to engage in ongoing ethical dialogues in our training institutes, journals, and conferences stems from the scientism that Cushman and Hoffman describe, and reinforces it. Discussion about ethics usually comes down to making the rules ever more precise—I have just seen the draft of a psychoanalytic institute's 20-page ethics code, which does attempt to be a statement of both values and rules. We keep hoping that precision in our rules will rescue us from needing to engage in moral discourse, and moral reasoning. But we must resort to genuine education. Cushman writes: "The absence of philosophically learned moral discourse in the profession leads to a thin, easily manipulated relation with ethics" (2018b, p. 13). Without practice in such ethical dialogue, leading to practical wisdom, we are like people who need to learn to swim when already drowning. With only rules to guide us, we become experts at bending them, as Cushman warns.

To summarize my first thought, I believe we should heed Cushman's call to take ourselves seriously as an alternative to the valueless, foggy, procedural, reductive, liquid "discourse" of postmodernity. We hermeneuts in psychology and in psychoanalysis (Cushman, 2007, 2011; Orange, 2010, 2011; Stern, 2013) can speak up for racial justice, climate justice, ethical treatment of patients, and opposition to torture, for example. We can invite those who think psychotherapy concerns more than techniques and technologies, and especially those who think it probably concerns something else entirely, to talk ethics with us. Perhaps our conversations, and ethical worries, will bleed out into the larger cultures where they are so urgently needed.

My second thought concerns the reading of history as an ethical project. Scientistic approaches to psychology, psychotherapy, and worst of all, to psychoanalysis, lose track of the old dictum that those who do not study history are doomed to repeat it—a good reason to read the Hoffman report, Cushman's article, and the writings of those closely familiar with this awful story. But worse, by not studying history, including this history, we are already repeating. We continue the fog, the obfuscation "bad things happened," and the evasions. Somebody else did it, far away. Chattel slavery, settler colonialism? Somebody else did it, long ago.

And yet, just this summer, wanting to know more about the history of Maine where I usually spend summers, and looking to Wikipedia as the handiest resource, I "learned" that Maine's history began with the French and the British. Surrounded by names like Penobscot and Kennebec and Passagassawakeag, and having read Wendy Warren's (2016) *New England Bound: Slavery and Colonization in the New World* I remembered that the earliest colonists from Massachusetts had sent others to Maine to take the land and eliminate those few indigenous people who had survived the plagues already brought from Europe. The beauty of Maine hides a brutal, criminal history of over-entitled Europeans appropriating communally held land in the name of religion, but for economic gain. Only a few of its original people remain to protect and honor their Penobscot, Wabanaki cultures. If we look beyond the surface of the history we have been taught, we prepare ourselves for moral questioning.

Thus, I believe that each of us must study some aspect of the history of moral oppression and crimes if we are to develop the needed sensitivities to stop repeating. We already know this in families. Because my nine siblings and I talk about the conditions of our past, it has become possible for one of my younger sisters to write a statement to be read at her funeral: "no one in our generation ever beat their children." Repeating can be stopped, usually through dialogic examination of what went wrong and what it all means, both individually and culturally. Lynching, and its more recent imitators, stops only if we study its history and the attitudes—conscious and unconscious—it expresses. Psychoanalytic devotion to this type of understanding means protecting our precious dialogic legacy from the threat of doublethinking, and from physics envy. In search of scientific legitimacy, we lose and betray the most precious gift we have to offer our patients and the larger world. We also refuse ethical responsibility.

This brings me to my title point, the Miranda warning: you have the right to remain silent. Yes, when I am being approached by law enforcement as if I were a criminal, this precious right may save me. Still, it cannot become my fundamental life organizing principle. When you are starving, falling, being mistreated, being tortured, I may not remain silent. Now we have crossed over from law into ethics. Cushman asks: "How did we allow this series of betrayals, humiliations, and sadistic acts to be thought of as a subject of legal debate, instead of recognizing it as an ethical scandal?" (2018b, p. 10). The difference between parsing out legal distinctions—important as these may be—and responding ethically, corresponds to the difference between machine-like rule-following and protecting the vulnerable Other, whose fate, directly or indirectly, may be in my hands. Learning, over and over, the relation and difference between law and morality requires conversation about such matters from childhood through graduate school and professional education to the end of life. Reading books like lawyer Bryan Stevenson's *Just Mercy* (2014) helps us understand that laws can be seriously unjust, and that, as he often repeats, each person is better than the worst thing he or she has ever done. No moral calculus here, but an ethical conversation about justice beyond law. Reading history, to return to my point above, stretches our moral sensibilities to include people we might not otherwise notice or include in our concerns. In the face of gross injustices all around us, in which we participate pervasively, we do not have the right to remain silent. We psychologists and psychoanalysts are citizens, and fellow human beings.

Philip Cushman has now spoken out, challenging the most fundamental attitudes and assumptions in our professions, breaking our silence on behalf of those who cannot speak for themselves. Who will be next?

In conclusion

Belatedly, we are learning to hear. "Philosophy," Merleau-Ponty wrote in his last work, *The Visible and the Invisible,* "is the reconversion of silence and speech into one another" (1968, p. 169/129).[12] Finding words for the unspeakably beautiful and the unspeakably horrible, inadequate as these words will always be, even perhaps poetic words, philosophy does only one half of its job. In the other half, we lapse back into silence, as Wittgenstein reminded us: whereof we cannot speak, thereof we must remain silent. Silent before that which demands reverence, silence before what exceeds words either by way of sublimity or horror.

The artist faces the same problem as the philosopher: on the wall of Beethoven's house in Heiligenstadt are Kant's words: the starry heavens above and the moral law within. In this very house where Beethoven wrote both his heart-wrenching Testament expressing his suicidal thoughts over his encroaching deafness, and also some of his greatest music, he faced the problem of silence. To break it he wrote music; to accept silence, the music ends, and he walks in the fields.

So a phenomenology of silence arrives at no definition, but finds an omnipresent feature of human life that punctuates and pervades it, under and beyond all the noise. Silence also threatens, as in deafness and in violence. It protects the guilty, often for generations, and creates false innocence. But it may, at times, express the profoundest reverence.

Notes

1 Bindeman (2017, p. 66) quotes: "We usually say that the painter reaches us across the silent world of lines and colors, and that he addresses himself to an unformulated power of deciphering within us that we control only after we have blindly used it—after we have enjoyed the work" (Merleau-Ponty, 1964, p. 45).
2 It remains to study the voice of Spinoza running through *The Phenomenology of Perception* (Merleau-Ponty & Landes, 2012), an influence perhaps deeper than that of Schelling.
3 "Language lives only from silence, everything which we cast to the others lives in this mute land which we do not leave" (Merleau-Ponty, 1968, p. 126).

4 There is far more to be said about Merleau-Ponty's phenomenology of silence, but space limitations and also respect force me to refer the reader on to Glen Mazis.
5 Many questions for the phenomenologist/clinician belong here: Does my silence about race, gender, history, violence, further silence my patient? Do I implicitly try to evade responsibility by my silence?
6 See also the thoughtful and challenging work on restorative justice, e.g. (Stauffer, 2015).
7 Here is the long version: "Whilst men are linked together, they easily and speedily communicate the alarm of any evil design. They are enabled to fathom it with common counsel, and to oppose it with united strength. Whereas, when they lie dispersed, without concert, order, or discipline, communication is uncertain, counsel difficult, and resistance impracticable. Where men are not acquainted with each other's principles, nor experienced in each other's talents, nor at all practiced in their mutual habitudes and dispositions by joint efforts in business; no personal confidence, no friendship, no common interest, subsisting among them; it is evidently impossible that they can act a public part with uniformity, perseverance, or efficacy. In a connection, the most inconsiderable man, by adding to the weight of the whole, has his value, and his use; out of it, the greatest talents are wholly unserviceable to the public. No man, who is not inflamed by vain-glory into enthusiasm, can flatter himself that his single, unsupported, desultory, unsystematic endeavours, are of power to defeat the subtle designs and united cabals of ambitious citizens. When bad men combine, the good must associate; else they will fall, one by one, an unpitied sacrifice in a contemptible struggle." (Burke, 1999).
8 Here I distinguish "states" from parts, with Onno van der Hart and others who expertly and compassionately teach us to treat those sufferers from extreme violence who live in parts not even remembered by other parts.
9 I (Orange, 2018) have discussed this problem at length elsewhere, and noted that Bromberg seems recently to be reversing course toward a more integrated sense of self. It is also true that some proponents of this type of postmodern theory involve themselves in ethical critique and political activism.
10 I am not claiming here that we possess a substantialized or reified thing called "a self" (see critiques by Stolorow, 1995), but rather that the phenomenological and ethical sense of more- or less-integrated selfhood, responsible for actions, attitudes, and bystanding, needs theorizing in psychoanalysis if we are to escape our ethical fog (Orange, 2013).
11 Cushman formulates our STEM aspiration problem perfectly when he writes: "when psychology claims a scientific warrant, it is in the unenviable position of trying to determine good ways for humans to live by using a method that claims it has bracketed off all ideas about good ways to live" (2018b, p. 19).
12 I am grateful to Sean Williams (2010) for alerting me to this passage as well as to Merleau-Ponty's important connection to Schelling.

References

Améry, J. (1980). *At the Mind's Limits: Contemplations by a Survivor on Auschwitz and Its Realities*. Bloomington, IN: Indiana University Press.

Apuzzo, M., Fink, S., & Risen, J. (2016, October). How US torture left a legacy of damaged minds. *The New York Times*.
Atwood, G. (2013). *The Abyss of Madness*. New York: Routledge.
Bindeman, S. (2017). *Silence in Philosophy, Literature, and Art*. Leiden, The Netherlands: Brill.
Bromberg, P. M. (1994). "Speak! That I May See You": Some reflections on dissociation, reality, and psychoanalytic listening. *Psychoanalytic Dialogues*, 4(4), 517–547.
Bromberg, P. M. (1998). *Standing in the Spaces: Essays on Clinical Process, Trauma, and Dissociation*. Hillsdale, NJ: Analytic Press.
Burke, E. (1999). Thoughts on the cause of the present discontents. Liberty Fund (Ed.), *Select Works of Edmund Burke* (vol. 1, p. 146). http://www.opencultu re.com/2016/03/edmund-burkeon-in-action.html.
Caruth, C. (2014). *Listening to Trauma: Conversations with Leaders in the Theory and Treatment of Catastrophic Experience*. Baltimore, MD: Johns Hopkins University Press.
Cushman, P. (2007). A burning world, an absent God: Midrash, hermeneutics, and relational psychoanalysis. *Contemporary Psychoanalysis*, 43(1), 47–88.
Cushman, P. (2011). So who's asking? Politics, hermeneutics, and individuality. In: R. Frie & W. Coburn (Eds.), *Persons in Context: The Challenge of Individuality in Theory and Practice* (pp. 21–40). New York and London: Routledge.
Cushman, P. (2018a). The earthquake that is the Hoffman report on torture: Toward a re-moralization of psychology. *Psychoanalysis, Self and Context*, 13(4), 311–334.
Cushman, P. (2018b). *Travels with the Self: Interpreting Psychology as Cultural History*. New York: Routledge.
Dauenhauer, B. P. (1980). *Silence, the Phenomenon and Its Ontological Significance*. Bloomington, IN: Indiana University Press.
Davoine, F. and J.-M. Gaudillière (2004). *History Beyond Trauma: Whereof one Cannot Speak, Thereof One Cannot Stay Silent*. New York: Other Press.
Dimitrijević, A., Cassulo, G., & Frankel, J. (Eds.) (2018). *Ferenczi's Influence on Contemporary Psychoanalytic Traditions: Lines of Development – Evolution of Theory and Practice over the Decades*. New York and London: Routledge.
Fanon, F. (2004). *The Wretched of the Earth* (R. Philcox, Trans.). New York: Grove. (Original work published 1961).
Fanon, F. (2008). *Black Skin, White Masks* (R. Philcox, Trans.). New York: Grove. (Original work published 1967).
Fromm, E. (1955). *The Sane Society*. New York: Henry Holt.
Fromm, E. (1966). *You Shall Be as Gods: A Radical Interpretation of the Old Testament and Its Tradition*. New York: Henry Holt.
Gibson, N. C. (Ed.) (2014). *Decolonizing Madness. The Psychiatric Writings of Frantz Fanon* (L. Damon, Trans.). New York: Palgrave Macmillan.
Gibson, N. C., & Beneduce, R. (2017). *Frantz Fanon, Psychiatry and Politics*. London: Rowman & Littlefield International.
Heidegger, M. (1994). *Bremer und Freiburger Vorträge*. Frankfurt am Main: Klostermann.

Hoffmann, I. (2009). Doublethinking our way to "scientific" legitimacy: The desiccation of human experience. *Journal of the American Psychoanalytic Association*, 57(5), 1043–1069.
Kleinberg-Levin, D. M. (2008). *Before the Voice of Reason: Echoes of Responsibility in Merleau-Ponty's Ecology and Levinas's Ethics*. Albany, NY: State University of New York Press.
Lévinas, E. (1990). *Difficult Freedom: Essays on Judaism*. Baltimore, MD: Johns Hopkins University Press.
Liebling, A. J. (Ed.) (1947). *The Republic of Silence* (R. Guthrie, Trans.). San Diego, CA: Harcourt Brace.
Mazis, G. A. (2016). *Merleau-Ponty and the Face of the World: Silence, Ethics, Imagination, and Poetic Ontology*. Albany, NY: SUNY Press.
Merleau-Ponty, M. (1964). *Signs* (R. McCleary, Trans.). Evanston, IL: Northwestern University Press.
Merleau-Ponty, M. (1964). *The Primacy of Perception, and Other Essays on Phenomenological Psychology, the Philosophy of Art, History, and Politics*. Evanston, IL: Northwestern University Press.
Merleau-Ponty, M. (1968). *The Visible and the Invisible: Followed by Working Notes*. Evanston, IL: Northwestern University Press.
Merleau-Ponty, M. (1973). *The Prose of the World*. Evanston, IL: Northwestern University Press.
Merleau-Ponty, M. & Landes, D. A. (2012). *Phenomenology of Perception*. Abingdon, Oxon/New York: Routledge.
Orange, D. M. (2010). *Thinking for Clinicians: Philosophical Resources for Contemporary Psychoanalysis and the Humanistic Psychotherapies*. New York: Routledge.
Orange, D. M. (2011). *The Suffering Stranger: Hermeneutics for Everyday Clinical Practice*. New York: Routledge/Taylor & Francis Group.
Orange, D. M. (2013). A pre-Cartesian self. *International Journal of Psychoanalytic Self Psychology*, 8(4), 488–494.
Orange, D. M. (2018). Multiplicity and integrity: Does an anti-development tilt still exist in relational psychoanalysis? In: L. Aron, S. Grand & J. Slochower (Eds.), *Decentering Relational Theory* (pp. 148–172). New York: Routledge.
Stauffer, J. (2015). *Ethical Loneliness: The Injustice of Not Being Heard*. New York: Columbia University Press.
Stern, D. B. (2013). Psychotherapy is an emergent process. *Psychoanalytic Dialogues*, 23(1), 102–115.
Stevenson, B. (2014). *Just Mercy: A Story of Justice and Redemption*. New York: Spiegel & Grau.
Stolorow, R. D. (1995). An intersubjective view of self psychology. *Psychoanalytic Dialogues*, 5(3), 393–399.
Warren, W. (2016). *New England Bound: Slavery and Colonization in Early America*. New York: Liveright Publishing Corporation.
Williams, S. (2010). *Silence and phenomenology: The movement between nature and language in Merleau-Ponty, Proust, and Schelling* [Doctoral dissertation, University of Oregon]. http://hdl.handle.net/1794/10917.

Chapter 2

Encountering religious and spiritual silences

Colum Kenny

Some people savour silence simply for the purpose of assisting relaxation. Others do so especially because silence is conducive to reflection and contemplation. Some savour it because they have experienced in an attentive or meditative silence a sense of being nurtured, guided or inspired, either by God (as they perceive and believe in God) or by another sacred force or spirit.

There are various kinds of silence and various ways in which silence may have value for the spiritual or religious person. While not resorting to an elaborate taxonomy of silence, I have elsewhere classified it by reference to a dozen different and clearly defined categories (Kenny 2011a, pp. 1–47). In the religious sphere alone silence may be valued, for example, as a signifier of receptivity and respect in the presence of a spiritual teacher, as a skillful means of calming the mind and body, or as a vehicle of divine or sacred communication, inspiration and transcendence. It is worth noting that experiences of silence in palliative and spiritual care, psychotherapy and counselling support the existing recognition in religious circles of the value of silence as not only a context but also as both a skill and a practice (Bassett, Bingley and Brearley 2018).

The ineffable

The understanding of the nuances of silence as a phenomenon is complicated by the fact that spiritual experiences may be represented by religious people as being an encounter with the 'ineffable', with that which defies or transcends precise expression in language. As the classic Chinese wisdom text known as the Tao Te Ching puts this, 'The name that can be named is not the enduring and unchanging name' and 'He who knows [the Tao] does not [care to] speak [about it]; He who is [ever ready to] speak about it does not know it. He [who knows it] will keep his mouth shut and close the portals...' (Lao Tse 1891, sections 1, 56).

That some people make assertions of the ineffable as a defensive means of protecting self-delusion by invoking mystery or as a way of defying rational discourse by resorting to mute defiance is clearly possible, but one may not assume from this that the experience of silence is therefore entirely explained by reference to blind faith, mental illness, denial or fantasy; for meditative experiences are frequently difficult to put into words adequately. It is like the difference between biting into an apple and just talking about tasting one. The *fact* of experience in the life of an individual is central to grasping the significance of theories of silence in religious and spiritual contexts. For this reason, amongst others, individuals who have had a spiritual experience may be reluctant to share it because they sense a gulf between themselves and those who have never experienced silence in the same way. For example, as the authors of an introduction to a special issue of the *Journal of Clinical Psychology* devoted to psychotherapy with religious and spiritual clients have put it, 'a hesitancy might stem from fear of being pathologized for their beliefs' (Worthington and Aten 2009, p. 125).

The sense of an eloquent existential silence is one that some poets and writers share with the overtly religious or spiritual. In the 1870s, for example, the novelist George Eliot strikingly proclaimed in her novel *Middlemarch* (1994, p. 162) that,

> If we had a keen vision and feeling of all ordinary human life, it would be like hearing the grass grow and the squirrel's heart beat, and we should die of that roar which lies on the other side of silence. As it is, the quickest of us walk about well wadded with stupidity.

In Africa the power of silence to move people was enunciated in Swahili verses of the nineteenth century entitled 'Silence'. These took as their starting point an old Swahili saying, 'Deep silence makes a loud noise' and cautioned people to respect silence because it has 'a future' (Harries 1962, p. 257; Madan 1903, p. 154).

Folk rituals

A belief in the efficacious power of silence has long been reflected in various folk rituals around the world, although some critics might classify these as superstitions rather than religious or spiritual practices. Among the Yucares people in what is now central Bolivia, the Franciscan friar Lacueva found in the early 1800s that the manufacture of pottery was a function reserved for women who solemnly sought appropriate clay in the most sequestered parts of the forest: 'While they are at work they observe certain ceremonies and never open their mouth, speaking to each other by signs, being persuaded that one word spoken would infallibly cause all their pots to break in the firing' (Frazer 1911–15, vol. 2, pp. 204–205). A similar custom existed in Europe with respect to the picking of certain plants for particular purposes. For example, in Germany, into modern times Thüringen, peasants held that 'if the root of the yellow *mullein* (Verbascum ["Our Lady's Flannel"]) has been dug up in silence with a ducat [gold coin] at midnight on Midsummer's Eve, and is worn in a piece of linen next to the skin, it will preserve the wearer from epilepsy' (Frazer 1911–15, vol. 11, p. 63).

Egypt to Greece

Priestly texts from ancient Egypt and Mesopotamia included many prescriptions of silence (McEvilley 2002, p. 285). Silence was a significant feature of worship in Egypt more than a thousand years before Christ: 'In the opinion of the sages… the most effective means of gaining the favor of God is contemplative silence and inner communion' (Breasted 1912, pp. 355–356). Egyptians depicted their god Horus as a child with a finger in, or to, his mouth. He was seen by the Greeks as the god of silence, whom they named Harpocrates. The Greek philosopher Pythagoras trained in Egypt and highly valued silence, his followers being satirized on that account. However, they were also respected for it, with Plutarch noting that Pythagoreans did not eat fish because they respected the fishes' silence, 'and they thought silence to be divine, since the Gods without any voice discover their meaning to the wise by their works' (Plutarch 2002, vol. 3, p. 422).

India

While various wisdom traditions have long encouraged people to sit or kneel in silence, to 'be still and known that I am God' as one Jewish text has it (Psalm 46, v.10), recent developments have seen a quiet 'mindfulness' being advocated for largely self-centered, secular objectives that include physical relaxation, good health and concentrated efficiency. However, whatever the ancillary personal benefits of mindful meditation, a religious or spiritual harvesting of silence is ultimately justified or judged by reference to its bearing fruit in compassionate action towards others. For example, Mahatma Gandhi wrote that:

> The sannyasi [Hindu ascetic] has renounced the society of men to live in silence and solitude. Even when he moves among men, he will not indulge in idle conversation… Yet the *sadhu*'s [holy man's] lack of interest in the personalities and events of the world does not at all mean that he is a self-centred egotist. Quite the reverse…
> (Abhishiktananda 1975, p. 8).

One of many Indians who have preached the virtues of silence was the influential Sri Aurobindo (1872–1950), yogi and activist for political independence. The aim of his method of practice is a spiritual realization that not only helps to liberate mankind's consciousness but also transform mankind's nature. An integral part of that practice is learning to be silent, for as he explained:

> The silence opens the mind and the rest of the being to greater things, sometimes to the cosmic consciousness, sometimes to the experience of the silent Self, sometimes to the presence or power of the Divine, sometimes to a higher consciousness than that of the human mind; the mind's silence is the most favourable condition for any of these things to happen.
> (cited at Chaudhuri 1960, p. 70)

Judaism

The Jewish 'Tractata Berakoth' tells us that, 'The pious men of old used to wait an hour before they said the Tefillah, that they might direct their hearts towards God [or The Place]' (Mishnah 1933, p. 5). This sentiment may owe something to the seminal experience of the prophet Elijah on the mountain called Horeb, that 'mountain of God' also known as Mount Sinai. He went there fearing for his life, under threat from Jezebel, and passed the night in a cave. Then, 'the word of the Lord' came to him and said (1 Kings 19: 9–15):

'Go out and stand on the mountain before the Lord, for the Lord is about to pass by.' Now there was a great wind, so strong that it was splitting mountains and breaking rocks in pieces before the Lord, but the Lord was not in the wind; and after the wind, an earthquake, but the Lord was not in the earthquake; and after the earthquake a fire, but the Lord was not in the fire; and after the fire a sound of sheer silence. When Elijah heard it, he wrapped his face in his mantle and went out and stood at the entrance of the cave. Then there came a voice to him that said, 'What are you doing here, Elijah?'.

One is reminded of Mohammed being folded in a cloak when he received visions in the cave at Hira (Surah 73, i; 74, i).

I have written elsewhere of the complexity involved in translating this remarkable passage about Elijah from the original, particularly where the concept of some kind of 'sheer' or pure or great silence is not a common one in the Hebrew scriptures (Kenny 2011a, pp. 237–244). Davies believes that the contrast here between silence on one side and wind, earthquake and fire on the other is significant in distinguishing the Jewish God from deities of the elements. The former transcends elements. However, Davies also acknowledges an 'unresolved interplay' between silence as an absence of noise and silence as a mode of God's speech, 'since the God who inhabits the silence is a God who speaks' (Davies and Turner 2002, pp. 207–209).

Judaism and certain other religions include the practice of a day dedicated to rest, a sabbath. This may be seen as useful even to secularists today as a means of encouraging therapeutic silence when public and private spaces are colonized by commercial and other noise. Mudge believes that 'In a world of busyness bordering on "madness" [referring here to fanatical and foolish behaviour and not to serious mental illness], technological dominance, and constant, unreflective activity, a renewed spirituality of the Sabbath is essential for a flourishing, fulfilling and spiritual life, for both children and adults' (Mudge 2018, pp. 260–274; Sim 2007).

Buddhism

Religious or spiritual respect for silence as a source of enlightenment is of course not confined to the West. It is also very much a part of Buddhism among other eastern traditions. For example, one of the central figures in the history of Tibetan Buddhism is Milarepa, whose story of hardship for the sake of spiritual enlightenment is often recounted and who is frequently depicted sitting in a meditative position while cupping his ear.

The Buddha is reported to have remained silent on at least one occasion when faced with a complex philosophical question, not because he had no answer to give but because he was concerned that the correct answer might have upset his questioner as it was beyond that person's level of spiritual understanding. In the same way, there are many stories of Zen monks responding enigmatically to their students' queries. In such cases of 'noble silence' the response of the master should not be judged to be high-handed or anti-philosophical but as considered and considerate.

A principal purpose of being silent in Buddhism is to quieten the mind and passions and encourage deliberation or 'right speech', meaning speech that is compassionate. Beyond that, mindful presence to the silence itself can be refreshing and inspirational in various ways. This is not to say that Buddhist traditions are without many texts that may be chanted and invocations that are spoken. Similarly, while Judaism and Christianity have a place for silence it is not the foremost feature of either, even if a particular movement such as that of the Quakers gives it a special place in its services of worship.

Christianity

One recently published work surveys a broad field within Christianity and thus reminds us of the great depth and breadth of teachings about silence in that tradition alone (MacCulloch 2013). Its teachings are associated with ways of life that respect silence, concerning which one leading cardinal of the Roman Catholic church today has expounded at length because he believes that '*Dieu est silence* [God is silence]' (Sarah and Diat 2016. Also see https://www.fayard.fr/la-force-du-silence-9782213701080 [Accessed 15 Oct. 2018]).

Jesus himself specifically cautioned against 'heaping up empty phrases as Gentiles do; for they think that they will be heard because of their many words. Do not be like them, for your Father knows what you need before you ask' (Matthew 6:7). He taught his followers the simple and short Lord's Prayer or Our Father. He told them, 'when you pray, go into your room and shut the door and pray to your Father who is in secret; and your Father who sees in secret will reward you' (Matthew 6:5–6). His advice has not deterred many of his followers from devising long and wordy prayers and loudly delivering these in public places of worship.

Jesus withdrew into the solitude of a desert to fast for 40 days and 40 nights, and silent retreats are a feature of some mature spiritual lives. Near the end of his life on earth Jesus also stayed silent when interrogated by the Romans. 'If I tell you, you will not believe; and if I question you, you will not answer', he says to his tormentors (Luke 22:67). Pilate asks him to confirm reports that he is purporting to be 'the King of the Jews' but he replies simply 'You say so'. He stays quiet when Pilate asks him 'What is truth?' (John 18:38). Pilate is 'greatly amazed' by this silence of Jesus (Matthew 27:11–14; Mark 15:1–5). Herod too gets no answer, even though he 'was hoping to see him [Jesus] perform some sign' (Luke 22:66–23:8). Signs and words at this point might have enabled Jesus to escape crucifixion, but his silence speaks eloquently of a spiritual reality that he experiences but his interrogators do not grasp.

From the earliest times, side by side with honoured verbal aspects of Christianity, silence has had a recognized place in religious practice. Isaac, bishop of Ninevah, wrote in the seventh century that,

> If thou lovest truth, thou must love silence. This will make thee illuminated in God like the sun and it will deliver thee from the idle thoughts of ignorance; silence will even unite thee with God... Love silence above all things. It brings thee near the fruit which the tongue is too weak to interpret. At first we compel ourselves to be silent. Then from our silence something is born which draws us towards silence. May God grant thee to perceive that which is born from silence
> (Isaac 1923, pp. 299, 302).

However, silence in all its forms is not always good, and Christians today are ashamed of those in their communities who have failed to speak out strongly against various types of abuse or who have silenced the abused and oppressed in any way.

The Greek appreciation of silence did not end with the demise of the Pythagorean school. The Orthodox Church, inspired in this respect by St Gregory Palamas of the fourteenth century and other practitioners, treasures the Hesychasm tradition of contemplative prayer that teaches the necessity of inner silence. A bishop of that church wrote not long ago that

> The *hesychast*, the person who has attained *hesychia*, inward stillness or silence, is *par excellence* the one who listens. He listens to the voice of prayer in his own heart, and understands that this voice is not his own but that of Another speaking within him.
>
> (Ware 1974, p. 184)

In a certain way the person becomes prayer rather than simply speaking it. Sacred silences such as these are welcomed by spiritual practitioners, and may be distinguished in nature from silences imposed by religious authorities according to hierarchical or gender criteria for example.

The monastic tradition of Christianity has clearly and particularly articulated and formulated the value of silence in an unsurpassed fashion.

While significant aspects of the requirement for silence in monasteries have been an emphasis on the avoidance of sinning by speech and a desire to ensure that teachings are received obediently, the holy nature of silence as a vehicle for divine inspiration has been praised by writers such as Teresa of Avila and John of the Cross. In a commentary, the latter Spanish mystic of the sixteenth century explained that:

> In that nocturnal tranquility and silence and in knowledge of the divine light the soul becomes aware of Wisdom's wonderful harmony and sequence in the variety of her creatures and works. Each of them is endowed with a certain likeness of God and in its own way gives voice to what God is in it. So creatures will be for the soul a harmonious symphony of sublime music surpassing all concerts and melodies of the world. She calls this music 'silent' because it is tranquil and quiet knowledge, without the sound of voices. And thus there is in it the sweetness of music and the quietude of silence. Accordingly, she says that her Beloved is silent music because in him she knows and enjoys this symphony of spiritual music… for even though that music is silent to the natural senses and faculties, it is sounding solitude for the spiritual faculties.
>
> (Kavanagh and Rodriguez 1991, pp. 535–536)

John of the Cross also wrote that 'The Father spoke one Word, which was his Son, and this Word he speaks always in eternal silence, and in silence must it be heard by the soul'. This Spanish mystic believed that 'the knowledge of God is received in divine silence':

> In contemplation God teaches the soul very quietly and secretly, without its knowing how, without the sound of words, and without the help of any bodily or spiritual faculty, in silence and quietude, in darkness to all sensory and natural things.... For him, silence can open one to a special kind of spiritual influence: ... the blessings this silent communication and contemplation impress on the soul, without its then experiencing them, are inestimable...
>
> (Kavanagh and Rodriguez 1991, pp. 88, 92, 439, 626, 689 citing *The Spiritual Canticle*, stanza 39)

A German film documentary, shot in a famous but reclusive Carthusian monastery and released in 2005, provides precious insights into the practical manifestation of beliefs about the value of silence. In that acclaimed production (*Die Grosse Stille*, English title *Into Great Silence*), its director Philip Gröning uses the passage about Elijah, quoted here earlier in English, as an onscreen device to frame the depiction of monastic life at the Grand Chartreuse monastery in France. It has been noted in this context that, 'The salience of Carthusian silence is that it is where they can discern divine presence' (Waistell 2018, pp. 211–228).

Meditation or contemplation

The concept of silence is interwoven with those of meditation and contemplation, terms so fluid that they are often used interchangeably. For its part, meditation may take the form of sitting or kneeling in silence. Behind the sitter's silence may be inner turmoil or a feeling of peace; the meditator may just observe the natural breath pattern or adopt a special breathing technique; he or she may entirely let go words and concepts as they occur or on the contrary may repeat particular holy words or dwell upon an observed or imagined object. The terms 'contemplation' and 'meditation' are each found being used sometimes to indicate active reflection on a particular text or image, and on other occasions to indicate the avoidance of any sustained train of thought and the gentle maintenance of a kind of mental equilibrium that cannot be forced. Some meditators find it helpful to adopt a mantra or to repeat a prayer during meditation or to rest their gaze on an object such as a candle or flower while observing the unforced flow of their breath or the arising and passing of emotions and thoughts—seen like white clouds floating in an otherwise clear blue sky. To some people meditation is a way of getting closer to their God or listening for divine or transcendent inspiration. To others it is just a way of calming the mind and seeing all things more clearly. Some regard such personal outcomes as sufficient, not least for their own mental health, while others insist that meditation is also a fundamental step towards the necessary recognition, development and expression of compassion for one's fellow beings.

Meditation need not be confined to silent locations. When understood as a form or method of mind-training and awareness conducive to compassion, meditation may be practised at all times, even in very noisy situations. The World Community for Christian Meditation is one of the organizations advocating it today.

It is certainly possible to project subconsciously into the silence of sitting meditation or contemplation a desired response to one's emotional needs or conceptual challenges. The voices of silence can then become the echo of one's own wishes or dispositions, a collection of perceptions to be analysed in the same way as reactions to inkblots in the Rorschach Test. However, many mature meditators are acutely aware of this possibility, and world religions include traditions that teach skillful means of avoiding the pitfalls of self-absorption, attachment, delusion and vanity in meditation and contemplation.

Fine, modern explanations of the forceful nature of silence in Christian religious practice have been offered by Thomas Merton and Roger Schütz ('Frère Roger') amongst others. Merton, a Trappist monk and writer who reached out through dialogue with the Dalai Lama and with Thich Nhat Hanh and other Buddhists to explore Asian traditions, wrote that:

> Then, in the deep silence, wisdom begins to sing her unending, sunlit, inexpressible song: the private song she sings to the solitary soul. It is his own song and hers – the unique, irreplaceable song that each soul sings for himself with the unknown Spirit, as he sits on the door-step of his own being, the place where his existence opens out into the abyss of God. It is the song that each one of us must sing, the song God has composed Himself, that he may sing it within us. It is the song which, if we do not listen to it, will never be sung. And if we do not join with God in singing this song, we will never be fully real: for it is the song of our own life welling up like a stream out of the very heart of God.
>
> (Merton 1956, p. 24)

Merton's openness to Eastern traditions complemented his awareness of some secular poetry that also drew sustenance from a well of silence, particularly the poems of Rainer Maria Rilke that echo with contemplative sentiments (McCaslin 2010, pp. 15–25). Rilke wrote, for example, that 'We are far from being able to bear the voice of God, but listen to the nascent message that ceaselessly forms itself from silence, its whisperings reach you…' (*Duisener Elegien: Die Erste Elegie*, translated in Crockatt 2012). For Merton, at times that whispering burned like a fire, as he expressed it himself in his own poem entitled *In Silence*:

> The whole
> World is secretly on fire. The stones
> Burn, even the stones
> They burn me. How can a man be still or
> Listen to all things burning? How can he dare
> To sit with them when
> All their silence
> Is on fire?
>
> (Merton 1957)

It has been claimed that 'More a suggestive than a systematic thinker, Merton generally evokes rather than analyses the meaning he finds in silence' (Teahan 1981, p. 364). During a remarkable trip to Asia that ended tragically in his accidental death, Merton met the Dalai Lama a number of times and noted in his journal that the latter had asked him about the monastic 'rule of silence'. Had he lived, Merton might have shared more of this conversation with his readers. After his death the journal that he had written during his Asian trip was published: it was through a passing reference in this that during the early 1970s the present writer discovered a Buddhist monastery in rural Scotland that Merton had hoped to visit (Merton 1973, pp. 323, 339). It had been founded recently by refugees. Merton's writings in general and that discovery in particular fueled my interest in the spiritual dimensions of silence, an interest that eventually led to my writing a book about the power of silence in many aspects of our daily lives (Kenny 2011a, 2011b).

In his old age Frère Roger (1915–2005), the founder and prior of the ecumenical monastic community of Taizé, also died suddenly, being killed by a deranged person during evening prayer. He once wrote that:

Jesus Christ is the Word of God, and we have to be passive and attentive if we want to hear him. We have to forget ourselves and our little kingdoms, and listen attentively... Strange as it may seem, it is in the silence that we can speak to him best: in the silence of meditation, when we respond to him; in questioning silence, when we wait for him to explain to us what it is he wants us to do or know; in troubled silence, when we know that we are confronted with our Judge, and our whole life is lit up and we see it for what it is, and God invites us to change our ways; in the silence which is a cry for help, when we see that we cannot possibly do what he is asking us, and realize that it is only he who can give us the strength; and in awed silence, when we see him as he allows himself to be seen, and we quail at our own nothingness, and then discover that he is asking us to live as his sons and daughters.

We need times of outward silence, if we are to know the inward sort. Some lucky ones can always find it, but all must be on the lookout for the silent moment that is possible, when no one and nothing can get at them; and it nearly always is possible to find it some time or somewhere.

(Schütz 1957, pp. 60–61)

Elected silence is not the exclusive preserve of religious contemplatives such as Thomas Merton and Brother Roger. Anyone may benefit from devoting time to being silent. Runcorn believes that 'in all the varied encounters of our lives of whatever the nature, silence is part of an inner response that invites us to *deepen* the moment' (Runcorn 1989, p. 4).

Forsaken silence

Even for the most religious spiritual practitioner, one who has a firm belief in the existence of God, silence may cease to be eloquent in any way or to communicate any sense of the ineffable. At such times the silence becomes terrible and a practitioner may feel as forsaken as Jesus himself is said to have felt on the cross. The Japanese novel *Silence*, by Shusaku Endo, takes this existential experience of emptiness as its theme in telling a story of persecuted Jesuit Christian missionaries in Japan. Yet paradoxically, and to the puzzlement of observers unfamiliar with mystical traditions, a person suffering what John of the Cross called '*la noche oscura del alma* [the dark night of the soul]' and who is immersed in such absolute spiritual silence may still see this optimistically as a rite of passage to enlightenment and salvation. Indeed, one psychiatrist has written that 'the dark night of the soul is not restricted to holy people. It can happen to anyone' and can be transformative (May 2004, p. 4). A familiarity with traditions that encompass that transformation may help a sufferer along the way.

Analysis and religious silence

A person who is in crisis concerning spiritual experiences of silence and who turns to another person for help with very personal and sensitive feelings may recoil about the subject if sensing that a friend or counsellor has an indifferent or even hostile attitude towards religion and spirituality. Such a person who seeks counselling and who for one or more reasons values being silent may be particularly receptive to therapists who deploy the 'poetics of pause' as part of their methodology (Carr and Smith 2014, pp. 83–114). What has been seen as an early psychoanalytic disdain for the mystical tradition was 'ominously heightened by [Carl] Jung's apostasy into mysticism and his fascination with its Indian varieties' (Kakar 1982, p. 289). A primary focus on speech may seem to run counter to the significance of silence in Buddhist, Hindi or other teachings. However, the cultural and professional insights of Girindrasekhar Bose, Viktor von Weizsäcker, Sudhir Kakar and others (Kumar et al. 2018, pp. 145–188; Nandy 1995, pp. 81–144) help to bridge any such rift and to encourage a scientific understanding of insights into silence in wisdom traditions and theories of consciousness that are therapeutic. In recent years, materials have been published to assist therapists in integrating spirituality in counselling (e.g., Helmeke and Ford Sori 2006).

Conclusion

The place of silence in religion and meditation is central to any understanding of its function for individuals who consider themselves to be religious or spiritual. Spiritual and religious traditions demonstrate that silence has long been understood to be an intrinsic aspect of everyday reality. Silence continues to be appreciated and cherished today, not only by conventionally religious people but also by some meditators and other 'mindful' people who are not actively a part of any particular religious tradition.

References

Abhishiktananda, S. [Le Saux, H.] (1975). *The Further Shore*. Delhi: ISPCK.
Bassett, L., Bingley, A. F., & Brearley, S. G. (2018). Silence as an element of care: A meta-ethnographic review of professional caregivers' experience in clinical and pastoral settings. *Palliative Medicine, 32*(1), 185–194.
Breasted, J. H. (1912). *Development of Religion and Thought in Ancient Egypt*. London: Hodder & Stoughton.
Carr, E. S., & Smith, Y. (2014). The poetics of therapeutic practice: Motivational interviewing and the powers of pause. *Culture, Medicine and Psychiatry, 38*(1), 83–114.
Chaudhuri, H. (1960). *Sri Aurobindo: The Prophet of Life Divine* (2nd ed.). Pondicherry: Sri Aurobindo Ashram.
Crockatt, I. (Ed.) (2012). *Pure Contradiction: Selected Poems of Rainer Maria Rilke*. Todmorden, UK: Arc Publications.
Davies, O., & Turner, D. (Eds.) (2002). *Silence and the Word: Negative Theology and Incarnation*. Cambridge: Cambridge University Press.
Eliot, G. (1994). *Middlemarch*. Ware, UK: Wordsworth Classics.
Frazer, J. G. (1911–15). *The Golden Bough: A Study in Magic and Religion* (3rd ed., 12 vols.). London: Macmillan.
Harries, L. (Ed.) (1962). *Swahili Poetry*. Oxford: Oxford University Press.
Helmeke, K., & Ford Sori, C. (Eds.) (2006). *The Therapist's Notebook for Integrating Spirituality in Counseling: Homework, Handouts, and Activities for Use in Psychotherapy*. New York and London: Routledge/Haworth Press.
Isaac of Nineveh. (1923). *Mystic Treatises* (A. J. Wensick, Ed. and Trans.). Amsterdam: Uitgave Der Koninklijke Akademie Van Wetenschappen.
Kavanagh, K., & Rodriguez, O. (Eds.) (1991). *The Collected Works of St. John of the Cross*. Washington, DC: ICS Publications.
Kakar, S. (1982). Reflections on psychoanalysis, Indian culture and mysticism. *Journal of Indian Philosophy, 10*(2), 289–297.
Kenny, C. (2011a). *The Power of Silence: Silent Communication in Daily Life*. London: Karnac.
Kenny, C. (2011b). Old silence: New story. *The Merton Journal, 18*(2), 21–28.
Kumar, M., Dhar, A., & Mishra, A. (Eds.) (2018). *Psychoanalysis from the Indian Terroir: Emerging Themes in Culture, Family and Childhood*. Lanham, MD: Lexington Books.
Lao-Tse. (1891). Tao teh king (J. Legge, Trans.). In M. Müller (Ed.), *Sacred Books of the East* (Vol. 39). Oxford: Clarendon Press.
MacCulloch, D. (2013). *Silence: A Christian History*. London: Penguin Books.
Madan, A. C. (Ed.) (1903). *Swahili-English Dictionary*. Oxford: Clarendon.
May, G. (2004). *The Dark Night of the Soul: A Psychiatrist Explores the Connection between Darkness and Spiritual Growth*. San Francisco, CA: Harper.
McCaslin, S. (2010). Transformative solitudes: Merton and Rilke at the pivot of silence. *The Merton Seasonal: A Quarterly Review, 35*(1), 15–25.
McEvilley, T. (2002). *The Shape of Ancient Thought*. New York: Allworth.
Merton, T. (1956). *Silence in Heaven: A Book of the Monastic Life*. New York: Studio Publications/ Thomas Y. Crowell.
Merton, T. (1957). *The Strange Islands: Poems*. New York: New Directions.

Merton, T. (1973). *Asian Journal*. New York: New Directions.
[*The*] *Mishnah* (1933) (H. Danby, Trans.). Oxford: Oxford University Press.
Mudge, P. J. P. (2018). 'Re-souling daily life': Towards a restored spirituality of the sabbath as a cure for 'societal madness'. *International Journal of Children's Spirituality*, *23*(3), 260–274.
Nandy, A. (1995). The savage Freud: The first non-Western psychoanalyst and the politics of secret selves in colonial India. In *The Savage Freud and Other Essays on Possible and Retrievable Selves* (pp. 81–144). Princeton, NJ: Princeton University Press.
Plutarch (2002). *Morals* (T. McEvilley, Ed.). Boston, MA: Little Brown.
Runcorn, D. (1989). *Silence*. Bramcote, UK: Grove.
Sarah, R., & Diat, N. (2016). *La Force du Silence: Contre la Dictature du Bruit*. Paris: Librairie Arthème Fayard.
Schütz, R. [Frère Roger] (1957). *So Easy to Love*. London: Longmans.
Sim, S. (2007). *Manifesto for Silence: Confronting the Politics and Culture of Noise*. Edinburgh: Edinburgh University Press.
Teahan, J. F. (1981). The place of silence in Thomas Merton's life and thought. *Journal of Religion*, *61*(4), 364–383.
Waistell, J. (2018). The salience of silence: The silence of salience. *Journal of Management, Spirituality and Religion*, *15*(3), 211–228.
Ware, K. (1974). The power of the name: The function of the Jesus prayer. *Crosscurrents*, *24*(2/3), 184–203.
Worthington, E., & Aten, J. (2009). Psychotherapy with religious and spiritual clients: An introduction. *Journal of Clinical Psychology*, *65*(2), 123–130.

Chapter 3

Forms and functions of silence and silencing

An approach from linguistics and conversation analysis with reference to psychotherapy

Silvia Bonacchi

Silence and silencing in communicative exchanges

Linguists do not use a single binding definition of silence. Silence is understood generally as an absence of sound (as in the phrase: "the silence of the night"), but in linguistics particularly as an absence of talk (as in the sentence: "She looked out the front window in silence"). This "absence" of talkativeness can be motivated by many reasons: linguistic taboos ("it is not allowed to speak about it"), inexpressibility ("no words can express it"), incapability of verbalising ("we are not able to speak about it"), fear ("we fear sanctions if we speak about it"), disinterest ("it's not worth talking about") and rejection of interaction ("I do not want to speak with you [about it]").[1] In all these cases, the various dimensions of silence become tangible in linguistics in relation to speech, from a "logocentric perspective" (Schmitz 1990, p. 12) that contrasts the *absence* of silence with the *presence* of speech. We can say that silence was "silenced" in linguistics and for a long time it has been considered simply as the abstention from speech, and therefore not relevant for interaction analysis. Although the need to integrate a theory of interaction with a broader assessment of the communicative functions of silence was highlighted as early as the mid-1980s (Tannen & Saville-Troike 1985), only in the last two decades silence has turned out to be an important research field not only for linguistic investigation (Ephratt 2008), but also for all research fields in which communicative exchange is essential, including the analysis of psychotherapeutic interactions between patients and psychotherapists (Alder & Buchholz 2017). In the present chapter I will give a linguistically informed overview of the forms and functions of silence and silencing on the basis of their communicative valence in order to understand how silence and silencing can be used in full awareness by psychotherapists in their work with patients. Silence is not always a sign of communicative failure, but can be very communicative.

Silence in non-dialogical situations (NDS) and in dialogical situations (DS)

Human communication can be verbal, i.e. based on words, and non-verbal, i.e. based on other body resources (gestures, facial expressions, movements, tactile signals). Silence has no voice, but it can relate to other communicative dimensions. When words are replaced by other communication resources (gestures, facial expressions, gaze, body position), silence is "eloquent" (Ephratt 2008) and its observation opens the field to wider multimodal analysis (Hall 1959; Scheflen 1973[2]; Kwiatkowska 1997), which can be useful for a broader investigation of the communicative processes during psychotherapeutic interactions, in particular as markers for fluency or dysfluency in the verbal exchange.

Regardless of whether the communication is verbal or nonverbal, we can distinguish between *dialogical* situations, in which our communicative behaviour (verbal and nonverbal) is Other-referential, i.e. directed to the Other, and *non-dialogical*, i.e. concerning self-referential situations in which we do not want to reach the Other.[3] A fundamental criterion for classification of the forms and functions of silence is therefore the difference between silence states that emerge in situations in which speech, i.e. interactional exchange through words, is considered not necessary (*non-dialogical* situations – NDSs) and silence states that emerge when speech is expected for the communicative exchange with the Addressee (*dialogical* interactions or situations – DS). In the following part, we will consider the moments in which silence can be a sign of communicative failure and should be interpreted in order to overcome this impasse.

Silence in non-dialogical situations (NDS)

Silence may accompany activities that do not require words. In German, the fundamental distinction between silence states in DS and NDS is reflected in the words *Schweigen* (abstaining from speech, remaining silent) and *Stille* (being quiet). Remaining silent is the absence of articulation, being quiet the absence of noise (Schmitz 1990, p. 6; Goppelsröder 2013). The writer who writes, the farmer who works manually, the athlete who trains and the intellectual who studies – all keep quiet just because they are too committed to make or put up with noise. Silence, the lack of articulation and sound, quietness – these are all very common clues to the effectiveness of an action. In these cases, silence is an expression of a state of consciousness characterised by attention, vigilance, concentration and devotion which can lead to production and creation.[4] Silence can also be motivated by ways of attunement with one's partner so as not to require words, therefore going beyond dialogicity ("embodied silence" according to Acheson 2008). This can explain why people who have a great degree of confidence can "sustain" more silent phases than people who are not as close to each other (Watts 1997, p. 110). This "eloquent silence" is the silence of lovers or of people who are sharing an aesthetic experience, for example being immersed in the contemplation of an artistic masterpiece. Silence can also be a sign of high attunement between psychotherapists and patients which go beyond the borders of expressibility.

Considering the differentiation between NDS and DS, it should be highlighted that there is no clear boundary between silence, inner monologue and dialogue. This interdependence is well expressed in the concepts of *endophasia* (inner speech) and *exophasia* (articulated speech), defined by De Mauro 1998 (for a wider discussion see Finocchi 2007, p. 98–100; Lœvenbruck et al. 2018). Endophasic moments are those in which we "use words" to think, like in one's inner monologue (unlike moments in which we think without words in an operational or procedural way, for example when we drive a car). Important forms of endophasia are mute reading or silent prayers. These forms often presuppose a pre-existing text that can be read or that is imprinted in the memory. Endophasic acts are an alternative type of verbal activity which should be, like exophasic ones, recognised and "respected"[5] ("the right to silence", Ephratt 2008, p. 1930) as moments of internally collecting thoughts and elaborating them, which is preliminary to the exophasic activity. There are people who have deep needs for endophasic moments (we often speak of these people as having "a rich inner life"), so their silence must be acknowledged (i.e. to "give people time and space to collect their thoughts") as an important moment for emotional and cognitive elaboration and particularly for the preliminary constitution of exophasic acts. It is interesting that research on psychotherapeutic processes and psychotherapeutic interactions only recently began to study processes invested by silence phases in which other communicative resources (such as facial expressions) are engaged as a context of environments of clarifying affects and emotional turmoil (Benecke & Krause 2005; Frankel et al. 2006).

Ritual or conventional (taboo-motivated) silence

A special case of silence not *sensu stricto* dialogical is ritual silence, which is a form of embodied social enacting. In every culture and in every community silence can have a deep ritual meaning, providing a form of "enacted" expression of socially shared cultural values. Silence is embodied, a mating of phenomenal bodies which affirm themselves as being situated in a common world (Acheson 2008). An example is the silence that accompanies funeral rites. In this case, silence can express astonishment at that which is addressed by verbal taboos, namely death. Silence expresses respect, while silent participation[6] enacts belonging to the group and sharing the values of the community. Silence can also have a religious meaning: silence during religious rites expresses the inexpressible mystery, the ineffability of the divine experience and dumb astonishment when faced with the secret of initiation.[7] There are forms of silence subject to social conventions such as silence on prohibited topics or silence as an off-record strategy (i.e. open interpretation) imposed by courteous norms or by norms of social tact ("it is not tactful to speak about it"). In cases of great difficulty in verbalisation, such as death, divorce between life partners, dismissal from work or other types of social failure, or in cases of clear difficulty in managing emotional reactions (such as bursting into tears or expressions of strong emotional upset), silence can be a relatively easy sustainable response to situations of strong emotional involvement.

The silence of the Speaker and of the Listener (Hearer), silence in interaction

In dialogical situations (DS) we have silence, or breaks in the verbal exchange, at two moments that we can define as the silence of the (expected) Listener and the silence of the (expected) Speaker. The expression "the silence of the Speaker" may seem to be an oxymoron, like "the runner is standing still" in reference to an athlete who stops running during a marathon. Anyway, the expressions "Speaker" and "Listener/Hearer" (here indicated with capital letters) are intended in conversation analysis to act as specialised terms. Conversation analysis is based on so-called sequential analysis, that is to say on the way interlocutors build sequences, organise Turn Construction Units (TCU) and manage turn exchange (turn-yielding and turn-taking). Thanks to this shared organisational effort we can distinguish in the interaction a Speaker (the person who is expected to speak) and a Listener/Hearer (a person who is expected to listen). A communicative interaction is a continuous negotiational process in which the two interlocutors define together conversational roles (who has to speak or listen and how), allocate conversational power (the power to decide turn organisation, conversational orientation and topics) and distribute conversational "space". Normally, the Speaker is expected to speak and the Listener is expected to listen. So, silence as absence of speech is considered "not marked" if it is produced by the expected Listener, but very "marked" if it is produced by the expected Speaker. Silence can occur in the Turn-Construction-Units of a Speaker and Hearer and in Transition Relevant Points (or Places, TRPs). TRPs are points where a turn may end and a new Speaker may take her/his turn.[8] TCUs contain the main content of the Speaker's utterance and are built using various unit types: verbal units (such as sentences), nonverbal units (such as gestures or facial expressions), chordal expressions (such as laughter) and silence (filled and unfilled pauses). In regard to the sequential organisation, we distinguish between initiating turns (such as questions), which express a certain grade of activity and interactional power, and responding turns (such as answers), which are characterised by passivity and lack of interactional power. The conversational power of the Speaker is the result of the Hearer's "giving space" in a mutual negotiation. In some cases, the Speaker's and Hearer's roles can overlap. A dialogue develops sequentially through an alternation of initiating and responding turns, and needs an alternation of interlocutors regarding the Speaker's and Listener's roles, which is guaranteed by a set of practices speakers use to construct and allocate turns. We will try to show which functions silence can have as a turn allocation component.

The *silence of the Speaker* is mostly located in initiating turns. With its heightened non-initiative character, the silence of the Speaker, when s/he is supposed to have the initiating turn, is mostly interpreted as a refusal to join the communicative exchange ("the Speaker does not want to speak [with me]") or as an expression of scepticism about the success of the verbal interaction ("the Speaker hesitates"). In many cases, the silence of the person who is supposed to open the interaction can cause a deep disturbance within the interlocutor, who is "forced" to break the silence and start the interaction herself/himself. It is a form of "burdening silence" which is typical of medical interactions (Bellebaum 1992, p. 161). The silence of the Speaker leads the interlocutor to speak in a slightly aggressive manner, often opening with questions about her/his role, for example: "why don't you talk?", "do you want me to talk?", "do I have to start talking?". A total or partial silence of the expected Speaker in the form of interruptions to the verbal flow can also convey closure, hostility, latent conflict and disinterest in the other through lapses and "disengaging". Hesitation signals of the Speakers can convey communicative discomfort – such as in the case of sentence and word breaks (anacoluthons) which lead to self-repairs. In anacoluthons the Speaker shows often a reformulation effort motivated by vigilance processes activated in the conversational exchange, or a certain unsatisfaction or fear about the present formulation and the effort to find a better or more adequate formulation, as in the famous passage from Shakespeare's *King Lear*: "I will have such revenges on you both, that all *the world shall – I will do* such things, What they are, yet I know not ..." [italics: S.B.] (Act 4, Scene 2). The reformulation effort can take place through the correction in a single lexical item or in a syntactic structure. In a similar way, breaks in the verbal flow can be shown by hesitation signals (filled and unfilled pauses). Through hesitation signals (normally filled pauses), the Speaker expresses her/his need for control of the verbal flow and the need "to take time". Sudden interruptions to the verbal flow can also be an expression of fear (Ephratt 2008, p. 1911). An interruption in the verbal flow in the form of silence ("to stop speaking") is an extreme form of hesitation signal.

The silence of the Speaker can also be an instrument of self-promotion and self-stylisation aimed at gaining power, such as in political discussions (Kenny 2011), and a way to show the acquisition or loss of discourse status (Watts 1997, p. 110). This "burdening silence" can also occur in psychotherapeutic situations, when a psychotherapist "forces" the patient to speak through her/his silence in opening turns. In psychotherapeutic interactions, the silence of the psychotherapist in initiating turns can lead the patient to take full responsibility for the initiation of the psychotherapeutic interaction, with all the consequences of it, above all confrontation with – and the overcoming of – fear and shame.

The *silence of the Listener* is in most cases located in responsive turns. Silence is the dimension of attentive listening: thanks to the silence of the

Listener the Speaker has the opportunity to develop her/his own communicative space in verbal flow. Silence can be an expression of the will to listen and "give (communicative) space" to the Other, as attested by filled pauses as feedback signals (Buchholz 2018). In these cases, silence can signal a high level of cooperation between interlocutors: during a conversation, the Listener has an obligation to support the Speaker by listening to and not interrupting her/him. An interruption impedes upon this obligation by infringing upon the wishes of the Speaker to be heard. Interruptions may be an expression of the initiation of Other-repairs and even lead to silencing. When silence occurs as non-fulfillment of conversational obligations, such as not answering a question, not returning a greeting, not replying to a compliment or not closing an adjacency pair, the silence of the Listener can be interpreted in contrast as a refusal to join the communication exchange and, from a psychological perspective, as a basic "withdrawal of resonance" (Buchholz & Gödde 2013). In such cases, silence violates social rules and conversational maxims, mostly that of relevance, in a similar way as the change of theme topic, and will be interpreted as: "I do not want to speak about it". If changes of topic reveal nevertheless the will to maintain the conversational exchange, silence is an off-record strategy which can be interpreted as lack of will of clear positioning in the communicative exchange or even a rejection of the interactional exchange.

In the margin of the proposed differentiation, it should be noted that silence often is not univocally attributable to the Speaker and the Listener, but is distributed among the participants in a dynamic way for joint construction of the interaction. The absence of talk (the phases of silence) is considered principally as the moment in which interlocutors in TRP "make space" for each other for the transition of "speakerness". Every filled moment in a dialogue requires "unfilled" frames, i.e. "silent phases", which turn out to be essential for the success of a communicative exchange. These silent phases can occur as filled or unfilled pauses. Unfilled pauses can be classified according to their durations. The interlocutors have the task of negotiating the quantity and duration of necessary and sustainable pauses so that the communicative space is arranged in such a way as to offer optimised possibilities of exchange. Generally, we can distinguish between prolonged silence moments (more than 3 seconds), long pauses (from 3 to 0.8 seconds), short pauses (0.8 to 0.3 seconds) and very short pauses (less than 0.3 seconds) (Bögels, Magyari & Levinson 2015; Butterworth 1980; Oliveira, 2002; Ruiter, Mitterer & Enfield 2006). The length of silence between turns depends on many factors (contextual, situational, interlocutional), affecting how turns are distributed, how transitions are signaled or how long the average gaps between turns are. The duration of the pauses and their function of structuring turns and segmenting the sequential order of a dialogue (Goodwin 1980) are not only related to idiosyncratic factors, but also to wider cultural features (Stedje 1983; Sifianou 1997; Tannen 2012). Watts suggests, based on Jefferson (1983), that an inter-turn silence of around 1.5 seconds is a convenient boundary between perceived fluency and dysfluency in Western/North American cultural frameworks (Watts 1997, p. 94). Vocal patterns – such as pitch – are specific to the individual, and also cue the Hearer to expect how the timing will play out in turn-taking. The organisation of conversation involves processes for constructing contributions, responding to previous comments, and transitioning to a different speaker, using a variety of linguistic and non-linguistic cues. Normally, the organisation of a conversation requires participants to speak one at a time in alternating turns. Interlocutors construct their contributions while holding their turn until the moment they open a TRP (Transition Relevant Place), that is to say a point at which a new speaker "gets space". Thanks to TRPs the interlocutor can begin to construct her/his turn. A turn-yielding signal (for example an unfilled pause) indicates that the speaker has finished speaking and that the other person may start talking. This involves using audible signals (decreased volume, slowed tempo, a lower pitch for declaratives, and a raised pitch for interrogatives), visible signals (cessation of gestures, a long gaze at the listener, or eyebrow raising), or an extended silent pause, which indicates that a TRP has been opened. Turn-taking can be cooperative (a joint effort for the success of the exchange) or competitive (a struggle for interactional power). Whether turn-taking is cooperative or competitive does not depend so much on what objectively happens, but on how what happens is perceived by the interlocutors, that is to say on the type of interaction, on the relationship between the interactants and on idiosyncratic and cultural factors. Between the two extreme situations in which the interactants might either speak simultaneously or remain silent, we have a range of intermediate forms.

How much "place" (silence moments) interlocutors need for turn-taking is managed by conversational rules that every interactant should know to manage successfully the communication exchanges. The violation of these rules is highly marked i.e. very expressive. The social importance of these rules is shown by politeness values. Violations are oft stigmatised as "interrupting" and condemned conversationally as impolite and not tactful. In a similar way, co-construction turns through the Listener, like to continue or complete a sentence formulated by the Speaker, who shows some disflows, can be perceived as very aggressive, even though motivated by a cooperative intention. The intention of the Listener who began as Co-Speaker a co-construction turn can be interpreted in the following way: "the Speaker is not able to formulate a full sentence alone, I must help him" as "The Speaker will not formulate a proper sentence, I have to intervene". It is obvious that a very accurate analysis of co-construction units in psychotherapeutic interactions would be very useful to understand the dynamic of the relationship between patients and psychotherapists.

In what follows, I will briefly summarise the forms of turn-taking in which silence (or absence of silence) plays an important role. By *overlapping* (two speakers speaking at the same time) we have to distinguish between competitive and cooperative overlaps. Competitive overlapping turns are generally to be avoided in a conversational exchange, because they signal a struggle for interactional power and lead to *interruptions* and breaks in the conversational units (Local & Kelly 1986). According to Goldberg (1990) there is a dynamic relationship between overlaps and power. "Power interruptions" are generally interpreted as hostile, because the goals of the power interrupter are both divergent from and contrary to the goals of the Speaker. Power interruptions are further categorised into two types: process control interruptions and content control interruptions. Process control interruptions involve attempts to change the topic by utilising questions and requests, while content control interruptions involve attempts to change the topic by utilising assertions or statements that are unrelated to the current topic, so they aim to silence the interlocutor. In this type of interaction none of the speakers opens a TRP, and therefore communicative space, to their interlocutor. The interlocutors do not listen to each other, each of them struggling for interactional primacy. Therefore *interruptions* (with resulting Other-initiated other- or self-repairs) are a form of competitive overlapping: an interruption or a forced change of topic has, in many cases, the effect of silencing the interlocutor (Maynard 1980, p. 264). A series of silences can indicate the failure of a prior topic to yield a successful transfer of speakership and difficult speaker transitions (Maynard 1980, p. 265). Finally, *prolonged gaps* (with longer moments of silence) can be interpreted as a signal of difficult communication and therefore are to be avoided according the existing conversational (and politeness) rules.

Overlapping is not always competitive. We have a variety of cooperative overlapping forms. *Terminal overlaps* occur when the Listener assumes the Speaker has or is about to finish their turn and begins to speak, thus creating an overlap. A similar case is a *transitional overlap*, which occurs when a speaker enters the conversation at a possible point of completion. This happens when speakers participate in the conversation enthusiastically and exchange speech acts with continuity. The Speaker does not perceive it as an interruption, but as a cooperative action to animate the dialogue. An explanation for this may be that the Listener actually starts preparing their next contribution much earlier than the Speaker stops speaking (Bögels, Magyari & Levinson 2015; Buchholz 2018, p. 99; Wilson & Zimmerman 1986). So, in every interactional exchange we have endophasic and exophasic moments, and "what we say" is just a surface phenomenon concealing deeper processing.

Sometimes it is the Speaker who invites the interlocutor to carry out a *co-construction* (for an overview see Jacoby and Ochs 2010), inviting her/him to speak out of turn by signaling a formulation difficulty, for example when searching for a word. In this case the overlap can also be defined as a *recognitional overlap*, which occurs when a speaker anticipates the possible remainder of an unfinished sentence, and attempts to finish it for the current speaker. Similarly, a *progressional overlap* can occur as a result of the speech dysfluency of the previous speaker when another speaker self-selects to continue with the ongoing utterance. In all these forms of cooperative overlaps a pause signalises the wish to yield the turn. *Conditional access* to the turn implies that the current speaker yields her/his turn or invites another speaker to interject in the conversation, usually as a collaborative effort. An unfilled pause can be a signal for conditional access. Filled pauses can occur amongst the feedback-signals (*continuers*) of the Hearer, which are a way for the Hearer to acknowledge or understand what the Speaker is saying. These are verbal signals of the Hearer that signal attention, but not a wish to take the turn. In psychotherapeutic interactions, this kind of pause and silent moment can express the idea that "my-mind-is-with-you" (MMWY-Principle, Sacks 1995; see also Buchholz 2018, p. 101ff.), that is to say empathic participation that does not require words, a "hidden dimension" (Hall 1990; see also Bonacchi 2020) which delivers a broad space for embodied communication and projection processes (Local & Kelly 1986). Finally, chordal signals (such as laughter) also signal nonverbally that the speaker and listener share *common ground*[9] and that the direction of the conversation is perceived as proper.

Interpreting silence

When it occurs in a conversation, silence is difficult to interpret, both for participants and for external analysts. It is an *off-record* act (Brown/ Levinson 1978, pp. 66–69), in which the interlocutors have substantial interpretative discretion. The Listener is required to have a high level of inferential effort in the reconstruction of *what is not said but meant*, and *why what is meant is not said*. As examples of how *implicatures of silence* can be reconstructed, we can cite the following conversations:

Conversation 1: a group of friends (A, B, C, D) is walking in a forest

1	A:	Which way should we go, left or right?
2	B, C, D:	[0.4]
3	A:	No one knows?
4	B, C, D:	[0.6]
5	A:	Ok, let's turn right then.

In this case, the absence of an answer (a pause of 0.4 seconds) after A's question is interpreted as a *responce latency*, i.e. an inability to answer (B, C and D do not know which direction is correct). It is imaginable that B, C and D express this state with nonverbal signals as well. As a result of the silence, speaker A closes (5) the obligation opened by the question, deciding alone what to do.

The implicature can be reconstructed in the following way:

[unfilled pauses in segments 2 and 4] +> B, C and D do not speak because they have no answer

Conversation 2: a mother and her teenage daughter

1	Mother:	Ann, what's up at school?
2	Daughter:	Hmm…
3	Mother:	Ann, I am speaking to you!

In this case the filled pause (hesitation signal) cannot be interpreted in an unequivocal way.

The implicature can be reconstructed in the following ways:

[unfilled pauses in segment 2] +$>^n$
where +$>^n$:

+>¹ Interlocutor does not answer because she does not know the answer
+>² Interlocutor does not answer because she does not want to speak with the Speaker
+>³ Interlocutor does not answer because she does not think it is worth answering such a (banal) question
+>⁴ Interlocutor does not answer because she thinks the Speaker should not ask this question
+>⁵ Interlocutor does not answer because she needs more time

The filled pause is, in these cases, an off-record act, which allows interpretative freedom and makes the Speaker (mother) responsible for the continuation of the interaction. In the examples above, the silence in the responsive turns provokes an intensification and a strengthening of the initiatory role of the Speaker, eliciting a further initiatory act (the question in Segment 3 in Conversation 1 and a reinforced disambiguation in Segment 3 in Conversation 2).

> Conversation 3 (Watts 1997, p. 97): R, B and D are speaking about friends M and S borrowing money
>
> 1: R: Well how much did they borrow from M and S?
> 2: B: I don't know [clears throat] [2.7] About a couple of hundred, wasn't it, David? Something like that
> 3:   [4.8.]
> 4: D: [clears throat]
> 5: R: Well, that's not very much, is it? I mean [.] a couple of hundred?
> 6:   [4.3.]
> 7: B: Sally doesn't like owing money. She wants to pay it back as soon as possible.
>   [6.8.]

In this conversation the inter-turn moments of silence between the shifts indicate a situation of dysfluency. The interlocutors speak about a taboo theme (the money borrowed), the prolonged pauses revealing their awkwardness.

The silence in the conversations can be reconstructed at the level of what is meant but cannot be said in the following way:

2: B: I don't know [clears throat] [2.7] About a couple of hundred, wasn't it, David? Something like that
3: [4.8.]
5: R: Well, that's not very much, is it? I mean [.] a couple of hundred?
6: [4.3.]

[unfilled pauses in Segment 3 and 6] +> B and R do not want to speak because it is not tactful to speak about these themes and ask exactly how much the friends borrowed]

In the following segment the silence can be reconstructed as an appeal to justify the friend's actions:

7: B: Sally doesn't like owing money. She wants to pay it back as soon as possible.
    [6.8.]

[unfilled pauses in Segment 3 and 6] +> Interlocutors should know that S does not like owing money and that she will pay it back as soon as possible.

In the analysed conversation, silence is therefore to be considered as "eloquent" (Ephratt 2008, p. 1913).

Silencing and communicative violence

An interesting form of interactional management marked by asymmetric power allocation is silencing. Silencing can be a reactive or proactive behaviour, and even rise to forms of aggression and offence (Wardhaugh 2010, p. 234). It is an act designed to "shut up" subjects when they raise issues that are not accepted or claim interactional roles that are denied them. In most cases persons perceived as "weak" or socially vulnerable (children, women, elders[10], socially disadvantaged people, patients) are silenced. Silencing encompasses harassment or intimidation and discourages these people from speaking out. Shaming and humiliation are targeted at vulnerable subjects to prevent them from speaking and at the same time deny the legitimacy of their speech. Silencing can be expressed in open (prototypically in limitative sentences, see Bonacchi 2013, p. 159) and in latent forms. In the latter case a silencing intention can take the form of benevolent advice, recommendation or psychological pressure.

In interactions between medical staff and patients forms of patronising with the aim of depriving patients of self-determination rights are often recorded (Sachweh 2005). In psychotherapeutic interactions, silencing can be a form of controlled "communicative violence", a refusal of communicative exchange which normally would be perceived as punitive or aggressive. Therapists sometimes use silencing as a confrontational intervention to initiate positive processes in the patient (Alder & Buchholz 2017, p. 193ff.).

Interpreting silence in the psychotherapeutic interaction

As described earlier, in everyday interactions, we have many situations in which silence occurs as expression of communicative distress: A child who comes home from school crying and can't speak because of his excitement, a declaration of love, a person fired from her/his job, a funeral, etc. In psychotherapeutic interactions, psychotherapists and patients often have to deal with situations at the limit of expressibility, with what in German is defined as a *Sprachnot*, a linguistic expression of distress: both the patient and the psychotherapist are called upon to search together for words to verbalise states and processes that escape expressibility – be it a trauma, a compulsive state or a dependence. To do this, they must first establish a relationship that guarantees proper conditions for this process of searching for words and to permit words to restore the psychological balance. This is a challenge[11]: psychotherapeutic action sometimes requires the transformation of silence into speech, and sometimes the transformation of words into silence, according to a targeted strategy of recover psychological balance. In this sense, psychotherapeutic interactions show a high vulnerability potential, in which both psychotherapists and patients have to negotiate properly their interactional power and roles. Even though all participants in psychotherapeutic interactions try to model their relationship in different ways, psychotherapeutic interactions are from the perspective of conversational analysis characterized by a clear framing, which defines actors and roles, space, time and the contents of the interactional exchange. Psychotherapeutic interactions take place in a particular physical space, normally psychiatric or psychotherapeutic clinics or practices, and are limited in time (the psychotherapeutic session, which takes place at fixed intervals). Between the actors, the psychotherapist and the patient, an exclusive interaction has to be established, in ideal circumstances characterised by trust and openness. Participants interact within a metacomplementary asymmetric relationship, since the psychotherapist has interactional primacy as long as the patient grants her/him this power. This interactional power over the patient is expressed in the patient's giving the psychotherapist the right to ask questions, to select the topics for conversation to a certain extent and to control the allocation of turns. For the attribution of these rights, the psychotherapist – for the duration of the psychotherapeutic interactions – is dedicated exclusively to the patient, listens to her/him and takes responsibility for the success of the therapeutic interaction. This is an interaction which, in the understanding of some psychotherapeutic orientations, has a strong strategic character: the psychotherapist acts on the psychological structures of the patient through targeted interventions, restoring the patient's will to live, reviving her/his feeling for their own psychological identity and recovering her/his ability to function in society. Although there are many forms of psychotherapeutic interventions (like art performing, theatre, enacting, etc.), verbal therapy – i.e. "healing through speech" (Gutwinski 1981, p. 224) – remains the main form of psychotherapeutic therapy for adults, in which the verbalisation of experience (mainly the emotional part of it) is a shared task for both patient and psychotherapist. In this form of therapy, the patient is called on to verbalise through words various traumas, disorders and psychological discomforts, blocks etc. The patient has to be supported in her/his efforts to verbalise in various ways: sometimes using a gentle and empathic technique, sometimes with controlled acts of "communicative violence" (Alder & Buchholz 2017, p. 200ff.). Conversational analysis can make a significant contribution to show that the silence of the patient must be interpreted by the psychotherapist in its various dimensions, forms and functions. From a conversational perspective, if the silence occurs in the conversational units of the psychotherapeutic session, it can reveal not only difficulties in verbalisation (motivated by inexpressibility, shame, traumas) and in fulfilling obligations (for example, refusing to answer a question), but also a mismatch between the conversational strategies "imposed" by the psychotherapist and the ones sustainable for the patient. The patient often experiences a series of feelings – such as fear or shame – that block verbal fluency,[12] especially when associated with a weak feeling of self-worth and extreme stress caused by the psychotherapeutic situation. In these cases, the patient's silence may be an expression of shame and resistance in respect to the pressure regarding self-disclosure and the demand for openness which the therapist exerts (Spitznagel 1986, p. 32). Furthermore, the therapist is often anxiously observed by the patient – due to their past experiences the traumatised patient (consciously or unconsciously) "expects" an assault. Therefore, a therapist remaining silent in combination with the smallest nonverbal signals (a "doubtful" facial expression, a bored look etc.) can be interpreted as being offensive and rejective.

Clearly, all this does not mean one must avoid silence and pauses in psychotherapy because they generally can be perceived as violative and "dangerous". On the contrary: the patient's struggle to verbalise content often requires prolonged endophasic phases of silence. In this case, "positive" silent feedback signals (gaze, gestures, facial expressions, small nonverbal comments, see Labov & Fanshel 1977) from the psychotherapist as Listener[13] can be perceived by the patient as a sign of interest, empathy and attuning and can therefore be interpreted as an MMWY-expression and "make space" for the development of the verbal flow of the patient. It is a part of the expertise of the psychotherapist to understand how much "silence" the patient needs, that is to say how long the pauses in TRP have to be, how many unfilled pauses are sustainable, if overlapping is accepted, how long the gaps between turns can be and how far the psychotherapist can go when intervening in moments of conversational disfluence with co-constructional units (for example, suggesting answers or completing units; for an analysis see Alder & Buchholz 2017, p. 179; Streeck 2001).

The psychotherapist should be aware that due to her/his role and the vulnerability of the patient, her/his interventions can have the effect of reducing the therapeutic interaction to silence, i.e. silencing the patient. At the same time, silent moments can be treated as a chance to renegotiate interactional space, as moments of openness, which can present a high affordance for verbal filling (Alder et al. 2016).

Notes

1. For an overview see Bellebaum 1992; Bergmann 1982; Grabher & Jessner 1996; Hart Nibbrig 1981; Jaworski 1992; Luhmann & Fuchs 1989; Zerubavel 2006. An extensive collection of studies on the forms and dimensions of silence is provided by Jaworski, 1997.
2. In his study *Communicational Structure* (1973), Scheflen described, through an analysis of video recordings, the role that nonverbal communication (body position, gestures, facial expressions, movements) plays in psychotherapy.

In this sense, silence can represent the background against which gestures, expressions and movements imbued with meaning stand out in the foreground.
3 In what follows, we will use the term Other in the sense of Other-referential Addressee as intended in Conversation Analysis.
4 Balint has defined this state as the "third area" and highlighted its importance in psychotherapeutic interactions (Balint 1958: 338). Balint's study provides many valuable indications on the use of language in psychotherapy. In the concept of "basic fault" (second area), which Balint sets in opposition to the oedipal level (first area), associations and even silence are fundamental because the experiences in this second area are not to be verbalised.
5 For the notion of "respect" and "disrespectfulness" in psychotherapeutic interactions see Alder & Buchholz 2017, p. 176.
6 See also Newman-Norlund et al. (2008), Kenny (2011).
7 In his book *Schweigen und Verschweigen,* Alfred Bellebaum describes the divine silence as being the basis of language (*Lingua Fundamentum Sancti Silentii*, Bellebaum 1992, 34–54; see also Neubaur 1999).
8 For an overview see Schegloff & Sacks (1973), Sacks, Schegloff & Jefferson (1974), Wilson & Zimmermann (1986), and Schegloff (2013).
9 The notion of Common Ground is essential for understanding language as a form of social interactive behavior. In every social exchange, it requires Speaker (S) to make some assumptions about Hearer's (H's) ability to understand utterances (U) (Clark 1996; Stalnaker 2002).
10 See Sachweh (2005).
11 The classic Freudian view of silence as an anal-retentive form of resistance, defence or opposition (Cremerius 1969) has been surpassed by new studies that highlight the multiplicity of forms of silence in psychotherapeutic interaction, see Bergmann, 2016; Alder & Buchhholz 2017, p. 24; Frankel et al., 2006; Gale & Sanchez, 2005; Jacobs, 2000; Lane, Koetting, & Bishop, 2002; Levitt, 2001a; Levitt, 2001b.
12 I would like to thank Thomas Fuchs for his valuable collaboration in preparing this part of the chapter based on his many years of professional experience as a psychotherapist.
13 Scarvaglieri (2013, p. 284ff.) sees a psychotherapeutic interaction as "listener-centered discourse".

References

Acheson, K. (2008). Silence as gesture. Rethinking the nature of communicative silences. *Communication Theory, 18*(4), 535–555.
Alder, M.-L., Brakemeier, E.-L., Dittmann, M., Dreyer, F., & Buchholz, M. B. (2016). Fehlleistungen als Empathie-Chance – Sie Gegenläufigkeit von "Projekten" der Patientin und der Therapeutin. Eine verhaltenstherapeutische Sitzung und ihr Anfang. *Psychotherapie Forum, 21*(1), 2–10.
Alder, M. L., & Buchholz, Michael B. (2017). Kommunikative Gewalt in der Psychotherapie. In: S. Bonacchi (Ed.), *Verbale Aggression. Multidisziplinäre Zugänge zur verletzenden Macht der Sprache* (pp. 171–207). Berlin: de Gruyter.

Balint, M. (1958). The three areas of the mind. Theoretical considerations. *International Journal of Psycho-Analysis, 39*(5), 328–340.
Bellebaum, A. (1992). Schweigen und Verschweigen. *Bedeutungen und Erscheinungsvielfalt einer Kommunikationsform*. Opladen: Westdeutscher Verlag.
Benecke, C., & Krause, R. (2005). Facial affective relationship offers of patients with panic disorder. *Psychotherapy Research, 15*(3), 178–187.
Bergmann, J. R. (1982). Schweigephasen im Gespräch – Aspekte ihrer interaktiven Organisation. In: H.-G. Soeffner (Ed.), *Beiträge zu einer empirischen Sprachsoziologie* (pp. 143–184). Tübingen: Narr.
Bergmann, J. R. (2016). Making mental disorders visible: Proto-morality as diagnostic resource in psychiatric exploration. In: M. O'Reilly & J. N. Lester (Eds.), *The Palgrave Handbook of Adult Mental Health: Discourse and Conversation Studies* (pp. 247–268). Houndmills, Basingstoke, Hampshire: Palgrave Macmillan.
Bögels, S., Magyari, L., & Levinson, S. C. (2015). Neural signatures of response planning occur midway through an incoming question in conversation. *Scientific Reports, 5*, 12881.
Bonacchi, S. (2013). *(Un)Höflichkeit. Eine kulturologische Analyse Deutsch – Italienisch – Polnisch*. Frankfurt: Lang.
Bonacchi, S. (2020). La costruzione dello spazio comunicativo a scuola. Considerazioni teoriche, metodologiche e prospettive di applicazione. In: M. Voghera, P. Maturi & F. Rosi (Eds.), *Orale e scritto, verbale e non verbale: La multimodalità nell'ora di lezione*. Firenze: Cesati.
Brown, P., & Levinson, S. C. (1978). Universals in language usage: Politeness phenomena. In: E. Goody (Ed.), *Questions and Politeness: Strategies in Social Interaction* (pp. 56–310). Cambridge: Cambridge University Press.
Buchholz, M. B. (2018). Kleine Theorie der Pause. *Psyche, 72*(2), 91–121.
Buchholz, M. B., & Gödde, G. (2013). Balance, Rhythmus, Resonanz: Auf dem Weg zu einer Komplementarität zwischen 'vertikaler' und 'resonanter' Dimension Des Unbewussten. *Psyche, 67*(9–10), 84–880.
Butterworth, B. (1980). Evidence from pause in speech. In: *Language Production: Speech and Talk* (pp. 155–176). London: Academic Press.
Clark, H. H. (1996). *Using Language*. Cambridge: Cambridge University Press.
Cremerius, J. (1969). Schweigen als Problem der psychoanalytischen Technik. *Jahrbuch der Psychoanalyse, 6*, 69–103.
De Mauro, T. (1998). *Linguistica elementare*. Bari: Laterza.
Ephratt, M. (2008). The functions of silence. *Journal of Pragmatics, 40*(11), 1909–1938.
Finocchi, R. (2007). *Linguaggio e comunicazione. Teoria, strutture e usi linguistici nelle pratiche comunicative*. Torino: Effatà.
Frankel, Z. E., Levitt, H. M., Murray, D. M., Greenberg, L. S., & Angus, L. (2006). Assessing silent processes in psychotherapy: An empirically derived categorization system and sampling strategy. *Psychotherapy Research, 16*(5), 627–638.
Gale, J., & Sanchez, B. (2005). The meaning and function of silence in psychotherapy – With particular reference to a therapeutic community treatment programme. *Psychoanalytic Psychotherapy, 19*(3), 205–220.

Goldberg, J. A. (1990). Interrupting the discourse on interruptions. *Journal of Pragmatics, 14*(6), 883–903.
Goppelsröder, F. (2013). *Eloquente Stille. Kleists literarische Geste. Merkur, 67*(769), 506–515.
Goodwin, C. (1980). Restarts, pauses, and the achievement of a state of mutual gaze at turn-beginning. *Sociological Inquiry, 50*(3–4), 272–302.
Grabher, G., & Jessner, U. (1996). *Semantics of Silences in Linguistics and Literature*. Heidelberg.
Gutwinski, J. (1981). Zum dialog im monolog. Redewiedergabe in fallpraesentation aus balint-gruppen. *Journal of Pragmatics, 5*(2–3), 223–242.
Hall, E. T. (1959). *The Silent Language*. New York: Doubleday.
Hall, E. T. (1990). *The Hidden Dimension*. New York: Anchor Books.
Hart Nibbrig, C. L. (1981). *Rhetorik Des Schweigens. Versuch über den Schatten literarischer Rede*. Frankfurt/M: Suhrkamp Verlag.
Jacobs, T. J. (2000). Unbewußte Kommunikation und verdeckte Enactments im analytischen Setting. In: U. Streeck (Ed.), *Erinnern, agieren und inszenieren. Enactments und szenische Darstellungen im therapeutischen Prozeß* (pp. 97–126). Göttingen: Vandenhoeck & Ruprecht.
Jacoby, S., & Ochs, E. (2010). Co-construction. An introduction. *Research on Language and Social Interaction, 28*(3), 171–183.
Jaworski, A. (1992). *The Power of Silence: Social and Pragmatic Perspectives*. Newbury Park, CA: Sage Publications.
Jaworski, A. (Ed.) (1997). *Silence: Interdisciplinary Perspectives*. Berlin: de Gruyter.
Jefferson, G. (1983). Notes on some orderlinesses of overlap onset. In: V. D'Urso & P. Leonardi (Eds.), *Discourse Analysis and Natural Rhetorics* (pp. 11–38). Padua: Cleup Editore.
Kenny, C. (2011). *The Power of Silence. Silent Communication in Daily Life*. London: Karnac.
Kwiatkowska, A. (1997). Silence across modalities. In: A. Jaworski (Ed.), *Silence: Interdisciplinary Perspectives* (pp. 329–338). Berlin: de Gruyter.
Labov, W., & Fanshel, D. (1977). *Therapeutic Discourse: Psychotherapy as Conversation*. New York: Academic Press.
Lane, R. C., Koetting, M. G., & Bishop, J. (2002). Silence as communication in psychodynamic psychotherapy. *Clinical Psychology Review, 22*(7), 1091–1104.
Levitt, H. M. (2001a). Sounds of silence in psychotherapy: The categorization of clients' pauses. *Psychotherapy Research, 11*(3), 295–311.
Levitt, H. M. (2001b). Client's experience of obstructive silence: Integrating conscious reports and analytic theories. *Journal of Contemporary Psychotherapy, 31*(4), 221–244.
Local, J., & Kelly, J. (1986). Projection and 'silences'. notes on phonetic and conversational structure. *Human Studies, 9*(2–3), 185–204.
Lœvenbruck, H., Grandchamp, R., Rapin, L., Nalborczyk, L., Dohen, M., Pierrer, P., Baciu, M., & Perrone-Bertolotti, M. (2018). A cognitive neuroscience view of inner language. To predict and to hear, see, feel. In: P. Lahland-Hassan & A. Vicente (Eds.), *Inner Speech: New Voices* (pp. 131–167). Oxford: Oxford University Press.

Luhmann, N., & Fuchs, P. (1989). *Reden und Schweigen*. Frankfurt/M: Suhrkamp Verlag.
Maynard, D. W. (1980). Placement of topic changes in conversation. *Semiotica*, *30*(3/4), 263–290.
Neubaur, C. (1999). Schweigen, Stille, Reverie. Erscheinungsformen einer sakralen und psychoanalytischen Kategorie. *Merkur*, *53*(608), 1155–1171.
Newman-Norlund, S. E., Noordzij, M. L., Newman-Norlund, R. D., Volman, I. A. C., Ruiter, J. P. d., Hagoort, P., & Toni, I. (2008). Recipient design in tacit communication. *Cognition*, *111*(1), 46–54.
Oliveira, M. (2002). The role of pause occurrence and pause duration in the signalling of narrative structure. In: E. Ranchhod & N. J. Mamede (Eds.), *Advances in Natural Language Processing. Third International Conference, PorTAL 2002* (pp. 43–51). Berlin, Heidelberg: Springer.
Sachweh, S. (2005). *Noch ein Löffelchen? Effektive Kommunikation in der Altenpflege*. Bern, Switzerland: Hans Huber Verlag.
Sacks, H., & Jefferson, G. (1992/1995). *Lectures on Conversation*. Oxford: Basil Blackwell.
Sacks, H., Schegloff, E. A., & Jefferson, G. (1974). A simplest systematics for the organization of turn-taking for conversation. *Language*, *50*(4), 696–735.
Scaravaglieri, C. (2013). *Nichts Anderes als ein Austausch von Wörtern. Sprachliches Handeln in der Psychotherapie*. Berlin: de Gruyter.
Scheflen, A. E. (1973). *Communicational Structure; Analysis of a Psychotherapy Transaction*. Bloomington, IN: Indiana University Press.
Schegloff, E. A. (2013). Ten operations in self-initiated, same-turn repair. In: M. Hayashi, G. Raymond & J. Sidnell (Eds.), *Conversational Repair and Human Understanding. Studies in Interactional Sociolinguistics* (Vol. 30., pp. 41–70). Cambridge: Cambridge University Press.
Schegloff, E. A., & Sacks, H. (1973). Opening up closings. *Semiotica*, *8*(4), 289–327.
Schmitz, U. (1990). Beredtes Schweigen – Zur sprachlichen Fülle der Leere. Über Grenzen der Sprachwissenschaft. *Schweigen. Osnabrücker Beiträge zur Sprachtheorie (OBST)*, *42*, 5–58.
Sifianou, M. (1997). Silence and politeness. In: A. Jaworski (Ed.), *Silence: Interdisciplinary Perspectives* (pp. 63–84). Berlin: de Gruyter.
Spitznagel, A. (1986). *Sprechen und Schweigen. Zur Psychologie der Selbstenthüllung*. Bern: Hogrefe AG.
Stalnaker, R. C. (2002). Common ground. *Linguistics and Philosophy*, *25*(5/6), 701–721.
Stedje, A. (1983). "Brechen Sie dies rätselhafte Schweigen" – Über kulturbedingtes, kommunikatives und strategisches Schweigen. In: I. Rosengren (Ed.), *Sprache und Pragmatik* (pp. 7–35). Stockholm: Alqvist & Wiskell International.
Streeck, U. (2001). 'Ja, genau, genau'. Bestätigungen als Versuche Des Patienten, die Kompetenz Des Psychotherapeuten als eigene zu deklarieren – Eine gesprächsanalytische Untersuchung. *Psychotherapie und Sozialwissenschaft*, *2*, 74–94.
Tannen, D. (2012). Turn-taking and intercultural discourse and communication. In: Paulston, Ch., Kiesling, S., & Rangel, E. (Ed.). *The Handbook of Intercultural*

Discourse and Communication (pp. 135–157). Chicester, UK: John Wiley & Sons.

Tannen, D., & Saville-Troike, M. (Ed.). (1985). *Perspectives on Silence*. Norwood, NJ: Ablex.

Wardhaugh, R. (2010). *An Introduction to Sociolinguistics*. Hoboken, NJ: Blackwell Publishing.

Watts, R. J. (1997). Silence and the acquisition of status in verbal interaction. In: A. Jaworski (Ed.), *Silence: Interdisciplinary Perspectives* (pp. 87–116). Berlin: de Gruyter.

Wilson, T. P., & Zimmerman, D. H. (1986). The structure of silence between turns in two-party conversation. *Discourse Processes*, 9(4), 375–390.

Zerubavel, E. (2006). *The Elephant in the Room. Silence and Denial in Everyday Life*. Oxford, New York: Oxford University Press.

Chapter 4

The many forms of silence in music

Helga de la Motte-Haber

Is this heading intended as a joke? The apparent paradox of silence and music was given form in 1897 by Alphonse Allais with his *Marche funèbre composée pour les funérailles d'un grand homme sourd* (Funeral March for the Obsequies of a Great Deaf Man). It is a piece made for laughter with 24 empty bars on sheet music paper and the performance direction *Lento rigolante* (laughing lento). *Silent Music* (1941) by the jazz musician Raymond Scott is in some ways comparable. Scott wanted to amuse his audience by having the musicians make movements without producing any sounds. And yet the *Marche Funèbre* comes across differently. Allais was a member of the short-lived group *L'art incohérent* that parodied the art of its time. Today this group is considered a historical precursor to the Dadaists.

The German-Bohemian musician Schulhoff was probably not familiar with Allais's march. He did, however, have contact with the Dadaists in Berlin. The *Pittoresken*, op. 30 for piano were composed in 1919 with the remark: "sincerely dedicated to the painter and Dadaist George Groß [sic]!" This suite, inspired by the popular dances of his time, contains a silent piece as the third movement: *In Futurum*. It is notated in an absurd manner with rests and the tempo indication "tempo – timeless". The upper staff is marked with a bass clef, the lower with a treble clef; the rhythms indicated – 3/5 and 7/10 – would scarcely be playable. The pause for breath after bar three is odd in a piano piece, as are the concave and convex double fermatas, interpolated exclamation marks and sketches of faces, including one in the "Marshal Rest". Schulhoff also called Grosz Marshal Grosz. While the notation of the rests cannot give the precise pitch, it does indicate differences in pitch, almost melodic phrases, which, however, appear to be contradicted by the direction *con espressione e sentimento*, because the rests indicate a very fast tempo. But a pianist could conceivably render it without pressing the keys. It is the revolt against tradition that makes this piece seem preposterous. With a title like *Ironien (Ironies)*, Six pieces for piano four hands, op. 55 (1920), Schulhoff identified his aesthetic approach. But he was a proponent of Dadaism only briefly.

The "visual scores" by musicians of a Dadaist bent that indicate music by way of association only, prefigure later musical artworks such as those paintings that have abounded since the twentieth century whose contemplation is meant to evoke sound. The collages of blank sheets of music, op. 106 (2008) by Michael Denhoff, are indeed conceived as silent music.

The title of my chapter, *Silent Music*, is not meant as a joke. There have been several publications devoted to this subject in recent years. Most of them are collections of essays that look at individual aspects of this problem (Losseff & Doctor, 2007; Schmusch & Ullmann, 2018). Salomé Voegelin (2010, p. XV) specifically explores the possibility of an immersive listening in silence. "In the quiet sound the listener becomes audible himself as a discrete member of an audience."

As well as the publications, there are also conferences, because the sounds of the past are currently capturing the interest of historians and social scientists. And yet silence and music still seem to be mutually exclusive – perhaps one reason why David Toop (2010) looks only at the visual representation of music in his chapter *Art of Silence*. It seems it is not so easy to answer the question of what silence is.

Definitions of silence

The Oxford Dictionary defines silence as "complete absence of sound". In the Cambridge Dictionary, silence is likewise described as "a period without any sound, complete quiet", but with the additional explanation "a state of not communicating", thus touching on a state that the meditation exercises prevalent in many cultures seek to attain. Silence would seem to be a prerequisite for religious contemplation, which can lead to a deeper understanding of the self and its conditions. In this context silence is defined as an experience of the presence of the supremely spiritually sublime, as something transcendental, that can only be experienced as the absence of all things and events.

In mediaeval times, at least, the opposition of silence and music was considered a given. Meister Eckart had demanded absolute silence: when the Lord speaks "all voices and all sounds must cease" (Kern, 2018, p. 87). Moreover, in the Middle Ages the Roman Catholic Church had the custom of "low Mass" in which the priests only moved their lips. Its most important characteristic was *sine cantu*. It was practised until 1963. But there are also other linguistic contextualisations of silence that prove useful for aesthetic matters.

When it comes to the definition of silence, German-language dictionaries differ from English-language ones in evincing a rich semantic field, as evidenced by the four-volume *Grammatisch-kritische Wörterbuch der hochdeutschen Mundart* (1793–1801) by Johann Christoph Adelung. In Old High German and ever since, silence has been associated with a state of movement (standing, motionless, inactive), without much noise, with peace and quiet (soundless, being undisturbed by any noise), with being silent, wordlessness, solitude and that which goes unnoticed, *sotto voce*, that which is subsiding, hidden, which happens quietly and without a fuss. This list encourages us to describe silence musically not only in terms of a lack of acoustic events, but also through a contemplation of dynamic and rhythmic, harmonic processes, through structural characteristics in general, and to ask what is thus kept secret or withheld, or perhaps not expressed at all. Jean-François Lyotard (1955) had grappled in the context of contemporary visual arts with the question that it is on the one hand impossible to truly represent an absolute, and yet, through that which is shown, an imagining of the ineffable can be evoked.

In connection with the inexpressible, it should also be remembered that there were fundamental changes in aesthetic thinking over the course of the centuries. These include the altered status of art since the eighteenth century, which no longer had to serve a purpose and now claimed autonomy. Music in particular was increasingly understood as a language above language that was capable of lending expression to the unspeakable and unsaid. Where it comes from – no longer bound to functional ends through words or as dance music – seems to have remained a mystery to twentieth-century composers as well. Many works by György Ligeti are born of the emptiness of a rest, into which they again disappear. It may have been religious sentiments prompting Karlheinz Stockhausen's openness to the ascending worshipper or worshippers at the conclusion of his meditative work *Inori* (1973/4). Echo effects and rests accompanied by a soloist within the piece contribute to its transcendental character.

Absolute silence was able to be integrated into the music as a conveyor of meaning, a signifier. Ferruccio Busoni (1911, p. 23) wrote in his *Sketch of a New Aesthetic of Music*:

> That which, within our present-day music, most nearly approaches the essential nature of the art, is the Rest and the Hold (Pause). Consummate players, improvisers, know how to employ these instruments of expression in loftier and ampler measure. The tense silence between two movements – *in itself music* in this environment – leaves wider scope for divination than the more determinate, but therefore less elastic, sound.

Busoni defined music as "signs": "an ingenious device to grasp somewhat of that eternal harmony.

Music's ability to capture the eternal harmony became a widespread *topos* in the nineteenth century and is still influential today, even if it is no longer explicitly voiced. With musical silence in particular, the same question was often raised that Charles Ives addressed in exemplary fashion in the preface to his instrumental piece *The Unanswered Question* (1906). "The perennial question of existence" that the solo trumpet poses in this piece, without the pursuit of an answer reaching the flutes, remains unanswered. The whole thing takes place over the quiet, triple-*piano*, heavily sustained, muted soundscape of the distant (offstage) strings. As a result of the increasingly forceful search for questions and answers, these muted tones are sometimes almost inaudible. They represent, as Ives writes in the preface: "the Silence of the Druids who know, see and hear nothing". They still resound after the last question, withdrawing to a quadruple *piano*. Ives was a confirmed transcendentalist. This went hand in hand with his belief that man and nature partook of a common spiritual principle that is untouchable by the human question-and-answer game. *The Unanswered Question* inspired many of the pieces that will be mentioned in the following, although they did not stem from the same religious beliefs as those underlying Ives's works.

The following begins by returning to Busoni's remark in examining the expressive qualities of non-sounding elements in music, or those which fade away. A strictly systematic classification, however, did not seem feasible. The elements common to all silent pieces sometimes emerged more clearly when individual works were discussed. This procedure also made it possible to better differentiate between different aesthetic convictions. Many more works than could not be accommodated in a chapter would also have merited attention.

One that shall not go unmentioned, however, is the *Symphonie Monotone-Silence* (1944/1961) by Yves Klein, orchestrated by Pierre Henry. It consists of a single sustained D-major triad. Henry's score bears the handwritten note "Durée: 5 ou 7 minutes/ Plus 44 secondes du Silence absolu" (Duration: 5 or 7 minutes/ Plus 44 seconds of absolute silence). It is unclear why it is sometimes played today in a version with 20 minutes of sound and 20 minutes of silence. The silence of the 44 seconds is much more intense than that of 20 seconds, because after the 10 to 12 seconds of the memory image fading away, attention can be maintained with effort, and an intense experience of something inaudible becomes possible, without being distracted by other thoughts. The symphony was performed for the first time at a performance, the *Anthropometrien* (1960), in a reduced version for strings. This was part of the context of the tireless search for immateriality that lead Yves Klein to blend Western and Eastern mysticism as a judo master and a member for a time of the Rosicrucian Order. *Saut dans le vide* (*Leap into the Void*, 1960) is symbolic: The photo document is a montage, and casts doubts on whether the empty ground of the world can be attained by means of reality.

From effect to signifying symbol: the rest

Musical silences are represented in a very direct way through rests, which, however, are part of the sound and do not merely signify an opposition. In the nineteenth century the rest was sometimes described as the "silent sign", as a form of eloquent silence. Because in music, the rest rarely denotes an empty period of time.

Various different meanings may be associated with the absence of sound. Nevertheless, it seems paradoxical that Joseph Haydn used a rest almost like a beat of the drum in his String Quartet in E-flat Major, op. 71 no. 3 (1793). A brief opening passage is followed by a rest lasting one and a half measures, followed by a *Vivace* which, however, integrates the play with the rest, legitimising it, as it were, purely in terms of the compositional structure. But its first occurrence confronts listeners with the surprise of a silence, thus awakening a sudden attention to the music at a time when audiences were not yet used to the later concentrated listening. Mozart also made use of such dramatization with rests within a work (e.g. Piano Concerto in G major, KV. 453, measure 224).

Rests provide an underlying structure and are therefore often used to herald the conclusion. Georg Friedrich Händel dramatically separated the final *Hallelujah* with a general pause. For Haydn it presented one possibility among others for the moments of surprise in his music. In the finale of his String Quartet in E-flat Major, op. 33 no. 2 (1781), general pauses are used to repeatedly postpone the ending. And then it seems the conclusion has arrived after all. But take care not to applaud too soon – it is only after another prolonged general pause lasting two and a half measures that the conclusion is actually reached. In England this quartet was nicknamed "The Joke", an epithet it has retained to this day. But might Haydn have also intended not only that music be understood as a bravura performance, but also that other meanings could be experienced, heard lingering on in rests?

The repetition of a general pause in Johann Sebastian Bach's motet *Jesu, meine Freude* (BWV 227) has a powerful exclamatory effect. The passage at the beginning of the second movement "Es ist nun nichts Verdammliches an denen, die in Christo Jesu sind" ("Now there is nothing damnable in those who are in Christ Jesus") contains a verbal repetition, and "nothing – nothing –" is emphatically underscored with two general pauses. Here, too, the absence of sound during rests is associated with tension and intensification. But here the general pause becomes an admonition, a call to devotion in the face of death. In the St John Passion of 1724 (BWV 245), the music suddenly breaks off at Jesus's death with the words of the evangelist: "And he bowed his head and passed away".

Music that falls silent

The structuring function of the rest became important for twelve-tone music with the relinquishing of tonality. Anton Webern strikingly realised his idea of the comprehensible form through the development of clearly demarcated musical forms. The rest at the beginning of many of his works and his frequent off-beat accents/lack of metric accents also liberate his music from the bonds of meter, and lend it a floating quality. And yet there is generally more than this implied. The beginning of the second movement of the *Bagatellen für Streichquartett,* op. 9 (1913) offers an easily described example of this. It begins with a rest, followed by an ascending eighth-note figure, decrescendoing from *mezzo forte* to *piano* and vanishing into a rest. The combination of a decrescendo with an ascending motion can be found for what is probably the first time in the late work of Beethoven. It reverses the usual combination of a sequence of notes at once rising and growing louder that had been used since the eighteenth century and known as the *Mannheimer Walze* (Mannheim roller) to open, or provide intensification within, a movement. It is probably such moments of turning inward that make Webern's music appear to be on the verge of falling silent. They stem from a Neoplatonic attitude that was already widespread in the nineteenth century, according to which all that was material appeared to be grounded in the spiritual. Webern was influenced by Goethe's pantheistic thought, but, as was not uncommon in his day, also by the continuing legacy of the symbolist movement that saw a spiritual truth behind the objective reality.

Changes in the conception of the world at the beginning of the twentieth century in both philosophy and science (including, not least, the theory of relativity) had raised doubts about the direct cognoscibility of the world. These changes affected the artists in very different ways. They inspired a new use of form that tended towards abstraction. Painters and musicians alike sought to put these thoughts into practice in various ways. One smallest common denominator can be found in the rejection of any form of positivism and in the belief in the ability to adumbrate the invisible. Pure creations of the mind independent of material circumstances were the aim. After the turn of the century the notion of evoking the invisible was also inspired by the reception of theosophical and anthroposophical ideas, particularly among Schoenberg's circle through the writings of Emanuel Swedenborg. The role of the publication of Wassily Kandinsky's *Über das Geistige in der Kunst* (1912) is also not to be underestimated. The book was quickly translated into other languages, including, in 1914, English (*Concerning the Spiritual in Art*). In this work, Kandinsky, himself inspired by theosophical and anthroposophical thought as well as by the occultism of Pyotr Demianovich Ouspenskii, highlighted many facets of the spiritual dimension behind the material phenomena whose inner sound he, too, sought to reveal. Webern's music, reduced as it is to the essential, also opens up a spiritual space. Moreover, the whole of Europe was gripped at this time by the French symbolist movement. Webern himself was profoundly impressed by a performance of Debussy's opera *Pelléas et Mélisande*, which he had heard in 1909.

Fermatas and reverberation: French "métamusique"

The sentence "music is the silence between the notes" is ascribed sometimes to Mozart but mostly to Debussy, and we should recall that the word *silence* in French, as in English, means both the absence of sound and abstaining from speech. The unsaid in or behind what is said was discussed as a characteristic of art in numerous French publications from the 1890s onwards (see Ergal & Fink, 2010), including by Camille Mauclair (1928) in his book *La Musique de Silence*.

On the face of it, the numerous *piano* and *pianissimo* directions in Debussy's music point to silence. The harmony, long durations, lack of metric accents may also create this impression. They are typical of Debussy's musical style. The third movement of *Suite Bergamasque* (1890), *Clair de lune*, anticipates his later compositional techniques. Like many other pieces by Debussy, it comes *con sordino*, out of the silence of a rest; its key is blurred because it is not based on the root note; the key remains in many cases obscured as the work progresses ("mediant" relationships), even though the piece has few chromatics. Tied notes obscure the metre and contribute to shifts in metre. As an aside, successive shifts in pitch, as a hazy chiaroscuro effect, may reflect the title of the piece. The lingering echo effect created in the middle and at the end of the piece with a flowing arpeggio followed by a rest was replaced by Debussy in other works with a fermata followed by a rest or a sustained chord. A heavily accented, dry eighth-note *sforzatissimo* (sff/ sec) of a sound followed by a rest also creates a sense of fading away to an unknown distance (*Préludes I*, 1910, *Ce qu'a vu le vent d'ouest*). These and other phrases give the impression that Debussy would like to overcome the common bookending finale effect of, in particular, dominants and tonics. His works emerge from an unknown space, into which they again fade away. Irrespective of innovations in compositional technique in the form of the use of whole tones and chromatic progressions, there are, as it were, openings to the inaudible in his works, in the form of unresolved seventh and ninth chords and free-floating arabesque melodies. In *Prélude à l'après-midi d'un faune* (1894), the opening flute arabesque is followed by a seventh chord that is not resolved, but instead gives way to a rest. This chord may be mistaken for dissonance; the seventh creates a soft susurration that invites attentive listening. Two performance directions, namely *laissez vibrer* and *en dehors*, are typical of Debussy's differentiation of the sound. The *laissez vibrer* fulfils similar functions of reverberation to the rest and fermata. But it implies a stronger suggestion that something is audible. The sound dies out twice shortly after the beginning in *Les collines d'Anacapri* (*Préludes II*, 1913). The *laissez vibrer* refers to the intangibility of the origin and emergence of the sound.

Creating distance effects by placing the instruments separately was nothing new in Debussy's day. But Debussy composed distance in so many different ways and even without placing the instruments at a distance, making it clear just how much dynamics were no longer merely a means of representation but, much like rhythm and pitch, had become a central composition factor – occasioning Debussy to frequently notate the *Préludes II* on three systems. In addition to descriptions such as *en dehors*, *lointain*, *s'éloignant* (prominently: outside; distant; becoming more distant), a detailed analysis would include the various indications of volume in the different parts. The *en dehors*, mostly soft, muted, belongs to a mysterious background (e.g. *Ibéria*, 1908, 3rd movement, *Marche lointain*, with mutes). But there is also a *dehors* played *forte*, as in the previously mentioned prelude *Ce qu'a vu le vent d'ouest*. It is the epitome of a generative process whereby a musical *form* appears *forte/fortissimo* behind a chromatically ascending demisemiquaver murmur in the left hand.

Theodor W. Adorno (1949/2006, p. 188) wrote critically and with acuity of the no-longer linear-time structure of Debussy's works and their purely suggestive gestures:

> Anyone who has been schooled in German and Austrian music and who has listened to Debussy will be familiar with the experience of frustrated expectation. Throughout any one of his compositions, the naïve ear listens tensely, asking whether 'it is coming'; everything appears to be a prelude [...] a juxtaposition of colors and surfaces such as are to be found in a painting. [...] There is no 'end'; the composition ceases as does the picture, upon which the viewer turns his back. [...] Through this swimming of notes into one another, the music produces something like a sensual infinity.
>
> (Ibid., p. 141)

Debussy was not an impressionist; rather, he was influenced by symbolism, an artistic movement that sought to evoke the deeper meaning of the world through symbols. Among the key librettists of Debussy's vocal works were the symbolists Charles Baudelaire, Paul Verlaine, Maurice Maeterlinck and Stéphane Mallarmé. Debussy also attended the symbolists' gatherings on Tuesday evenings at the apartment of Stéphane Mallarmé.

What Adorno viewed with criticism yet also perceptively discerned in Debussy's music is at the heart of symbolist thought, namely the attempt to evoke allusions to a "sensual infinity" through sensate signs. The phenomena were intended to be merely referential in nature in order to hint at the impenetrable. In musical terms, this meant breaking up the fixed syntax in order to let a silence show through that cannot be attained by any sound expression. In the anthology of his older writings *La Religion de la Musique*, Camille Mauclair (1928, p. 68) spoke of "métamusique", whose silence can be expressed in music at best as an allusion: "There is above music a supreme language to which this allusion refers. This is the generating rhythm of the universe, in respect of which our sounds are merely echoes. And only this rhythm is metamusic."

What Mauclair is referring to here is, in the terminology of philosophy, the distinction between *natura naturata*, which is secondary, produced by a *natura naturans*, which is understood in turn as a creative power at the original source of all things. Whether one wants to read this as an allusion to pantheism, Neoplatonism or monism need not be considered further here. Elements of these movements were present at the time, even if there is no evidence of them having a direct following.

Olivier Messiaen viewed his music as metaphysical in a religious sense, as indicated by the title of his cycle for piano, *Vingt Regards sur l'enfant-Jésus* (1944). Fermatas, pregnant pauses are used here, as well as the direction *laissez vibrer, long* with a fermata, as for example at the end of no. XXVII: *Regard du Silence*. Overall, however, this quiet contemplation of the infant Jesus reveals itself with its motley abundance of chords and its alternation between very slow and virtuoso, fast passages, to be a picture of constantly shifting colours. In some of his earlier works, Messiaen had explicitly named the colours associated with his sounds. That would be scarcely possible in this piece given the kaleidoscopic brilliance of the colours of the rainbow. Messiaen signalled this appearance of the *arc-en-ciel* (the rainbow) in the score, and he describes it in the preface to *Vingt Regards* as multicoloured gemstones blending into one another, and also as "impalpable". The *laissez vibrer* with fermata of the ending is preceded by a longer, almost mono-rhythmic passage with constantly changing chords which is, however, in turn blurred by pedalling and only intended to convey an impression of the play of colour that decelerates before the fermata and evokes sparkling effects in the treble with short appoggiaturas. Messiaen had sometimes spoken concerning his "musique de couleur" of an *éblouissement* (dazzlement) effect, comparable to being dazzled by the rose windows of French Gothic cathedrals. He associated the quiet contemplation of the manger with a similar effect. Quiet or silence here implies the intense experience that entails a form of being overwhelmed.

Maurice Ravel, like Debussy, had a close connection to symbolism. Theo Hirsbrunner (1989, pp. 170–183) has demonstrated this with regard to his settings of symbolist poetry, particularly with an extensive analysis of *Gaspard de la nuit* (1908), a piano piece based on the poems of Aloysius Bertrand, who the symbolists saw as their predecessor. This note shall suffice. For we shall turn now to the fading away that Ravel handled in a very nuanced manner in his works that deal with death. An unusual passage in the *Pavane pour une infante défunte* (1899) involves the detailed composition of a rising crescendo from *pianissimo* to *fortissimo* to an ultimate fading away in a fermata followed by a rest. The individual movements of *Le Tombeau de Couperin* (1914/17) have surprisingly subtle endings, the suggestion of an elusive Somewhere. They are briefly listed here in the order of the movements: A single, very low tone; a quivering tremolo with fermata followed by garlands of notes resonating in the treble. / Tempi alternately hesitating – accelerating – hesitating, unsteady extended conclusion on the light part of the measure, with an empty fifth. / Brief gestures of farewell in *pianissimo*, then a solitary, dry staccato tone, as if it had fallen out of the "static" sound, it is not possible to continue. / Instability of a *fortissimo* sound on the light part of the measure. / A "frozen" trill: *sans laisser vibrer*. / A toccata, not in its usual function as an introductory movement, plunges with a short appoggiatura into the depths: a definitive conclusion.

All in all, an echo of the past blows over Ravel's *Le Tombeau de Couperin,* a suite of baroque dances. It is reminiscent of a memorial. Ravel is said to have dedicated the individual movements to friends who fell in the war. And yet the suite is not sombre, but rather highly nuanced in tone, often atmospheric with the many *pianissimos*. The very carefully developed finales also exude merely a sepulchral aura. The silence cannot be directly conveyed through the senses. Both the music and the sounds of nature are merely a translation of the silence into perceivable sounds,

Monclair wrote. But the soul perceives the silence nevertheless; it is metamusical (*métamusicale*).

The All-One of space and time in the work of Iannis Xenakis

A great leap in time brings us now to a piece from 1961. In connection especially with the rest's function of providing an underlying structure, which has further philosophical implications, it is of almost exemplary significance. It is not necessary to consider whether an entirely different source other than that of Neoplatonic thought is relevant for the relationship of that which can be perceived to the non-sensory, as Platonism, is Iannis Xenakis's point of reference.

His piano piece *Herma* is based, like other works, on a mathematical method, namely the logic of the sieve theory. This was used to "sift out" categories of notes and their relationships and arrange them in a temporal order, creating the impression for the listener of clouds or linear sequences. Xenakis (1992, pp. 175–177) described the method in detail, also summarising it more briefly in the preface to the score. The abstract structural connection was clearly important to Xenakis. The pitch categories changing in accordance with the sifting procedure are indicated in the score with letters.

Despite the mathematical method he used, however, Xenakis always viewed himself as a composer in the true sense of the word. *Herma* is a virtuoso, blistering piece of great compass; at the beginning it strives with increasing density/fullness towards what constitutes the climax of the first section, a single sustained semibreve. This formal structure can be easily followed by the listener. The following section becomes less dense towards the end. The structure of the rests sets it apart. Rests lasting one or two measures allow silence to shimmer through despite the rapid tempo. But there are rests lasting as many as four measures that test the listener's memory span. The piece thins out towards the end, a four-bar rest serves as the conclusion; into this silence, however, breaks a recollection of a traditional stretto with a wild triple *forte*. It lingers on in a rest, which is not, however, as unusual as the translucent places of the whole-measure rests.

Construction and auditory comprehension, whereby the work is reconstructed through listening, coalesce in Xenakis's work. The mathematical structure may sometimes be too complicated to be understood in detail. But it is important to know that his music has an abstract foundation. Xenakis viewed his pieces as symbolic music, i.e. understood them as a symbol for something not directly present. Like his architectural constructions, they too are rooted in the idea of the identity of space and time in an All-One, as described by Parmenides, whom Xenakis frequently cited. Parmenides postulated an indivisible, homogenous, omnipresent original source; having not yet "become", it contains space and time. It is no coincidence that Xenakis bases his piano work on this idea. He ruled out a purely temporal differentiation with a performance direction: The individual tones are not to be accented. In the preface to the score, we read: "The name Herma means bond, but also foundation, embryo etc." What do these weighty reflections mean for the unusual rest structure? Suffice it to draw a parallel to the musically cadenced window façade that Xenakis designed for the monastery at La Tourette. The view through the glass dissolves the solid concrete into a whole that is organised in terms of space and time.

The fermata: dreaming spaces and sudden ecstasies in the work of Luigi Nono

There is probably no other work specifying as many fading fermatas as Luigi Nono's *Fragmente – Stille, an Diotima* (1980). Moments of pausing and fading away permeate this string quartet, often in combination with the tempo indication crotchet = 30, which is rarely used by composers because pieces then appear to be on the verge of falling apart. The constant changes of tempo prevent the flow of a pronounced metre from developing. In 52 places, specified as inaudibly silent, like directions to the performers, are 47 fragments of Hölderlin citations: "das weisst aber du nicht…" ("but you don't know that… ") is repeated five times.[1] Concerning the quotations, Nono noted in the preface: "never to be spoken aloud during the performance – under no circumstances to be taken as programmatic performance indications […]. The players should 'sing' them inwardly in their autonomy…" As the concertgoers normally read the references to Hölderlin in the programme, but can only guess which passages they pertain to, this level of eloquent silence demands an increase in attention and hence also in immersion in the music. The fermatas, for which Nono used special signs up to four times as long as a standard fermata, and often indicated a duration in seconds, often follow a sustained note. The two fermatas just after the beginning, with a duration of 15 seconds and 17 seconds, are commensurate with that of echoic memory, which can last up to 18 seconds. They demand that the sound, mostly performed softly and therefore already vanished, continues to be heard after it has gone. But are indications of endless 25- or 27-second rests meant to call memories back?[2] The subsiding *al niente* also explicitly substitutes silence for auditory events. The dilation of time through the fermatas *al niente* is also, as it says in the preface, meant to sound different each time, namely "with free fancy – of dreaming spaces – of sudden ecstasies – of unutterable thoughts – of tranquil breaths – of silences 'intemporally' sung." The expressive qualities of the string quartet, of distance, silence, tranquility, depth, etc., continue to be felt by the listener in the experience of silence. Does the quotation of the chanson "Malor me bat",[3] used in many masses during the Renaissance, mark a nadir of grief? Nono cites it with a reference to Ockeghem: "*sotto voce, dolcissimo, ... wenn ich trauernd versank...*" ("*sotto voce, dolcissimo, ...* as I sank down in grief"). But it is not the experience of absolute nothingness. "*Mit innigster Empfindung*" ("with the utmost feeling"), the performance direction borrowed from Beethoven's "Heiliger Dankgesang", or "holy song of thanksgiving" from op. 132, soughs in Nono's piece in quarter tones *sotto voce*, sometimes with great shifts in pitch, fades *al niente* four times, but also erupts into a triple *forte*:[4] An ecstatic outburst that testifies to the fact that these moments of "silences, 'songs' of other spaces, other skies / to otherwise rediscover the possible, do not 'say farewell to hope'" (preface to the score). This remark by Nono was initially ignored when his string quartet was interpreted as revealing his hopes for social and political change. With the string quartet, he simply took a different approach to that of the calls to revolution of some of his earlier works, which sought to effect a direct overpowering. Helmut Lachenmann (1999, p. 27), a student of Nono's and extremely well acquainted with his work, has expressed this very compellingly:

> The silence into which Nono's late works lead us is a *fortissimo* of agitated perception. It is not the sort of silence in which human searching comes to rest, but rather one in which it is recharged with strength and the sort of restlessness which sharpens our senses and makes us impatient with the contradictions of reality. [...]. However, a topos arises which is also characteristic of the change in Nono's Art and at the same time redefines the continuity: that moment of erring – in a double sense – goalless searching, in directions where there are

neither paths nor signposts; and also erring in the sense of a priori failure because the goal surpasses the imagination. It is only in the strength displayed by the seeker to continue to err that the reality and latent presence of the goal reveals itself as hidden inside ourselves.

This restless silence of a jolting awareness is evoked, among other things, by the constant tritones of the string quartet. These derive from the *scala enigmatica* from Giuseppe Verdi's *Requiem* that Nono takes as a basis for the piece, a scale comprising elements of both major and minor scales, as well as the whole-tone scale. Many sound constellations can be derived from this. If we listen with a concentrated, heightened awareness, we can even hear in the background in Nono's work an allusion to a harmony that is quite unusual in new music. Almost inaudible, in quadruple *piano*, a fifth relation somewhat roughened with quarter tones puts in an appearance:[5] "wenn aus der Tiefe ..." ("when out of the depth..."). It seems to be linked to places that mark a section in transition. This fifth, a timeless interval and one that is often also felt to be intercultural, fades away *al niente* at the quartet's conclusion: "eine stille Freude mir ... wieder..." ("quiet joy comes back to me"). The interval emerges repeatedly from the *scala enigmatica*. It is not the aim of Nono's string quartet in the narrower sense, but perhaps an indication of hope: "to otherwise rediscover the possible, do not 'say farewell to hope'".

The meaning of silence in Nono's work is different to the way in which it is put to use in the work of Ives, Debussy and Webern to listen intently to the primaeval source of a non-sensory, spiritual metamusic of being. We might speak here of "deep listening". Nono's string quartet, on the other hand, demands the intentional act of a "detecting hearing", a listening as a concentrated, effortful quest to discern a hidden message in reality. It is surprising that non-sound, the absence of sound, in music can express very different forms of an eloquent silence.

Silent music – the introduction of new forms of silence

Nono's string quartet encouraged composers to give greater attention to silence in Europe in the last third of the twentieth century. But a mixture of different influences was at play.

It wasn't until the 1980s that the recorded piano and ondulina improvisations by Giacinto Scelsi, rendered in traditional notation by ghostwriters, became known. Scelsi believed in the theory of reincarnation and was very heavily influenced by Indian philosophy. He was also inspired by American music, including La Monte Young's conceptual pieces. Some of the verbal scores of his *Compositions* (1960) aim for a spiritual meditation practice: No. 2, listening to a crackling fire; No. 5, watching butterflies flying; No. 6, the musicians watching the audience in the way that the audience usually watches the musicians. The *Compositions* have no fixed duration. The best known is No. 7, consisting of the notes B and F#, with the instruction "to be held for a long time". Young had turned to Indian music at this time. In 1964 he founded *The Theater of Eternal Music*, a group of artists and musicians that became known for their long-duration music. They had sometimes already begun playing before the audience was admitted; there was no fixed end; the soundscape was characterised by sustained drone tones.

Other tendencies in minimal music also suggested new directions. The 1972 European tour by Steve Reich's ensemble, which was influenced in turn by African music, was significant, as were the *Metamusik Festivals* in 1974 and 1976, which gave a very broad scope to minimal music, including works by Terry Riley and Philip Glass. Interest at the time focused on the connections between Far Eastern cultures and those of the West. Silence meant committing oneself to a form of almost trance-like meditation.

John Cage indisputably made the most widely discussed contribution to the subject of silence with his so-called silent piece, *4'33"* (1952). It influenced European composers when the subject of silence re-emerged in the 1990s. The works of Morton Feldman were now also known in Europe. But they were often placed in the context of John Cage, although Feldman's music should be seen rather as mediating European and American thought. He (1985, p. 137) rarely spoke of silence – at most of stasis, a state of abeyance. For him, however, the concept of "abstract experience" is central. In connection with silence, it provides fertile ground for reflection. By the way, it should be mentioned that also the fade out of pop music leads to an attitude of immersion into the indeterminate (Kopiez et al., 2013).

Abstract experience: Morton Feldman

As always in Feldman's music, the beginning is quiet, yet clearly set out, although admitting of exceptions such as the piece *Intermission 6* (1953), which places 15 sounds, freely distributed on a page, at the disposal of the pianist or the two pianists. The endings, on the other hand, disappear into the open with the different parts thinning out and with *ritardandi*. Feldman (1985, p. 89) was heavily preoccupied with the way in which all sounds decay as they fade away. This is also relevant within a piece if there are no tempo indications and the sound has to fade away before the next one follows. The fading away should, at the same time, make the sound appear to start without a beginning. The fact that the sound departs from us, instead of moving towards us, creates the impression of a landscape vanishing from sight. The fading away suggests an unknown place of origin (Feldman, 1985, p. 87), whose atmosphere is merely alluded to in the sensory present. There are indications that Feldman believed there was a different reality behind the one accessible to us through the senses.

The most striking characteristic of Feldman's system of notation is the grid technique of his pattern compositions. For a whole piece, before he began composing in the strict sense, Feldman drew vertical lines, mostly nine arrangement lines, on sheet music paper. This grid maps a spatiotemporal structure; as an image in noted form it offers something external to hold onto. Feldman (ibid., p. 125) described the grid as a "ruler". This supporting structure extends into the piece, albeit mostly inaudibly, for instance through the metre indication 3/8. Tom Hall (2007) has examined the relationships between the grid and the musical construction, and identified a neutralisation of the grids through asymmetrical overlays of groupings of patterns, creating a shifting auditory impression. In some pieces, however, such as the four-hour trio *For Philip Guston* (1984), the grid emerges at the beginning, over the course of 35 bars, in the form of interrupting rests, albeit not entirely regular and intact. These rests are one of the few instances in which Feldman (ibid., p. 129) used the word "silence". He spoke of "silent frames". Does this mean that the audible sound elements stand out, as it were, from a background of silence? The patterns are in turn to be understood as relatively self-contained units. A linear passage of time in the sense of a consistent development is not intended.

Feldman often mentions in his writing Henri Bergson and his concept of time, which replaced the forward movement of a linear, chronological progression with the *durée* as a temporal fabric – a changing interpenetration of many different, shifting qualities. The totality of the patterns in Feldman's work embedded in the structure of the grid, their repetitions, superimpositions and permutations, have the effect for the listener of the experience of an undirected sound, ultimately of an experience in which time is suspended. The composer, who described himself as "very Kierkegaardian", was heavily influenced by Søren Kierkegaard, whose story *Repetition* (1843) established a new philosophical category. Kierkegaard considered true repetition to be impossible, because it implies a confluence of past and present, whereby that which is present is always also that which is absent at the moment in which, according to Kierkegaard, eternity manifests itself. Feldman (ibid., p. 107) used Kierkegaard's image of the leap for this experiencing in an undefinable state: "The leap into the Abstract is more like going to another place where the time changes. Once you make that leap there are no longer any definitions. [...] It has to happen."

Another important intellectual ally for Feldman was Piet Mondrian, whose paintings with their purely horizontal and vertical grids hide nothing and show nothing. They abstract from any traditional pictorial representation. Feldman (ibid., p. 115) said of Piet Mondrian's "plus/minus" series that it even neutralised our ability to visually complete the paintings: "It is all there, so to speak, but *where* or *how* to look at them, is not."

Feldman pointed out that Mondrian's abstract constructions have blurred elements that are easily overlooked, because, for instance, the grids with their black borders may be slightly blurred with the white and are also frayed the edges. For Mondrian, a confirmed Calvinist and anthroposophist, the frayed edges of the grid (also outwards) signified an opening up to the spiritual. Feldman (ibid., p. 81), who for his part considered art to be merely a metaphor, raised questions that were at least similar to Mondrian's: "How can you bridge what is real with what is only a metaphor? Art is only a metaphor." Of interest in this context is a remark by the art historian Rosalind E. Krauss (1979/1986, p. 10) about grid paintings, which were increasingly used by artists in the 1960s in an attempt to encourage viewers to see something non-visible. She described them as spiritually, "religiously" motivated, because a grid could ultimately extend in all directions and potentially to infinity, thus using the real sensory representation merely as a means to evoke something abstract. This can by all means be extended to Feldman's idea of his music being rooted in an abstract experience, allowing us to understand his grids in terms of Krauss's (1979/1986, p. 52) interpretation: "The grid is a staircase to the universal."

The image of a staircase is an apposite symbol for the fact that much of American art production – including in the second half of the twentieth century – refers theoretically to the notion of the sublime, accompanied by scholarly publications dedicated to the same subject. The concept was already being redefined in the nineteenth century, and *sublimitas* was now no longer equated with the kind of delightful horror produced by lightning or the Alps, but rather with an inner experience of the ineffable, the inexpressible. A grid laid out by the artist has the effect of the limiting frame of a window, evoking a tension between something which can be perceived and a sensory non-present present. In his seminal essay *The Sublime Is Now*, however, Barnett Newman (1948, p. 53) presented this inner experience of seemingly immaterial *sublimitas* as an exclusively American achievement, "free from the weight of European culture […] we are making it out of ourselves, out of our own feelings". It is no coincidence that this description did not seem satisfactory among Feldman's closer circle of friends. Mark Rothko frequently used a similar choice of words with regard to his paintings, as in 1947 (p. 84), when he spoke of "transcendental experience", which surpasses empirical experience while at the same time remaining bound to it. This definition of the sublime, which has been the standard definition since the nineteenth century, also applies to Feldman's work. It is therefore no surprise that it also includes musical techniques that recall traditions despite the fact that they fundamentally change the musical material.

In his investigation of sound and silence in Beethoven's oeuvre, William Kinderman (1995) described open closing cadences that want to go beyond the frame, similar to those found in Feldman's work. And he demonstrated how deeply they penetrate into the compositional structure, as for example in the last variation of op. 109, *Mit innigster Empfindung*, where there is a veritable decay of the cantabile theme. The sonata ends with a subsiding pedalled *ritardando* in an elusive Somewhere. The inaudible that cannot be represented, but only felt, is a metaphor in the sense of a catachresis, namely not directly given, but subject to the condition of the audible. Feldman (1985, p. 89) not only associated this idea with the fading away of the sound; rather, an audible, "sounding" piece of music can point to this indefinite, inaudible dimension:

> What concerns me is that condition in music where aural dimension is obliterated. What do I mean by this? The obliteration of the aural plane doesn't mean the music should be inaudible – though my own music may sometimes seem to suggest this. Offhand, I think of the

Schubert *Fantasie in F Minor*. The weight of the melody here is such that you can't place where it is, or what it's coming from.

The common conception of silence as the lack of sensory information is not what is meant by the inaudible ineffable. It presupposes the leap to another place that cannot be forced: "It has to happen." Nevertheless, the composer demands of the listener maximum concentration. That Feldman's later works often lasted many hours, to symbolise an infinite scope, presents a challenge for their reception, because it demands complete absorption, absolute immersion. Only then is the leap to the other place possible.

4'33" – The buzzing of ambient sounds

At the end of the 1940s, Cage intended to sell a "silent prayer" in the form of uninterrupted silence, lasting the length of a vinyl record of the time, to the company MUZAK. The idea is considered the initial catalyst for the three silent movements of *4'33"*, demarcated by pianist David Tudor at the world premiere in 1952 by lowering and lifting the keyboard lid (ending with an open piano). The fact that there was nothing to hear in the concert hall except for the sounds of the audience was felt to be scandalous, especially as it was meant to be a benefit concert.

4'33" seems to have been a key work for Cage for sounds that did not pursue any compositional intention, stirring up nothing but sounds that already existed in reality, albeit in a set time frame. Other pieces whose titles referred to *4'33"* followed, though they could be of different lengths and use different settings to produce sound with the intention of reconciling sensory perception and meditative stillness.

It was evidently difficult, however, to find the framework for the purged, silent piece of music, *4'33"*, in which a pianist was to play nothing. Thomas M. Maier (2001, p. 137 ff.) has reappraised the three versions of the score and discussed them in detail. The first version of 1952 has been lost and is known only from accounts. David Tudor's recollection is important here. This version was written in conventional notation on manuscript paper and contained empty bars without rests. The second version, printed in landscape format and also dating from 1952, uses graphic notation with vertical lines, whereby Cage specified that 1 page = 7 inches = 56". For Cage, as for other artists, the relationship between space and time had become self-evident. The duration of the individual movements is indicated at the end of each one. But is the number 60 on the top horizontal line a metronome marking for the tempo with which a page should be read? The third version from 1960 indicates the order of the movements one below the other with the direction "Tacet". The total length is now indicated only by the title, which in one edition, however, is abandoned as well. The tremendous effort Cage put into creating the scores challenges us to understand the genesis of *4'33"* in part as a process of purification from any and all musical rules and regulations. Performed *tacet*, the music becomes a meditative yet buzzing/humming silence that just needs a frame by means of specified durations to bring out the play of ambient sounds.

4'33" – The pure experience

As well as Meister Eckart, the theorist of Zen Buddhism Daisetz Teitaro Suzuki also had a crucial influence on Cage. It is not known precisely when exactly Cage came into contact with Zen Buddhism (possibly as early as the late 1940s), but we do know that he attended Suzuki's lectures in 1952. Much has been written about this, and often repeated. But the fact has mostly been overlooked that Suzuki, who had already spent 11 years in the US from 1897 onwards, blended Eastern and Western views in his thought, lending Japanese Buddhism a special focus. Suzuki, who had known William James personally, had studied James's writings and passed his ideas on to his students. As only some of Cage's books have been preserved, it is difficult to establish outright whether he was directly influenced by James's writings. Only recently has the importance of pragmatism for the development of American music been pointed out (Brooks, 2016; Clarkson, 2001). It would appear that this requires a rethinking of Cage research. Remarkably, however, these more recent studies neglect the writings of Van Meter Ames (1954), a philosopher informed by both pragmatism and Buddhism, who was a close friend of Cage's. The correspondence between the two has not even been published yet, despite its importance for Cage's understanding of Buddhism. Ames had in fact given a lecture on Cage and pragmatism at the *Sixth Congress of Aesthetics* in Uppsala in 1968. Of central importance to Ames (1956, p. 306) was James's concept of "pure experience" (James, 1904). This undoubtedly describes the experience Cage was aiming for with *4'33"*.

For Cage, however, Suzuki (1994, p. 20) was presumably the most important source of information on the spiritual aspects of pragmatism;

for his part, Suzuki repeatedly pointed out the impact of William James's work on Zen Buddhist theory. He concurred with James's idea of mystical experience: "That there is a noetic quality in mystic experience has been pointed out by James in his *Varieties of Religious Experience* and this also applies to the Zen experience." In the book mentioned earlier, Suzuki characterized James's "illumination" and "revelation" as "noetic qualities": "They are states of insight into depths of truth, unplumed by the discursive intellect" (1902, p. 371). In Japanese Zen Buddhism in particular, James's idea of "pure experience" was adopted by Nishida Kitarō, a philosopher and friend of Suzuki and proponent of the so-called Kyoto school. This "pure experience" could not be clearly attributed to a material basis but was rather a state of consciousness. In it, external things are presented, but in such a way that these impressions are broken up and reassembled, i.e. processes take place that are difficult to appreciate and understand individually. In the version proposed by the Kyoto school, world and consciousness are integrated in these processes, i.e. satori is anchored in them.

William James (1890, vol. I, p. 488) first described the "pure experience" of the untarnished perception of a stream of consciousness free of all concepts in relation to new born babies: "The baby [...] feels it all as one great blooming, buzzing confusion... [...] the original extents or bignesses of all the sensations which came to our notice at once, coalesced together into one and the same space." And he did not bar the possibility of this unspoilt, pristine unity of experience (ibid.) for adults. He spoke of the fact "that any number of impressions, from any number of sensory sources, falling simultaneously on a mind which has not yet experienced them separately, will fuse into a single and undivided object for that mind" (ibid.). The assumption that before every act of perception and consciousness a "pure experience" precedes without a subject–object polarity is one of the premises of his thinking. In 1904 he explicitly stated this thought once again.

4'33" creates a prototypical situation for very different impressions to blend in unison, free of any form of conceptual distinction or classification. They make possible what James described as "pure experience", a "blooming, buzzing", that leads to an unmediated unity of consciousness and sensation. As a prime reality (1890, I, p. 263), this experience is without self-brand. Thus, it does not entail a dualism between world and individual, either: It is "a sense of existence in general without the least trace of distinction between the me and the not-me." This aspect of intentionlessness, without self-brand, was one of Cage's most fundamental aesthetic beliefs.

4'33" is not silent in the sense of soundlessness. The idea is, rather, that in the buzzing of the ambient sounds, freed from human conceptualisation, a sense of the wholeness of the existence of the world and humanity can be experienced. Cage also sought with chance procedures to dismantle the accustomed categorial relationships of compositional technique and to expand consciousness to include possibilities of genuine knowledge, which differs from that with which we are already familiar. The parallel to James, whose "psychology" is a wrestling with existential questions, is astonishing. In his published lectures *A Pluralistic Universe* (1909, p. 212), James disputed that conceptualising, rational, logical thought could afford any fundamental knowledge of the world:

> I have finally found myself compelled to give up the logic, fairly, squarely, and irrevocably. It has an imperishable use in human life, but that use is not to make us theoretically acquainted with the essential nature of reality. [...]. When you have broken the reality into concepts you never can reconstruct it in its wholeness.
>
> (Ibid., p. 261)

This led to his call to "install yourself in a phenomenal moment" (ibid.) – a call that could serve as an epigraph to Cage's work.

The perennial question of existence

Silence in the form of a rest can have the effect of dramatising the music, because it creates tension. In the twentieth century in particular, however, it often assumed a spiritual significance. It was believed to evoke religious, transcendental notions of an immaterial, otherworldly beyond, or, in the tradition of Eastern religions, occasion a meditation on the existence inherent in things. Silence can also be associated with the attempt at a symbolist reference to an inherently spiritual component in things, and with a monistic/pantheistic intention to penetrate reality with a spiritual dimension. Silence as mediator of an experience of immanence that encompasses *Dasein* and being can also serve as an indication of the all-encompassing unity of space and time, or indeed simply suggest the search for a better reality that could be hidden in the given reality. Even if a composer has explicitly rejected metaphysics, the musically composed silence still carries the implicit idea of something that cannot be expressed in words. It suggests the attempt to imbue something that is musically inaudible nevertheless with a trace of the sensate. What is always intrinsically inherent is the perennial question of existence.

Notes

1 At numbers 34, 36, 38, 43, 45.
2 At number 40: "endlos" ("endless").
3 At number 48.
4 At number 43.
5 At number 8 (1st and 2nd violin).

References

Adelung, J. C. (1793–1801). *Grammatische-kritisches Wörterbuch der hochdeutschen Mundart* (4 vols.). Leipzig: Breitkopf & Härtel.
Adorno, T. W. (2006). *Philosophy of Modern Music* (A. G. Mitchell & W. V. Blomster, Trans.). London-New York: Continuum. (Original work published 1949).
Ames, V. M. (1954). Zen and pragmatism. *Philosophy East and West*, 4(1), 19–35.
Ames, V. M. (1956). Zen and American philosophy. *Philosophy East and West*, 5(4), 305–320.
Brooks, W. (2016). Pragmatics of silence. In: N. Losseff & J. Doctor (Eds.), *Silence, Music, Silent Music* (pp. 97–126). Aldershot: Ashgate.
Busoni, F. (1911). *Sketch of a New Esthetic of Music* (T. Baker, Trans.). New York: Schirmer.
Clarkson, A. (2001). The intent of the musical moment: John Cage and the transpersonal. In: D. E. Bernstein & C. Hatch (Eds.), *Writings through John Cage's Music, Poetry, and Art* (pp. 62–112). Chicago: University of Chicago Press.
Ergal, Y.-M., & Finck, M. (2010). *Écriture et silence au XXs siècle*. Strasbourg: Presses Universitaires.
Feldman, M. (1985). *Essays* (W. Zimmermann Ed.). Kerpen: Beginner Press.
Hall, T. (2007). Notational image. Transformation and the grid in the late music of Morton Feldman. In: L. Kouvaras, R. L. Martin, & G. Hair (Eds.), *Current Issues in Music* (Vol. 1, pp. 7–24). Amaroo and Sydney: Southern Voices.
Hirsbrunner, T. (1989). *Maurice Ravel. Sein Leben. Sein Werk*. Laaber: Laaber Verlag.
James, W. (1890). *Principles of Psychology* (2 vols.). New York: Holt.
James, W. (1902). *The Varieties of Religious Experience. A Study in Human Nature*. New York/London: Longmans, Green.
James, W. (1904). A world of pure experience. *The Journal of Philosophy, Psychology and Scientific Methods*, 1(20), 533–543.

James, W. (1909). *A Pluralistic Universe. Hibbert Lectures at Manchester College.* New York/London: Longmans, Green.
Kern, U. (2018). *Meister Eckart. Der transzendentale Aufklärer.* Münster: LIT Verlag.
Kinderman, W. (1995). Über den Rahmen hinaus. Das Verhältnis von Klang und Nicht-Klang bei Beethoven. In: E. Schmierer, S. Fontaine, W. Grünzweig, & M. Brzoska (Eds.), *Töne – Farben – Formen* (pp. 59–78). Laaber: Laaber Verlag.
Kopiez, R., Platz, F., Müller, S., & Wolf, A. (2013). When the pulse of the song goes on: Fade-out in popular music and the pulse continuity phenomenon. *Psychology of Music, 43*(3), 359–374.
Krauss, R. E. (1986). Grids. In: *The Originality of the Avant-Garde and Other Modernist Myths* (pp. 8–22). Cambridge, MA: MIT Press. (Original work published 1979).
Lachenmann, H. (1999). Touched by Nono. *Contemporary Music Review, 18*(1), 17–30.
Lyotard, F. (1985). *Les Immatériaux* [Exhibition Catalogue]. Paris: Centre Pompidou.
Losseff, N., & Doctor, J. (Eds.) (2007). *Silence, Music, Silent Music.* London-New York: Routledge.
Maier, T. M. (2001). *Ausdruck der Zeit. Ein Weg zu John Cages stillem Stück 4'33".* Saarbrücken: Pfau.
Mauclair, C. (1928). *La Religion de la Musique.* Paris: Librairie Fischbacher.
Newman, B. (1948). The sublime is now. *Tiger's Eye, 1*(6), 52–53.
Rothko, M. (1947). The romantics were prompted. *Possibilities, 1*, 84.
Toop, D. (2010). Art of silence. In: *Sinister Resonance. The Mediumship of the Listener* (pp. 73–107). New York: Continuum Publisher Group.
Schmusch, R., & Ullman, J. (Eds.) (2018). *Stille / Musik.* Büdingen: Pfau Verlag.
Suzuki, D. T. (1994). *The Zen Koan As a Means of Attaining Enlightment.* Boston/Rutland, Vermont/Tokyo: Charles e. Tuttle.
Voegelin, S. (2010). *Listening to Noise and Silence. Towards a Philosophy of Sound Art.* London/New York: Continuum.
Xenakis, I. (1992). *Formalized Music: Thought and Mathematics in Music.* Stuyvesant, NY: Pendragon Press.

Chapter 5

Silence in an age of distraction

Patrick Shen

Any modern person with a healthy set of ears can attest to the scarcity of silence. The silence which once blanketed nearly every aspect of our lives – and was intimately linked to survival for our ancestors – has long been replaced by the sound of industry and transportation. Nearly 150 years of rapid technological growth void of any real checks and balances in regard to the health impacts of its ever-expanding sonic footprint has ensured that this silence will likely never return. Some may be skeptical of the actual costs associated with living in a world without silence. Others may suggest that the advantages which technological innovation brings far outweigh the benefits of silence. Perhaps they are right on some level. Regardless, I am less interested in pitting technology against silence than I am in exploring the ways in which the two can co-exist. More fundamental to that, a case must be made for the restoration of silence into the fabric of our experience. For once silence and the gravity of its vanishing is understood, perhaps then may we devise methods to restore and protect that silence for future generations.

What do we mean by *silence* anyway? One could easily fill an entire volume on the slippery nature of this word alone. For those of us in the Western world, the word silence is often associated with the cessation of sound or noise. The silence between speech, between two notes of music, or the silence that falls on the battlefield after the last shot is fired. Indeed, there are aspects of this notion of silence which offer an important dimension to the way we navigate experience, aspects that are under threat today. These spaces give definition to and inform our experience. If not for the pause in someone's speech, for example, we would not be afforded the time to reflect and form a proper response. Yet in the modern era, for each momentary pause in the soundtrack of our lives, there is something in nearly every instance – from elevator music to nervous finger tapping – designed to replace it. In this age of rapid-fire communication, silences between speech have become "awkward." In fact, just three to four seconds of silence for the average English speaker is what it takes for verbal exchanges to get awkward according to Michael Handford, professor of linguistics at the University of Tokyo.[1] Whether it's an *um*, *ah*, or a comment about the weather, we feel compelled to fill the silence with something, anything to avoid the discomfort a break in conversation brings. Indeed, fast and frequent talkers find themselves garnering more attention than their slower counterparts, increasing in power and influence as the meeting goes on. Not only does the nearly continuous speech directed toward us demand our attention, those on the receiving end even consider these fast talkers more intelligent, more likable, and even better looking. "All of this would be fine if more talking were correlated with greater insight," Susan Cain (2013) writes in her best-selling book *Quiet: The Power of Introverts in a World That Can't Stop Talking*, "but research suggests that there is no such link."

In the same way that artists and photographers use negative space to give shape and definition to their subjects, silence has a way of setting one thing apart from another. It is in this space in which we engage with what came before and anticipate what comes next. Without the ceasing of one note we cannot anticipate the delight of the subsequent note when enjoying a favorite piece of music. Without a break in conversation, we cannot reflect and form a thoughtful response, and move a conversation forward in a fruitful manner.

While many of our commonly shared notions of silence may suggest that it is more to do with an absence of something, scientists, philosophers, theologians, and writers through the ages have found plenty to say about what is contained by this word, paradoxically leaving us with volumes upon volumes of literature exploring the complexities of this ineffable concept. The seventeenth-century Spanish mystic Miguel de Molinos distinguished three degrees of silence related to our everyday experience: silence of the mouth, silence of the mind, and silence of the will. For the American composer John Cage, silence had more to do with an awakening of sorts, as he referred to it as "a change of mind, a turning around." As for acoustic silence, after a life-altering experience inside a soundproof room in which he heard only the sounds of his own body, Cage famously concluded that there is in fact "no such thing as silence." In his book *The Way of the Heart*, Theologian Henri Nouwen speaks of an ancient silence with more existential implications which he gleans from the teachings of the Desert Fathers and Mothers of third-century Egypt. Nouwen writes, "In the sayings of the Desert Fathers, we can distinguish three aspects of silence. First, silence makes us pilgrims. Secondly, silence guards the fire within. Thirdly, silence teaches us to speak." For Nouwen, words were an instrument of the present while silence was "the mystery of the future world," in which words are no longer necessary. If the proliferation of words which continue to "form the floors, the walls, and ceilings of our existence," as Nouwen wrote back in 1981, is any indication, the future world clearly remains elusive.

Many have understood this paradox of examining silence through words and have attempted in numerous other ways to explore the varied dimensions of silence. Religiously devout men and women have spent lifetimes bathing in silence in order to, as Nouwen might say, bridge this world with the future world. Painters like Robert Rauschenberg and Ad Reinhardt have explored nothingness by stripping their processes of all technique, offering us "blank" white and black canvases. An essay is not the place for a deep investigation of these ideas which speak to the deepest aspects of the human experience and that are perhaps best understood through experience itself. What I'm sure becomes glaringly apparent to the reader is that silence is more than what we have been led to believe and when considered in the aforementioned ways is evidently much more inclusive than exclusive. Put another way, silence has much to say to those willing to listen.

It is this expansive, transcendental element of this vast subject which I found most intriguing when in 2012 I set out to make a feature-length film to investigate silence further. Aware of the inherent paradox in using images and sounds to paint a picture of silence, I was only interested in adopting a cinematic language which would embody the subject and invite viewers into an experience of silence rather than attempt to demystify it. As I began to imagine a film which would embody silence, it quickly became apparent the challenges I'd face in attempting to give form to a formless material or concept, to demystify that which is the embodiment of mystification itself. When considering the film's soundtrack, I wondered if there should be any sound at all. If I were to make a purely silent film, stripped entirely of a soundtrack, wouldn't then the subjects I chose to photograph and the juxtaposition of those images express something of me rather than of silence? In every scenario I imagined, I found myself imposing my own artistic sensibilities upon silence. Making matters more problematic, the mountain of books and decades of highly revered works of art devoted to this very subject elevated silence to that of something sacred, way beyond the reach of the intellectualizing and demystifying that most documentaries are known for.

As the Japanese would suggest, the shape and personality of the silence we encounter draw their identity from our surroundings, our past experiences, our memories, and even our emotional state. Hushed voices gently reverberating through the halls of a museum heard just moments after you've waited in line outside amidst a cacophony of the bustling city, may instantly calm the nerves and quiet the mind while someone who's seen too many horror films may find the dead quiet of a cemetery rather unsettling. The characteristics of the silence one experiences depends wholly on the individual; where she has been and how she is feeling factor directly into the unique shape of one's encounter with silence. And so I began to ponder my own journey with silence for some clues. I thought about the existential yearnings of my adolescence which sparked my journey inward. The theater listing in the newspaper that led to my visiting a movie theater one afternoon in 2007 to see *Into Great Silence* the beautiful film by Philip Groning. The words of authors, filmmakers and poets like Max Picard, Nathaniel Dorsky, Mary Oliver, Rainer Maria Rilke, Henry David Thoreau, John Cage, and Pico Iyer, to name a few. Those who write in a manner that embodies silence rather than attempts to demystify it. Then there was the music of John Cage and others like Arvo Part who treat silence as a collaborator rather than a space with which to fill their egos. It appeared that my own journey into silence had been informed and fueled by experiences unique to me, experiences which gave me insight, context, and the freedom to explore the spaces in-between. What I eventually discovered was that silence and sound were inextricably tied to one another and that silence was intimately connected to one's experience in the world.

One begins to see now, I hope, the grand implications of silence and that silence – at least of a particular variety – can bring immeasurable value to the human experience. In fact, one might say that it is integral to the human experience. Further, one should begin to see that if this silence continues to be engulfed by the noise of the modern world, we stand to lose an aspect of our humanity. How bad is the noise problem? Noise has become so pervasive in our lives, it's hardly noticed. We have somehow been convinced that shouting at our dinner companions just to be heard amidst a cacophony of background music, voices, and the screech of chairs dragged across hard reflective surfaces is a sure sign that we have "come to the right place." It's no wonder why friends gathered around a table with heads down buried in their devices is such a common sight now. Shouting is exhausting. The social implications of noise aside, the World Health Organization has ranked noise pollution the second most hazardous environmental toxin – just below air pollution – elevating noise to a legitimate health concern. It's no longer a matter of annoyance or impaired concentration when the neighbor's stereo is too loud. Nearly half a century of research on the deleterious health effects of noise undeniably establishes noise as a serious danger to children's cognitive development and our health, leading to, among others, a host of cardiovascular problems.[2]

With all the wonderful things that technological innovation has brought us, we've also inherited a host of social, political, environmental, and spiritual challenges that have altered the very fabric of being human.

We needn't look too far back to gain some perspective on how we got here. In the years between the late 1800s and the mid-1900s – an era which Aldous Huxley would refer to as "The Age of Noise" – the world had seen more technological and scientific innovation than all the previous centuries combined. Between the proliferation of the automobile, commercial air travel, radio, television, and amplified rock'n'roll, people were introduced to a barrage of sounds the world hadn't seen or heard before in their everyday lives. The twentieth century also marked the first time we experienced the horrors – and noise – of a large-scale global war made possible by the mass production of military hardware, one of the many fruits of the Technological Revolution. It wasn't just physical noise Huxley warned us against 75 years ago however. New varieties of "mental noise" were also introduced into our collective psyches via these advances in technology. For the first time in history, sounds – and the often commercially driven messages they carried with them – could be beamed into homes from miles away over the airwaves and, thanks to the telephone, those previously separated by geography could connect in an instant and converse in the same casual fashion as they did face-to-face. The entire world from which we drew our identity accelerated and expanded by leaps and bounds virtually overnight inflicting humanity with a new disease which writer and futurist Alvin Toffler termed "future shock," a psychobiological condition he described as a "dizzying disorientation brought on by the premature arrival of the future" (1970, p. 11).

Anyone alive today who has ever tried to do anything can attest to the dizzying state we find ourselves in. The reader of this essay need only tally up the number of disruptions she's encountered thus far while reading this book. Whether a leaf blower, the dings and whooshes of a smartphone, the relentless click-bait of our social media echo chamber, or the incessant inner dialogue about what's for dinner, this modern age appears to be marked less by its innovations than the deleterious effects of those innovations. Urban dwellers seem to exist in a nearly constant elevated state, triggering a host of responses within the nervous system once designed to pool certain bodily resources to help navigate a threat to life and limb. And what of the writer of this essay? Unforeseen forces seem to keep taking a hold of me as I write this and strange lapses in consciousness perforate the process. What I seem to experience each time my mind is redirected from the task at hand is more akin to a hypnotic state of sorts as I'm often unable to recall where my mind had gone exactly. It's no different than sleeping really. Except actual sleep is a restorative process whereas this constant deluge of stimuli and reactivity is causing stress to our bodies not to mention killing our productivity. As I attempt to retrace my actions, I'm not exactly surprised by what I find but I do feel disappointed that I had so unwittingly fell into this trance that is so prevalent in modern life. What came between me and the task at hand is probably what comes between you and what you'd prefer to be doing on many occasions. A handful of emails that require my "immediate" attention, a string of text messages which required my brain to shift cognitive gears each time; the constant dings, whooshes, and pings beckoning you to engage and respond.

Just as the need for knowledge spawned the digital age, attention is the new commodity driving innovation and the new axis upon which our world spins. Now that so much of our lives take place in the virtual space, industries are pouring millions of dollars into understanding the rhythms and psychological underpinnings of what drives us to click and keep clicking. Building off the research of behavioral scientists employed by advertising agencies in the mid-twentieth century, industries battling it out in the attention economy are employing hundreds of engineers and designers to dictate our every move in the digital space. Things like reward, punishment, aversive stimulation, and ingratiation are just some of the strategies directly linked to the core principles behind the persuasive design employed to create popular online platforms.

If you've read this far, bravo to you. That's more than most, who according to studies only read about 20 percent of the text on the page before getting pulled away by the next ding or whoosh.[3] What is the actual cost of these momentary lapses in attention? In the new field of "interruption science" researchers have found that the average worker switches tasks every three minutes and once distracted, needs approximately a half-hour to effectively reorient their attention back onto the original task.[4] Those interruptions and the subsequent recovery time now take up 28 percent of a worker's day, according to business research firm Basex. For a species which seems to prize its intellectual ability, there is surprisingly little time and space in our lives, homes, and workplaces to actually think. "By fragmenting and diffusing our powers of attention," says Maggie Jackson (2010), author of *Distracted: The Erosion of Attention and the Coming Dark Age*, "we are undermining our capacity to thrive in a complex, ever-shifting world."

It's not just our work lives that suffer from this "dizzying disorientation." With so much of our human sensibilities and rhythms now being driven by mechanical and technological devices, we have begun to adopt new rhythms which exceed our human limits and transfer technological expectations to areas of our lives which are not technical. "When we come home at the end of the day, it may not be just work we bring with us, but also our high-speed frustrations and electronic expectations," says Stephen Bertman, author of *Hyperculture: The Human Cost of Speed* (1998, p. 8) "In short," Bertman continues,

> we may come to expect the imperfect human beings in our lives to operate as efficiently as our equipment, quickly losing patience with those we might otherwise live because they do not answer as swiftly, or respond as rapidly, or obey as readily as the machines we know.

The modern phenomenon of declining relationship satisfaction[5] and increasing reports of isolation and loneliness[6] all seem to boil down to one thing in this author's opinion: mental noise brought on by an accelerated lifestyle we simply can't keep up with.

If you're not convinced, try spending 20 minutes doing nothing in a relatively quiet space like a library or empty church. Or better yet, get yourself to an anechoic chamber. An anechoic chamber is an acoustically constructed room designed with painstaking effort to be nearly soundproof. Those who own them pride themselves on how quiet their rooms can get, some of them vying for the distinction of being the quietest place on earth. Orfield Labs in Minneapolis, Minnesota with their rating of −13 decibels held the record for a number of years. Microsoft's audio lab in Redmond, Washington now holds the record with a rating of −20 decibels, approximately three decibels shy of the level of sound made when air molecules bounce off of one another. Of course, the human ear isn't capable of experiencing such low levels of sound. In fact, the majority of people even with perfect hearing are unable to detect sounds that measure below zero decibels, the human threshold of hearing. I visited several of these rooms during the making of my film *In Pursuit of Silence* – including Orfield Labs – and it's remarkable what rises to the surface when the white noise of the external world is removed from the soundtrack of our experience. Even in zero decibels of silence, the dings and whooshes find a way to persist. If not the sound of blood flowing through your veins or your tinnitus – that ringing auditory residue in your ears that millions of modern people suffer from – you'll most certainly encounter what writer Tim Parks calls, "The interminable fizz of anxious thoughts or the self-regarding monologue" made up of thoughts that are "destructive in their insistent revisiting of where we've been a thousand times before." Inner speech researchers estimate that we spend approximately 25 percent – roughly 4 hours – of our day talking to ourselves at the rate of about 4,000 words per minute or ten times faster than verbal speech.[7] According to that math, we're engaging in the outer-world equivalent of 40 hours of conversation with ourselves every day. Just as the words we exchange with others can easily slip into idle chatter, so too can our inner dialogue. "And if the unspoken words of our mind's endless, idiot monologue are counted," suggests a rather cynical Aldous Huxley, "the majority for idleness becomes, for the most of us, overwhelmingly large" (1945, pp. 216–217).

The concern over distractions is nothing new of course. Around 400 BCE Socrates lamented that the advent of writing and the Greek alphabet would diminish the mind. The invention of the printing press in 1440 spawned similar warnings of a mass information overload that would weaken our memory as books would release us from the responsibility of remembering things. The level of distractions available today however have reached a level of sophistication rivaled only by the sophistication of the technology which has spawned it. Today 5 billion people around the globe carry a pocket-sized computer millions of times more powerful than the world's first computers making it both a technological marvel and tool of mass distraction. As we are beginning to see, the ripple effects of those distractions have far-reaching consequences. For technology ethicist James Williams, it is the cumulative impact of distractions that should have us all concerned. "In the short term," Williams says (2018, pp. xi–xii), "distractions can keep us from doing the things we want to do" while in the longer term, they can accumulate and keep us from living the lives we want to live, or even worse, undermine our capacities for reflection and self-regulation."

How will we escape the dizzying effect of this accelerated path we find ourselves on now, the path toward what we may call an "Age of Mental Noise"? What role does silence play in helping us to deal with the rising tide of mental noise and disorientation? If we are to break out of this "future shock" and find ourselves firmly seated back in the driver's seat of human progress, we must find a way back to silence. For as long as our technological innovation is driven by commercial interests and our daily actions continue to devolve into idle responses to the noise around us, our heads will continue to spin, unable to effectively deal with the challenges of the modern world and the continued exponential growth we're sure to see.

With so much vying both externally and internally for our attention, it's no wonder why we have forgotten all about the silence missing from our daily experience. To quote from a letter I recently received from my friend, writer and poet Jonathan Simons, "One can only imagine what else might exist if we peeled our hands away from the gears of these image making machinery." What does the world even sound like beneath all the noise, the disorientation? I wouldn't dare suggest that I know what it sounds like for you exactly – that's up to silence to determine – but I imagine that person you meet there is probably the most authentic version of yourself you'll find anywhere else. If Pico Iyer is right when he says, "Silence is where we hear something deeper than our chatter," and "Where we speak something deeper than our words,"[8] I think we owe it to ourselves and each other to quiet the mental noise to explore whether we can see the path more clearly.

In the anechoic chamber, I did experience some momentary respite from the mental noise eventually. When I did, I encountered a part of my being I hadn't seen in some time. It was awkward at first, like seeing an old friend with whom you've exchanged a few emails but have had little three-dimensional contact. It was the part of me that is content with who he is and with life as it is lived as opposed to the spectacle we engage in each day. The "house of mirrors," as my wise friend Jonathan Simons suggests we'll be able to "pull ourselves in and out of" so long as we "maintain familiarity with what's real." This part of me I encountered in the chamber is also quieter, able to resist the need to fill my consciousness with narrative, content with simply engaging with the world in the spaces between the dings and whooshes, and open to the lessons those encounters may hold for me. It didn't require any sophisticated or exotic technique to get there. It did take time and some effort to shift my attention away from the noise, but I became convinced that with time and practice, I could learn to quiet the "interminable fizz" in perhaps any environment or situation and eventually move from the occasional encounter with silence to more prolonged engagements.

Our collective disorientation is intimately wrapped up in our treating technology as a lifeline rather than a useful tool. If we continue to allow our online existence to inform the offline one and surrender our natural rhythms to that of our machines, this dizzying enchantment will persist as if it is our only option. The house of mirrors is tempting and vast, but with an ear toward silence we stand a better chance at breaking free from the allure of its reflections.

Notes

1 https://www.japantimes.co.jp/community/2010/10/16/community/professor-finds-meaning-in-silence/#.XOheMS3MxoN
2 http://healthland.time.com/2012/06/21/study-traffic-noise-linked-to-heart-attack-risk/
3 https://www.nngroup.com/articles/how-little-do-users-read/
4 https://www.nytimes.com/2008/06/22/jobs/22shifting.html
5 https://www.womenshealthmag.com/relationships/a19981620/more-are-unhappy-in-their-marriage-than-ever-before/
6 https://www.forbes.com/sites/karenhigginbottom/2018/10/08/a-lack-of-connection-in-a-digital-world/#5bb9a08a4b21
7 https://www.theatlantic.com/science/archive/2016/11/figuring-out-how-and-why-we-talk-to-ourselves/508487/
8 From an interview Pico Iyer gave to the present author that appears in the latter's film *In Pursuit of Silence*.

References

Bertman, S. (1998). *Hyperculture: The Human Cost of Speed*. Westport, CT: Praeger.
Cain, S. (2013). *Quiet: The Power of Introverts in a World That Can't Stop Talking*. London: Broadway Books.
Huxley, A. (1945). *The Perennial Philosophy*. London: Harper & Brothers.
Jackson, M. (2010). *Distracted: The Erosion of Attention and the Coming Dark Age*. Buffalo, NY: Prometheus Books.
Nouwen, H. J. (1981). *The Way of the Heart*. New York: Ballantine Books.
Toffler, A. (1970). *Future Shock*. New York: Random House.
Williams, J. (2018). *Stand out of the Light: Freedom and Resistance in the Attention Economy*. Cambridge: Cambridge University Press.

Part II
Clinical

Part II

Introduction to Part II

Now that we have resolved those most fundamental questions about silence in the first part of the book, we turn to psychoanalysis. The questions, hopefully, remain the same: is silence in the psychoanalytic process natural to it, or is it just a side-effect? Should we try to deal with it – avoid it, fight it, enjoy it? – somehow, or is it simply to be highly valued and nourished? Is silence only a break in the psychoanalytic session or a message of a kind, sometimes possibly even the most profound one? Should the practitioners of what is called "the talking cure" encourage patients to develop their capacity to be silent? And will that change the name of their profession into the "being-silent-together cure"?

The clinical part of the book opens, in analogy to the previous one, with phenomenology. We decided to reprint the 2006 paper by Elsa Ronningstam, possibly the best known and frequently quoted paper on silence in psychoanalysis in the last 20 years. It offers an overview of the cross-cultural meanings of silence and a review of psychoanalytic literature on silence, yet its central part is a detailed case presentation, and we hope that this will provide an inspiring overture to all subsequent chapters.

The next chapter brings Salman Akhtar's classification of the types of silence in the psychoanalytic setting, enriched with two clinical vignettes. Akhtar distinguishes between the following: structural silence, unmentalised silence, defensive silence, enactive silence, symbolic silence, contemplative silence, regenerative silence, and blank silence. We hope that this will both help practitioners and inspire parallels with classifications based on empirical psychotherapy research.

Aleksandar Dimitrijević writes about the topics that, especially in the first several decades of the development of psychoanalysis, was seen as an equation—silence as the manifestation of resistance. His review of classic papers on the topic is organized into three parts: he discusses silence as a possible manifestation of resistance in the patient, in countertransference, and as an intersubjective phenomenon, offering clinical illustrations for many of his points.

The topic of the chapter that follows is almost the opposite of Dimitrijević's. Standing on the shoulders of Ferenczi and the Independents, as well as Norbert Freedman, Jay Frankel writes about all things good that silence in psychoanalysis can bring. Frankel elaborates creatively on the ideas such as silent holding or the necessity of silence for self-reflection and symbolizing, but he also introduces notions such as renegotiating internalized object relations and his innovative idea of "the analytic state of consciousness."

Margaret Boyle Spelman, the author of two books and co-editor of another one Winnicott, focuses here only on silence in the oeuvre of this pediatrician-psychoanalyst. Infants are, of course, often silent and never verbal, so it is not surprising that Winnicott's developmental theory emphasized the importance of this phenomenon. The chapter discusses developmental aspects, as well as silence and growth. Also interesting is the elaboration of the idea that silence can be counted among potential transitional objects. There are also more direct clinical contributions, such as the ideas of the silent holding between the analyst and patient, or the idea of the silent self, which are only going to prove that Winnicott never ceases to inspire.

Howard Levine has written a chapter about the psychology of the analyst (and we always lack those) focused on silence. Apart from his explorations of Bion (specifically, the ideas of reverie and negative capability), Levine mostly deals with the (non-Lacanian) French psychoanalytic tradition, particularly Green, and sees Freud as the foundation for them all. He acknowledges the other possible roles of silence in the psychoanalytic setting, most of which are thoroughly discussed in previous chapters, and focuses on the notion of silence as a condition for analytic listening.

The part closes with a chapter entirely devoted to the concept of silencing—an active and deliberate attempt to make it impossible for a person or group to articulate her voice and, thus, identity. Aleksandar Dimitrijević writes about the role of this malignant mechanism in transforming trauma into a mental disorder. Silencing is here explored on three levels: first, in the domain of attachment trauma, then as the conspiracy of silence on a group level, and finally in psychoanalysis itself, mostly when it comes to education but also with the concern that treatments can sometimes be retraumatizing. The reviewed empirical evidence shows that 1) traumatic experiences can be overcome when recognized and acknowledged, 2) they are predictive of mental disorders when, in the case of abused children, caregivers behave as if nothing happened or actively prevent the child from expressing her story and her feelings.

This whole part is, however, only one side of the story. The research part that follows is complementary to it, and the two of them should be read together, as two ways of listening to the same composition. Being able to hear both will, we hope, be enriching.

Chapter 6

Cultural function and psychological transformation of silence in psychoanalysis and psychoanalytic psychotherapy

Elsa Ronningstam

The Swedish poet Gunnar Ekelöf (1959) wrote an important poem about silence:

> It is in the silence you should listen
> the silence behind the apostrophes, allusions
> the silence in the rhetoric
> or in the do called formally perfected
> This is the search for an unmeaning
> in the meaningful and the reverse[1]

In the above lines, the poet gives his readers a directive, to listen to the silence that is behind the words, in the rhetoric. These lines have special meaning for psychoanalysts who are often trained to think more about the words than about the spaces between them. And yet, silence has, over the past decades, interested scholars and scientists representing several areas of inquiry. By now their documentations bear evidence of the wide range of meanings and functions of silence. While silence in cultural contexts has been considered legitimate and understandable, its position as a psychological and psychoanalytic phenomenon has been much more controversial, raising questions about whether it is a resistance and obstacle to treatment, a symptom, or whether in and by itself silence can be considered a meaningful occurrence. In this chapter, I hope to bring together cultural and psychoanalytic thinking about silence. In my clinical experience I have often been impressed by my patients' experiences of silence (both their own and others') in their original families and communities, in their marriages and workplaces, and in their own internal lives. I have also often wondered how these experiences affect their participation in psychotherapy/psychoanalysis. I propose that silence can be understood as an active and meaningful psychological process that can be productively integrated into the course of a psychotherapy or psychoanalysis. More specifically, my hypothesis is that silence can function as a protection of an inner space and promote an inner transformation and connection between experiences, affect and verbal language that enables changes in interpersonal relationships.

Cross-cultural meanings of silence

In some cultures, silence is highly regarded and even idealized, like a virtue. In others, where talking is socially desirable, silence is considered an indisposition, equivalent to a handicap. In several countries it is a human right to remain silent. In others, influenced by threats and terror, silence can represent the narrow line between life and death, i.e. the means to survival. Some cultures are stereotyped as exceptionally silent—such as parts of the Finnish culture (Lehtonen and Sajavaara, 1985; Sajavaara and Lehtonen, 1997), while in others, like the Japanese culture, a complex, historically, and religiously determined use of silence and nonverbal communication may be nearly impossible to decipher for the less initiated (Morsbach, 1988).

In the recent film *Fast Runner*, filmed in the Nunavut territory in Northern Canada, we follow the lives of the Inuit people and the legend of the man who runs naked over the ice to escape his deadly enemies. The people harbor their experiences and process feelings of longing, grief, fear, and humiliation, all without speaking. In the course of silence, beautifully intertwined in the film with seasonal changes and daily chores, powerful personal realizations and transformations take place. The question is whether justice and coexistence will supersede deceitfulness and violence in the tribe. In another recent film, *Kandahar*, which documents a woman's efforts to reach her suicidal sister in Afghanistan, silence contains the fear and torment of a risk-taking and potentially deadly commitment. People's silence, equally beautifully intertwine with the desert landscape and the striking colors of the women's burkas (which effectively suppress their speech); courage and decisiveness coexist with terror, dread, and the anguish of uncertainty and waiting. Is she going to be able to hide her true identity and reach her sister before it is too late?

Some anthropological studies describe the *containing function* of silence. Among the people in the Northern Italian village Valbella (Saunders, 1985), an emotionally warm, intense, and expressive culture, both exuberant noise and grim silence are functionally equivalent. Silence is the strategy to manage emotionally difficult and tense situations. People feel it is better to remain silent than to lose control and risk the tragedy of separation or estrangement. On an individual level, silence helps control strong feelings, settle disputes, and allow more passive expression of discontent. In less serious situations, people prefer the 'noisy-avoidance' style, i.e. to express intense emotions while focusing on non-conflictual issues. Another cultural aspect of silence is captured in the British expression 'to send someone to Coventry', i.e. to refuse to associate with a person (Encyclopedia Britannica, 1945, p. 617) or to treat someone as if he/she does not exist. In this context, silence represents a hostile act of ostracism and exclusion, sometimes also found in extreme religious sects.

In studies of politeness, well summarized by Sifianou (1997), silence is regarded as being particularly ambiguous. It can be used in interpersonal interactions as a means to protect personal territory, to demonstrate deference, or to preserve emotional neutrality (negative politeness). This type of silence is highly valued in England, where it is considered polite to avoid intrusion. In Greece, however, where people enjoy being involved with each other through conversation, this silence is perceived as distancing and considered impolite or even insulting. Interestingly, some Greek proverbs imply that silence can be even more threatening than arguments, i.e. 'a dog that barks does not bite.' Silence can also relate to being understood and indicate solidarity and common ground (positive politeness). The British respect for privacy and non-expression of strong or negative emotions is an example of such silence. In Finland, silence is considered harmonious and an expression of mutually positive attitudes. Being together without speaking is highly accepted. Furthermore, silence can also be a manifestation of polite indirectness[2] in which, by saying nothing, you still convey something (off-record politeness), i.e. to avoid asking for something because of shyness, embarrassment, or unwillingness to impose.

In Sweden the search for meaning in silence has a long tradition. Crafoord (1994) identified several types of silence: the *searching silence* where the vocabulary is not enough; the *gray silence* that reflects an inner absence of words; the *passionate silence* which contains strong, even dangerous feelings and impulses, often of an erotic nature; the *pondering silence* which contains a wordless and mutually shared certainty about its content; the *creative silence* that should not be disrupted, because something is about to take shape and form; the *threatening silence* that harbors resistance, protest, and detachment, as well as rage, envy, and revenge; and the *black silence* that conveys the ultimate rejection and self-destructiveness, the presence of death.

The cultural significance of silence in psychoanalysis and psychotherapy

We usually think about silence in the context of speech, i.e. an absence of something that should be present. However, silence can also define the context in which talking takes place, as with the silent patient who suddenly begins to speak and whose silence had a specific significance. People who begin a 'talking cure' usually have more or less complex experiences related to both talking and silence, which influence the way they form an analytic alliance and pursue the analytic process.

A woman who grew up in a family with a very secretive, secluded, and silent lifestyle conveyed that she was to be neither seen nor heard. Her father had, during his upbringing in an Asian country, experienced discrimination and terror. Despite his protected and successful life in the new world, he continued to enact his earlier experiences within the family. Starting analysis and breaking the silence was for this woman associated with strong feelings of guilt for revealing family secrets, but also with ambivalence and fear. As she began to change, she realized that she had been breaking several of the silent, invisible prohibitions that formed the foundation of the monumental family barrier. 'I am not supposed to do this,' she said, when noticing that *she* no longer was either invisible or silent. Another woman learned early that, being quiet and without feelings, she was considered a 'good girl.' Her silence was highly rewarded in her family, while her feelings were strongly criticized and punished to suppression. Psychotherapy was a specific narcissistic challenge. By talking, she was doing something less valuable and even dangerous, and she was no longer in control of her own status and self-protection. Another woman, an immigrant from Eastern Asia, repeatedly surprised me as she retreated into long silence after most of my interventions. Following each such long silence her comments were remarkably thoughtful and emotionally integrated. When I asked her what was happening, she smiled and said, 'I am thinking about what you were saying,' but she did not want to reveal the inner process that had led to these insights and transformations.

An additional complexity concerns the person's *selective silence*, i.e. the avoidance of certain modes of interaction or experiences and feelings that for a long time can remain embedded in silence. It may be a challenging task to identify the meaning of such non-spoken material in the context of the patient's regular talk and silence. This is specifically relevant for people from 'high shame cultures' who are used to hiding shameful experiences.

Silence as a psychoanalytic phenomenon

The first panel on the 'Silent Patient' held at the American Psychoanalytic Association meeting in 1958 (Loewenstein, 1961; Waldhorn, 1959) addressed a groundbreaking question: Is silence a resistance or can silence have meaning that grants fruitful exploration? Although most reports thereafter agreed that silence is a form of communication or a way of relating to others, including the analyst, some authors still interpreted silence as a hindrance. For Hadda (1991), silence was a *resistance*, representing the patient's fear that the analyst would not be sensitive to her need for mirroring, and for Kurz (1984), a resistance towards changes in the personality and opposing the curative goals of treatment.

The *narcissistic function* of silence as a *protection of self-esteem* has also been recognized. Weinberger (1964) suggested that silence is a form of defense against the fear of loss of self-esteem and status. Modell (1975, 1976, 1980) found that a specific non-communication of affects in certain narcissistic patients promotes a 'cocoon-like state' aiming at *omnipotent control of the affects*. This cocoon is like a grandiose illusion of self-sufficiency motivated by fear of closeness and intrusion from others, and it serves to regulate self-esteem and maintain inner control. Coltart (1991) identified *feelings of shame* as one cause of silence in a patient who remained speechlessly ashamed following several unprocessed losses and rejections. Morrison (1984, 1989) confirmed that shame feelings can remain hidden, rationalized, or otherwise defended against. The significance of shame-inducing events may also remain unknown (Tangney, 1991). Studies have identified shame as an overwhelming, painful emotion that triggers a desire to hide (Lewis, 1971; Tangney, 1996; Tagney et al. 1992) or withdraw from interpersonal relationships to protect from the anticipated painful additional exposure of shame (Schore, 1994). Furthermore, studies of *loneliness and isolation* have highlighted the narcissistic dilemma in relationships, i.e. the 'inability to either be with the object or without it' (Erlich, 1998) or the inability to tolerate emotional expressions where isolation represents a pre-semantic level of affect organization (Killingmo, 1990).

Ascribing a *communicative function* to silence has stimulated studies of its subjective significance and integration into the analytic process. This is in line with interdisciplinary perspectives that define silence as a 'metaphor for communication' (Jaworsky, 1997). Closely related but not identical to silence is nonverbal communication. Winnicott (1958, 1963) noticed that significant relating and communicating can be silent, and he differentiated between simple non-communication, i.e. being alone in the presence of another, and active non-communication, which is more defensive and accompanied by anxiety. He also identified an authentic non-communicated core in the developing self that may remain isolated in silence. The unconscious, symbolic, or affective meaning of nonverbal interactions has recently been underscored (Jacobs, 1994; Pally, 2001), and, as Rizzuto (1995) pointed out, part of the complex task of the analyst's listening involves paying attention to what the patient cannot say, maybe even to himself. Both research in neuroscience and studies of early infant behavior have signified the role of nonverbal indicators for self-regulation and attachment. A complex process of activating and signaling nonverbal cues occurs in the transference–countertransference matrix between patient and psychoanalyst/therapist, which promote empathy and understanding, as well as interfering reactions, such as dysphoria, anxiety, or detachment (Pally, 2001).

Interpersonal and intersubjective psychoanalytic approaches have paradoxically inspired further studies of the meaning of silence. For some authors, silence represented an *early identity formation or developmental arrest*, and through the silence the patient disclosed to the analyst an early disturbed or lost relationship. Kahn's (1963) patient conveyed how it felt to live with a severely depressed mother, and Weinberger's (1964) patient re-enacted a partial loss in relationship to his mother due to changes in her presence and attitude.

Silence as part of an *active developmental process or therapeutic transition* is analogous to speech, with its own relational qualities in a nonverbal line of development. Silence can be like a respite, providing a chance to rebuild walls that have been ruptured catastrophically. Hence, silence can resemble a retreat or a space for resolving dilemmas that words cannot comprehend (Kurz, 1984), or it can provide a protection and legitimization of the core authentic self (Gabbard, 1989). Leira believed that the sensory interaction, her own attentiveness, and the nonverbal interaction between her and her patients promoted a 'working through of elements in early attachment' (1995, p. 60) that led to the development of emotional depth and greater autonomy in the patients.

As noticed, the distinction between silence as a defense or resistance versus silence as a protection has some major theoretical and technical implications. While interpretation of the function of silence to underlying aggressive or sexual aims is beneficial in cases of defensive silence, the function of protective silence to maintain self-cohesiveness and shield nonverbal aspects of the authentic self requires a different technical approach involving nonverbal interaction, sensitive attentiveness, and gradual exploration. Jacobs noted that 'silence in the analyst not uncommonly contains elements of countertransference' (1998, p. 68), and that the patient's silence can have its counterpart in the psychotherapist's/ analyst's silence. Understanding of the transference–countertransference matrix between the patient and the therapist, and identifying the patient's internal object relationships as they are expressed in projections and projective identifications (Gabbard, 1989) can reveal additional meaning of the silence that may not be readily discernible.

In this chapter I apply a transference–countertransference model to further explore different ways silence may *contribute* to transformation and change during psychoanalysis or psychotherapy. The question is: What can occur in the silence that might promote and account for changes in the personality? I am proposing that, in the case of Susan, which I discuss, silence serves two functions: first, to protect the patient's core self and provide a space to resolve early problems in attachment, affect, and self-regulation, and second, to contain a transference–countertransference matrix that includes projections of Susan's internalized mother- and father-related objects on to me. Later this inter-relational matrix promoted affect regulation and enabled transformation in the patient's capacity to internally access and to verbally convey her own experiences and affects in relationship to me. I attempt to describe how this specific process of affect desomatization, affect differentiation, and affect verbalization developed. I also propose that my own culturally based tolerance for silence and ability to remain attentive and actively exploring while silent contributed to this transformation.

Susan—A case of silence in the sixth year of treatment

For Susan, silence had both a cultural origin and served several psychological functions. Before the phase of silence that began in the sixth year of treatment and lasted for about one and a half years, Susan communicated by *describing* life events and interactions with others. She was a watcher, an eyewitness of events and she made elaborate, precise, and witty descriptions of others and their whereabouts, while she preferred not to be seen or involved. Her words were in a subtle way separated from her inner affects, and she used global labels (I hate this/love that) to express preferences or inner states.

Susan, a single woman in her late thirties, diagnosed with narcissistic personality disorder, major depression, and chronic suicidality, began intensive psychoanalytic psychotherapy with me, four times a week, shortly after she had made a near-lethal suicide attempt by overdose. Two events preceded this attempt—her mother had died of cancer and Susan had opted to leave her job as a director of a chemical laboratory. Her departure was prompted by a demotion. She found the proposal extremely humiliating, but she chose to hide her strong reactions in silence while she walked out of the laboratory, never to return. After unsuccessfully applying for several jobs, she felt lost, and secretly began to make detailed plans to end her life. She remained silent about these plans, even to her previous psychotherapist whom she saw twice a week at the time. Susan described how she withdrew and fell into a pleasant state of isolation. She felt superior, calm, in control, protected from all defeats, and free from feelings of agony, anger, and hopelessness.

Childhood and adult history

Susan was the middle of seven siblings. She learned from her mother that she was a 'replacement' for an older sibling who had died shortly after birth. The mother repeatedly told Susan that she was strange looking, different from the rest of the family, and never able to do things right. The mother also accused Susan of having caused her burdensome stress and constrictions both before and after birth, especially as the mother secretly feared that she would lose this child too. Susan learned to take pride in not showing emotions, and, when disciplined, she relished watching her mother's anger escalate into uncontrolled fury as she faced Susan's undefeatable silent non-responsiveness. The father was more distant but respectful towards Susan, and through others she learned that she actually was the father's pride and favorite daughter. Although this was never openly admitted or discussed within the family, Susan was much aware of her mother's envy towards her. Susan described herself as a lonely and unprotected child, often singled out for various negative reasons, and never feeling that she belonged. She always had a strong need for 'a way out' inasmuch as she often was the scapegoat, accused of being bad or wrong, or the target of cruelty and humiliation by others. Her major 'way out' was silence and withdrawal into solitude.

Susan told me about the many functions of silence in her family. One was to hide shameful family scandals. Another was to withhold praise and positive attention, e.g. that Susan was her father's favorite, which she learned from his colleagues. A third function of silence was to manage strong feelings such as pain and humiliation, e.g. that Susan for several months was the target of daily cruelty from a housekeeper. The family also kept boundaries through silence, and Susan learned not to talk to her father when he read the newspaper. In addition, decisions about major changes and plans were kept in silence, such as plans for family vacations or a move to a different house. Susan learned early in life to navigate herself in this complex matrix of family silence and secrets, and to protect her own space and integrity by spending time alone boating, hiking, or biking outdoors, or indoors in her room. Nevertheless, from her early teens she engaged in baseball coaching and became highly regarded among children and families in the community.

I understood that Susan had developed a cocoon-like position in her family, a narcissistic space that protected her own self and helped to prevent intrusion from others. Susan had obviously learned to neither reveal nor even feel her own feelings, and to organize her observations of herself and others as descriptions of events rather than conveying her own experiences. What remained unclear to me at this point was whether Susan felt that she was not allowed to talk or sensed that she should avoid or withhold talking due to loyalty, shame, guilt, or fear of loss of inner control; or whether she was indeed not able to talk, i.e. did not have the connections between the words and her inner experiences and feelings.

After working in the computer business for a few years, Susan shifted her career to research and worked for ten years in a chemical corporation. She began as a research assistant, but gradually advanced to become a director with independent responsibility for one section of the chemical operations. Although she preferred work to socializing, she had several close long-term friends whom she had met either through her family or at work. She described that they met regularly, shared a sense of humor, and traveled together. She never married, but dated a man for several years who died in a car accident. When her mother was diagnosed with cancer, Susan became her primary carer. Although their relationship changed as the mother became appreciative, and help-seeking, Susan was relieved when the mother passed away. Six months later, she abruptly walked away from her job as she faced an unexpected demotion. One and a half years later, she made a serious suicide attempt while in psychotherapy twice a week.

The first five years of treatment

Following her suicide attempt, Susan participated in a long-term intensive treatment effort including a group and milieu-focused partial program, family therapy, cognitive behavioral therapy, and intensive psychoanalytic psychotherapy with me for four sessions a week. It also included psychopharmacological treatment with antidepressants and mood-stabilizing drugs. Several gains occurred as she separated and moved away from her family, established her own living quarters, and developed independent relationships with those family members she appreciated.

Susan formed a compliant alliance with me, and, as she gradually connected with and accepted me, she faithfully attended her sessions. My attempts to explore transference reactions, or feelings and fantasies about the therapy and me, were usually unsuccessful, as Susan either rejected my suggestions or in other ways made it clear that my interventions did not make sense to her. Equally fruitless were my efforts to interpret or relate Susan's behavior to inner feeling states. However, although no visible transference had developed, following Rizzuto's (1988, 1995) expanded definition of transference, and Modell's (1975, 1976, 1980) observations of the 'cocoon transference,' I still considered a type of transference present, i.e. one that in the context of Susan's history indicated her need to protect herself from intrusion from me, to hide her feelings, to avoid interactions and dependency, and to maintain inner control. I sensed that she had developed a cocoon-like transference in which I was like a function in her life, a new object to whom she related out of a sense of duty. She experienced her treatment in general and the psychotherapy in particular as unpleasant, 'like a religious chore I am supposed to do,' she said, and 'hopefully something good will come out of it in the end.' I understood this to be either a defensive stand or an aspect of her negative attachment, but I also noticed her expression of hope.

Susan had a long history of warding off any type of wishes or longings vis-à-vis other people, which now seemed applied to me. I sensed that she felt endangered by getting close to or beginning to depend upon or long for another person, believing that she would get severely hurt and disappointed, or lose control and fall apart. She was secretive and selectively silent, but she often surprised me when she unexpectedly revealed new secrets. I often wondered what created those moments when Susan accessed new memories, alternative perspectives, or significant additional details; was it a sign of altering or deepening transference that enabled her to evoke memories or other experiences vis-à-vis me, or was it a transformation that took place in Susan due to our interaction?

During this part of the treatment, Susan recovered and reconstructed memories and personal history in an effort to establish a sense of herself. She discussed in depth her conflictual relationships to her mother and brother, including feelings of anger and envy, and she gained some distance and understanding. She gradually began to recognize changes in her mood and affect states and identify some of the causing events. However, her affects remained separated from her words and it was unclear what contributed to Susan's ability on one level to actively participate in such an intensive and interactive residential partial program and get stronger, and seemingly gain understanding and ability to manage herself, and yet on another level remain untouched. Her capacity to differentiate and regulate feelings, especially anger, remained poor. She turned anger inward into excruciating humiliation and self-scorn and suicidal ideations. Although Susan was capable of doing skilled and advanced work tasks, her attempts to get back into the professional field usually ended in sudden functional collapses. Moreover, she also suffered from a series of unexpected losses of close friends and relatives who died during a period of two years.

The phase of silence

In the sixth year of treatment, Susan suddenly became very quiet. This occurred in the context of her terminating the partial program and moving into her own apartment. Although the treatment plan included both work and group therapy, she chose to spend a lot of her time home alone, and she became protective of her time and space. It was more important for her to *be* and *have* her time than to *do* something with her time (Erlich, 1998). She isolated herself and did not let anybody in. She had only sparse contact with very few people, and said that she usually preferred and enjoyed her time alone, as she felt in control. For long periods she literally secluded herself in a narcissistic cocoon that encompassed her home. However, she also noted that, if she spent too much time by herself, she began to feel detached and suicidal, wishing to join her dead relatives and friends. Her relationship with me changed; during the sessions she was present but more emotionally flat and constricted, and much less interactive compared to the previous years. She appeared to 'be in herself,' and I noticed that the connection to me was tenuous and in contrast to her sense of belonging to her dead relatives, foremost her mother.

The silence was noticeable in Susan's use of fewer words and shorter sentences. Her language lost its former rich and diverse intellectual and symbolic quality and became sparser and more concrete. Her words were detached from her feelings. She replaced descriptions of experiences with accounts of headaches, binge eating, and suicidal ideations. Sometimes she only hinted at more global physical or psychological states, like 'I am having a very bad day,' or 'I feel better today.' During her sessions she had long periods of no speech, usually without eye contact. In some sessions of 45 minutes, she could say as few as three to four sentences; in others, she became involved in periods of brief interaction with long intermittent silences; while in still others there was a very slowly emerging dialogue that could occupy a major part of the session. I usually looked at Susan most of the time throughout the sessions; she sometimes looked at me when she talked, but usually she looked down, straight in front of her, or to the side, and often she had her eyes closed. This 'silent period' lasted about one and a half years, during which a gradual shift took place as Susan initiated more interaction and was more able to communicate her feelings and experiences.

The transference–countertransference matrix

Initially, I had strong concerns about Susan's silence, and I felt confused and painfully frustrated. As she maintained this isolated position in which she put herself out of reach of my interventions, I felt 'disarmed' and incompetent. I also felt confused by the paradox of her faithful and predictable attendance of the sessions, combined with her emotional distancing and verbal non-communicativeness. My efforts to interpret her silence or suggest reasons for her not talking, i.e. 'Maybe it is more difficult to talk because the treatment is just you and me now,' or 'Maybe you miss the intensive interactions with the others in the group program,' felt intrusive. She adamantly rejected my suggestions, as they did not seem to make sense to her, but, yet, I also noticed that she did not reject me. Still, I felt as if I was hanging on a very thin relational string.

As the treatment continued, I realized that Susan's silence was more profound and existential and, to my surprise, I noticed that I continued to feel present, curious, and creative. That contrasted to my experiences of silence with some of my other patients with whom I could feel empty, constricted, numb, or dreadfully bored. With Susan, however, I intuitively sensed it was crucial to respect and understand her silence. Baker's (1993) suggestion that the presence of the analyst/therapist provides a constancy that could allow a new type of object relation seemed relevant, as did the idea of silence as a respite or sanctuary for rebuilding ruptured ego and self-regulatory functions.

I experienced a complex range of projections and projective identifications; my sense of helplessness, powerlessness, and frustration seemed to reflect in part Susan's own experiences in relationship to her critical aggressive mother and to her distant but idealized father now projected on to me. On the other hand, my sense of perseverance, presence, and participation during this phase was probably associated to Susan's projection and my identification with her idealized father and her being his favorite and idealized daughter and with her idealizing aging mother for whom she had been the special carer. On a deeper level, I felt let in and included in Susan's withdrawn, silent, and lonely space that she had adopted as a protection in early childhood. On the other hand, I also felt that our relationship was reduced to a minimum. Her dutiful attendance could easily turn into a powerful aggressive rejection that would erase me from her internal world. Nevertheless, I sensed that I also was partly trusted and needed for something that at the time I was not able to fully identify. More than before, I felt like a 'lifeline' or 'lifesaver' especially since for days or even weeks in a row I was the only person Susan had contact with.

In addition, in the countertransference I noticed an aspect of the silence that was strongly influenced by my experiences in my own cultural background. I grew up in a Protestant farming village in Northern Sweden, close to the Arctic Circle, on the same latitude as Northern Alaska, Middle Greenland, and Northern Siberia. The Gulf Stream contributed to a relatively warm climate with marked contrasts between the seasons. At the winter solstice, the sun barely reached over the horizon, and at midsummer it barely reached under the horizon, providing 24-hour daylight. Although I was fortunate to grow up in a community where people did speak and communicate, still, silence was a predominant phenomenon. Some silences were restful and thoughtful, and words were not necessary. Other silences were empty because words were missing, especially for conveying feelings. Still other silences could be described by a truism, i.e. 'speech is silver but silence is gold.' But silence could also represent distancing and/or elimination of threatening, painful, or hateful matters and experiences. People embedded their losses, failures, or scandals in silence. They treated their enemies with silence, and managed overwhelming conflicts and threats in silence. They waited in silence, grieved in silence, and rejoiced or prided themselves in silence. In anthropological terms, I have a high, culturally determined tolerance for silence and, in psychoanalytic terms, silence is to a high degree ego-syntonic to me. I was used to waiting in silence and I had learned to observe details and look for context, meaning, and communication in the silence. My experience of silence related to people's survival and perseverance. I grew up in the aftermath of the tuberculosis and the Spanish influenza epidemics that heavily affected Northern Sweden during the early twentieth century. Thousands of people lost their lives, and most families were in some way affected, including both my mother's and my father's. As much as silence served survival and protection against the unbearable, uncontrollable, and threatening, it was also related to distancing and erasing, but, foremost, it was closely related to hard work, faithful collaboration, and persistence, and to tenuous hope and confidence in the future. As an immigrant, I brought into the psychoanalytic psychotherapy with Susan my understanding of the complexity of silence that I so closely had seen and experienced among the people I grew up with. The silence was also brought to me in my relationship to my father, who then was in his nineties and gradually had lost his ability to speak. During my visits to the far North, this new silence between us provided a space for me to be in his presence and reflect upon my own cultural inheritance. In our silence, I also wrote a narrative of my father's life for a historical anthology of the village.

I felt embarrassed as I reported on this new phase of silence to my supervisor. Silence was not supposed to occur at this time in Susan's treatment. My supervisor was an experienced psychoanalyst, and extensive knowledge and deep devotion to my work was enormously valuable, as was his interest in the silence and attention to the sparse interaction in the therapy. Following his advice, I focused on exploring the shifts that Susan reported in her mood, motivation, somatic state, or eating behavior, or in other aspects of her life. Doing so aimed at helping Susan to identify and express her reactions, and to begin to verbalize feelings and inner experiences in relationship to me. My supervisor also strongly advised me to 'not let her get away,' but instead to systematically and actively encourage and involve Susan in explorations of her reactions and feelings. This strategy influenced the transference–countertransference matrix. Rather than being critical and intrusive and trying to explore her feelings in relationship to me, my active exploratory position helped me to balance my countertransference and be aware of the major risks for enactments. I felt it was important to respectfully stay with the material she brought to the sessions, the manifest content of her experiences. I accepted that she needed to keep me on the outside and I intuitively felt it was important to respect her self and space. I sensed the risk of being too intolerant and intrusive, like her mother, or too disengaged and idealizing, like her father. As I was waiting and attending to her silence, I was balancing between, on the one hand, engaging Susan in our relationship and pulling her into life, and risking the eruption of her underlying unintegrated rage that could have led to her erasing me and our relationship. On the other hand, I believe that a less interactive approach might have promoted her detachment into a psychotic process and suicide.

Vignette I

This vignette is a slowly emerging dialogue during a 45-minute-long session a couple of months into the silent phase. (For the purpose of clarity, I present process notes with my comments.)

As usual, I opened the session by asking how Susan was doing and what she wanted to talk about. This was followed by her initial silence (6–8 minutes).

[*I am looking at Susan, noticing that she looks pale and burdened.*]

Patient: Today I feel horrible ... yesterday was a better day.

[*Following my supervisor's strategy, I focused on exploring the context of the shift from 'better' to 'horrible.'*]

Analyst: When did you notice this change?
P: I don't know ... Maybe yesterday evening ...
A: What were you doing when you noticed the difference?
P: I don't know ... nothing special ... [Long silence.]

[*I wondered if Susan actually did not know, or if she did know but was unable to tell me, if she indeed did not want to tell me, or if she wanted to tell me but on her own terms. I also wondered whether during the silence she was just keeping me away and protecting her inner self from me, or whether and in what way she was influenced by my interest in her shifting state.*]

A: Was something happening or going on around the time of the shift?
P: Not really ... [Silence.] Yes, actually ... my brother called. It was about my car.

[*I wondered what enabled this memory and contributed to Susan's willingness to convey the event to me.*]

A: Was it something about your brother's phone call that you reacted to?
P: No ... [Long silence.] I had a huge bowl of ice cream.

[*I had previously noticed that Susan's eating in response to sudden craving or hunger usually represented a non-specific way of regulating affect, i.e. a regression in affect in the context of some unexpected or disturbing event or experience.*]

A: Hmmm. [Silence.]
P: Then I got a headache. [Silence.]

[*Obviously S's reactions to her brother's phone call were overtly expressed in urges of uncontrolled eating which usually also led to a migraine headache, but what did she actually experience during and after her brother's phone call?*]

A: Maybe you had feelings and reactions to your brother's phone call?
P: He thinks that I am completely incompetent!

[*Susan identified and described her observation and interpretation of her brother's communication and intentions.*]

A: Incompetent? [Silence.]
P: He wants to look at my car and decide about the repair.

[*Susan continues to describe her understanding of the brother's intentions.*]

A: You obviously have some feelings and reactions to that.

[*I am focusing on trying to link Susan's somatic reactions to her understanding of her brother's intentions.*]

P: [She sighs. Silence.] I hate that!! I just feel awful.

[*Susan expresses a global undifferentiated state of dissatisfaction, displeasure and frustration without being able to convey her own emotional experiences and feelings.*]

A: So you got angry with your brother.

[*I continue my attempts to translate her comments into feelings.*]

P: He intrudes in my life. I wish I did not have to deal with him.

[*Susan responds with a description of her brother's behavior and a passive and vaguely expressed wish to be able to set boundaries in relationship to her brother. Obviously, it was premature of me to focus on her emotional reaction.*]

A: In other words, you felt intruded upon by your brother.
P: Something like that …

[*Finally, we reached an agreement about Susan's experience. I decided not to ask whether she also felt intruded upon by me in the same way as by her brother, because I had previously noticed that she turned down such parallels as if they represented too much intrusion and control on my part upon her inner experiences and/or as if she needed to avoid or prevent feelings of rage towards me and the risk of disrupting the relationship. I also sensed that it was too early to connect her episode of eating and her accompanying headache as a reaction to having been intruded upon by her brother. Instead, I decided to focus on exploring her efforts to take ownership of and communicate her experience to her brother.*]

A: Did you tell him?
P: Oh noooo! I would never do that!!

In the countertransference I felt as intrusive as her brother now and her mother in the past, and I sensed that my presence was in many ways a painful and aggravating experience. Nevertheless, she maintained an alliance with me throughout the session, as did I, and we reached an agreement. Several years later she confirmed that my questions evoked her strong aggressive reactions. I felt I had a hard task as I balanced between being an active explorer, a lifesaver, and a protector and participant in her silence, balancing between her potential distrust and rage, and working towards establishing a new type of relationship that also could involve more of Susan's affects and emotional experiences, including her rage.

Vignette 2

This vignette of a session a few months later presents a step further in Susan's ability to experience inner longing, and her accompanying reactions and feelings about being rejected.

Susan mentioned for the first time ever that she missed her father who had left for his annual winter vacation. She was bothered by his absence in her internal world, and she said, 'I feel as if I have lost my father's spirit in me.' She mentioned how she experienced herself as different from her father. Before, she used to feel more similar and equal to him, especially professionally. While on vacation, the father forgot to call Susan on her birthday. First, she described feeling hurt, as if she did not matter to him. Then she struggled with inner feelings of anger. 'I don't want to get angry at someone,' she said, 'especially not at my father. I will start to dislike him and it may lead to that I don't talk to him, and that will be most painful for me.' I asked if she associated feelings and expressions of anger with total loss and silence, and she said, 'I used to erase people from my mind if I got angry at them.' I asked myself whether she believed that if she got angry with me, she would erase me too or that she would erase me instead of expressing her anger towards me, but I sensed that it was too early to discuss this with her.

This vignette further reveals an aspect of my countertransference that Susan's silence could represent me being erased from her internal world. I was impressed by her fragile and dangerous balance; exposing and protecting her newly emerging experience as an existing human being with own feelings and longings, and anticipating her powerful rejection of her father and me out of fear of being rejected, or condemned because of her longings. Several years later, in the termination phase, she confirmed this by saying that I had 'passed the test,' and if I had behaved differently, she easily could have become frustrated and resentful towards me and consequently erased me too. In other words, Susan contained in the silent relationship her anger and rage towards me to be able to maintain the relationship with me. She was not able to handle her intense, unintegrated anger, and the silence probably enabled the anger to *be*. Susan did not ignore her anger, but nor did she directly express or experience it.

Epilogue

Susan gradually began to interact differently with me and initiate her talking to me more frequently. This was still a very fragile capacity that easily overwhelmed her and she was still prone to retreat to silence in complex or challenging situations. Nevertheless, in the end of what I defined as the 'silent phase,' Susan was able to identify an inner experience and accompanying feelings and convey this in her verbal interaction and relationship to me. She had begun to feel, tolerate, and process her affects and to process inner psychological conflicts, and she was on her way to becoming the owner of her own feelings. This was like an embryo of internal change that she gradually continued to develop during the following years of treatment. A special milestone occurred four years later when Susan discovered me as a separate person, who was able to see and hear her. She suddenly said, 'This is embarrassing, but I just realized that I have been talking to another person—you!—for all these years. This is horrible! I have to stop psychotherapy immediately.' She felt guilty for having revealed secrets, and ashamed for having exposed herself to me and she foresaw her ending our relationship. A few weeks later, she forcefully and emphatically told me, 'I hate you when you ask questions!!' I realized that Susan's new ability to express her feelings of rage and hatred towards me while continuing to stay in the relationship with me was a major sign of progress. Obviously, by verbalizing feelings of shame and discussing the shame-triggering events, Susan was able to identify and process other feelings, foremost rage and envy (Morrison, 1984, 1989). This ability also enabled her to more independently explore her feelings and experiences with me, and she began to ask, 'What am I reacting to?' and 'Why am I feeling this?' In the termination phase several years later, Susan spontaneously acknowledged the value of the silent phase and expressed her gratitude to me for respecting her silence and for my capacity to be silent with her.

Conclusions

Susan's silence has to be understood in its context: following termination of a more than four-year intensive multimodal treatment during which she had uncovered conflicts and verbalized experiences that never before had been put into words. While remaining in continuing intensive psychoanalytic psychotherapy, within this silence context, she gradually began to develop a new and more genuine relationship with me.

I see this development as representing a multilevel complex process. First, the silence served to protect and provide space for Susan's inner transformation and development. This was made possible because Susan in the silence gradually could make connections between her inner experiences, her verbal language, and her affects (Rizzuto, 1988). The silence served like a sanctuary or a retreat that provided a space for searching for and accessing her private, non-communicative core of herself (Gabbard, 1989).

Second, the silence also involved a transference–countertransference matrix that represented a delicate and tenuous balance between maintaining and erasing the relationship between Susan and myself. As much as I represented a hope of a possible new object relationship for Susan, I also represented an intrusive threat that easily could trigger her anger and fear by assuming the projective identification of her critical mother. Or

I could have assumed the role of someone unreachable and longed for, like her representation of her father. On the other hand, as much as Susan represented hope for me, she also represented a challenge: at any time I could have rejected and erased her by being too intolerant or intrusive; in addition, in the silence, I could have distanced myself vis-à-vis Susan and devoted my attention to interests of my own.

Third, the silence phase was highly influenced by my own cultural background and what I brought into the relationship: my tolerance and acceptance of being silent in the presence of another, and my gradual acknowledgment of the internal complexity and pressure that Susan may have experienced in the silence. While this objective cultural experience made me less sensitive to and more accepting of the threatening or aggressive aspects of the silence, it also helped me in several ways: to identify the patient's need for protection of her internal space; to control my own enactment; and to maintain an empathically appreciative therapeutic stance. The image that Susan presented, of erasing her father from her internal life, conveyed to me the nature of her rage and anger. In retrospect I believe that my familiarity with a more silent culture enabled me to appreciate and identify with Susan's protective efforts of her internal space, and it helped me to control my impulses to be too intrusive or too rejecting.

It is difficult to determine the mode of therapeutic action in the case of Susan with any certainty. However, some aspects suggest that the silence phase served an important purpose: the context and the timing of the phase, after more than four years of intensive multimodal treatment; the length of the phase; and the gradually emerging changes that become more explicit in the therapeutic alliance several years later, and especially notable and verbally confirmed during the termination phase. The absence of obvious connections between silence–intervention–change indicates that the nature of change may be more complex, especially in a patient like Susan with narcissistic defenses, unintegrated rage, a fragile internal self, and tenuous object relationships.

Notes

1 Reprinted with permission from Suzanne Ekelöf. Translated from Swedish by E. Ronningstam.
2 Cf. the chapter by Sylvia Bonacchi in this volume and her references to her studies of politeness (editors' note).

References

Baker, R. (1993). The patient's discovery of the analyst as a new object. *International Journal of Psycho-Analysis, 74*(6), 1223–1233.
Coltart, N. (1991). The silent patient. *Psychoanalytic Dialogues, 1*(4), 439–453.
Crafoord, C. (1994). *Människan är en berättelse — Tankar om samtalskonst* [The Human Being Is a Narrative — Thoughts about the Art of Conversation]. Stockholm, Sweden: Natur och Kultur.
Encyclopedia Britannica (1945). The new survey of universal knowledge. Chicago, IL: University of Chicago Press.
Ekelöf, G. (1959). Opus incertum: Poetik. In: *Dikter*. Stockholm, Sweden: Bonniers Förlag AB, 1984.
Erlich, H. S. (1998). On loneliness, narcissism and intimacy. *American Journal of Psychoanalysis, 58*(2), 135–162.
Gabbard, G. (1989). On 'doing nothing' in the psychoanalytic treatment of the refractory borderline patient. *International Journal of Psycho-Analysis, 70*(3), 527–534.
Hadda, J. (1991). The ontogeny of silence in an analytic case. *International Journal of Psycho-Analysis, 72*(1), 117–130.
Jacobs, T. J. (1994). Nonverbal communications: Some reflections on their role in the psychoanalytic process and psychoanalytic education. *Journal of the American Psychoanalytic Association, 42*(3), 741–762.
Jacobs, T. (1998). On countertransference enactments. In: S. J. Ellman & M. Moskowitz (Eds.), *Enactment. Toward a New Approach to the Therapeutic Relationship* (pp. 63–76). Northvale, NJ: Aronson.
Jaworsky, A. (Ed.) (1997). *Silence — Interdisciplinary Perspectives*. New York, NY: Mouton de Gruyer.
Kahn, M. (1963). Silence as communication. *Bulletin of the Menninger Clinic, 27*, 300–317.
Killingmo, B. (1990). Beyond semantics: A clinical and theoretical study of isolation. *International Journal of Psycho-Analysis, 71*(1), 113–126.
Kurz, S. (1984). On silence. *Psychoanalytic Review, 71*(2), 227–245.
Lehtonen, J., & Sajavaara, K. (1985). The silent Finn. In: D. Tannen & M. Saville-Troike (Eds.), *Perspectives on Silence* (pp. 193–201). Norwood, NJ: Ablex.
Leira, T. (1995). Silence as communication: Non-verbal dialogue and therapeutic action. *The Scandinavian Psychoanalytic Review, 18*(1), 41–65.
Lewis, H. B. (1971). *Shame and Guilt in Neurosis*. New York, NY: International UP.
Loewenstein, R. M. (1961). Introduction to panel: 'The silent patient'. *Journal of the American Psychoanalytic Association, 16*, 2–6.
Modell, A. (1975). A narcissistic defence against affects and the illusion of self-sufficiency. *International Journal of Psycho-Analysis, 56*(3), 275–282.
Modell, A. (1976). 'The holding environment' and the therapeutic action of psychoanalysis. *Journal of the American Psychoanalytic Association, 24*(2), 285–307.
Modell, A. (1980). Affects and their non-communication. *International Journal of Psycho-Analysis, 61*(2), 259–267.
Morrison, A. P. (1984). Working with shame in psychoanalytic treatment. *Journal of the American Psychoanalytic Association, 32*(3), 479–505.

Morrison, A. P. (1989). *Shame, the Underside of Narcissism*. Hillsdale, NJ: Analytic Press.
Morsbach, H. (1988). The importance of silence and stillness in Japanese nonverbal communication: A cross-cultural approach. In: F. Poyatos (Ed.), *Cross-Cultural Perspectives in Nonverbal Communication* (pp. 201–216). Toronto: Hogrefe & Huber.
Pally, R. (2001). A primary role for nonverbal communication in psychoanalysis. *Psychoanalytic Inquiry*, *21*(1), 71–93.
Rizzuto, A. M. (1988). Transference, language, and affect in the treatment of bulimarexia. *International Journal of Psycho-Analysis*, *69*(3), 369–387.
Rizzuto, A. M. (1995). Sound and sense: Words in psychoanalysis and the paradox of the suffering person. *Canadian Journal of Psychoanalysis*, *3*(1), 1–15.
Saunders, G. R. (1985). Silence and noise as emotion management styles: An Italian case. In: D. Tannen & M. Saville-Troike (Eds.), *Perspectives on Silence* (pp. 165–183). Norwood, NJ: Ablex.
Sajavaara, K., & Lehtonen, J. (1997). The silent Finn revisited. In: A. Jaworsky (Ed.), *Silence — Interdisciplinary Perspectives* (pp. 263–283). New York, NY: Mouton de Gruyer.
Schore, A. N. (1994). *Affect Regulation and the Origin of the Self. The Neurobiology of Emotional Development*. Hillsdale, NJ: Erlbaum.
Sifianou, M. (1997). Silence and politeness. In: A. Jaworsky (Ed.), *Silence — Interdisciplinary Perspectives* (pp. 63–84). New York, NY: Mouton de Gruyer.
Tangney, J. P. (1991). Moral affect: The good, the bad, and the ugly. *Journal of Personality and Social Psychology*, *61*(4), 598–607.
Tangney, J. P. (1996). Conceptual and methodological issues in the assessment of shame and guilt. *Behaviour Research and Therapy*, *34*(9), 741–754.
Tangney, J. P., Wagner, P., Fletcher, C., & Gramzow, R. (1992). Shamed into anger? The relation of shame and guilt to anger and self-reported aggression. *Journal of Personality and Social Psychology*, *62*(4), 669–675.
Waldhorn, H. F. (1959). The silent patient. *Journal of the American Psychoanalytic Association*, *7*(3), 548–560.
Weinberger, J. L. (1964). A triad of silence: Silence, masochism and depression. *International Journal of Psycho-Analysis*, *45*, 304–309.
Winnicott, D. W. (1958). The capacity to be alone. *International Journal of Psycho-Analysis*, *39*(5), 416–420.
Winnicott, D. W. (1963). Communicating and not communicating leading to a study of certain opposites. In: *The Maturational Processes and the Facilitating Environment* (pp. 166–170). New York, NY: International Universities.

Chapter 7

Varieties of silence in the analytic setting

Salman Akhtar

While cognizant of the fact that the categories of silence I am about to propose might neither be completely exclusive of each other nor exhaustive of the phenomena under investigation, I nonetheless find it heuristically as well as technically useful to view silence along the following typology.

Structural silence

Since "structure" merely implies a relatively predictable and recurring set of processes, it is both quizzical and understandable to speak of "structural silence". It is quizzical because how can something become organised if it is quiet and not adequately mentalised? It is understandable because aspects of mind do exist that are entirely process-oriented and not content-based. An illustration of this is Winnicott's (1960) concept of "true self". Denoting the "going-on-being" (Winnicott, 1956) and un-thought psychosomatic continuity of existence, the "true self" is indescribable. It reflects living authentically with a lambent corporeality and unimpeded psychic life (both operating in peaceful unison); indeed, the essence of true self is "*incommunicado*" (Winnicott, 1963, p. 187, my emphasis).

Another illustration of "structural silence" or silent structures is constituted by the "area of creation" (Balint, 1968). In this realm of psychic experience, there is no external or internal object present. "The subject is on his own and his main concern is to produce something out of himself; this something to be produced may be an object but not necessarily so" (p. 24). Besides artistic creation, mathematics, and philosophy, this mental sphere includes "understanding something or somebody, and last but not least, two highly important phenomena: the early phases of becoming—bodily or mentally—'ill', and spontaneous recovery from that 'illness'" (p. 24). Even when the subject is without an object, he is not entirely alone. He is most probably with "pre-objects", dim fragments of non-self representation that congeal into objects only after much preconscious work. The "area of creation" appears in the clinical situation, at times, when the patient is silent and pensive. Such a patient might not be running "away" from disturbing mental contents but might be running "towards" the state of having tangible mental content. This type of silence need not be ruptured by an "intervention"; the analyst must wait patiently till the patient "returns" from his reverie with a "solution" to his malady of the moment.

A third example of "structured silence" is constituted by the psychic material under the domain of "primal repression" (Breuer & Freud, 1895). There is little preconscious representation of the material under "primal repression" and the prefix "primal" (as opposed to "primary") underscores not only the early but also the ubiquitous nature of the phenomenon in human experience. "Primal repression" is associated with the nonverbal period of infancy; the elements under it cannot be verbally recalled but only be relived. In Frank's (1969) terminology, this is "the unrememberable and the unforgettable" (p. 48) substrate of the human psyche.

Unmentalised silence

We know from Bion (1962a, 1962b) and, more recently, from Fonagy and Target (1997) that it takes the maternal processing of a child's spontaneous, even though incoherent and "un-thinkable" psychic material to cohere in sustainable and intelligible thoughts. In Bion's terms, this is turning beta elements into alpha elements, or incomprehensible and vague affect-sensations into formed narratives that can be reflected upon. It is this maternal attitude that ultimately bestows the gift of the ability to think about one's mental goings-on. In its absence or pronounced limitation—such as in the case of a "dead mother" (Green, 1983)—the child grows up to be an individual who has little to say in response to others' thoughts and even, as a follow-up, of his own inescapable spontaneity. In clinical situations, we see such individuals interrupt their half-hearted forays into free association with an exasperated "anyway", "so that's it", "I have nothing more to say about this", followed by a sigh. It is as if they have run out of ideas and are staring—puzzled and clueless—at the abyss of wordlessness. Interventional strategies with such patients falter if their "silence" is regarded as a resistance. It is more productive to gently encourage them to "think" more. The analyst, for instance, might say to such a patient: "Next time, instead of saying that 'I have nothing more to say about it', try saying 'I have nothing more that *I know* to say about it'", or "The next time you are about to end what you are saying by sighing and saying 'anyway', and then changing the topic, try saying 'I was about to say anyway but will try to go on and see what more—even if seemingly unrelated to the topic—can come to mind'". Such "educative" measures convey to the patient that the analyst is not only interested in the un-mined (pun unintended) areas of his mental field but genuinely believes that the patient can develop the ability to look at this realm himself.[1]

Defensive silence

This is the most recognised type of silence in terms of clinical psychoanalysis. Such silence might appear spontaneously and is then a response to the emergent unacceptable wishes and fantasies in the patient. It serves to keep in abeyance those drives, drive-directives, and the transference wishes consequent upon them that are felt morally repugnant or shameful by the patient. For instance, a patient talking about his drive to succeed and be famous might suddenly stop talking. Anxiety takes over and his ability to free-associate is transiently compromised. He seems to have lost his train of thought. Gentle encouragement, along with some "defense analysis" (A. Freud, 1936) might result in the patient's revealing that he wishes to win a Nobel Prize. In turn, such revelation makes it possible to analyse the patient's motives in this regard but also, and perhaps more important, his transference-based fears of rejection and criticism for his ambition. Seeming to hinder the progress of analysis, the silence of resistance affords the analyst a wonderful opportunity to bring deep and conflicted material to the surface.

Guilt, shame, and fear of retaliation are, however, not the only motivators of silence in the service of resistance. Loving and feeling loved can also appear threatening, especially to schizoid and masochistic patients, and become the subject of mental erasure. Just as the patient begins to feel loved, anxiety rises and drowns the capacity for verbalisation.

Finally, there is the phenomenon of deliberate withholding. Here the patient refuses to share with the analyst something that he knows (e.g., an extramarital affair, cheating in exams) is emotionally significant and can impact upon his treatment. Prevalent among patients with pronounced, even if compensated, narcissistic and sociopathic traits (Kernberg, 1984; Stone, 2009) such withholding can manifest through "silence" but can also exist under the mask of pseudo-cordial verbalisation. However, it should be remembered that relatively "intact" neurotic patients can also consciously withhold information (e.g., the price of a recently purchased house) out of anxiety and transference-based fears of shame, competitiveness, and hostility.

Clinical vignette 1

Rebecca Cohen,[2] 26-year-old daughter of a Holocaust survivor father, was in analysis with me. The course of early treatment was filled with anxiety-laden fantasies about her father's experience in the Nazi concentration camp. Dreaded scenarios of ethnic hatred and violence preoccupied Rebecca and this readily spread to the transference. She feared and hated me, regarded me as a Jew-hating Muslim or Arab, and suspected that I supported anti-Israeli violence by Palestinians. Projections of her own trans-generationally given post-traumatic Jew–Nazi split of the self were constantly active in her relatedness with me. One day, I was hated and viciously attacked. Next day, I was deeply feared.

During one session while talking of the Holocaust, she suddenly jumped up from the couch and ran to the corner of the office that was farthest from me, trembling and obviously shaken by something she had just experienced internally. Rebecca stood there crying. I remained silent. Then she found a box of tissues on the desk nearby, cleaned her face, and began to look a bit composed. I did not say anything and waited patiently for things to unfold. Rebecca jumped up, sat on my desk, and asked me if I knew what had happened. I shook my head, telling her that I did not. She then revealed that she had felt that I was going to take out a knife and stab her while she was on the couch and that's why she had to get away from me. As she was narrating this, I noted that she had become much calmer. I remained quiet. Rebecca went on to say,

"You know, I have never seen your office from this end. It looks so strange ... you know, what it looks like ... it looks so still.

Everything is unmoved, quiet. It is like a dust cover jacket of a best-seller murder mystery. And you know what, sometimes when you read the whole book, you find out that all the clues were already shown in the photograph on the cover of the book. Yes, your office, from this side, looks like a photograph of just that sort, with all the clues intact."

Now I spoke. I said, "And, I guess I would be the corpse in this murder scene." Rebecca smiled, stretched her arms, and aiming her clasped hands at me, made a noise indicating that she was shooting me with a gun. I responded by saying

"You know what, a little while ago you thought that I was going to kill you and now that you have taken some distance from that position, you find yourself killing me. Look, this murder and murderer are both parts of your own self and, for the work we have mutually undertaken, it is my hope that we hold on to both these views and see how they are related to each other, where they came from, and what purposes do they serve."

Rebecca got off the desk, walked back to the couch, and lay down. The session continued in the "usual" way.

Enactive silence

The "deliberate withholding" mentioned above might be a way of avoiding personal shame, anticipated ridicule by the analyst, or behind-the-back gossip or mocking by real or imagined third parties (e.g., the analyst's colleagues or spouse with whom the analyst is assumed to share secrets). Until the time such motivation governs withholding, the practice falls under what Arlow (1961) has called "silences which serve primarily the function of defense" (p. 49). However, if the aim of deliberate withholding is to mislead the analyst, control him, and render him impotent, then the phenomenon belongs to the category of "silences which serve primarily the function of discharge" (p. 49).

In contemporary terminology, silences of the latter type constitute enactments. By becoming or remaining silent, the patient is putting something into action and, at the same time, pulling the analyst into a reactive or reciprocal response. Such silence may be used to cause a "reinstinctualization of the process of empathy" (ibid., p. 51) in the analyst. It might be a way of teasing and hurting the analyst. Hiding under the cloak of "verbal invisibility", a tenaciously silent patient might attack the analytic process, freeze its progress, "kill time", and paralyse the analyst's "work ego" (Olinick, Poland, Grigg & Granatir, 1973). The activation and discharge of primitive sadomasochism is difficult to miss under such circumstances.

While it is hardly possible to exhaustively list the relational scenarios that are played out through relentless—and, often motionless (with the patient lying absolutely still on the couch)—silences, common "messages" from such patients include: (i) "Please do not try to kill me; I am already dead", (ii) "I am going to make it impossible for you to do your work; you will feel as worthless as I felt growing up in my family", (iii) "I am not going to talk no matter how much you want me to; I will make you feel how I felt when my father would become silent for days upon the slightest infraction of rules on my part", and so on. In other words, enactments in the form of silence can reflect self-protection, important identifications, reversals of traumatic childhood scenarios, "attacks on linking" (Bion, 1958), and destructiveness towards the treatment process.

Instinctual discharge and enactment of identifications (e.g., with silently hostile parents) are, however, not the only factors in the aetiology of such silence. Superego dictates might also contribute to it. Arlow clearly states that:

> I do not wish to leave the impression that silence in the service of discharge is related exclusively to gratification of id-impulses. Clinical experiences abound to show that failure, suffering, and provocation in analytic situations may serve the self-punitive demands of the superego, and transference repetition may represent a persistent need to expiate guilt by using silence as a provocation of punishment
>
> (1961, p. 51).

Clinical vignette 2

In the throes of a regressive transference, Jill Schwartz entered my office enraged and waving a finger. Approaching the couch, she said, "I have a lot on my mind today and I want to do all the talking. I don't want you to speak even a single word!" A little taken aback, I mumbled, "Okay." Jill shouted, "I said, 'not one word' and you have already fucked up this session!" Now sitting on my chair behind her, I was rattled. "Did I do wrong by speaking at all?" I asked myself. As she lay on the couch, angrily silent and stiff, I started to think. Perhaps she is so inconsolable today, so intent upon forcing me into the role of a depriving person, that she found a way to see even the gratification of her desire as its frustration. I was, however, not entirely satisfied with this explanation and therefore decided to wait, and think further. It then occurred to me that maybe she was rightly angered by my saying "Okay". In my agreeing to let her have omnipotent control over me, I had asserted my will and thus paradoxically deprived her of the omnipotence she seemed to need. I was about to make an interpretation along these lines, when it occurred to me that by sharing this understanding, I would be repeating my mistake: making my autonomous psychic functioning too obvious. As a result, I decided to only say, "I am sorry", and left the remaining thought unspoken. Jill relaxed and the tension in the room began to lessen. After ten minutes of further silence, she said, "Well, this session has been messed up. I had so many things to say." After a further pause, she said, "Among the various things on my mind ..." and thus the session gradually "started". By the time we ended, things were going pretty smoothly.

Symbolic silence

The contemporary eclipse of the "drive theory" perspective[3] should not make one overlook that what appears as silence might be a displaced, symbolic derivative of other instinctual aims. For instance, silence in obsessional neurotics is often a manifestation of anal erotism (Ferenczi, 1916): mouth replaces the anus and words get equated with faeces under such circumstances. "Retaining words" becomes a vehicle of controlling a mother who insists upon proper toilet habits. Sharpe enlarged the scope of the drive-based aims that could be expressed via silence.

> When the ego stabilizes the achievement of body-control and it becomes automatic, the emotions of anger and pleasure which heretofore accompanied bodily discharges must be dealt with in other ways. At the same time as sphincter control over anus and urethra is being established, the child is acquiring the power of speech and so an avenue of "outerance" present from birth becomes of immense importance.
>
> First of all the discharge of feeling tension when this is no longer relieved by physical discharges can take place through speech. The activity of speaking is substituted for the physical activity now

restricted at other openings of the body, while words themselves become the very substitutes for the bodily substances.

(1940, p. 157)

Thus, silence can represent an open mouth waiting for the milk of the mother-analyst's voice, a tightly closed anus refusing to yield faeces for a pleading mother, or a welcoming vagina ready to receive the father-analyst's "phallic" interpretations. However, such thinking has become sidelined in the current fervour of object relations, intersubjectivity, and an overall pallor of psychoanalytic interest in the body (Paniagua, 2004). Sharpe's perspective that silence might symbolise other bodily phenomena has lost its audience. Even less recognised is the fact that traffic moves in the opposite direction as well. In other words, other organs can be enlisted to express silence. Eyes are particularly important in this regard. Averting gaze and refusing to look at someone can be deployed as a form of not talking to them; this can have devastating effects upon the one who is thus shut out. A growing child, encountering such "visual silence" might find it hard to sustain self-esteem, and his capacity for object constancy might suffer (Abrams, 1991; Riess, 1978). Even during adulthood, being subject to such relational silence can be very disconcerting (Patsy Turrini, personal communication, February, 2012).

Such dreadful turning-away of the object and the resulting "torture by separation" (Sartre, 1946, p. 8) bring to mind that silence can symbolise death. Wurmser's (2000) observation that the German word *Totschweigen* stands for "to kill by silence" is also pertinent here. Wurmser notes that such "soul blindness"—a sustained and profound insensitivity (including visual aversion) to someone's individuality—can lead to structural disintegration in the recipient. Within the clinical situation, a tenacious silence often transmits a sense of putrefaction and deadness. The patient seems to be "playing possum" and thus avoiding an imagined attack from the analyst while at the same time "killing" the analyst off.

Contemplative silence

A slowing down of perceptual and cognitive traffic as well as a certain "low keyedness" (Mahler, Pine & Bergman, 1975) of affect is essential for fresh insights to emerge from within (Ronningstam, this volume) and/or new information from outside to be metabolised. The associated stoppage of active speech falls under the rubric of "contemplative silence". The individual, in this state, is involved in a private and subliminal dialogue with his subjectively experienced inner objects (Mahler, Pine & Bergman, 1975; Winnicott, 1963) or turning attention inward to comprehend and catalogue what he has just heard or seen.

The pensive quietude that follows reading poetry, looking at a striking piece of art, and even upon hearing seriously bad national news is an illustration of "contemplative silence". In the context of our clinical work, such silence appears spontaneously and is followed by a meaningful revelation or enhancement of associations. Or it appears in response to the analyst's intervention.

> Some patients need some "silent time" to mull over, to contend with, to digest the new insight. This will be followed by confirmatory material if the interpretation is correct. It is a much more frequent occurrence, however, to find that patients will react with silence to an incorrect interpretation. In this situation, silence usually indicates the disappointment in not being understood. Usually such silences in response to interpretation are transient. Prolonged silence after an interpretation always means that the interpretation has been incorrect.
> (Greenson, 1961, pp. 82–83)

Clearly, the clinical situation is not the sole arena for contemplative silences to emerge. As stated above, appreciation of art and literature is regularly reliant on such quietness of mind. Rapt absorption in pondering over scientific and mathematical problems, as well as seeming oblivion before a writer puts pen to paper, are also instances of contemplative silence.[4] The "recess" a judge takes before giving his judgement in a court of law is also pertinent in this context.

Nowhere is "contemplative silence" more evident than in the state of mourning.[5] Withdrawal of cathexis from the external world and the need to shuffle the relational cards involving the lost objects lead to a certain quietness on the bereaved person's part. Feeling humbled by the awesome power of death, one loses faith—for a moment—in spoken words. Communion with the internal representations of the deceased, and the awareness of one's own mortality render one wary of platitudes. Attention turns towards the changed reality, and the gaping hole produced by the loss is covered over by silence.

Regenerative silence

Within psychoanalysis, the notion of an ego-replenishing quietude was first introduced by Winnicott (1963). According to him, genuine communication only arises when objects change over from being subjective to being objectively perceived. It is at this point that the two opposites of communication also appear. One is active or reactive not-communicating and the other "simple not-communicating" (p. 183). This is what I have termed "regenerative silence" here. In Winnicott's words:

> Simple not-communicating is like resting. It is a state in its own right, and it passes over into communicating, and reappears as naturally ... One should be able to make a positive statement of the healthy use of non-communication in the establishment of feeling real.
> (pp. 183–184)

Such not-communicating is seen by Winnicott as restoring the vitality of true self which by its very nature is incommunicado and most worthy of preservation. His notions in this realm have been further developed by Khan (1983a, 1983b). In describing the state of "lying fallow", Khan declared that this:

> is not one of inertia, listless vacancy or idle quietism of soul; nor is it a flight from harassed purposiveness and pragmatic action. *Lying fallow* is a transitional state of experience, a mode of being that is alerted quietude and receptive wakeful lambent consciousness ... We need to be somewhat idle and feel our way out of this benignly languid passive mood. If we are forced out of it, either by our own conscious or the environment, we feel irritable and grumpy.
> (pp. 183, 185, italics in the original)

Khan regards the experience of "lying fallow" to be "a nutrient of the ego" (p. 185) and important for the process of personalisation in the individual. Unlike Winnicott, he suggests that while silent inactivity is the most frequent pathway to such experience, it can also be reached by pictorial expression, as through doodling. Moreover, the experience, while deeply personal and private, can be facilitated by the silent companionship of someone—a spouse, friend, or even an unintrusive pet. This is "silence in the service of ego" (Shafii, 1973, p. 431) *par excellence*.

Blank silence

The consideration of diminished content and velocity of thought in the "lying fallow" state leads to the next logical step of total absence of activity in the mind: no verbally encoded thoughts, no visual images, no affective currents. To be sure, a proposal of this sort causes puzzlement and raises flags of scepticism. One wants to protest. Would not such a state be equivalent to "psychic death" (Guntrip, 1969) or betray a withdrawal from object cathexes that is of psychotic proportions? How could the mind become still to this extent, unless there was a "negative hallucination of thought" (Green, 1993) operative *in toto*? In other words, the theoretician amongst (and within) us might reluctantly concede that "blank silence" exists but only if he can declare it to be seriously pathological.

Such thinking can certainly explain a certain form of "blank silence", a "malignant" one, I suppose. However, there might be a benign type of "blank silence" also. Indeed, it was in this latter sense that Van der Heide first proposed the term. He regarded it as representing a blissful merger of the self and object, also seen in close proximity to sleep. Such silence usually occurs in response to a concise and correct transference interpretation.

> The patient falls into a silence of many minutes or lasting for the remainder of the session. His position on the couch is relaxed, often the habitual one of sleep; there is no sign of motor activity, speech has vanished and is not attempted. It looks like "time out". If the analyst succeeds in terminating the silence by urging verbalization (which rarely succeeds), he is told that thoughts were absent and there is no evidence of conscious withholding of thoughts or fantasy. If after a time the silence breaks spontaneously, the spoken thoughts appear distant from the content of the interpretation. Sometimes the patient ends the silence with a remark evidencing awareness of the analyst's thoughts or momentary affective state.
>
> (1961, p. 86)

Concluding remarks

In this chapter, I have addressed the multifaceted phenomenon of silence and described eight types of silence: (i) structural silence; (ii) silence due to the lack of mentalisation; (iii) silence due to conflict; (iv) silence as enactment; (v) symbolic silence; (vi) contemplative silence; (vii) regenerative silence, and (viii) blank silence. I have placed silence on an equal footing with speaking—especially as these occur in the psychoanalytic setting—by emphasising that both possess the ability to serve similar aims. Both can hide and both can express psychic contents. Both can defend against drive-related pressures and both can help discharge such tensions. Both can convey transference and both can become vehicles of enactment. Both can induce and evoke countertransference feelings. Both can be responded to appropriately or inappropriately by the patient. Both can facilitate or impede the progress of the analytic process. Through all this and more, both silence and verbalisation become integral to our clinical enterprise.

Now, I wish to conclude by noting some questions that have remained unaddressed in this discourse. These include the following. Does gender play a role in the capacity for expressing oneself through silence or in bearing others' silences? Are there developmental phases where silence, at least in regard to spoken language, is inevitable (e.g., early infancy) or preferred (e.g., old age)? Is silence (around oneself or in parts of oneself) conducive to creative work? Is silence an integral component of that ubiquitous human process called mourning and that elusive character attribute called "dignity"? To be sure, future contributions might provide answers to such questions but we must leave the possibility open for some of those answers to come without the veil of words. We must allow our knowledge to be enriched by a new manuscript of silence.

Notes

1 Talking of the generally alexithymic psychosomatic patients, Baranger and Baranger (2009) speak of interventions that "supply words to describe experiences that never had any. In this type of interpretation, the analyst proceeds *per via di porre* and not only *per via di levare*, as Freud (1905) demanded in referring to neurotics" (p. 102).
2 The names given to patients are fictitious.
3 Pine (1988, 1997) continues to remind us, however, that the heuristic corpus of psychoanalysis consists of four psychologies: drive psychology, ego psychology, object relations psychology, and self psychology. They overlap but each adds something new to the understanding of development, psychopathology, and technique.
4 The well-known psychoanalyst-philosopher, Allen Wheelis, told me that he often sits quietly for hours before beginning to write (personal communication, January 2008).
5 Note in this connection the ritual "moment of silence" observed in honour of the deceased. Its purpose is to enforce—temporarily at least— respectful attention upon the memories of the departed one.

References

Abrams, D. M. (1991). Looking at and looking away: Etiology of preoedipal splitting in a deaf girl. *Psychoanalytic Study of the Child, 46*(1), 277–304.
Arlow, J. A. (1961). Silence and the theory of technique. *Journal of the American Psychoanalytic Association, 9*(3), 44–55.
Balint, M. (1968). *The Basic Fault: Therapeutic Aspects of Regression*. London: Tavistock.
Baranger, M., & Baranger, W. (Eds.) (2009). *The Work of Confluence*. London: Karnac.
Bion, W. (1958). On arrogance. *International Journal of Psycho-Analysis, 39*(2–4), 144–146.
Bion, W. (1962a). *Learning from Experience*. London: Karnac, 1984.
Bion, W. (1962b). The psycho-analytic study of thinking. *International Journal of Psycho-Analysis, 43*, 306–310.
Breuer, J., & Freud, S. (1895). Studies on hysteria. In: J. Strachey (Ed.), *The Standard Edition of the Complete Psychological Works of Sigmund Freud* (Vol. 2, pp. 1893–1895). London: Hogarth Press, 1955.
Ferenczi, S. (1916). Silence is golden. In: *Further Contributions to the Theory and Technique of Psychoanalysis* (pp. 250–251). London: Hogarth Press, 1948.
Fonagy, P. & Target, M. (1997). Attachment and reflective function: Their role in self-organization. *Development and Psychopathology, 9*(4), 679–700.
Freud, A. (1936). *The Ego and the Mechanisms of Defense*. New York: International Universities Press.
Frank, A. (1969). The unrememberable and the unforgettable: Passive primal repression. *Psychoanalytic Study of the Child, 24*(1), 48–77.
Green, A. (1983). *Narcissisme de vie, Narcissisme de mort*. Paris: Minuit.
Green, A. (1993). *The Work of the Negative*. London: Free Association.
Greenson, R. (1961). On the silence and sounds of the analytic hour. *Journal of the American Psychoanalytic Association, 9*(1), 79–84.
Guntrip, H. (1969). *Schizoid Phenomena, Object Relations and the Self*. New York: International Universities Press.
Kernberg, O. F. (1984). *Severe Personality Disorders: Psychotherapeutic Strategies*. New Haven, CT: Yale University Press.
Khan, M. (1983a). On lying fallow. In: *Hidden Selves: Between Theory and Practice in Psychoanalysis* (pp. 183–188). New York: International Universities Press.
Khan, M. (1983b). Infancy, aloneness and madness. In: *Hidden Selves: Between Theory and Practice in Psychoanalysis* (pp. 181–182). New York: International Universities Press.
Mahler, M. S., Pine, F., & Bergman, A. (1975). *The Psychological Birth of the Human Infant: Symbiosis and Individuation*. New York: Basic.
Olinick, S., Poland, W., Grigg, K., & Granatir, W. (1973). The psychoanalytic work ego: Process and interpretation. *International Journal of Psycho-Analysis, 54*(2), 143–151.
Paniagua, C. (2004). What has happened to the body in psychoanalysis? *International Journal of Psycho-Analysis, 85*(4), 973–976.

Pine, F. (1988). The four psychologies of psychoanalysis and their place in clinical work. *Journal of the American Psychoanalytic Association, 36*(3), 571–596.
Pine, F. (1997). *Diversity and Direction in Psychoanalytic Technique.* New Haven, CT: Yale University Press.
Riess, A. (1978). The mother's eye: For better and for worse. *Psychoanalytic Study of the Child, 33*(1), 381–433.
Sartre, J. -P. (1946). *No Exit and Three Other Plays.* New York: Vintage.
Shafii, M. (1973). Silence in the service of ego: Psychoanalytic study of meditation. *International Journal of Psycho-Analysis, 54*(5), 431–443.
Sharpe, E. F. (1940). Psychophysical problems revealed in language: An examination of metaphor. In: *Collected Papers on Psychoanalysis* (pp. 155–169). London: Hogarth, 1950.
Stone, M. (2009). Lying and deceitfulness in personality disorders. In: S. Akhtar (Ed.), *Lying, Cheating, and Carrying on* (pp. 69–92). Lanham, MD: Jason Aronson.
Van der Heide, C. (1961). Blank silence and the dream screen. *Journal of the American Psychoanalytic Association, 9*(1), 85–90.
Winnicott, D. W. (1956). Primary maternal preoccupation. In: *Collected Papers: Through Paediatrics to Psychoanalysis* (pp. 300–305). New York: Basic, 1958.
Winnicott, D. W. (1960). Ego distortion in terms of true and false self. In: *The Maturational Processes and the Facilitating Environment* (pp. 140–152). New York: International Universities Press, 1965.
Winnicott, D. W. (1963). Communicating and not communicating leading to a study of certain opposites. In: *The Maturational Processes and the Facilitating Environment* (pp. 166–170). New York: International Universities Press, 1965.
Wurmser, L. (2000). Magic transformation and tragic transformation: Splitting of the ego and superego in severely traumatized patients. *Clinical Social Work Journal, 28*(4), 385–395.

Chapter 8

Silence as a manifestation of resistance

Aleksandar Dimitrijević

Very early on in its development, psychoanalysis was described as a *talking cure*. Sigmund Freud and his followers adopted this formulation ascribed by Josef Breuer to his patient Bertha Pappenheim (fictitiously called "Anna O."). They developed a doctrine of curing mental disorders with the use of talking (i.e., interpreting), as opposed to various forms of early medical treatments for mental disorders. This was probably meant to indicate that they were not using any means other than conversation, be it hypnosis, suggestion, baths, or genital stimulation (see Aron & Starr, 2013), and psychoanalysts invited their patients to talk incessantly. This was named free-associating and is considered the basic, or even the only, rule of psychoanalysis. It requires of a patient nothing less than to "relax and to say everything that occurs to him as it occurs to him, observing what thoughts, feelings, and impulses come up in his mind" (Reik, 1948, p. 122). This stream (or, sometimes, an avalanche) of words constituted, together with interpreting dreams, the principal method for discovering the secrets of the unconscious, and brought forth the blind spots and transferences, as well as an occasional fashionable novelistic masterpiece, or whole artistic movements, like surrealism.

Opposite to this, every prolonged silence coming from a patient was considered a deviation from the basic rule, a suspicious anomaly, or even the "enemy of therapeutic success" (Arlow, 1961, p. 44). Ultimately: a manifestation of resistance. The concept of resistance, in the meantime widely discussed, pertains to "all verbal material and action that blocks the analysand's access to his or her unconscious" (Akhtar, 2009, p. 247). Analysts think that behavior, including behavior in the analytic setting, is not passive or automatic, but active and meaningful; this is even true in the apparent *absence* of action, like missing a session, forgetting to pay—or being silent. We put unconscious work into forgetting precisely this or that detail that is most central to understanding the conflict we are struggling with and we are silent about something that would be revealing too much too early.

In this chapter, I review the traditional view of silence as manifestation of resistance in the patient, but also as a possible manifestation of resistance in the analyst, and, finally, the more contemporary conception of silence as intersubjective impasse in psychoanalytic treatments.

Silence as resistance in the patient

To say that silence is a manifestation of resistance means that we consider a break in a patient's free associations to be full of meaning, for instance, an unconsciously motivated effort not to share something that could lead to uncomfortable or anxiety-provoking insights. And this is indeed very frequently a plausible interpretation of silences in sessions.[1] For instance, imagine this:

> A thirty-year-old, successful businesswoman comes to four-sessions-per-week psychoanalysis, initiated by somatic ailments and anxiety that reaches the level of panic. From the earliest sessions, she develops intense idealizing transference. Sometime into the third year, however, she starts feeling extremely bored. She cancels a session at least every week or fails to show up without prior announcement. When she does come, she feels there is nothing to be said. One day, after she is six minutes late, the following conversation ensues:

> I do not know what to say. (She is then silent for about five minutes.) I have no idea what to talk about. (She is then silent for two or three minutes.) I didn't feel like coming today. I can only repeat what I have already told you. (She is then silent for about five minutes.) I am so tired. I barely slept last night. (She then turns aside.) May I lie like this?
> That is up to you.
> Thank you. (The patient is then silent for several minutes before she starts snoring. She wakes up ten minutes before the end of the session.) Oh, excuse me! This is so embarrassing!

> In what way do you feel embarrassed?
> You don't visit other people and doze off in their houses or offices.
> What made you fall asleep here, now?
> I don't know. (She is then silent for about three minutes.) I won't be able to come on Friday. I will have to go on a business trip. I better not forget to tell you so that I won't have to pay for that session. (She is then silent until the time is up.)

Silence as a form of resistance does not have to relate to one single session only. Nina Coltart (1991, p. 439) described a group she called silent patients—those who speak for no more than 10 percent of the analytic time (or five minutes per regular session). She has seen eight of them over the 30 years of her career, and one of them was completely silent for three-and-a-half months straight. Torhild Leira (1955, p. 41) writes about a patient who was silent for as long as one year.

If a patient uses silence to indeed express resistance, that decision can have different meanings[2]:

1. Initial resistance, as readjustment to an unfamiliar situation—being on the couch, talking about dreams, etc.—which should be the mildest of all problems when silence reflects resistance, as free associating is not frequent in social communications and almost everyone needs time to get used to it;
2. An effort to conceal relevant information or insight from the analyst or from the patient's consciousness (by probably keeping it in the preconscious). The repressed thought is believed to interfere with the process of thinking, so much so that the person cannot say anything (Reik, 1949)[3];
3. Silence can also be a consequence of unconscious efforts to resist recollection, which is problematic as it leads to repeating instead of understanding and working through;
4. Resisting the awareness and disclosure of transference that the patient feels is developing. This can be a result of mechanisms that stem from different developmental layers (Bergler, 1938; Fliess, 1949):
   a. phallic mechanisms: avoiding erotic transference; using masochistic acting out for feelings of being overpowered, and, eventually, castrated); renouncing negative transference;
   b. anal mechanisms: retaining thoughts, as a sign of stubbornness and aggression, or even ambivalence or paranoia;

c. oral mechanisms: silence as a sign of enjoyment in receiving or revenge for not having received.
5. A passive-aggressive protest against the analyst, not expressed in words or behavior, though one can learn to recognize when the non-verbal communicative gestures are full of tension and anger;
6. Avoidance of the relationship with the analyst after having experienced frustration, though still not a complete abandonment of it, or the projection onto the psychoanalyst of one's dissatisfaction with the capacity to improve in the analysis.

Freud (1912, p. 102) viewed silence as "the most powerful resistance," especially to transference.[4] Although the silence Freud had in mind is related to the lack of verbal activity, wordless, although not necessarily soundless silence, to use Greenson's important distinction (1961, p. 80ff.), Freud connected it to resistance against anal erotic wishes. Karl Abraham (1919/1949) subscribed to the idea that one of the functions of speech was the discharge of affect displaced from the original erogenous zones to the organs and functions of speech, and suggested that silence served the opposite purpose: it was a form of repression.

Clinical and technical issues were, as was usual, most elaborated by Sándor Ferenczi. In his first, brief papers about speech and silence, Ferenczi repeated Freud's positions. He claimed to have learned from Freud about "connections between anal erotism and speech" (1916–17, p. 251), talking being a form of discharge of drive impulses, and silence retention, "retention of all emotion" (ibid.). Still, Ferenczi also connected silence with oral eroticism: the fear of uttering obscene words (1911), as well as the repressed sexualization of mouth, tongue, and teeth (1919).

From Ferenczi come several iterations of advice as to what to do when a patient is repeatedly silent. He first suggested interpreting, the usual strategy psychoanalysts used at that time: "if the patient is silent for a more prolonged period, it usually signifies that he is withholding something. A patient's sudden silence must, therefore, always be interpreted as a *passagere* [transient] *symptom*" (1919, p. 179). On the same page, however, he adds that it is sometimes best to "encounter the patient's silence with silence." In one of the last pieces he had written, a diary entry from October 1932, he mentioned "my (occasionally used) technique of silence" (1988, p. 259), but it remains unclear what he meant. His explanations that this technique is no different than free associations in leading to more profound insight into the unconscious, and that very long silence can lead to the states of trance are, unfortunately, too cryptic. The same is true of the following note from the same month:

> Longish 'keeping quiet': deeper relaxation, dreams, images, somewhat more 'dreamlike'– far from the conscious thought material.
> But when afterwards must it come to speaking?
> Should the analyst interrupt (surprise) the silence? (Not so bad.)
> When should such 'silent sessions' begin?
>
> (1988, p. 258)

Silence as a form of countertransference resistance

Everything expected of psychoanalysts when it came to talking and silence was utterly opposite to what I have just described as having been expected from patients. Not only "the analyst is not afraid of silence" (Reik, 1948, p. 124), but in popular culture, in books, films, cartoons, and jokes, psychoanalysts were portrayed as notoriously silent, and this was frequently very accurate, probably more in Paris and New York City than elsewhere. And inside the world of psychoanalysis, there was pride that the absolute silence "was never made a methodological principle before Freud" (Reik, 1948, p. 124).

The silence of the analyst was almost regarded as the defining dogma of psychoanalytic practice. Theodore Reik, whose authority came partly from his close contact with Freud himself, wrote that the analytic process depended more on the analyst's silence than on what s/he said, and that the process of each psychoanalytic treatment started when the patient realized that not only was the analyst silent but s/he intended to remain silent (Reik, 1948, p. 126). This apotheosis of silence was soon echoed in two papers that got to be frequently quoted since their publication. Zeligs (1961) considered silence the baseline psychoanalysts always return to, and Pressman wrote that "if there is one thing that makes the analytic situation unique, it is the silent listening objective attitude on the part of one of the partners" (1961, p. 168).

This attitude was justified in different ways, as the silence of the analyst was considered to have the following effects:

1. Helping the patient calm down in the presence of the analyst's calmness and peace of mind;

2. Give the analysand an impression of being in contact with a person who is loving without words, like a mother to a preverbal child, in a state of merger, with inarticulate emotional states and physical sensations; if the analyst recognizes this transference dynamic, he/she should better not use interpretations or even questions for quite some time (Dimitrijević, 2019);
3. Making "the world outside the [analytic] room [be] put into the background" (Reik, 1948, p. 125), so that the patient could focus on exploring his/her Unconscious via free-associating;
4. Analyst's silence serves as a sounding board that makes the thoughts of the patient obvious, "loud";
5. Analyst's silence is a tool for obtaining "confessions," as patients are expected to feel listened to and cared for by an expert who is not imposing his/her personal or professional agenda but is open to learning about the patients; this can presumably work only once the therapeutic alliance is firmly established;
6. If the analyst would talk frequently and a lot, that was believed to make patients defenses stronger through interference with the free association (Pressman, 1961, p. 171), and encourage drive or emotional discharges.

For all these reasons, it was considered wisest for those working in this constellation to develop a capacity for being taciturn and provide interpretations of supposedly deep unconscious material only sparingly, if not frugally. Even the strongest proponents of the silent attitude of the analyst, however, opened the question of possible patients' interpenetrations of analysts' silence, and admitted it can be seen as persecutory and coercive (Reik, 1949), as well as a sign of the analyst's boredom, anger, depriving the patient, sadism, deadness, being displeased and/or threatening (Pressman, 1961, p. 176). It seems that any of these interpretations would cause painful emotions in the patient, as was recognized by Ferenczi, who, as his understanding of psychoanalysis changed toward the idea of elasticity, approached the patient's silence with a modicum of tenderness: "when one should keep silent and await a further association and at what point the further maintenance of silence would result only in causing the patient useless suffering" (Ferenczi, 1928, p. 89). But all this was treated as collateral damage, an inevitable by-product of psychoanalytic treatment.

As this was the era of Ego-psychology, there was a belief that "ideally, the analyst's silence should always be cognitive. The better trained and more experienced the analyst, the more do cognitive factors supervene" (Pressman, 1961, p. 178) over emotional. In the other psychoanalytic jargon, Kleinian, every ripple on the supposedly perfect surface of the analyst's psyche was a consequence of the mechanism called projective identification.[5] This in essence means that "the analyst (should) take special cognizance of that mood which the patient's silence evokes within him" (Arlow, 1961, p. 52), because the patient has supposedly "evacuated" some of his/her unbearable inner contents into the analyst, and it is the task of the analyst to recognize those contents alien to him/herself and give them a name ("the anger/fear/boredom I am feeling at this moment my patient feels regularly" or the like). Although this mechanism (without going into explanations of its possible origin and functioning here) does play a specific role, there is more to all this.

Today, the confidence and optimism of previous generations of psychoanalysts sound like a belief that the unconscious of the analyst can be switched off so that it will leave no shadow, much less influence, on his/her behavior. Cremerius (1969) was more cautious, writing that silence is but one of the tools, "technical operations," that must be applied with careful assessment of the actual situation so that it supports and improves the analytic process. Yet the idea of the analyst's mistakes is still obscure, and their possible intentional character unmentioned even in this classic paper on silence. In the US, Merton Gill (1984, p. 168) wrote that "silence is of course a behavior too ... silence too can be plausibly experienced as anything ranging from cruel inhumanity to tender concern." Finally, one can think of the analyst's silence as in nature opposite to cognitive, when it is a result of reverie, as described by Bion, so that it is almost artistic, full of fantasy and "free-floating attention."

Although the focus on countertransference experiences has become a rule over the last several decades, connecting it explicitly with resistance is not something many authors deal with. When it comes to the analyst's resistance to dealing with his/her countertransference, there are only a handful of papers about that topic. Still the most notable is the 1985 article by Darlene Ehrenberg, where countertransference resistance is considered to

> include, of course, those forms of resistance to awareness of collusive involvements such as identification and reaction formation. It would include also those defensive ways of avoiding engagement such as

detachment, resistance to awareness of one's own affective reactions, resistance to utilizing countertransference awareness, that is, resistance to dealing with any aspect of the nuances of the transference-countertransference interaction.

(1985, p. 564)

These precious lines bring the unconscious motivation of the analyst center stage, and with it every individual decision to remain silent or not. It is at least possible, and sometimes probable, that psychoanalysts are silent for personal reasons.

The first to write about resistance in countertransference was Sándor Ferenczi. After an impasse in his analysis of Elizabeth Severn, he agreed to her suggestion about mutual analysis (for further details see Ferenczi, 1988, and Severn, 2017), so that she analyzed him for one hour and then he analyzed her for another hour. During this process, Ferenczi discovered his resistance in countertransference in the form of hatred. He believed this was a consequence of the fact that Severn reminded him of the bad parts of his mother, which he, for a long time, was not capable of admitting to himself, because he was afraid of her like he was afraid of his mother. Ferenczi then started believing in the high importance of open sharing of negative feelings with patients as a strategy for overcoming "negative countertransference." He considered this so important that it is in the focus of the very first entry to what is now known as "Clinical Diary":

> Mannered form of greeting, formal request to "tell everything", so-called free-floating attention, which ultimately amounts to no attention at all, and which is certainly inadequate to the highly emotional character of the analysand's communications […] has the following effects: 1. the patient is offended by the lack of interest […], 2. since he does not want to think badly of us, he looks for the cause in himself […]; 3. finally he doubts the reality of the content, which until now he felt so acutely.
>
> (1988, p. 1)

Silence, admittedly, is not explicitly mentioned here. But I find this to be at the same time the earliest and the most revolutionary general statement about the three ideals of Ego-psychology (anonymity, neutrality, abstinence) as re-traumatizing for the patient. Ferenczi goes even one step further, and lists possible symptoms of this resistance in the analyst: "loss of enthusiasm, silence, irritation, the feeling of having done the best one could and still being criticized for it. Desire to break off the analysis, and perhaps really doing so" (1988, p. 200). And the root of this all is, as Donnel Stern, one of the most creative representatives of relational thinking in contemporary psychoanalysis, wrote, in our lack of self-reflection:

> The analyst unconsciously denies himself access to the context, to the state of his own self—to the other within himself—from within which it would be possible to construct the experience of the analysand. In more familiar terms, the analyst does not understand himself well enough to understand the patient.
>
> (2003, p. 846)

To improve this situation, we can accept the definition which says that "silence is a resistance on the part of the analyst if it interferes with new and relevant communication from the patient" (Liegner, 1974, p. 234).[6] We can, and definitely should, use this impetus to specify reasons and situations when the silence of the analyst is a sign of resistance:

1. The analyst does not like the patient as a person, or even detests him/her, and communicates with him/her only when that is unavoidable;
2. The analyst can be silent to unconsciously express punishment or revenge (Racker, 1968, p. 138), for instance after being offended, attacked, not paid, underestimated, denigrated, etc.;
3. The analyst can repeat in his/her work the trauma of his/her training analysis, which as a rule were and still frequently are full of silences;
4. Silence can be the sign of an analyst's awkward distancing at moments when he/she unconsciously feels too much closeness with a patient, whether closeness was the objective of the patient or not;
5. Silence can contain challenge and/or spite when the analyst unconsciously wants to prove to the patient that he/she is more powerful;
6. Silence can be a result of situations or patient behaviors that for the analyst are anxiety-provoking when he/she feels "on the thin ice";
7. Some analysts, as noted by Pressman (1961, p. 1978), have narcissistic fantasies about the omnipotence of their interpretations and, therefore, enjoy their silences and do not want to spoil them by anything "less" than interpretations;

8. Silence is just a by-product of the sleep of the analyst during a psychoanalytic session, a phenomenon on which not a single publication indexed on PEP-Web has ever focused.[7]

Here is another brief illustration of a concrete clinical situation:

> A female psychoanalytic psychotherapist, middle-aged and experienced, reports in peer-supervision that she has made a strange mistake working with a patient. She usually feels comfortable with her patients' maternal transferences and quickly identifies with patients, though she has never been prone to acting out on that. Now she reports that she has become strangely silent and withdrawn throughout a session with a female client 20 years her junior. Although she had previously liked talking to this patient, this time she even shortened the session by five minutes. It was this act (shortening the session) that motivated her to ask the group for advice, while she did not pay too much attention to her silence. After being asked to focus on what was new immediately before or during the session, the therapist, after offering several answers, "stumbled upon" the detail that she had noticed the patient checked her knees, although, she added, her skirt was not improperly short. With support, she then figured out that she had not been prepared for possible erotic transferences in work with female clients, and that this time she felt embarrassingly unprofessional and withdrew into silence because she had no prepared answers.

Much work is needed to overcome this fundamental avoidance of the psychoanalytic community and face it openly and rigorously. Because, we should have no doubts, "the patient hears that the analyst's silence is speaking to him. He listens to the analyst's silence or interpretations and reinterprets them according to the history that contributed to the constitution of his psyche" (Faimberg, 1988, p. 114). Analysts' resistances and consequently their silences most often go unnoticed, and we are not well prepared to detect them and reflect on them, while they can cause much pain and destroy many otherwise valuable treatment efforts. For this reason, supervision and/or peer-supervision should be asked for even by the most experienced of the analysts,[8] and one should never pretend to be above and beyond them: if silence is a sign of resistance, it must be translated into words, at least in another relationship.

Analytic silence as an intersubjective impasse

Silence, when it is a sign of resistance, can come from the patient, which is more frequent, as well as from the analyst, which our profession is less focused on. But this can also be an intersubjective phenomenon, coming from both sides at the same time. In other words: Just as any other couple immersed in long-term and emotionally intense social interaction, a psychoanalyst and a patient can end up locked in a profound, or total, silence for long periods of time. A couple may even wish to dissolve, but this turns out to be impossible because there is still intense attachment between them; and when they try to overcome the silent impasse, it turns out to lay in such darkness that, for a certain time, they cannot see any exit.

Despite contributions from the relational school, it seems to be a reason for concern that PEP-Web does not contain a single paper focused on this problem. And the problem definitely exists. If we agree with the classical attitude that says that "the analyst may become confused, fatigued, seduced, or otherwise psychically immobilized by a patient's prolonged silence and immobility" (Zelig, 1961, p. 20), we must not forget that this immobilization of the analyst that includes silence as a powerful symptom, can have deeply personal roots in the analyst's unconscious, and can lead to further silence in the patient. Although initially they can be considered two separate silences, they merge into one, joint, intersubjective silence. Therefore, it is impossible to overcome it just by a unilateral attempt to address the problem, be it interpreting or supervision.

I call this a problem because meeting silence with silence can quickly escalate, turn into a therapeutic impasse, an interpersonal battle, therapist against client, and client against therapist (Glover, 1955). Luckily, the problem has finally been recognized in all its depth: "But genuine analysis never proceeds smoothly, from either side of the couch. Transference mirrors countertransference; resistance mirrors counterresistance; anxiety, counteranxiety, mental states shift and collide" (Bass, 2003, p. 664). Ubiquitous though this may be, it can lead to various sorts of acting out reactions, and it can possibly cause drop-outs at different stages of treatments:

> [Resistance] gives voice to opposing realities within the patient's inner world that are being enacted in the intersubjective and interpersonal field between analyst and patient. The negativity of resistance thus represents a dialectic tension between realities that are not

yet amenable to a self-reflective experience of intrapsychic conflict and are, at that moment, in a discontinuous, adversarial relationship to each other. Optimally, and most simply, it is a dimension of the ongoing process of negotiation between incompatible domains of self- experience.

(Bromberg, 1995, p. 174)

If silence is a form of intersubjective resistance, it can have the following possible reasons:

1. Analyst and patient have been a bad match from the beginning, their personalities, patterns of social interaction and emotion expression, and/or traumatic histories, all can lead to silent impasse that even the most thorough training analysis could not have prevented;
2. The initial progress of the analysis was too fast, positive transference was analyzed before therapeutic alliance was firmly established and resistances were overcome, which led to swift yet superficial improvement (e.g., when the patient wants to be perfect, and the analyst narcissistically enjoys the illusory effectiveness), but once this phase is over they both experience disappointment and turn distant and silent;
3. The matching was proper, the progress was optimal, but the analyst and the patient have the same psychological weak point, which was not thoroughly or competently addressed during training or was (re)activated afterward, and they make one another additionally helpless in facing it;
4. The irreversible loss of the analytic third, this "product of a unique dialectic generated by/between the separate subjectivities of analyst and analysand within the analytic setting. It is a subjectivity that seems to take on a life of its own in the interpersonal field, generated between analyst and analysand" (Ogden, 1994, p. 169). It can be jeopardized by an enactment, flaw, or slip (e.g., the analyst forgetting the patient's wife's name, which the patient feels is inexcusable, which the analyst feels is sadistic, which the patient feels is accusatory, etc.), that leads to further silence;
5. Jay Frankel (1993, p. 228) writes about inevitable collusions at the beginning of every psychoanalytic treatment, and defines them in the following way: "I suggest that collusion involves an unconscious deal – a mutual denial, by patient and analyst, of some aspect of their

relationship that frightens them both." These collusions will hopefully evolve into intimacy, but they will never completely disappear and may remain hidden sources of intersubjective resistance, while other parts of the process develop well.

It is not easy to come up with solutions for a problem that psychoanalysis has not addressed, described, or defined. As the usual psychoanalytic supervision probably does not have the means necessary, help might better be asked through consultations with couple counselors or group therapists. And since analysts involved might be biased and blind for certain aspects of their communicative patterns, recordings might be of more help than transcripts or notes.

Conclusion

Silence in the analytic space can have many meanings and many functions. Just one, though the most frequently discussed, of its possible roles is that it can be a sign of resistance. Silence in the analytic room, when it is resistance, can stem from different persons and constellations. If that turns up to be so, the silent patient should be invited to explore thoughts and words he/she is quiet about. The silent analyst, however, must monitor his/her proneness to silence, search for his/her resistances relentlessly, and, if necessary, ask colleagues to help him/her regain the capacity to explore and express limitations openly. Because silence is inspiring and nurturing only when it is not a resistance, while it can destroy even the best of our therapeutic efforts if not reflected upon and worked through.

Notes

1 Other options include: quiet as a sign of shame; fear due to low self-esteem that the analyst will be bored by what one has to say; silence as a protection of the inner space and autonomy; silence as an effort to be like the analyst.
2 That some of the items on this list give primacy to psychosexual dynamics is a consequence of the fact that the list is a review of papers published in the 1950s and '60s, or even earlier, when this topic was prominent in psychoanalysis.
3 We should also note that the same purpose (concealing a thought) can be achieved by talking too much under the guise of free-associating.
4 In a similar literary style, Arlow (1961, p. 46) writes that "silence was resistance carried to the nth degree."
5 There is not enough space here to elaborate on the criticism of the traditional ("pre-Bionian") use of the idea of projective identification, which limits a

fundamentally intersubjective situation of a psychoanalytic session to a one-sided process in which the unconscious of the analyst barely participates and never initiates.
6 Countertransference feelings as a form of resistance can, thus, mean both interference with empathy for the patient and with knowing something about the patient.
7 The only exemption from this silence about the sleep of analysts is still Ralf Zwiebel's 1992 book, which, to the best of my knowledge, has never been translated from German into other languages.
8 Ferenczi (1988, p. 115) also recommends returning to personal analysis: "If six to eight years (of training analysis) required, impossible in practice. But should be corrected by repeated supplementary analyses. But even so, not quite satisfactory."

References

Abraham, K. (1919/1949). A particular form of neurotic resistance against the psycho-analytic method. In: *Selected Papers on Psychoanalysis* (pp. 303–311). London: Hogarth Press.
Akhtar, S. (2009). *A Comprehensive Dictionary of Psychoanalysis*. London: Karnac.
Arlow, J. A. (1961). Silence and the theory of technique. *Journal of the American Psychoanalytic Association*, 9, 44–55.
Aron, L., & Starr, K. (2013). *A Psychotherapy for the People: Toward a Progressive Psychoanalysis*. New York: Routledge.
Bass, A. (2003). "E" enactments in psychoanalysis: Another medium, another message. *Psychoanalytic Dialogues*, 13(5), 657–675.
Bergler, E. (1938). On the resistance situation: The patient is silent. *Psychoanalytic Review*, 25(2), 170–186.
Bromberg, P. M. (1995). Resistance, object-usage, and human relatedness. *Contemporary Psychoanalysis*, 31, 173–191.
Coltart, N. (1991). The silent patient. *Psychoanalytic Dialogues*, 1(4), 439–453.
Cremerius, J. (1969). Schweigen als Problem der psychoanalytischen Technik. *Jahrbuch der Psychoanalyse*, 6, 69–103.
Dimitrijević, A. (2019). The spectrum of loss in war-torn societies. In: M. K. O'Neil & S. Akhtar (Eds.), *Loss. Developmental, Cultural, and Clinical Realms* (pp. 79–95). London / New York. Routledge.
Ehrenberg, D. B. (1985). Countertransference resistance. *Contemporary Psychoanalysis*, 21(4), 563–576.
Faimberg, H. (1988). The telescoping of generations: Genealogy of certain identifications. *Contemporary Psychoanalysis*, 24(1), 99–118.
Ferenczi, S. (1911). On obscene words. In: *Sex in Psychoanalysis* (pp. 132–153). New York: Basic Books.
Ferenczi, S. (1916–17). Silence is gold. In: J. Rickman (Ed.), *Further Contributions to the Theory and Technique of Psycho-Analysis* (J. I. Suttie & Others, Trans., pp. 250–251). London: Hogarth.

Ferenczi, S. (1919). On the technique of psychoanalysis. In: J. Rickman (Ed.), *Further Contributions to the Theory and Technique of Psycho-Analysis* (J. I. Suttie & Others, Trans., pp. 177–188). London: Hogarth.

Ferenczi, S. (1928). The elasticity of psycho-analytic technique. In: M. Balint (Ed.), *Final Contributions to the Problems and Methods of Psycho-Analysis* (pp. 87–101). London: Hogarth.

Ferenczi, S. (1988). *The Clinical Diary of Sándor Ferenczi* (J. Dupont, Ed., M. Balint & N. Z. Jackson, Trans.). Cambridge, MA: Harvard University Press.

Fliess, R. (1949). Silence and verbalization: A supplement to the theory of the 'analytic rule'. *International Journal of Psycho-Analysis, 30*, 21–30.

Frankel, J. (1993). Collusion and intimacy in the analytic relationship: Ferenczi's legacy. In: L. Aron & A. Harris (Eds.), *The Legacy of Sandor Ferenczi* (pp. 227–247). Hillsdale, NJ: The Analytic Press.

Freud, S. (1912). Recommendations to physicians practicing psycho-analysis. In: J. Strachey (Ed.), *The Standard Edition of the Complete Psychological Works of Sigmund Freud* (Vol. 12, 1911–1913, pp. 107–120). London: Hogarth Press, 1958.

Gill, M. M. (1984). Psychoanalysis and psychotherapy: A revision. *International Review of Psycho-Analysis, 11*, 161–179.

Glover, E. (1955). *The Developing Technique of Psychoanalysis*. New York: University Press.

Greenson, R. R. (1961). On the silence and sounds of the analytic hour. *Journal of the American Psychoanalytic Association, 9*(1), 79–84.

Leira, T. (1995). Silence and communication: Nonverbal dialogue and therapeutic action. *The Scandinavian Psychoanalytic Review, 18*(1), 41–65.

Liegner, E. (1974). The silent patient. *Psychoanalytic Review, 61*(2), 229–245.

Ogden, T. (1994). The analytic third. Working with intersubjective analytic facts. *International Journal of Psycho-Analysis, 75*(1), 3–19.

Pressman, M. D. (1961). Silence in analysis. *Bulletin of the Philadelphia Association of Psychoanalysis, 11*, 101–115.

Racker, H. (1968). The meanings and uses of countertransference. In: *Transference and Countertransference* (pp. 127–173). New York: International Universities Press.

Reik, T. (1948). *Listening with the Third Ear*. New York: Pyramid Books.

Reik, T. (1949). *The Inner Experience of a Psychoanalyst*. London: Allen & Unwin.

Severn, E. (2017). *The Discovery of the Self: A Study in Psychological Cure*. London: Taylor & Francis.

Stern, D. B. (2003). The fusion of horizons: Dissociation, enactment, and understanding. *Psychoanalytic Dialogues, 13*(6), 843–873.

Zeligs, M. A. (1961). The psychology of silence: Its role in transference, countertransference and the psychoanalytic process. *Journal of the American Psychoanalytic Association, 9*(1), 7–43.

Zwiebel, R. (1992). *Der Schlaf des Analytikers. Die Müdigkeitsreaktion in der Gegenübertragung*. Stuttgart: Verlag Internationale Psychoanalyse.

Chapter 9

Silence is golden (usually)

Jay Frankel

Historically, psychoanalysts have thought about their patients' silences, especially prolonged ones, in different ways. We can group these approaches to into three categories: silence as resistance; silence as benign regression in search of an analytically necessary experience, often requiring silent "holding" (Winnicott, 1955) by the analyst; and silence as a move in an interpersonal negotiation with the analyst, in the underlying hope of renegotiating one's internalized bad-object relations. The latter two perspectives view silence as facilitating analytic process in some way. In actual clinical practice, a given silence can be complex and multifaceted. Following a discussion of the different analytic perspectives on silence, I will discuss the ways in which silence is essential in the process of the deepening self-reflection and insight in analytic treatment.

Silence as resistance

Since the resistance aspect of silence has been addressed in the previous chapter, I will limit my comments here to noting two essential points that will be important in the discussion to come. First, resistance is a concept that arose from a conceptual framework based on intrapsychic conflict—unconscious wishes opposed by anxieties; and this idea of conflict points us to seeing the patient's silences as the result of inner conflicts that interfere with his following the fundamental rule of analysis: to say everything that comes to mind. This view invites an analyst to respond to a patient's silence by exploring or interpreting the conflict behind it. The second aspect of the resistance view that I want to note here is a corollary to the first: that thinking in terms of resistance tends to discourage analysts from understanding the pre-conflictual (i.e. object-relational or developmental-arrest) or intersubjective causes of a silence, or from appreciating its inherent place in the natural process of deepening self-reflection.

Silence as a pathway to a necessary therapeutic object relationship

The object-relational approach developed as analysts began to grasp how early trauma and subsequent regression block patients from fully participating in, and benefiting from, analytic treatment; and consequently, what accommodations regressed patients need from their analysts. This perspective begins with Ferenczi (1929, 1930, 1931). In his 1931 paper on "Child-analysis in the analysis of adults," he described how analytic treatment, at least during periods of regression, could be understood as a kind of game in which earlier experiences of self emerged. Such experiences of self were expressed in a shift to a "childlike attitude" (p. 131), most likely accompanied by his choosing simpler words, and altered tones of voice, ways of speaking, and bodily attitude—including the presence of silence as an expression of this regressed experience of self.

Ferenczi had recently come to appreciate the therapeutic value of such regressions, which offered the opportunity to work through analytically the earlier traumas that had created these undeveloped or split off "selves," and for analytic progress to take place. As such, Ferenczi emphasized that analysts must take special care to protect these regressions (1931, p. 130). He adjusted his manner, "entering into a game" (p. 129), speaking gently and simply, as if to a child of the age the patient then seemed to be psychologically. He seemed to be trying to foster the patient's feeling of safety and to protect the regressed state. Certainly, a resonant "holding" silence would also be one way to remain in tune with a silent, regressed patient. My impression is that a somewhat accommodating approach, and the openness to at least some degree of regression that lies behind it, are now widespread among analysts, whether they do this intuitively or have been directly influenced by Ferenczi's ideas or by the other thinkers I now turn to.

Winnicott's (1953) ideas of transitionality—transitional objects and transitional space—can be seen as a development and articulation of Ferenczi's thinking. (See Boyle Spelman's elaboration of Winnicott's contributions to understanding the place of silence in development and in analytic treatment, this volume). Winnicott understood that the baby lives in a world of self-generated illusion—she feels *she has created* the breast she needs. She will accept external reality and the limits of her own omnipotence only gradually, and *only when her natural need to feel omnipotent is first recognized by the mother*. Without this, the baby will never embrace the external world, which will remain a constantly threatening entity which she withdraws from behind a "false self," keeping her "true self" hidden (1960); and she will not achieve the feelings of being integrated, and of living within her own body (1945, p. 140). The child's omnipotence must never be challenged by the mother's question: "'Did you conceive of this or was it presented to you from without?'" (p. 95). This approach—for analysts, not just mothers—emphasizes what must not be said and can easily be understood to include the view that there are times when the analyst must not say anything at all.

Indeed, Winnicott spoke explicitly about the need for analysts sometimes to be silent with regressed patients.

> In almost all our psycho-analytic treatments there come times when the ability to be alone is important to the patient. Clinically this may be represented by a silent phase or a silent session, and this silence, far from being evidence of resistance, turns out to be an achievement on the part of the patient. Perhaps it is here that the patient has been able to be alone for the first time.
>
> (Winnicott, 1958, p. 416)

Indeed, his concept of the "holding" environment (1955, p. 19) emphasizes the times when the analyst must not impinge in any way upon the patient's transitional state, even by talking at all:

> In one vitally important hour near the beginning of the treatment I remained and knew I must remain absolutely still, only breathing. This I found very difficult indeed, especially as I did not yet know the special significance of the silence to my patient. At the end the patient came round from the regressed state and said: "Now I know you can do my analysis."
>
> (p. 24)

Michael Balint further elaborated the value of the patient's silence, and of the analyst's silent response. The background is Balint's (1979) concept of benign regression: a state in which the patient returns, inwardly, to a simpler approach to life, before his internalized object relations were distorted by attempts to cope with early traumatic experiences. In benign regression, the patient seeks out the particular kind of object relationship he needs with the analyst, that he senses will allow him to "be able to find himself, to accept himself, and to get on with himself" (p. 180)—to find, in Balint's words, a "new beginning" (e.g. p. 71). In malignant regression, in contrast, the patient chiefly seeks "gratification by an outside object" (p. 187)—the analyst—as an end in itself: the analyst will provide the cure, rather than being a vehicle or medium through which the patient can "reach himself" (p. 142). Malignant regressions lead "to the development of addiction-like states which [are] very difficult to handle, and in some cases … intractable" (p. 138). Consequently, silences during malignant regressions have a different feeling, and a different meaning, than those that occur during benign regressions, and need to be dealt with differently by the analyst. I'll say more about that when elaborating silence as a form of interpersonal negotiation.

During states of benign regression, in order to facilitate the patient reaching himself, "the analyst must do everything in his power not to become, or to behave as, a separate, sharply-contoured object" (p. 167). "Environment [i.e. the analyst] and individual penetrate into each other, they exist together in a 'harmonious mix-up'" (p. 66). The patient must be allowed his regressed state and the precise therapeutic object relationship he seeks, and needs, without interference.

Balint illustrates such an approach in response to a patient who was quiet for the first 30 minutes of a session. The analyst, understanding what might be happening, also remained silent. Eventually, the patient started to sob,

> relieved, and soon after he was able to speak. He told his analyst that at long last he was able to reach himself; ever since childhood he had never been left alone, there had always been someone telling him what to do. Some sessions later he reported that during the silence he had all sorts of associations, but rejected each of them as irrelevant, as nothing but an annoying superficial nuisance.
>
> (pp. 177–178)

Balint notes that the patient's silence here could have been understood and interpreted—indeed, correctly—"as resistance, withdrawal, a sign of persecutory fear … etc." But doing so, he emphasizes, would have destroyed the silence and the patient would not have been able to 'reach himself', at any rate, not on that occasion. [Interpreting] would inevitably reinforce the patient's strong repetition-compulsion, there would again be someone there, telling him what to feel, to think, in fact what to do.

(p. 178)

In these lines Balint goes straight to the heart of the difference between the intrapsychic-conflict model and a developmental/object-relational model, in their approach to silence. As he elaborates,

The pedestrian analytic attitude is to consider the silence merely as a symptom of resistance to some unconscious material stemming either from the patient's past or from the actual transference situation. One must add that this interpretation is nearly always correct; the patient is *running away* from something, usually a conflict, but it is equally correct that he is *running towards* something, i.e. a state in which he feels relatively safe and can do something about the problem bothering or tormenting him.

(Balint, 1979, p. 26)

In Balint's (and others') developmental/object-relational model, the way to foster safety and the patient's natural healing processes generally means a less intrusive clinical approach, often including silence.

Balint (1979) also developed the concept of the "area of creation" (p. 24)—the opaque inner space where new insights and approaches to problems are somehow generated. Protecting this process in patients may also require noninterference, and often silence, by the analyst. "[A]ny intrusion ... inevitably destroys for the patient the possibility of creating something out of himself" (p. 176).

Kohut's (1971) idea that narcissistically disturbed patients must be allowed to experience "selfobject" transferences—feelings of kinship with, idealization of, or admiration and mirroring by the analyst—unchallenged and unexplored, perhaps for extended periods of time, in order to reanimate arrested developmental processes, also belongs to this broad noninterfering clinical approach.

In a wider sense, drawing on these ideas, I (Frankel, 2011) have proposed an "analytic state of consciousness"—a universal state for analytic patients generally, akin to a transitional or play space, characterized by an increased sensitivity and reactivity to impressions arising from both the inner world and the analyst, a heightened sense of dependence and vulnerability, a permeability of boundaries in regard to the analyst, … a shift toward functioning on the basis of omnipotent fantasy in the analytic relationship [and] a feeling of realness of one's psychic reality, but without any true loss of reality testing.

(p. 1411)

It not only occurs during special periods of regression or in deeply regressed patients, but is an inherent and basic aspect of analytic process, providing a matrix and foundation for more articulated transferences. If this state is indeed a foundation for analytic process, then the analyst, much of the time, must lean toward a "reticent," non-intrusive stance of emotional accompaniment that tolerates the patient's silence as essential in fostering this state of consciousness—and this often requires the analyst's silence.

Silence as an element of interpersonal negotiation with the analyst

Analysts associated with the relational tradition, like Mitchell (1991a), Pizer (1992), and Frankel (1998), have discussed intersubjective negotiation, not least on the nonverbal level, as an essential therapeutic process in the task of restructuring the patient's internalized bad-object relations—what relational analysts may refer to as "relational configurations" (Mitchell, 1991b, p. 140). Relational analysts understand that analyst and patient are in a real (though analytic) relationship which includes both conscious and, notably, unconscious intersubjective dialogue — what Ferenczi (1915) called the "dialogue of unconsciouses" (p. 109). In his *Clinical Diary* (1932), Ferenczi detailed his discovery of how extensive two-way unconscious communication between patient and analyst can be. In this light, everything the patient does, or says, or does not say, can be understood as part of a largely unconscious, intersubjective dialogue with the analyst, intended to communicate something or to influence the analyst in some way. In this, the patient's silence is no different from his words.

The analyst's silence, too, whatever its conscious intention—for instance, to provide a holding or non-intrusive space for the patient—may also be doing double duty, communicating or acting on the patient in unintended or even disavowed ways—her "lines" in a "conversation" that may lie largely outside the awareness of both people but are nevertheless "heard" by the patient on some level, and may say something very different from what the analyst says out loud. In such cases, clearly, the analyst's efforts to remain a nonintrusive, facilitating, and benign presence are undermined (Ferenczi, 1933). Indeed, in the analytic dialogue, it is the nonverbal elements that may speak most forcefully.

Ferenczi's discoveries about the inevitable unconscious communication in analytic treatment may be the deepest foundation upon which the relational position is built, but the relational viewpoint—especially regarding negotiation—also has more recent conceptual pillars. Among them, Weiss, Sampson, et al. (1986), in their research program, explored the idea that much of what patients do in therapy constitutes *behavioral* tests of pathogenic beliefs, in the hope of disproving these beliefs. The emphasis on these tests as behavioral indicates that silence is no less part of therapeutic process and therapeutic action than words; both words and silence are actions; and as such, both play a central role.

Beatrice Beebe (Beebe and Lachmann, 2014), in her groundbreaking studies of mother–infant interactions, based on frame-by-frame analysis of videotaped communication in a standardized situation, has discovered a high degree of communication—and mutual influence—that occurs very rapidly and outside of conscious awareness. Greatly amplifying Ferenczi's long-ago insight, Beebe's mother–infant research can serve as a model of the extent of two-way nonverbal communication and influence that occur in adult analytic treatment (and which interact with verbal communication in complex ways). The implicit, largely nonverbal "unconscious dialogue" exists even despite the limits imposed by most analytic models on what the analyst expresses to the patient. Unavoidably, the timing, rhythm, and nonverbal accompaniments of silences are powerful tools of communication and influence by analyst as well as patient.

If the patient's silence is a statement, and a forceful one, in the ongoing nonverbal engagement between patient and analyst, what roles can silence play in the ongoing analytic negotiations? I note before addressing this question that in actual clinical situations, roles often overlap and interact.

Silence can be an attempt to find a sense of autonomy or influence when these feel shaky, or to resist a compulsion to be obedient—a silence that may appear defiant. Or through silence, a patient may struggle for a sense of authenticity or honesty when speaking feels false. A patient may fear that others cannot bear the separation that he needs, and his silence expresses. Such patients are likely to pay close attention to the analyst's reactions: will she accept his silence, and the frightening aspects of himself he expresses through this silence? Does she really want to know this side of him? Is she more able than the inner objects he projects onto her to accept his wishes and needs? Further therapeutic progress will be facilitated by later exploration of these interactions, but it may be necessary, and valuable in its own right (Frankel, 1998), for the patient to live out these interactions with the analyst.

Such motives for, and negotiations around, silence can be seen in the following brief vignette. A young woman emerging from a period of great inner struggle and fragility is uncharacteristically silent in her session— after a friendly hello, not another word for the whole hour. But her face, far from being empty or distracted, seems reflective, attentive to her unspoken thoughts and feelings. Surprisingly, I feel relaxed, engaged, free to observe her and my own thoughts. I even have a vague sense of following the flow of her experience, as revealed through her face and slightly shifting posture. Next session, silence again. Now I am not so relaxed. After a few minutes I ask: "Do you want to say what's happening?" She asks why she should. I explain, unnecessarily, that saying what's on her mind could help us better understand it. She says: "Don't you think my silence has meaning?" We both remain silent for the rest of the hour. The close relationship of the attempt to find necessary conditions for growth, and to renegotiate problematic internalized object relations, is clear in this example.

A patient may also use silences to try to make the therapist feel something the patient feels, perhaps in order to feel understood and less alone. Or he may need the therapist to feel something he has dissociated and cannot face within himself—projective identification (Klein, 1946, Ogden, 1979)—either to find contact with this dissociated experience through the therapist's experience of it, or to try to get rid of the intolerable feeling.

Silence may be an especially effective way for the patient to feel some kind of closeness to the therapist, or understanding by the therapist. This is true in certain therapeutically necessary narcissistic transferences, like twinship or idealization, where the patient imagines that the therapist simply knows his thoughts, and speaking could spoil this feeling. A silent feeling of closeness may also include romantic feelings; while these may reflect a workable underlying narcissistic transference that is a prerequisite for analytic progress, they may also be a sticking point, if the patient holds onto a sense that love between patient and therapist is the solution to the patient's problems.

Indeed, not all negotiations move patients toward helpful goals. A patient may use silence to try to control or punish the therapist. We may be sympathetic to a patient's underlying anxieties, and his fantasies of reversing roles in internalized traumatic scenarios, but this negotiating tactic is ultimately likely to be self-defeating, and to undermine his ability to develop stable feelings of autonomy, trust, calm, and intimacy.

There are undoubtedly more potential meanings of what patients express, and seek, through silence. What are the therapeutic implications of those I have mentioned? What guidelines can help the therapist think about how to respond to the patient's use of silence as a negotiating tactic to achieve each of these goals?

When the patient uses silence as a way to establish some kind of relationship with the therapist as an end in itself, rather than as a way to establish conditions for safety and self-reflection—for instance controlling or punishing the therapist, or expressing romantic feelings *as the final answer to one's problems*, we should look to Balint's (1979) idea of malignant regression; in such cases, the analyst's silent response may be taken as an indication that she submits to control or accepts guilt—a collusion (Frankel, 1993) with the patient that can intensify the patient's resistance and entrench his pathology (Frankel, 2018).

When the patient is trying to negotiate what feel to him like necessary therapeutic conditions—establishing trust and safety, a sense of being thought about, cared for, or understood, a feeling of authenticity, or an analytically necessary transitional selfobject transference—the analyst should not interfere with the silence. The analyst may need to be silent herself (often alongside her own inner identification with some aspect of the patient's conscious or unconscious experience). Here, Winnicott's concepts of transitional space and holding environment, and Balint's concept of benign regression, are likely to be good guides for the analyst.

Integrative: The roles played by silence in the process of symbolizing: The work of Norbert Freedman and his colleagues

Psychoanalyst and clinical researcher Norbert Freedman, along with Wilma Bucci and other colleagues, conducted a research program in which they developed a particular idea about the role of silence as facilitating the patient's symbolizing activity, and thus the analytic process. Freedman briefly summarized his later thoughts about this in a 2011 proposal for a conference panel; but he died suddenly before this panel could be further developed. I think it is important that these ideas find a hearing among clinical psychoanalytic thinkers, so I will go into some detail about them. In terms of the current chapter, Freedman's ideas can be seen as intersecting with, and integrating, all of the above ways of viewing silence: as resistance; as facilitating a needed, safe object relationship with the analyst so that the treatment may deepen; and as interpersonal negotiation of unresolved internalized object-relational issues.

In earlier empirical research, Freedman and his colleagues (Gilani et al., 1985) demonstrated that analytic silences can be signs of consolidation—a "pre-narrative activation period" (p. 100). "Analyzing the observable external kinetic and movement behavior" (p. 101) during a silence can provide a sense of the internal processes, as judged by the narrative activity that follows the silence. "The pattern of discharge movements followed by self-stimulating body-focused movements [was observed to lead to] more organized and cohesive verbal performance during the [ensuing] monologue" (p. 101, and see pp. 106 and 108).

In his later panel proposal (Freedman, 2011), based on his subsequent clinical-empirical research program, which included systematic analysis, on a number of dimensions, of audio recordings of a complete psychoanalytic treatment, Freedman suggested that "moments of silence at critical junctures during an analytic hour—the concurrent muteness by both patient and analyst—represent a particular state of consciousness that offers an opportunity for the deepening of the analytic process."

Freedman elaborated, proposing three different dimensions, or dynamic structures, in relation to silence in analytic treatment. Working in a coordinated way, these dynamic structures promote the progressive symbolization of intolerable or dissociated experience, and thus of transformation, in psychoanalytic treatment. Freedman proposed that a

> symbolizing silence [the first of these states] arises from a sense of implicit relational connectedness to the analyst—in some sense it mirrors the transference. The symbolizing silence, thus, is a kind of communication that invites analyst participation—a signal for closer interaction. Further, the consequent of the silence—when speech

resumes—reveals a progression toward metaphoric thought.[1] Thus, the symbolizing silence is one step in a linear process of transformation involving both thinking and object-relational aspects—a fact that places the inherent facilitating function of 'silent thought' within the transference.

Freedman also talked about a defensive

> desymbolizing silence [which] is part of a fragmented and frozen psychic constellation. It arises in the experience of a barren object relation, in which the analyst in fact withdraws from interaction (whether a reaction to the patient or analyst-initiated). There is minimal object relation to nourish reciprocal silent exploration (e.g. sleepiness). The desymbolizing silence reflects a mode of ego organization marked not only by fragmentation of thought, but also a defense against intolerable affect. ... Whereas in the symbolizing silence, there is a wish for the analyst's participation, here discharge of intolerable affect can result in alienating the present other—the analyst. However, in spite of momentary paralysis, a desymbolizing silence is necessary in order for the patient to confront intolerable affects and bring them into the analytic dialogue.

And he talked about a transformative silence that encompasses both symbolizing and desymbolizing silences:

> the transformative silence involves the confrontation with both states in sequence. ... while the symbolizing silence is the mirror of the transference, the transformative silence is the mirror of the countertransference. It is through the intrusion of countertransference that a new direction is sparked and a new course set. ... the transformative silence can be spelled out in successive phases. It begins with a symbolizing silence (reflecting initial analyst engagement), then a paralysis of meaning, followed by resymbolization. It is the unexpected confrontation with 'newness'—a discordant countertransference reaction—that triggers a transitory regression, followed by resymbolization. Transformation always involves the confrontation with the dialectic of meeting an incompatible experience needing resolution.

Freedman credits Glover with the idea that "silence may mirror the impact of the countertransference—the latter acting as a discordant element that must be accommodated and integrated," thus contributing to the patient's symbolizing activity.

Conclusion

What I have discussed as different functions of silence are often, in fact, different aspects of one and the same dynamic. While one function may be most visible at any given moment, others are likely to be operating in the background; which one seems clearest may simply reflect one's angle of view. For instance, to label a silence as resistant—as avoiding self-exploration: the very task that the patient has set for him- or herself—indicates that we see the silence as a manifestation of an internal conflict; in other words, the silence reflects the current state of a negotiation between the patient's *wishes* related to disclosing his inner life to the analyst, and his *fears* about doing so—a conflict that has become externalized and enacted with the analyst, and is being fought out in the transference relationship. It is partly *because of*, and *through*, this enacted silence, in tandem with self-reflection *about* the enactment, that these unresolved inner conflicts can be reworked in relation to the analyst. We can paraphrase Michael Balint's (1979) idea of "regression for the sake of progression" (p. 132) here and talk about *resistance for the sake of progress*.

Further, a patient's wish and attempt to renegotiate internalized bad-object relations through his relationship with the analyst—to free himself from his internalized bad objects—is the same as saying that the patient is hoping to find facilitating conditions, for instance a sense of safety, that will allow greater inner freedom and authentic analytic self-exploration. And when the analyst provides a safe, holding environment she may, from a different angle, be disconfirming the patient's pathogenic beliefs and helping the patient to renegotiate his internalized bad-object relations.

However, what the analyst feels outside of her own full awareness can be very different from the facilitating presence the analyst wishes to have, or believes she is communicating; and these disavowed feelings can be unwittingly communicated to the patient. Analysts, therefore, regardless of their preferred clinical stance, must always try to be attentive to, and reflect on, what they may be feeling and expressing outside of what they intend, and how this may be affecting the patient. Analysts' self-reflection can be aided by listening for disguised observations of themselves in their patients' associations (Ferenczi, 1933).

Finally, Freedman's work underlines the multiple essential roles that silence plays in the process of analytic symbolizing and working through—roles related to all the views of silence I have described.

Note

1 See the chapter by Dreyer and Franzen in the research section of this volume (editors' note).

References

Balint, M. (1979). *The Basic Fault. Therapeutic Aspects of Regression.* London: Tavistock.
Beebe, B., & Lachmann, F. (2014). *The Origins of Attachment: Infant Research and Adult Treatment.* New York: Routledge.
Ferenczi, S. (1915). Psychogenic anomalies of voice production. In: J. Rickman (Ed.), *Further Contributions to the Theory and Technique of Psycho-Analysis* (J. I. Suttie & others, Trans., pp. 105–109). London: Hogarth.
Ferenczi, S. (1929). The unwelcome child and his death instinct. In: M. Balint (Ed.), *Final Contributions to the Problems and Methods of Psycho-Analysis* (E. Mosbacher & others, Trans., pp. 102–107). London: Hogarth.
Ferenczi, S. (1930). The principles of relaxation and neocatharsis. In: M. Balint (Ed.), *Final Contributions to the Problems and Methods of Psycho-Analysis* (E. Mosbacher & others, Trans., pp. 108–125). London: Hogarth.
Ferenczi, S. (1931). Child-analysis in the analysis of adults. In: M. Balint (Ed.), *Final Contributions to the Problems and Methods of Psycho-Analysis* (E. Mosbacher & others, Trans., pp. 126–142). London: Hogarth.
Ferenczi, S. (1932). *The Clinical Diary of Sandor Ferenczi* (J. Dupont, Ed., M. Balint & N. Z. Jackson, Trans.). Harvard University Press.
Ferenczi, S. (1933). Confusion of tongues between adults and the child. In: M. Balint (Ed.), *Final Contributions to the Problems and Methods of Psycho-Analysis* (E. Mosbacher & others, Trans., pp. 156–167). London: Hogarth.
Frankel, J. (1993). Collusion and intimacy in the analytic relationship: Ferenczi's legacy. In: L. Aron & A. Harris (Eds.), *The Legacy of Sandor Ferenczi* (pp. 227–247). Hillsdale, NJ: The Analytic Press.
Frankel, J. (1998). The play's the thing: How the essential processes of therapy are seen most clearly in child therapy. *Psychoanalytic Dialogues, 8*(1), 149–182.
Frankel, J. (2011). The analytic state of consciousness as a form of play and a foundational transference. *International Journal of Psycho-Analysis, 92*(6), 1411–1436.
Frankel, J. (2018). Thoughts on the limits of a mutual technique. *The American Journal of Psychoanalysis, 78*(4), 350–360.

Freedman, N. (2011). Silence and the deepening of the analytic process: Psychoanalytic and convergent empirical evidence Proposal for panel presentations. In: *IPA clinical research conference on analytic evidence, at that time scheduled to be held in San Francisco.*

Gilani, Z. H., Bucci, W., & Freedman, N. (1985). The structure and language of a silence. *Semiotica, 56*(1–2), 99–113.

Klein, M. (1946). Notes on some schizoid mechanisms. *International Journal of Psycho-Analysis, 27*(3–4), 99–110.

Kohut, H. (1971). *The Analysis of the Self.* New York: International Universities Press.

Mitchell, S. A. (1991a). Wishes, needs, and interpersonal negotiations. *Psychoanalytic Inquiry, 11*(1–2), 147–170.

Mitchell, S. A. (1991b). Contemporary perspectives on self: Toward an integration. *Psychoanalytic Dialogues, 1*(2), 121–147.

Ogden, T. H. (1979). On projective identification. *International Journal of Psycho-Analysis, 60*(3), 357–373.

Pizer, S. A. (1992). The negotiation of paradox in the analytic process. *Psychoanalytic Dialogues, 2*(2), 215–240.

Weiss, J., Sampson, H., & The Mount Zion Psychotherapy Research Group. (1986). *The Psychoanalytic Process: Theory, Clinical Observation, and Empirical Research.* New York: Guilford.

Winnicott, D. W. (1945). Primitive emotional development. *International Journal of Psycho-Analysis, 26*(3–4), 137–143.

Winnicott, D. W. (1953). Transitional objects and transitional phenomena — A study of the first not-me possession. *International Journal of Psycho-Analysis, 34*(2), 89–97.

Winnicott, D. W. (1955). Metapsychological and clinical aspects of regression within the psycho-analytical set-up. *International Journal of Psycho-Analysis, 36*(1), 16–26.

Winnicott, D. W. (1958). The capacity to be alone. *International Journal of Psycho-Analysis, 39*(5), 416–420.

Winnicott, D. W. (1960). Ego distortion in terms of true self and false self. In: *The Maturational Process and the Facilitating Environment* (pp. 140–157). New York: International Universities Press, 1965.

Chapter 10

Winnicott's capacity for silence in understanding and healing human nature

Margaret Boyle Spelman

Silent communication

As witnessed by the contents of this book, silence has been given much attention in many spheres and particularly within 'the talking cure' professions. At the inception of Freud's psychoanalysis the emphasis was on what was said; the interpretation. Silence was considered to be a sign of the patient's pathology and resistance to treatment. I propose in this chapter that Winnicott's thinking has contributed significantly to the reshaping of the profession's idea of silence, seeing silence and the capacity for silence differently now; it is a sign of health and an important developmental milestone for the human subject with important ramifications for treatment and technique in the psychoanalytic consulting room.

Although the concept of the individual human subject is a relatively recent one in human history, it is precisely this period of life, the fragile beginnings of individual subjectivity that Donald Woods Winnicott privileges (Boyle Spelman, 2013a, 2013b). His thinking of 40-plus years (Boyle Spelman and Thomson-Salo, 2014) is therefore also inevitably an important consideration of silence.

The experience of writing this chapter can be described thus: I went to make my own creation, 'my own cake', so to speak; my 'twist' on Winnicott's original recipe, a unique perspective using clinical vignettes from my professional life. But instead, in what I trust was a necessary step involving the postponement of my original conscious intention, I became enthralled by the individual ingredients and the original recipe of Winnicott's elaborate and enduring creation on the subject of human nature and silence. Reflecting my distraction and absorption and intending to be of clinical and general use, this chapter is a chronologically ordered whistle-stop tour of a personal selection of Winnicott's ideas on silence and on pre-Oedipal psychical life. The 'tour' foregrounds three themes; the importance of silence for the individual patient, silence as a transitional object and the function of silence in the consulting room between the patient–analyst dyad.

The importance of silence for the individual patient

Relatively ignored by Freud in favour of the later stage of the Oedipus complex, the baby's earliest developmental period journeys from late pregnancy, through the individual's birth into what for Freud was 'auto-eroticism' and 'primary narcissism' and then on to the establishment of a rudimentary boundary (the first recognition of the 'me'/'not me' distinction) in the context of the first object choice within the environment of the nursing couple; the baby's absolute and then relative dependence on the mother's care. Freud's relative inattention to this earliest developmental time is recognized by Goldman (1993) when he suggests that Winnicott made it his life's work to elaborate what Freud put in a footnote.

Winnicott does indeed bring to life this important pre-Oedipal stage that is 'preverbal, unverbalized and unverbalizable' (1967, p. 112) and a silence interspersed with sounds; he emphasizes all that happens outside language and before words. Winnicott includes early behaviour and the rich variety in the quality of silences that occurs within the nursing couple. His oeuvre is a passionately observed exposition of the development of the unique human subject in the early environment of the 'ordinary devoted' mother and her habits of baby care. In parallel Winnicott explored the traces of this earliest time of life and its vagaries as they manifest between the analytic couple, the therapist and patient, in the clinical psychoanalytic encounter.

Although eventually a fully-fledged human being, what Winnicott saw as the newly born 'bundle of anatomy and physiology' can only be considered a psychical entity as an infant–mother unit and when one includes along with the baby, the care of the 'ordinary devoted' mother; Freud's aforementioned footnote (Freud, 1911, p. 220). In detailing the prehistory and early history of the human being and in exploring its lessons for psychoanalytic technique, Winnicott believes that as a Freudian, he is simply taking up where Freud left off.

In his early days as a pediatrician, as shown in his first book *Clinical Notes on Disorders of Childhood*, Winnicott (1931) wished to inform his medical colleagues of how, by history-taking and observation of the child's clinical presentation, one can differentially diagnose the emotional disorder which speaks silently through bodily symptoms from ordinary organic disease.

Winnicott shows that so much is happening between the baby and the mother at the beginning. The good enough mother by her perfect adaptation to the baby's needs creates a situation for her baby, an illusion of unity, which allows the baby the experience of omnipotence and to simply 'be' in demand-free relaxed identification with their mother. From their own perspective, the absolutely but obliviously dependent baby 'is' the mother and the mother 'is' the baby. Through this reliable care experienced over time, the baby builds a confidence that what they need they will create/find (with creating and finding being paradoxically considered identical). In unconscious fantasy, the baby also 'destroys' the mother who repeatedly survives the greedy primitive loving of feeding.

Over time there is important growth which is met by a very significant change in the mother's approach; the mother's reliable care and her survival of these instinctual attacks allow the baby's rudimentary personal boundary to begin to build so that what Winnicott calls 'unit status' is gradually achieved and the child is their real self, with a boundary and an inside and an outside. The baby will also begin to understand that as the baby of quiet baby care or the baby of ruthless instinctual greed they are always one and the same baby. The baby will also slowly come to understand that the mother of quiet baby-care (environment mother) and the mother the baby 'destroys' (in unconscious fantasy) by feeding (object mother) are one and the same. Attuned to her baby's momentary fluctuations and growing understanding, the mother makes a very important change which signals the baby's entry into the stage of relative dependence: She now awaits a signal of need from her baby when – from the baby's perspective – they are separate rather than immediately anticipating and gratifying her baby's need as she does when they are merged in unity. The sensitive and adaptive mother titrates her response to a separate or merged baby, knowing how much waiting and how much anticipating is appropriate at any given moment. This in turn adds to the baby's growing sense of self in what is now a time of relative dependence.

Winnicott emphasizes the importance of a prerequisite silence for authentic experience. In his paper 'The observations of infants in a set situation' (1941) Winnicott shows that in deference to the scientific method, he set up his ordinary professional encounter with the mother–baby couple in his office as a 'controlled experimental environment' with a 'standard procedure' by which to observe the baby's mental health. He would offer and then leave a spatula (tongue depressor) for the baby as they sat on their mother's knee across from him. From this situation Winnicott made far-reaching deductions about the nature of healthy human experience. There are three parts to the full experience which involves communication which is outside language and is simply in behaviour; first the baby delays taking an interest in the spatula and allows their desire and curiosity to build until such time as they then take the spatula and play intently with it before finally losing interest and discarding it.

Winnicott recognized the importance of all three parts of the baby's experience. But what is particular to Winnicott is that he notes the necessity of the first part, the period of hesitation and the baby's distress if urged to take the spatula before they are ready. Applying his finding to all human experience, Winnicott deduces that any creative, spontaneous approach to the world, anything arising from the 'true self' – rather than from the 'false self' (of conformity or demand) – can only arise after this important 'period of hesitation'. With silent waiting the experience and self-experience is transformed. Something is happening before anything appears to be happening. In life or in the consulting room, within simply 'being' – while apparently 'doing nothing' – is the spring of all that is alive, enjoyable, creative and real in human experience.

It has often been noted that Winnicott's thinking on human nature consists of an elaborate system of interrelated concepts which seems to have existed within Winnicott in its entirety from the beginning (Boyle Spelman, 2013b). The system is given in embryonic form in his paper 'Primitive emotional development' (1945). Winnicott remarks here that he is saying something new within psychoanalysis: he attends not to relationships with others but to the patient's relationship with their own self and their conscious and unconscious phantasies about it. This existential psychoanalysis gives attention to the earliest stage of human development prior to language and to its new edition within psychoanalytic treatment.

Winnicott details the environment that pertains in the mother's sensitively adaptive care for both her baby's instinctual life and the illusion of unity needed for support of the baby's immature ego. The mother provides her baby with a sufficiently long experience of their own omnipotence within a relaxed identification with her. From the baby's perspective they provide for their own need to feed and to be cared for. It is understood that 'creating' and 'finding' amount to the same thing for the baby. By the mother's 'ordinary devoted attention' the baby grows in three ways:

Integration – the baby begins to experience the continuing, 'going-on-being' nature of their self, whether hungry and distressed or sated and sleepy.
Personalization – by the quality of baby care, the baby begins to feel the contours of their self, living in and from their body.
Realization – the baby begins to feel oriented in time and in space and to feel real.

Also the mother provides the facilitating environment for this by the holding (ego support), handling (reinforcing her baby's boundary through baby care) and object-presenting (showing the baby what they mean to their mother by the nature of her gaze and by her demeanour when she looks at her baby).

Difficulties arising for the adult patient from this early time have been detailed by Winnicott and expanded on by others including Masud Khan (1979). In the clinical encounter they are addressed by the reliability of the setting. The setting can here be seen as the silent constant in the relationship, a framing device. It is not often mentioned directly but there can be much action around it. Features can become very significant: the plants in the garden on the way in, the pictures in the room, the scent of the hand cream in the bathroom, seasonal light, noises off; the analyst's interested aliveness and reliability as well as the physical details of the couch, the room, session arrangements, beginning and ending times. More than anything spoken, the most important aspect often is the opportunity provided for the analytic dyad to live through experiences together.

The road to mature subjectivity is a long and gradual one with progressions and regressions during which the mother becomes less and less a subjective object which the baby finds/creates and becomes more and more an object objectively perceived, a whole and separate person. Winnicott details the baby's psychological growth from the first relative silence-with-noise featuring blurred vision, smell, kinaesthetic and tactile impressions to the baby later sitting in their mother's lap and, later still, taking turns with her in a game to which they both contribute and which is the prelude to the to and fro of conversation. It is the detail of this early 'good enough' environment which accounts for much individual difference and distinguishes the individual who can approach life creatively and with enjoyment from one who cannot.

Silence as a transitional object

Towards the end of the 1945 paper referred to earlier, Winnicott mentions features in the baby's environment which seem to ease the journey into separateness and to soften the 'me'/'not me' divide. These aspects of the environment bridge the inner and external worlds and are mysterious; e.g. clouds, breath, fluff. In the mother's role of easing and softening her baby's emergence from merger with her into being a separate individual, there are two stages; the creation of the illusion of unity is followed in a timely way by a gradual and sensitive disillusioning. These first 'not-me' objects seem to at once separate and connect, to soften the boundary and bridge inside and outside, reality and fantasy, and are the precursors to social, artistic, creative and fruitful living. These transitional phenomena, the baby's first 'not-me' possessions are famously further developed by Winnicott.

In his paper 'Transitional objects and transitional phenomena' (1951) Winnicott speaks of this universal journey into subjectivity – from the thumb to the teddy bear – and of the way in which the first 'not me' object stands for the mother and can substitute for short periods. The transitional object extends and elaborates the baby's experience of mother's presence. Winnicott first speaks of these transitional phenomena in relation to human development in the first transitional space which connects and separates mother and baby. He then generalizes this prototype space between the mother and her baby to include all human experience. He later expands on what he says here, that we live in this third intermediate area of experience which lies between inner and outer realities and is contributed to by both (Winnicott, 1967b). The area acts as a resting place for the subject's constant task of keeping inside and outside separate yet interrelated; it is the area between what is subjective and what is objectively perceived. The meaning and function of this first space which is filled with playing, dreaming and transitional phenomena is eventually neutralized when its meaning and function is inherited by and diffused out over the individual's whole community and cultural field.

If things have not gone well in the original instance it will be silently revisited in the course of the psychoanalysis and the analyst's tasks will reflect those of the adaptive mother. What is at issue here is the first part of the growing individual's lifetime journey from the illusion of unity (when it will never be asked 'Did you find this or create it?') through sensitive disillusionment, i.e. from feeling merged or at one with their mother and environment to true object relating with a mainly objectively perceived mother.

In his 1951 paper on the subject, Winnicott speaks of the journey from the baby's primary unawareness of indebtedness to their mother to their recognition of and concern for their mother as a whole separate person to whom they are indebted. The baby now has concern for her and has a retrospective understanding that their parents cared for them out of love.

In his paper 'Withdrawal and regression' (1954) Winnicott presents the case of a patient who had momentary 'sleep-like' withdrawals during analytic sessions. The withdrawal was an example of a patient providing himself with ego support and 'holding'. If the analyst can recognize the regression to dependence and meet the patient's need to be held then the patient can profit from the experience of the analyst's adaption-to-need and regress in service of their ego. By virtue of the holding and the silence a previously split-off part of the patient can be integrated into their personality.

Silence between the analyst and patient

Silent holding

In his paper 'The capacity to be alone' (1958) Winnicott begins by explaining that the arrival of silence in the consulting room shows the patient's capacity for solitude. It can happen variously; as a long period of silence or even in one completely silent session. A person may be solitary and unable to be alone. Far from viewing the silence as it had been viewed heretofore as a defensive or a pathological resistance, Winnicott celebrates silence as the important achievement of 'unit status'. Winnicott rejects the idea that the capacity to be alone – with silence as its outward manifestation – is a very sophisticated thing achieved after the time of the Oedipus Complex; rather it is Winnicott's view that the capacity to be alone, or in absorbed silence, is a phenomenon arising in earliest life when little or no ego maturity can be assumed.

The essential prerequisite for this capacity is a sufficiency for the baby and small child of a paradoxical experience of being alone in the presence of the mother/primary caregiver. This person is reliably present even if sometimes only represented by the crib or the buggy. The baby's ego immaturity is balanced against the ego support of the mother and this support is then gradually introjected. The later capacities – to play, to dream, to relax, to enjoy one's self, to become creatively absorbed in a task – all come from the child's repeated experience of forgetting their mother and surroundings while playing or day-dreaming and of then finding everything as they left it and mother receptive and welcoming when remembered having been temporarily forgotten.

Silent integration

It must be emphasized clearly here that for Winnicott an important prerequisite for the achievement of the capacity for silence is the integration into the personality of the aggressive and libidinal instincts through what he calls ego-relatedness and id-relatedness. This requires a good enough experience of an 'environment mother' of quiet baby-care and ego support and also of an 'object mother' who survives and welcomes the baby's instinctual loving feeding attack. It is worth noting that this plays out when there is no recognition of the mother and no realization that these two 'mothers' are one and the same mother. Winnicott gives the example of the ego-relatedness of the post-coital couple when one or both of the individuals are alone but in the crucial presence of the other.

Winnicott examines three statements ('I', 'I am' and 'I am alone') connected to the achievement of the capacity to be silently alone. 'I' refers to the achievement of one's personal unit self. 'I am' implies one's continuing existence facilitated by the unacknowledged mother. The statement 'I am alone' represents a state of affairs which is only possible after the mother is recognized as a whole, separate person. But it is based in sufficient early experiences of being alone in the presence of another who adapted to one's need without making demands or seeking recognition.

Winnicott explains that the 'internal environment' that eventually allows the child to forgo the need of the presence of the mother or her symbols is a more primitive phenomenon than is an 'introjected mother'.

And theoretically, even when able to be alone, the person with whom one was in identified unity as a young baby, is always present, consciously or unconsciously. Winnicott uses the term 'ego orgasm' for these enjoyable quiet experiences such as close friendship.

The patient's and the child's silence

In his paper 'The theory of the parent-infant relationship' (1960) the child's journey (and the parallel journey in undergoing psychoanalysis), is from absolute dependence, through relative dependence towards independence. Winnicott reminds us that before word representation the infant is dependent on care that is based on empathy rather than understanding. Anxiety related to this time is not one of separation or castration but rather the anxiety of annihilation. Winnicott explains that in his technique for classical psychoanalysis Freud wrongly took for granted that everything goes well in infancy. He quotes Freud who – in the famous footnote – notes that given the baby's neglect of the Reality Principle and enslavement to the Pleasure Principle, they can only be considered as a psychical organization 'provided that one includes with [them] the care that [they] [receive] from [their] mother – [and that then they] [do] almost realize a psychical system…' (1911, p. 220).

Winnicott details in this paper the way in which the analyst must wait, often for a long time, to allow for the patient's needed experience (perhaps for the first time) of the good enough environment – the physical features of the setting and the analyst's attitude – as dependable and reliable over time. It is only after this is sufficiently experienced that the patient's ego strengthens and they can benefit from interpretations and the 'talking' part of the therapy.

There must first be the 'holding' of environmental provision for inherited potential to naturally unfold in both human development and in psychotherapy. Winnicott speaks about the indwelling of the psyche in the soma with the skin as the limiting membrane. Then comes living an experience together and then the Oedipal situation of father, mother and baby all living together.

In this paper Winnicott draws the parallel between the patient struggling with difficulties from a developmental stage before the Oedipus complex and the baby at the stage of absolute dependence. The sensitivity that naturally occurs in the mother/analyst of the reliable setting is first based on empathy for a sufficient period before the understanding of a later stage and its technique of analytic interpretation is suitable or useful.

Winnicott's paper entitled 'Fear of breakdown' (1963a) addresses five primitive agonies; anxieties that are often silently experienced in the course of therapy. For Winnicott the breakdown that the patient fears may be one that has already been experienced at a time when the person was not sufficiently 'there' or present in terms of ego formation. It is 'unconscious' to the extent that ego integration cannot encompass it. Within the therapy the original experience is feared as if coming sometime in the future. And it cannot be relegated to the past until the ego can gather it into present-time omnipotent experience by means of the auxiliary ego function of the mother/analyst. Progress can be made if the patient can accept this strange truth and have the experience in the transference in relation to the analyst's mistakes and failures. Winnicott suggests that the analysis succeeds when the bottom of the trough is reached and that which is feared is experienced in the present within the transference. Sometimes the silent 'event' that caused a kind of psychical death is a non-event, a nothing. Something was needed but not provided creating a silent emptiness. In this case the silence in the session can be a useful re-enactment of the experience but this time held in a situation where it can be worked through.

The analyst's silence

'Two notes on the use of silence' (Winnicott, 1963b) features the use of silence as a technique and the crucial importance of the analyst's capacity to wait in silence. At the time of his writing Winnicott has just been silent all week in the sessions of one particular female patient. This patient, who has read Winnicott's writing, feels that what she is seeking is a sufficient experience of early mothering. She feels that she is achieving something she needs from Winnicott's silence. She reacts less violently now – no longer threatening to leave – to interpretations which she calls mistakes or 'blobs'. At this time in the analysis, for this regressed and dependent patient, interpretations are like 'a penis bursting across the field of the breast'. The particular 'breast' in question for this patient is a breast which is not to be eaten (nor to be eaten by, in retaliation), rather the breast is like a general field or a cushion; the ego support provided to the infant from the mother in early life. In this example we can see how silence in the presence of the analyst felt entirely necessary to the patient, something she had waited her lifetime for.

In their silence the analyst must sometimes tolerate the patient believing things that are not true – this same patient believes that Winnicott cannot bear being silent and that this accounts for a paper-crinkling noise heard on Friday. She also believes that he is jealous as she is getting something from him that he himself has never had. Winnicott explains here the importance of the analyst's capacity to wait in silence. He says that the listening done in silence is of a different order and includes an understanding of the function of the patient's regression to dependence. Interpretation will simply not work and might cause suffering while the patient is relating to part-objects and when the experience of omnipotence is projected out and, as with this patient, manifesting in a feeling of being 'doomed'. Also in these circumstances of merger, the patient's experience of omnipotence may involve a delusional transference and then the very important function of the interpretation is often simply to let the patient know of the limits of the analyst's understanding.

Essential silence

In his 1963 paper 'Communicating and not communicating leading to a study of certain opposites' Winnicott (1963c) makes important complex and sophisticated statements about the essence of the human subject and their communication. Recently Thomas Ogden (2018) has beautifully crafted an expanded exploration of the riches and nuances within this paper. Ogden says that Winnicott provides in this paper a theory of the state of being at our core; two states of a human being's being after the achievement of communication with subjective objects and objective objects – one is the enjoyment and use of being able to communicate with an external world and the other state, which surprises Ogden, is the non-communicating self, and the absence of communication is an essential quality of this state of being. Ogden translates Winnicott as suggesting that the earliest precursor idea of communication lies in the infant's communicating with the environment-mother. This 'communication' takes the form of 'going-on-being'. This is the most undifferentiated state of being experienced by the infant and is at the core of the isolate self (Ogden, 2018).

Winnicott first lists the benefits to the patient of the analyst's capacity for silently waiting; the interpretation is more creative and successful when it is the patient who makes it; sensitive environmental failure can lead to growth and integration; at a certain stage the most creative experience of the potentially good object is the refusal of it. But the truly vital message is about the non-communicating core of each individual and the need to protect it. Winnicott, while recognizing the sense of self that comes from communicating with external objects, also represents the sense of self that comes from the opposite need not to communicate. He protests against the horrifying idea of being infinitely exploited; eaten up, swallowed, found.

Winnicott gives the rationale for his claim: to the degree that the object is subjective, communication does not need to be explicit (Ogden usefully explains it as 'cul-de-sac' communication, not meant for any real or internal object but which nonetheless allows one's experience to feel real). But to the extent that the object is objectively perceived the communication is either explicit (communication as we ordinarily think of it) or dumb (e.g. the silence of private non-compliance).

Winnicott discusses two new ideas; the individual's use of different modes of communication and the concept of the individual's core self as being a non-communicating 'isolate'.

There are two opposite modes of non-communicating as the object becomes an object objectively perceived:

(1) A simple non-communicating which is a natural resting between communications
(2) A not-communicating that is active or reactive.

This second type can be either pathological or healthy. In the unhealthy situation the infant has developed a split because of environmental failure and there is no real communication in shared reality. Rather there is a communication with a subjective object and also a compliant false self which is actively non-communicating with the objectively perceived object.

Winnicott sees a need on occasion for an active non-communication which shows in the consulting room as a withdrawal or in compliant object-relating when silent communication with subjective objects takes over to restore balance. The healthy person also needs something corresponding to the unhealthy person's split; a healthy use of non-communicating which helps one to feel real. Winnicott reminds us that in health the transitional phenomena of childhood give way to cultural phenomena. He sees paradoxical trends in the artist which he eventually considers to be universal; the urgent need to communicate and the still more urgent need not to be found.

Silent communication

The silent subjective communication which Winnicott explores here comes from the time when the baby has no ego boundary and the mother's ego support is still essential. There is no projection or introjection and without a boundary the word 'inner' has no real meaning. Winnicott has in mind an earlier version of that which Klein calls 'internal'. Here 'inner' means 'personal' as it includes the mother's essential ego-support. Winnicott notes how mystics can withdraw into an inner subjective world. Then the loss of contact with the world of shared reality is counterbalanced with a gain in feeling real; wanting to communicate and wanting to not communicate.

Winnicott says that it is a joy to be hidden and a disaster not to be found: his female adolescent patient writes poetry just for herself, she says. And he explores with her possible bridges by which she might keep connection between her imaginative life and her everyday existence. All the while Winnicott's main point is that there is a healthy isolated core, a protected area of silence in each of us. Thus, although healthy people communicate and enjoy communicating, each individual has a core that never communicates and is an unfound isolate.

Violation of the self's core when communication seeps through the defences is a serious sin against the self to which parents and psychotherapists must give serious consideration. By the time they are objectively perceived, mothers have mastered the art of indirect communication through language. Transitional phenomena are there at the place where the infant begins to feel whole and separate and continuing communication with subjective phenomena enriches the feeling of being real.

Silent self

Winnicott explains the needs of the being who is growing in interrelatedness so very well. Here he brings the needs of the private silent part of the self into the picture. In the best situation there are three lines of communication: one that is forever silent; one that is explicit, direct and pleasurable; and one that derives from playing and comes into all cultural experience.

Furthermore, Winnicott suggests that it is vital that the psychoanalyst must acknowledge that the patient's silence makes a positive contribution in the consulting room; and analytic technique must allow the patient to communicate that they are not communicating and must distinguish this state from a patient's distress over a failure in communication. What begins as the capacity to be alone becomes a capacity for a withdrawal that is without loss of identification with that from which one has withdrawn.

In an analysis where there is a schizoid element, a period of silence may be the most positive contribution the patient can make and the analyst is then in a purposeful waiting game. Winnicott explains that in healthy development the infant starts off without life and becomes lively because of being alive; the liveliness of the child of a depressed mother is a communication that is unnatural and an intolerable handicap to the immature ego. The vagaries of the original situation may be worked through in silence in the consulting room. If the analyst fails to wait, however, there is a danger that they will suddenly become 'not me' and dangerously near to the patient's central still and silent spot of ego-organization. It is in such a case that an important function of the interpretation is to let the patient know the limits of the analyst's understanding.

This theme of the individual as an isolate has importance in the study of infancy and in the patients who have difficulties with negotiation of their personal boundary. The necessary defence is against being found before being 'there' to be found. Winnicott insists that at the core of the healthy individual there is a central self in silence, stillness and with no communication to the not-me world.

Conclusion: the rest is silence

This chapter may or may not appear in the pre-histories or 'periods of hesitation' of future creations. In any case, the tour is at an end and on reflection, my distraction was probably inevitable as Winnicott's assembly of constituent ideas to produce an explanation for the entire of human nature, was by his own admission an overly ambitious project (1988, p. 1). But he privileged and detailed the earliest time of silent dependence in human development and, I suggest, in so doing, made an enduring and significant contribution.

This is the time of the baby's pre-boundary experience of omnipotence and primary creativity when there was no 'other' to communicate with and silent dependence was a fact of life. Winnicott's psychoanalysis can therefore accommodate the private and nonverbal part of the development of human subjectivity and experience. Although interpretation has always been a part of 'the talking cure', Winnicott does not stress verbal prescription or remedy. Rather he emphasizes the part of cure that involves reliable live care, listening and silent holding while living an experience together.

References

Boyle Spelman, M. (2013a). *Winnicott's Babies and Winnicott's Patients*. London: Karnac.
Boyle Spelman, M. (2013b). *The Evolution of Winnicott's Thinking*. London: Karnac.
Boyle Spelman, M., & Thomson-Salo, F. (Eds.) (2014). *The Winnicott Tradition*. London: Karnac.
Freud, S. (1911). Formulation on the two principles of mental functioning. In: J. Strachey (Ed.), *The Standard Edition of the Complete Psychological Works of Sigmund Freud* (Vol. 12, 1911–1913, pp. 213–226). London: Hogarth Press, 1958.
Goldman, D. (1993). *In Search of the Real: The Origins and Originality of D. W. Winnicott*. Northvale, NJ: Jason Aronson Inc.
Khan, M. M. R. (1979). *Alienation in Perversions*. London: Hogarth.
Ogden, T. H. (2018). The feeling of real: On Winnicott's "Communicating and not communicating leading to a study of certain opposites". *International Journal of Psycho-Analysis*, 99(6), pp. 1288–1304.
Winnicott, D. W. (1931). *Clinical Notes on Disorders of Childhood*. London: Heinemann.
Winnicott, D. W. (1941). The observation of infants in a set situation. In: *Collected papers: Through Paediatrics to Psychoanalysis* (pp. 52–69). London: Karnac Books, 1984.
Winnicott, D. W. (1945). Primitive emotional development. In: *Collected Papers: Through Paediatrics to Psychoanalysis* (pp. 145–156). London: Karnac Books, 1984.
Winnicott, D. W. (1951). Transitional objects and transitional phenomena. In: *Collected Papers: Through Paediatrics to Psychoanalysis* (pp. 229–242). London: Karnac Books, 1984.
Winnicott, D. W. (1954).Withdrawal and regression. In: *Collected Papers: Through Paediatrics to Psychoanalysis* (pp. 255–261). London: Karnac Books, 1984.
Winnicott, D. W. (1958). The capacity to be alone. In: *Maturational Processes and the Facilitating Environment* (pp. 29–36). London: Karnac Books, 1984.
Winnicott, D. W. (1960). The theory of the parent-infant relationship. In: *Maturational Processes and the Facilitating Environment* (pp. 37–55). London: Karnac Books, 1984.
Winnicott, D. W. (1963a). Fear of breakdown. In: C. Winnicott, R. Shepherd & M. Davis (Eds.), *Psycho-Analytic Explorations* (pp. 87–95). London: Karnac Books, 1989.

Winnicott, D. W. (1963b). Two notes on the use of silence. In: C. Winnicott, R. Shepherd & M. Davis (Eds.), *Psycho-Analytic Explorations* (pp. 81–86). London: Karnac Books, 1989.

Winnicott, D. W. (1963c). Communicating and not communicating leading to a study of certain opposites. In: *Maturational Processes and the Facilitating Environment* (pp. 179–192). London: Karnac Books, 1984.

Winnicott, D. W. (1967). The location of cultural experience. In: *Playing and Reality* (pp. 128–139). London: Routledge, 1971.

Winnicott, D. W. (1988). *Human Nature*. Free Association Books.

Chapter 11

Silence as a condition for analytic listening

Site, situation and process

Howard B. Levine

I

In a recent paper published in the *Revue Francaise de Psychanalyse*, Evelyne Sechaud (2018) argued that as a *behavior*, the silence of the psychoanalyst "encompasses complex and highly varied aspects." She distinguishes "between silence as a speech act [i.e., a refusal to speak] and silence as a condition of analytic listening" (p. 89)[1] and thereby calls attention to what we might describe as the "active" and "receptive" dimensions of the analyst's silence. (Of course, "being receptive" is also an action, but it has the connotation of "taking in" rather than "doing to" and this is a distinction that I wish to emphasize).

Sechaud further notes that like the fundamental rule, the use of the couch, frequent meetings and the fixed and limited time of the sessions, the analyst's silence "is among the conditions *required* for the analyzing situation" (p. 90, italics added). That is, the role and function of the analyst's silence occupies a place in the analysis that we can qualify as *metapsychological*. In this chapter, I will attempt to build upon Sechaud's observations and explore the ways in which the analyst's silence structures the analytic setting, draws the patient's attention to the dimension of psychic reality and relates to the analytic process. In so doing, I hope to demonstrate the sense in which the analyst's silence is a necessary component of the analytic situation and a *resource of the analytic site* (Donnet 2009).

The *analytic site* is a term introduced by Jean-Luc Donnet (2009) in his book, *The Analyzing Situation*. There, he suggests that the structure of the analytic situation offers to patients a unique functional *ensemble* that includes:

- The presence of the analyst as a transference object available for both repetition and the creation of new experience.
- The functional capacities of the analyst's psyche as a more highly developed psychic organization (Loewald 1960) – i.e., the analyst's alpha function (Bion 1962) and capacity for figurability[2] (Botella and Botella 2005) – that may be temporarily placed at the patient's disposal to aid the latter in his or her psychic regulation and homeostasis.
- The analytic frame and space, which often first begins inside the mind of the analyst and later extends to the intersubjective and interpersonal space that forms between analyst and analysand, in which the opportunity for transference development and analysis, for self-discovery and recollection and for the creation and strengthening of the psyche may occur.[3]

In regard to the patient, Winnicott (1958) noted that the capacity to be alone in the presence of the other is both a developmental achievement and an important sign of emotional growth. Its appearance in the analysis "may be represented by a silent phase or a silent session, and this silence, far from being evidence of resistance, turns out to be an achievement on the part of the patient." (p. 416). But in order for this experience to occur, it requires the reciprocal participation of a silent, accepting, non-intrusive object (analyst).

In a well-functioning analytic process, the *absence* produced and the *space symbolized and created by the silence of the analyst* are essential to the strengthening and/or creation of the patient's *framing structure* (Green 1980) and to the capacity to create meaningful personal narratives that reinforce one's sense of subjectivity and identity.[4] In addition, the silence of the analyst symbolizes and is needed to maintain what Laplanche (1992) called the *hollow of the transference* ("*transference en crue*"): i.e., the open space in which new translations of the enigmatic may emerge into saturated, ideationally represented forms.

A further essential function of the analyst's silence relates to the analyst's management of the potentially obstructive dimensions of the countertransference and the maintenance of proper technique. Silence offers the analyst the time and space in which to transform and "tame" his or her own excitations of infantile sexuality (love and hate) that inevitably arise from the analytic encounter and so allows the analyst the possibility of maintaining a capacity for analytic thinking (Sechaud 2018, pp. 91–93).[5]

If properly used, the analyst's silence and other resources of the site can help the patient create a useful and usable transference-based dynamism, so that a *psychotherapeutic conversation* can develop into an *analytic discourse* and "the working situation *becomes analyzing*" (Donnet 2009, p. 36, italics in original). The capacity to use the resources of the site, however, cannot be taken for granted. Especially when working with non-neurotic patients and states of mind, the patient's incapacity to use the resources of the site is often at the heart of the very problems that need to be addressed within the treatment.

When the analyst fails to recognize and address this incapacity – and this failure may at times be abetted by a theory that fails to take into account the technical implications of the functional difference between neurotic and non-neurotic character structures and levels of psychic organization[6] – the necessary, facilitating place and role of the analyst's silence may be lost sight of and become confused with the analyst's personal difficulties, conflicts and countertransference. For example, Green (1977) notes that borderline patients

> are dependent on affective communication [and] seem to need a sharing of their experience, which does not mean collusion with it, in a non-intrusive exchange which gives them a feeling of existence, in which sufficient space can be formed, albeit manufactured space, for their silent self, and where the defensive meaning of their state can be acquired without their being a compression of their inner world.
>
> (pp. 200–201)

In the past, the indiscriminant and overly stringent application of a draconian idea of abstinence and neutrality was responsible for precipitating crises in the treatment of some borderline and psychosomatic patients, giving rise to the mistaken assumption that psychoanalysis was not an appropriate treatment for these diagnoses.[7]

II

In classical formulations of the treatment of neurotic patients, the manifest rationale of the analyst's silence – e.g., the analyst's refusal to answer questions, meet demands for advice, offer opinions, and so on – is meant to convey a stance of abstinence and is "the warrant of … [the analyst's] neutrality" (Sechaud 2018, p. 94). Viewed from this perspective, we can see the analyst's silence as an expectable, consciously applied component of analytic technique that aims:

1. To deny overt or covert gratification to unconscious drive-related impulses.
2. To mark the difference between analytic discourse and the manifest speech of "ordinary" social conversation, so as to better draw out and frame the latent meanings of the latter (Sechaud 2018).

However, as contemporary analytic experience has shown, the matter is more complicated.

As a refusal to speak (*Versagung*), the analyst's silence may, of course, also reflect – or be presumed by the patient to reflect – personal factors, conflicts or countertransference in its original, narrow sense. For example, silence may result from or signal the analyst's fatigue, illness, boredom, confusion, frustration, anger, retaliation, hatred, defense against erotic feelings, etc. From this perspective, these silences or dimensions of the analyst's silence may be seen as impediments to the analytic process that arise from inevitable moments of human imperfection.

When viewed through the lens of unconscious enactments and actualizations of transference configurations, however, these silences may also be seen as appearing under the aegis of the repetition compulsion. That is, as necessary *scenic presentation* (Argelander 2013) that direct attention to and offer opportunities for analytic reworking of the traumatic disruptions caused by object absence and the failure of provision of once-needed facilitating environmental responses. Recall Freud's (1914) comment that one cannot slay the enemy in absentia, Sandler's (1976) description of role responsiveness, Winnicott's (1974) "Fear of breakdown" paper, etc. Each of these formulations implies that "the past" relevant to the therapeutic action of psychoanalytic is not that of the *historical* past, which is no longer present, but the ever recurring "past" of the here-and-now transference enactment and repetition.

Under such circumstances, the "micro-failures" that occur within the analytic process – including countertransference driven enactments – are often painful, unconsciously created moments of negative transference relationship and anti-process that in retrospect may simultaneously be seen as inevitable and even essential occasions of actualization, role responsiveness and enactment. To the extent that they reflect the mobilization of past traumatic experiences and maladaptive internalized object relations that need to be unconsciously conjured into life and repeated and relived in the transference in order to be noticed and addressed, they are analytic opportunities. If recognized and treated successfully as such, they may become the seeds from which representations, thoughts and psychic structure may potentially evolve.

Although contemporary psychoanalysis, from Heimann (1950) and Racker (1988) down to our present day, has recognized a great deal about the inevitability, value and use of the analyst's countertransference, it remains an open question and matter of debate about whether or to what extent there is a difference between the analyst's subjectivity, the analyst's unconscious countertransference and the analyst's receptivity to the absorption and enactment of the patient's projective identifications.

I have argued (Levine and Friedman, 2000) that these concepts each reflect the unitary phenomena of intersubjectivity and inter-affectivity, as seen from a somewhat different perspective and applied with a somewhat different purpose in mind. So, for example, if we are considering the analyst's contributions to the anti-process of a session or analysis, we may talk of countertransference. If we speak of the mobilization and enactment of a negative transference relationship that is then recognized and addressed, we may talk of projective identification, receptivity, actualization and enactment. The difference between these designations may depend upon whether or to what extent any given analytic pair will be able to recognize and make good analytic use of the scene and situation that has been unconsciously created and brought to life.[8]

From the perspective of the psychology of the analyst, the underlying dynamics of any given situation, whether it turns out to be a contribution to the obstructive countertransference or to the progressive movement of the analytic process, are one and the same. Based on personal history, internal dynamics, analytic theory, etc., each analyst has a unique subjectivity, associative tendency and unconsciously preferred channels of listening, hearing and responding that will offer to the patient's unconscious the specific "hook" within that analyst on which the patient's projections, once they are absorbed by the analyst, will hang. These hooks offer a unique contribution to the creation of what will be the narrative of each particular analysis. In so doing, they will, along with the patient's specific dynamics and history, contribute that analyst's subjective "flavor" to the "dialect" of action, affect and verbalizable meanings that will constitute and describe the actualizations and/or enactments of that analysis.

III

In order to further advance and deepen our exploration of the analyst' silence, I would like to suggest the existence of two dialectical spirals that will define and describe the opportunities and problematic challenges of the analyst's silence in relation to the enigmatic and emergent potential of the analytic situation and relationship. One spiral is between silence and speech (silence <–> speech); the other is between silence as action or *thing* and silence as receptive waiting indicating potential space (silence as action or thing <–> silence as potential space). At any given moment, the force and meaning of the analyst's silence will occupy an ever-changing kaleidoscopic position within these different poles.

As Green (1986) has noted "silence can be experienced differently by each" member of the analytic dyad (p. 19). The patient has the conflicted desire to be in touch with the analyst and to avoid that contact; to be in touch with him or herself (especially the unconscious parts) and to avoid that contact. The same applies to the analyst. As a result, interpretation (i.e., the analyst's speech) will inevitably have "paradoxical goals, for it must maintain the contact with the analysand while allowing the necessary distance so that this form of contact can lead to insight" (ibid., p. 19). At times, of course, this distance will require "no speech" or silence on the analyst's part.

For the patient, conditioned by the transference, the analyst's silence may speak volumes. Thus, Faimberg (1981) reminds us that the patient may "hear" something behind and within the analyst's silence: "The patient hears that the analyst's *silence is speaking to him.* He listens to the analyst's silence or interpretations and *reinterprets* them according to the history that contributed to the constitution of his psyche" (p. 24).

For the analyst, silence is an essential component of listening and receptivity. It

> coincides with evenly suspended attention ... [and] appeals to the unconscious ... [by] invoking the representations and affects of repressed infantile sexuality... [It elicits] "the actualization of drive-related representatives, affects, acts and bodily states that will then

be pending representation. This silence is a silence of openness to the unexpected, if not the unknown. The point is to let oneself be infused by the patient's speech and by anything that comes from him. This includes words, speech acts, the voice, affects, bodily sensations, all those attractive, seductive and/or repulsive aspects. Silence allows the analyst to perceive the associative thread amid the flow of speech, to unravel the representations and the affects and retie them differently within constructions that can either be named or not. *The analyst's silence therefore consists of a speech that remains unsaid but whose verbalization is always pending in keeping with its timeliness.*

(Sechaud, 2018, p. 91, italics added)

This is the silence of Bion's (1970) reverie and negative capability, listening without memory or desire: a state of passive, but alert openness and receptivity, a readiness for absorption of unconscious projections from the patient and a "making room for wild thoughts" within oneself (intuition). It is a silence that allows time and space for the possibility and unconscious working of alpha function (Bion 1962) and the transformation of raw existential experience, emotion and somatic sensation into ideational representation that can become integrated into a personally meaningful narrative.

This silence is present even when the analyst is speaking. It is the silence behind the analyst's words; the silence of what is not being said. It is the intersubjective corollary of and often forerunner for non-neurotic patients of the enlarging and even creation of a psychic space in which thoughts, phantasy and feeling may appear: the interpersonal corollary of Green's "framing structure" (*encadrement*).

Perelberg (2017) describes the framing structure and the process of its creation as follows:

> Green states that when holding her infant, the mother leaves the impression of her arms on the child, and this constitutes a framing structure that, in her absence, contains the loss of the perception of the maternal object and a negative hallucination of it. ... *The negative hallucination creates a potential space for the representation and investment of new objects and the conditions in which the activities of thinking and symbolisation can take place.*
>
> (p. 51, italics added)

The

> negative hallucination of the mother is a pre-condition for Freud's hallucinatory wish-fulfillment, for images, for phantasy life, and for thinking. It is also an indication of thirdness, as the mother's absence implicitly poses the question: "Where does she go when she goes away?"
>
> (Perelberg 2017, p. 52)

At its most constructive, then, the silence of the analyst stands in for and/or reinstates the resonance of the process of creation and enlargement of this potential space, which Green (1980) qualified as the "primordial matrix of the cathexis to come" (p. 166).

Once developmentally achieved, each of us maintains this silent zone within ourselves, thereby guaranteeing the possibility of "the crucial experience of solitude in the object's presence" (Donnet 2009, p. 35).[9] In a progressive analytic process, "the analysis develops as though the patient had delegated this silent function to the silence of the analyst" (Green 1975, p. 17). But, as noted earlier, this developmental achievement is not always present or secure and it is often the goal and work of the analysis that is needed to establish its functional presence.

Non-neurotic patients are caught between the twin fears of fusional impingement and annihilating abandonment; between the intrusive presence of the object "which leads to delusion (*délire*) – and the emptiness of negative narcissism which leads to psychic death" (Green 1975, p. 17). Consequently, in borderline situations (*situations limités*), the analyst's silence "can be experienced … as the silence of death" (Green 1975, p. 16). When the latter is the case, the threat of death and annihilation must be transformed into more ordinary absence. This transformation not only requires the creation and maintenance of an internal representation of the absent external object, but may also require the internal creation of the potential space within which the object may be framed; that is, the "stage" upon which the internal object and its associated phantasy movements may come to exist.

Freud offers us a theoretical model of how this comes about in his description of the "perceptual identity" in hallucination through which the infant attempts to deal with the stimulus of hunger that follows the first successful feeding experience. This model of the wish for the missing breast that preserves the concept of the breast and is the precursor of thought also requires a silent space within which the breast-object may internally appear.

Freud's psychoanalytic formulation of what is needed for the creation of thought is dependent upon a double absence: the negative hallucination of the mother's physical holding, which reappears internally as the framing structure and the image of the object (breast, mother, milk) that was once there to satisfy and is now absent. Hence, Green (1975) writes: "Absence is potential presence, a condition for the possibility not only of transitional objects but also of potential objects which are necessary to the formation of thought" (p. 17).

In order to assist this transformation, the analyst must tread a fine line between speech and silence, presence and absence, mediating between what the patient can tolerate and use at any given moment and what the treatment requires. At some moments, for some patients, for whom too much speech may feel annihilating, the analyst's silence may offer a much-needed relief of decompression. For others, silence may lead to feelings of abandonment, disintegration and falling away into infinite space. Thus, Green reminds us that: "Language is situated between the cry and the silence. Silence often makes heard the cry of psychic pain and behind the cry the call of silence is like comfort" (Green 1977, p. 205).

Notes

1. All quotations from Sechaud 2018 are the present author's translations from the French.
2. "Figurability" refers to the psychic capacity to transform a drive derivative or sensory impression into a mental content (idea; representation) that is saturated in meaning and has the potential to be verbally expressed and symbolically linked to other mental contents. (See Levine et al. 2013 for elaboration of Freud's theory of representation and the implications of unrepresented states).
3. For readers unfamiliar with developments of non-Lacanian contemporary French psychoanalysis, Donnet's contribution might be seen as the culmination of a movement in analytic formulation from the idea of an objective, one-person psychology analyst "analyzing a patient" to a two-person psychology, in which a working alliance was necessary, to an even more complex formulation of an intersubjective encounter that included transitional space and the consideration of an analytic third.
4. These processes are included in part, for example, by Green (2005) in his concept of the objectalizing function, by the Paris Psychosomatic School (e.g., Aisenstein 2010) in their references to the competent functioning of the

pre-conscious and De Masi (2009) in his description of the emotional unconscious.
5 Of course, if this transformation does not occur and the opportunity is not realized, then the analyst's silence could actually reflect a countertransference-derived hostility or actualization of a rejecting and/or destructive wish.
6 See for example Green (1975), Levine et al. (2013).
7 See Lipton 1977 for a discussion of Freud's technique vs. so-called "classical" technique.
8 This assertion is analogous to the view that one cannot know whether or to what extent a painful and disruptive event will deserve to be called traumatic until the environmental response is factored in and the future happens (see Levine 1990).
9 "The analyst's silence sustains the crucial experience of solitude in the object's presence. But this experience is not necessarily made explicit or interpreted. As with an iceberg, only a small part of the density and complexity of the process appears on the surface. Discourse on the method tends to ignore the silent process of working-through on the intra-psychic level" (Donnet 2009, p. 35).

References

Aisenstein, M. (2010). The mysterious leap of the somatic into the psyche. In: M. Aisenstein & E. Rappoport de Aisemberg (Eds.), *Psychosomatics Today* (pp. 47–62). London: Karnac.

Argelander, H. (2013). The scenic function of the ego and its role in symptom and character formation. *International Journal of Psycho-Analysis*, 94(2), 337–354.

Bion, W. R. (1962). *Learning from Experience*. London: Heinemann.

Bion, W. R. (1970). *Attention and Interpretation*. New York: Basic Books.

Botella, C., & Botella, S. (2005). *The Work of Psychic Figurability*. London: Routledge.

DeMasi, F. (2009). *Vulnerability to Psychosis*. London: Karnac.

Donnet, J. -L. (2009). *The Analyzing Situation*. London: Karnac.

Faimberg, H. (1981). *The Telescoping of Generations*. London: Routledge.

Freud, S. (1914). Remembering, repeating and working through. In: J. Strachey (Ed.), *The Standard Edition of the Complete Psychological Works of Sigmund Freud* (Vol. 12, 1911–1913, pp. 145–156). London: Hogarth Press, 1958.

Green, A. (1975). The analyst, symbolization and absence in the analytic setting (on changes in analytic practice and analytic experience). In memory of D. W. Winnicott. *International Journal of Psycho-Analysis*, 56(1), 1–22.

Green, A. (1977). Conceptions of affect. In: A. Green (Ed.), *On Private Madness* (pp. 174–213). London: Karnac, 1997.

Green, A. (1980). The dead mother. In: A. Green (Ed.), *On Private Madness* (pp. 142–173). London: Karnac, 1997.

Green, A. (1986). Psychoanalysis and ordinary modes of thought. In: A. Green (Ed.), *On Private Madness* (pp. 17–29). London: Karnac, 1997.

Green, A. (2005). *Key Ideas for a Contemporary Psychoanalysis. Misrecognition and Recognition of the Unconscious* (A. Weller, Trans.). London and New York: Routledge.
Heimann, P. (1950). On counter-transference. *International Journal of Psycho-Analysis, 31*, 81–84.
Laplanche, J., Trans. (1992). Transference: Its provocation by the analyst. In: J. Fletcher (Ed.), *Essays on Otherness* (L. Thurston, Trans. pp. 218–237). London: Routledge, 1999.
Levine, H. B. (1990). *Adult Analysis and Childhood Sexual Abuse*. Hillsdale, NJ: Analytic Press.
Levine, H., & Friedman, R. J. (2000). Intersubjectivity and interaction in the analytic relationship: A mainstream view. *The Psychoanalytic Quarterly, 69*(1), 63–92.
Levine, H. B., Reid, G., & Scarfone, D. (Eds.). (2013). *Unrepresented States and the Construction of Meaning*. London: Karnac.
Lipton, S. D. (1977). The advantages of Freud's technique as shown in his analysis of the Rat Man. *International Journal of Psycho-Analysis, 58*(3), 255–273.
Loewald, H. W. (1960). On the therapeutic action of psycho-analysis. *International Journal of Psycho-Analysis, 41*, 16–33.
Perelberg, R. (2017). Negative hallucinations, dreams and hallucinations: The framing structure and its representation in the analytic setting. In: R. Perelberg & G. Kohon (Ed.), *The Greening of Psychoanalysis* (pp. 51–73). London: Karnac.
Racker, H. (1988). Transference and countertransference. *The International Psycho-Analytical Library, 73*, 1–196. London: The Hogarth Press and the Institute of Psycho-Analysis.
Sandler, J. (1976). Countertransference and role responsiveness. *International Review of Psycho-Analysis, 3*, 43–47.
Sechaud, É. (2018). Le silence du psychanalyste. *Revue Française de Psychanalyse, 82*(1), 89–97.
Winnicott, D. W. (1958). The capacity to be alone. *International Journal of Psycho-Analysis, 39*(5), 416–420.
Winnicott, D. W. (1974). Fear of breakdown. *International Review of Psycho-Analysis, 1*, 103–107.

Chapter 12

Silence and silencing of the traumatized

Aleksandar Dimitrijević

Trauma and silence

Silence is rarely as present and prominent as in cases of trauma. All too often, everyone involved, victims as well as perpetrators or witnesses, avoid talking about the experience at all costs. The silence surrounding trauma also leads to silencing insidiously, far more dangerous than explicit prohibitions or punishments. The problem is, however, that these connections are frequently neglected and for manifold reasons:

- our attention is focused on the horrors of trauma and not on the surrounding silence, which may not look like background as much as emptiness;
- silence is often a consequence of the inability of the listener to contain the personal experience of the traumatized person;
- silence can also be due to an active effort, be it conscious or unconscious, to make it impossible for the victim, and sometimes even the perpetrator, to break the silence surrounding his/her traumatic experience.

Out of this range of possible reactions, from benign to violent, this chapter will be focused on the darker end of the spectrum, the one where silencing can lead to the development of mental disorders. The discussion will be organized so that we follow this process in three dimensions: in the cases of attachment trauma, in groups experiencing social trauma, and in patients for whom psychiatric or even psychoanalytic treatments can be re-traumatizing.

Silencing the victims of attachment trauma

One type of trauma has, in recent studies, been emphasized as particularly important, and that is attachment trauma, especially if a child is repeatedly traumatized by a person to whom he/she is attached. Consequences seem to be most disturbing when trauma is inflicted in closest relationships, those from which children expect safety and encouragement for exploration. Children exposed to attachment trauma frequently develop a so-called disorganized attachment pattern, characterized by a complete lack of strategy in close relationships, freezing out of movement and expression, and incomprehensible behavior. About 15 percent of children in nonclinical samples are classified as disorganized (Schuengel, Van Ijzendoorn & Bakermans-Kranenburg, 1997, p. 136), but this number rises to an astonishing 82 percent of maltreated children (Lyons-Ruth & Jacobvitz, 1999, p. 526).

Researchers have found various consequences of childhood trauma (Osofsky, 2011; Read *et al.*, 2004, p. 223; Lieberman, Chu, Van Horn, & Harris, 2011):

- higher likelihood of being given up for adoption by one's parents, child fatalities, developmental delays;
- poor attachment and socialization, low self-esteem;
- distortions in sensory perception and meaning, constrictions in action, deficits in readiness to learn, attention, abstract reasoning, and executive function;
- HPA/cortisol dysregulation, smaller frontal-lobe volume, asymmetry of left and right brain centers included in the cognitive processes of language production;
- more self-mutilation, higher symptom severity, more suicide attempts;
- earlier first psychiatric admissions;
- higher dosages of medication;
- more prolonged and more frequent psychiatric hospitalizations and seclusions.[1]

Attachment trauma is the most detrimental type of trauma because it occurs inside the most important relationship a child can have: family. Due to this, the person who is the source of comfort and love for the child, maybe even the secure base (Bowlby, 1979), becomes the source of fear and terror as well. The child is thus in an unbearable position of having to reconcile these two opposite images of the parent: the loving one and the abusive one. Because this is impossible to do, the only way out for the child may be to dissociate the two parts of his/her psyche related to the corresponding parental images. Each child depends more on the benevolent parent than on his/her mind, so it is less painful to dissociate the mind in two (or more) and preserve the positive parental image than to admit to oneself: "My dad sometimes doesn't love me."

Painful though this may be, the presence of only one benevolent and caring adult can be of decisive help. In cases where attachment trauma does occur – and these cases are alarmingly frequent – children's mental health seems to depend on one factor more than anything else: acknowledgment or silence. If, in the family of the child, there is a source of recognition, the traumatic experience may be overcome. This person should no doubt do something – hopefully, report the perpetrator, protect the child, or in some cases, leave the household and relocate. What is, however, of even higher psychological importance is that this person talks to the child, hears everything he/she wants to share, and takes it seriously and responsibly. This will establish the status of trauma as an external, interpersonal event, and this can turn out to be of crucial importance for many reasons. First, the child can talk to other people about the trauma, look for help, and hopefully learn how to use that help. Second, the child can learn what to avoid in order to raise the chances of being protected: persons (usually men), places, times, conditions (e.g., drunk people). Third, this can prevent the development of the irrational belief in the child about her/him being guilty of the traumatic event, which may forever undermine the growing sense of self-respect. Fourth, the child will not lose trust in her/his mind but can use it to fight off the effects of this trauma and possibly future ones.

We now know a bit more about those helpful adults. On the one hand, evidence suggests that mothers of securely attached children do not suffer from unintegrated trauma. Furthermore, they are not particularly helpful in extreme situations, while securely attached mothers who had experienced significant loss(es)[2] were able to show the least frequency and intensity of frightening or frightful behavior, and proved to be most helpful to their distressed or traumatized children (Coates, 1998). On the other hand, the majority of psychotherapists come from the third generation of social trauma victims. They are usually resilient and highly mentalizing children of depressed mothers or chronically ill siblings (Dimitrijević,

2018), because in these families "the parent unwittingly and against her conscious will positions her trauma within the child; the child sets out to cure the parent and undo her trauma by placing himself in the parent's position" (Kaplan, 1996, p. 224).

For many children, however, benevolent, emotionally available, and mentalizing adults are not present in their social world, and preventive programs have not reached many others. Ferenczi claimed that traumatized children additionally suffer from the lack of empathic understanding by other adults: "Usually the relation to a second adult [...] is not intimate enough for the child to find help there, timid attempts towards this end are refused by her as nonsensical" (1933/1949, p. 163). It is highly likely, as we have seen above, that they will develop one or several forms of somatic illnesses, deviant behaviors, or mental disorders.

Mental disorders are not inevitable and direct consequences of traumatic experiences. A traumatized child will develop symptoms or disorders only if his/her experience is denied and remains isolated in silence. If this is what the child encounters in the family environment, he/she is left with little or no choice. Small children, especially preschoolers, usually perceive adults as benevolent, all-knowing giants. Not only can the adults read and know many facts, but they have social skills and can perform such complicated tasks as tying shoe-laces, brushing teeth, or buttoning a shirt. With such striking disproportion between them, the child naturally trusts the mind of the parent more than his/her own. Therefore, if the parent says that something has never happened, the child will inevitably start believing that the traumatic event has indeed never happened. Consequently, the recollection of the traumatic event will have to be either repressed or split off, and in the future, much energy will have to be invested in maintaining repression instead of developing or being creative. There is, unfortunately, more.[3]

When the child accepts the denying words of the other caregiver(s) ("that is impossible," "he never would have done that," "what else did you expect", and the like) as true, and represses the memories, he/she must also accept that something is fundamentally wrong with his/her mind. The image of both parents is again positive, possibly totally positive, and the child feels equivalent to what adults would phrase as: "I must be awfully evil to spread such horrible lies about the nicest person in the world" or "I must be completely crazy to hallucinate such horrible things involving the nicest person in the world." As a direct consequence of this, the child becomes afraid of his/her mind and may lose curiosity about it altogether. That is the beginning of the possibly life-long superficiality in introspection and emotion recognition. The child becomes internally silent about what parents wanted him/her to be silent externally.

These children may split their memory, cognition, and emotions in order to separate two types of experiences with the parent: loving father from abusive father. There is, then, one part of themselves they do not dare admit even to themselves, one part they believe is too horrible to face. The traumatized child first defensively inhibits his/her capacity to think about the inner states of others and her/himself, trying to avoid the insight that the parent may wish to hurt her. Consequently, trauma impedes deeper processing of emotional experiences and interferes with the (further) development of mentalizing capacity or can even destroy it (Fonagy, Gergely, Jurist, & Target, 2002).

This experience may generalize, and the child then feels that "looking inside" is dangerous under any circumstances. Being unaware of inner psychological processes means, of course, that one cannot control or regulate them.

> A daughter of two English literature professors and an avid reader always impressed me as brilliant in expressing every idea and impression about the world and people she met. She, however, started stuttering every time I would ask about her feelings. The same with a native English speaker who found solace in a local library from a very early age. During sessions I sometimes felt like writing down his creative phrases and expressions. This capacity was, however, utterly lost as soon as it came to describing his inner pain and sadness. He still told me almost immediately "I'm at a loss for words. This was never practiced with my parents."

Precisely this is considered to lead not only to disorganized attachment but to some form of mental disorder as well.

The message from both parents can, thus, be that of silencing. The perpetrator, usually the father, demands of the child not to reveal his criminal behavior. This silencing is most usually followed by threats, bribes, or lies. The other parent, usually the mother, silences for different reasons and with the use of other methods. The reason for the parent who is not the perpetrator to silence the child can vary widely:

- it is natural to find it challenging to listen and think about trauma, and we are all prone to denying it with words like "I cannot believe that," "I am completely stunned," or "Impossible." Indeed, for many people it is unbearably painful to imagine themselves in the position of the traumatized child;
- this parent can be a victim of torture from the same person and unable to protect the child due to the fear of revenge;
- women were historically forced into financial dependence, between the impossibility of returning to parents as divorcees and difficulties of living on their own without profession and income. From that position, they were not able to protect either themselves or anyone else;
- the violence against the child can be a part of the dyadic or triadic dynamics: it can psychologically get the meaning of the mother's revenge by proxy, her relief from suffering, or be a consequence of her jealousy or envy.

These findings led many authors to come up with a new etiological hypothesis, which claims that the cause of many mental disorders is a combination of (a) severe and repeated childhood trauma, and (b) lack of a person who could provide the interpersonal foundation for mentalizing (Fonagy et al., 2002; Levine, 2014). Trauma, thus, does not have to lead to a mental disorder and will not do so in cases when there are adults ready to face and recognize a child's traumatic experience and offer help in thinking about and overcoming it. However, it will very probably turn into a mental disorder if it is followed by silence and silencing.

Social trauma and the conspiracy of silence

A process analogous to the attachment trauma exists in the social sphere as well. It happens as a rule that incidents of social trauma are followed by long-term denial and silence. Several elements distinguish social trauma (see Dimitrijević & Hamburger, in press):

1) it is organized perpetration by one social group (for example, a nation);
2) against another social group, and not an individual;
3) it always includes the element of intentionality, which is not present in traumatic events caused by, for instance, natural elements.

Social trauma can have devastating consequences because it destroys societal and cultural foundations whose support and comfort we are otherwise used to having at our disposal and taking for granted: home, language, shared memories, as well as hospitals, counseling and psychotherapy services, or the legal system. While we may hope that a victim of individual trauma, even a child, can find some support and comfort in the immediate environment or from professionals, in the cases of social trauma the individual additionally suffers from the feeling of isolation, because everyone around him/her is equally traumatized, and, in cases of war trauma, everything around him/her can be destroyed (Dimitrijević, 2019).

There can be no doubt that events like wars, persecutions, or the Holocaust leave horrible consequences on their own, but the problem gets much more prominent if they are veiled by silence. It is a phenomenon recorded in various societies around the globe that both victims and perpetrators end up unable and/or unwilling to talk and listen about traumatic experiences.[4] Listening to the memories of trauma, especially in the case of such massive social trauma like the Holocaust, can cause disbelief in the listener, and later in the victim as well.[5] In the words of one survivor:

> "I survived a concentration camp but I regularly made the observation that people did not really want me to talk about my experiences, and whenever I started they invariably showed their resistance by interrupting me, by asking me to tell them how I got out."
> (E. Rappaport, quoted in Mucci, 2013, p. 141)

Again, the possible reasons are manifold:

- the definition of trauma says that it is an experience that cannot be integrated with the rest of personality. Therefore, it is to be expected that traumatic experiences will appear in dreams and flashbacks rather than in dialogues;
- the traumatized group avoids talking about that experience, hoping to protect the others, especially children and grandchildren, with the help of silence[6];
- people hope that the traumatized will be helped by silence, or at least that in this way they will not be repeatedly exposed to suffering;
- humanitarian and social organizations, which often claim that it is more important to address the future than the past, can induce silencing and cause more harm than cure;

- some groups or nations that have caused the trauma never mention what had been done, usually for about 20 years.

A very intelligent yet deeply traumatized patient told me that the first thing he wanted to share with me was a dream from ten years earlier. When he was still living in Israel, "before Berlin was anything to him," he dreamt the most powerful dream situated there. In the dream, he was at an underground party in an ample space full of young people. He tried to leave, but on the street level, he noticed that there was a massive fire in the city. Returning downstairs, he tried to talk to others, but this was not possible, as everyone had taken Ecstasy, their faces were motionless and eyes glassy. At that moment, "another him" came out of his body, visibly, and became a sort of his spiritual leader.

Believing that "a party" could stand for "the Party," and knowing that Ecstasy can come in the form of a crystal, I asked the patient whether any of his relatives had lived in Berlin in 1938. It turned out that, luckily, his grandparents had managed to escape two years before the burnings of the "Crystal Night." He initially could not accept the idea that the dream was not about his individual psychological life, as he had not heard anything about these experiences at the time of dreaming. Our work, however, later focused on the ways trauma echoed through the silent family, and on his dissociations.

Closely connected to this is also the phenomenon known as the transgenerational transmission of trauma. It undoubtedly has several components, but the most prominent among them seems to be the incapacity of the generation of the victims of social trauma to clearly think about anything related to their traumatic experience, and consequently, to talk about it. Trauma, thus, becomes inextricable from silence: "Survivors often claim that they experience the feeling of belonging to 'a secret order' that is sworn to silence. [...] They have become 'the bearers of a secret'" (Laub, 1992, p. 83).

Because of this, they are both unable to share the experience with their children, and later grandchildren, and, as was mentioned earlier, also believe that they will protect the young by not exposing them to details. However, as one title eloquently says, whereof one cannot speak, thereof one cannot stay silent (Davoine & Gaudillière, 2004).

Small children learn least from direct instruction.[7] They observe faces, listen to the tone of voice, even to silences, they see in the eyes of adults which topics inspire and which frighten them. Few things can be more potent than "knowing what you are not supposed to know and feeling what you are not supposed to feel" (Bowlby, 1979). It is in this way that silence of one generation, often planned as protection, becomes a prohibition to another, and often a silent, unrecognizable burden as well.[8]

The person or a group which tries to talk about crimes openly and admit in-group crimes, usually is treated as malevolent and as a traitor. After World War II, a new term was introduced in German: *Nestbeschmutzer*, "the one who makes the nest dirty." It labeled and put pressure on those who would not be silent, but also to implicitly claim that the nest (i.e., the home country and individual family homes) were actually clean (i.e., without guilt).

The silence usually comes to an end with the arrival of the next generation and their questions, usually about 20 years after the atrocities were enacted. It is not incidental that the first psychoanalytic study of the Holocaust was published in 1968 (Krystal's *Massive Psychic Trauma*). Even then, however, the dialogue comes slowly and much remains obscure forever. This prolonged societal silence makes the importance of audacious artists more evident than anything else. Their works provide what society dearly needs. Such is the case of containment for the pain of the suffering group (like Goya's paintings *May 2nd* and *May 3rd*), denouncement of the criminals at the moment when the majority claims disinterest or ignorance (like Thomas Mann's radio broadcast speeches "German listeners!"), uplifting the almost broken spirit (like *Shostakovich 7*), or opening discussion on a censored theme (like Eugene O'Neill's play *All God's Chillun Got Wings*). It is the art that can provide a safe space for feeling, thinking, and speaking about the unbearable pain or guilt of a large group, when it is still too early for the more rational work of psychoanalysis, sociology, and philosophy.

A precious example of the pioneering fight against the conspiracy of silence in the field of mental health comes from the work of Amra Delic, Bosnian psychiatrist and psychotherapist. After the wars in the former Yugoslavia, Dr. Delic encountered, among other groups of the victims of war, a large number of victims of systematic war rape (Delić & Avdibegović, 2015). Although political structures on all sides recognized the existence of this crime, none recognized individual victims or, subsequently, their associations. Ironically, in the deeply divided country of Bosnia and Herzegovina, even though one would expect this would have given them political "points," no institution of the two entities that were in a war against one another would grant their citizens this status or offer any form of support or psychotherapy.

A particular case in this painful situation is the existence of not only camps where both women and men were repeatedly raped, but also a large number of children born out of these rapes. The very existence of these children was long denied by almost everyone, so that their exact number is now impossible to discover. Many mothers were not capable of overcoming the ambivalence they felt toward their children who were fathered by those who had tortured them in the cruelest of ways. The rejection of their husbands and parents to accept children conceived in this way (many thought this was the ultimate family disgrace) made things even worse. When children remained with their mothers, their origin was, in most cases, never spoken of either in private or in the public sphere.

In these circumstances, Dr. Delic founded and coordinated an association where both female and male victims of war rape could meet and share their memories and emotions, which was the earliest forum that made it possible to break the conspiracy of silence against war rape in their country. No wonder the association was named "Our Voice."

The exceptional importance of this achievement can better be appreciated if it is contrasted with the time official policies require to achieve the same effectiveness. A very positive initiative of opening a memorial for the psychiatric patients murdered in the Third Reich, at the very place in Berlin where the plan for the "final solution" had been made, was realized in September 2019 – more than 74 years after the end of the war. That is probably the exact measure of how difficult it is to undo the conspiracy of silence.

Silence in the psychoanalytic treatment as a form of silencing and re-traumatization

One might say that, implicitly, psychoanalysis was created to break this silencing and help the victims articulate their voices. I believe that is what the author of the earliest psychoanalytic papers about silence meant when he wrote that "the patient himself comes into the psychoanalytic situation, which is unique in our civilization, out of silence" (Reik, 1948,

p. 125). It can (and should) be called "talking cure" not because of its technical properties as much as because it allowed the traumatized persons an opportunity to finally, sometimes after years of solitude, leave the hypocrisy behind and genuinely start talking about themselves and what really matters. Psychoanalytic listening can, in a nutshell, be described as openness to hear and acknowledge stories about traumatic experiences and silences related to them. It is precisely this form of listening that made psychoanalysis important and helpful: many victims could not find such an opportunity for a dialogue anywhere else. It is also precisely this form of listening that has special importance for the listener, as a source of both privilege and exhaustion.

This may even have been the revolutionary ethos of early psychoanalysis, as well as the reason for resistances against it: the awareness that the fight against silencing has to be political (Herman, 1992, p. 9ff.). Freud challenged the hypocrisy of Catholic Vienna; Reich did the same so passionately that he was repeatedly exiled and ultimately incarcerated; Ferenczi described psychoanalysis as a "science that is austerely honest and wages war on all hypocrisy" (1926, p. 11); Fromm and the members of the Frankfurt School persisted the longest.

However, this spirit seems to have disappeared at a particular moment, and psychoanalysis is not the societal force it once used to be (except possibly in France or Argentina). It is difficult to tell what exactly led to this. Some of the factors that first come to mind include: that "Freud glimpsed th(e) truth (about the subjugation of women) and retreated in horror" (Herman, 1992, p. 28); the once subversive discipline became well established, bringing high income and reputation; many psychoanalysts became immigrants and were not willing to risk their precarious existence or had language problems to express their political positions; psychoanalysis became a profession for people older than 50, sometimes active in their nineties, not exactly the ages passionate for revolution.

That the focus on opposing silencing is lost in psychoanalysis will here be discussed on two levels: first, when it comes to psychoanalytic treatments, and second, related to psychoanalytic institutions and education.

The clinical fight against trauma is undoubtedly demanding and requires experience and stamina from a psychoanalyst. As was mentioned in the previous section of this chapter, listening about traumatic experiences can "arouse defensive repudiation and avoidance not only in the traumatized person but also in the analyst, so that in many cases traumatic experiences in the treatments do not receive the therapeutic status that is actually their due" (Bohleber, 2007, p. 347). This alone could be enough of a reason for losing the battle against the silence that surrounds trauma.

Is it also possible that there is something rotten in the very state of psychoanalytic clinical work? The first discussion of the hypocritical elements of psychoanalytic treatments can be found in Ferenczi's *Clinical Diary* (1988). Indeed, its first note, the one of January 7, 1932, opens with the following thoughts:

> Mannered form of greeting, formal request to "tell everything," so-called free-floating attention, which ultimately amounts to no attention at all, and which is certainly inadequate to the highly emotional character of the analysand's communications [...] has the following effects: 1. the patient is offended by the lack of interest [...], 2. since he does not want to think badly of us, he looks for the cause in himself [...]; 3. finally he doubts the reality of the content, which until now he felt so acutely.

The basic idea here is that many patients come to treatment because they were, as children or adolescents, exposed to the malignant combination of (attachment) trauma and silencing and that psychoanalysis needed alternative techniques for working with them. Namely, Ferenczi believed that the silence of the classical analyst could be experienced by the traumatized patient as the repetition of his/her initial experience, in a way as re-traumatizing, and psychoanalysts not as allies in the battle against traumatic pain but as identical to the silent parent/environment of the past.[9]

> Coming to his third couch session, a young male client asked me, very apprehensively, whether he had to use the couch. He repeatedly offered to follow my advice, if I insisted on using the couch, but told me that he had felt the last two times that sessions were not nearly as helpful as in the beginning. His interpretation of this was that the dialogue has disappeared, that the initial sessions had been precious because I asked him questions and offered him the chance to inquire too. Now, all of a sudden, from his point of view, I was silent and he had no idea what to do with it. As we explored this, it turned out that conversations about personal issues, or simply about him, were curative because they had never occurred in his childhood home.

The same idea was also present in the work of Heinz Kohut (1959), who claimed that the attitude of anonymity, neutrality, and abstinence not only was not helpful for patients who had developed narcissistic transference but could even be harmful to them. Kohut, thus, introduced empathy as the most critical developmental and clinical concept, and in his clinical work was far more open and personal. This, later on, had a profound influence on the schools of self-psychology, American intersubjectivity, and relational psychoanalysis, where analysts disclose much more about their own experiences and emotions.

> A female client, for whom it was not uncommon to be silent for several minutes, would often break the quiet by asking me "What are you thinking about?" In the beginning, I returned the focus onto her and told her that it was more important we explored her thoughts. After this repeated a few times, I replied, honestly, "I am thinking about whether you are more curious about my mind than about yours, and if so – why." She said nothing to this, but several sessions later said, "I have been alone in my silence for long enough." She not only lived alone now but many of her childhood memories were about being alone in her room, reading. The question returned in the coming months, though less frequently, and if I gave her a candid reply, she would remain silent. My impression was that she was taking her time to enjoy a present.

We must also not forget the problem of silencing in psychoanalytic institutions. Candidates in training all too often encounter demands related to loyalty and uncritical acquisition of knowledge, while methods of testing and criticizing it (or appreciating wisdom coming from other psychoanalytic traditions or psychotherapy schools) are almost never taught. The situation is so critical that one former president of the International Psychoanalytic Association wrote about the systematic destruction of creativity of candidates and about the suicidal crisis of psychoanalysis (Kernberg, 1992, 1996). Indeed, persons at the beginning of their careers certainly become aware of:

1) the strange, church-like hierarchy in the institutions devoted to liberation, the constant listing of status in the association, the strange power of training-analysts;
2) very often non-transparent criteria for being accepted into the training and for advancement, which I find closely connected to the mystify-

ing language of psychoanalytic theory: where Freud had used everyday German terms, his translators often used Latin, and his followers developed a set of terms no one else understands: projective identification, transmuting internalization, *l'objet petit a*, etc.[10];

3) decades-long lack of a dialogue with other disciplines, arrogance toward other psychotherapy schools, sentiment of being attacked from the outside (first described by Freud himself), refusal to use scientific methodology, all of which have only partly been remedied in recent times;

4) a prominent tendency toward ostracism of those who challenge the dogma, or toward *Totschweigen*, death by silencing (Rachman, 2018), which happened to the dissidents of Freud (like Adler, Steckel, Jung, Ferenczi,[11] Rank) and of Melanie Klein (like Bowlby and, to a certain extent, Winnicott).

The most significant problem throughout the history of psychoanalysis is the attempt to silence creativity in its ranks. For more than half a century, almost all other psychotherapy schools were founded by disappointed or exorcized psychoanalysts: Otto Rank, Carl Rogers, Abraham Maslow, Aron Beck, Eric Bern, Alexander Lowen, and probably many more. Many authors' papers get rejected by journals, many books never enter training curricula, and some colleagues, like Frieda Fromm-Reichman and Ann-Louise Silver, are derisively asked: "What right do you have to call yourself a psychoanalyst?" (Silver, 2018). We would have been able to achieve so much, had we only been capable of containing, fostering, and utilizing their creativity for the cause of revising and improving the clinical and theoretical aspects of psychoanalysis, when it comes to the treatment of trauma, silencing, and many other aspects.

Conclusion

Trauma is not only widespread and ubiquitous but possibly also inevitable. Heavenly life, devoid of any frustration and trauma, exists only in religious and artistic fantasy, and is unattainable in the everyday life of nature or societies. It turns out, however, that trauma is not so malignant in itself and can be overcome with the help of a psychologically minded other, a group, or a service.

The silence that follows trauma is never natural, but it can only be a consequence of an action – silencing. Those – perpetrators, victims, or witnesses – who find talking about trauma too discomforting may – consciously or unconsciously – strive to make articulating the narrative about trauma impossible. There are various methods for this: from denial, minimizing, threats, begging, bribes, to propaganda, dehumanization and reducing one to a number without a personal name, social pressure, marginalization, ostracism, and censorship. The outcome is, however, always the same: the traumatized person or group will take the blame and start splitting, a child with the wish to preserve the image of the parent untarnished, and a group with the effort to reduce uncertainty.

Psychoanalysis started, probably more incidentally than deliberately, as a healing process focused on talking about what was heretofore blanketed by silence, on the articulation of traumatic experiences. Listening to those is, however, probably too demanding, so much so that psychoanalysis has mostly lost its early revolutionary character. It must, therefore, at every step, be reminded that both its training institutions and its treatments require genuineness and open-heartedness to meet the most sensitive and least familiar silences in the patient.

Notes

1 A meta-analysis that included 2048 case studies, 41,803 patients followed into adulthood, and 35,546 patients from cross-section studies (all of these with corresponding control samples), found (1) that all types of studies showed significant correlations between childhood adversity and incidence of psychosis in adulthood, and (2) that the risk for developing psychosis that came just from belonging to the population of traumatized was estimated at 33 percent (Varese *et al.*, 2012).
2 This pattern is now labeled "Earned Secure," to be distinguished from the "Continuous Secure."
3 Closely connected to all this is also the mechanism of the identification with the aggressor (Frankel, 2018).
4 There is empirical evidence that in the stories of the Holocaust survivors, "differentiation between what was purposely left unsaid and what was unconsciously avoided was not always possible" (Pisano, 2015, p. 149).
5 A detailed and insightful case presentation of the situation related to the Spanish Civil war can be found in Valverde & Martin-Cabrera, 2015.
6 A very eloquent example of this can be found in Grosz, 2013, where this London-based psychoanalyst describes visiting the Ukraine with his elderly father, who had been forced to flee the country and now pretends not to recognize anything.
7 It is also essential that silencing minorities sometimes occurs through a language barrier.

8 Vamık Volkan has masterfully described psychotherapy cases where patients were acting out the experiences of their grandfathers or parents, having no idea why they were doing what they were doing (2018a, 2018b).
9 For a connection between this and the mechanism of the identification with the aggressor, see Frankel, 2018, p. 138.
10 In this respect, ironically, the psychoanalyst most similar to Freud is probably John Bowlby, whose writing is crystal clear and terminology so understandable that every layperson can follow it.
11 There is, unfortunately, not enough space here to elaborate on the problem for the development of psychoanalysis of Ferenczi's ostracism and the silence that surrounded it between his death in 1933 and the publication of the *Clinical Diary* in French in 1985.

References

Bohleber, W. (2007). Remembrance, trauma and collective memory: The battle for memory in psychoanalysis. *International Journal of Psycho-Analysis*, *88*(2), 329–352.

Bowlby, J. (1979). On knowing what you are not supposed to know and feeling what you are not supposed to feel. *The Canadian Journal of Psychiatry*, *24*(5), 403–408.

Coates, S. (1998). Having a Mind of One's Own and Holding the Other in Mind: Commentary on Paper by Peter Fonagy and Mary Target. *Psychoanalytic Dialogues*, *8*, 115–148.

Davoine, F., & Gaudilliere, J. (2004). *History Beyond Trauma. Whereof One Cannot Speak, Thereof One Cannot Stay Silent* (S. Fairfield, Trans.). New York: Other Press.

Delić, A., & Avdibegović, E. (2015, June 5). Shame and silence in the aftermath of war rape in Bosnia and Herzegovina: 22 years later [Conference paper]. In: *Interdisciplinary Perspectives on Children Born of War – From World War II to Current Conflict Settings*, Hannover.

Dimitrijević, A. (2018). Why devote your life to psychoanalysis, an impossible profession. A lecture given at Chicago Psychoanalytic Society, June 18th, 2018.

Dimitrijević, A. (2019). The spectrum of loss in war-torn societies. In: M. K. O'Neil & S. Akhtar (Eds.), *Loss. Developmental, Cultural, and Clinical Realms* (pp. 79–95). London, New York: Routledge.

Dimitrijević, A., & Hamburger, A. (2020). Trauma. In: B. J. Carducci (Ed.), *Wiley Encyclopedia of Individual Differences*. New York: Wiley.

Ferenczi, S. (1926). To Sigmund Freud on his seventieth birthday. *International Journal of Psycho-Analysis*, *7*, 297–302.

Ferenczi, S. (1933/1949). Confusion of tongues between the adults and the child: The language of tenderness and of passion. *International Journal of Psycho-Analysis*, *30*, 225–230.

Ferenczi, S. (1988). *The Clinical Diary of Sándor Ferenczi* (J. Dupont, Ed., M. Balint, & N. Z. Jackson, Trans.). Cambridge, MA: Harvard University Press.

Fonagy, P., Gergely, G., Jurist, E., & Target, M. (2002). *Affect Regulation, Mentalization, and the Development of the Self*. New York: Other Press.

Frankel, J. (2018). Psychological enslavement through identification with the aggressor. In: A. Dimitrijević, G. Cassullo, & J. Frankel (Eds.), *Ferenczi's Influence on Contemporary Psychoanalytic Traditions* (pp. 134–139). London: Routledge.

Grosz, S. (2013). *The Examined Life: How We Lose and Find Ourselves*. London: Chatto & Windus.

Herman, J. L. (1992). *Trauma and Recovery: From Domestic Abuse to Political Terror*. New York: Basic Books.

Kaplan, L. J. (1996). *No Voice Is Ever Wholly Lost: An Exploration of the Everlasting Attachment between Parent and Child*. New York: Simon & Schuster.

Kernberg, O. F. (1992). Authoritarianism, culture, and personality in psychoanalytic education. Reprinted in: O. F. Kernberg *Psychoanalytic Education at the Crossroads. Reformation, Change and the Future of Psychoanalytic Training* (pp. 66–74), 2016. London: Routledge.

Kernberg, O. F. (1996). Thirty methods to destroy the creativity of psychoanalytic candidates. Reprinted in: O. F. Kernberg *Psychoanalytic education at the crossroads. Reformation, change and the Future of Psychoanalytic Training* (pp. 75–88), 2016. London: Routledge.

Kohut, H. (1959). Introspection, empathy, and psychoanalysis an examination of the relationship between mode of observation and theory. *Journal of the American Psychoanalytic Association, 7*(3), 459–483.

Krystal, H. (Ed.) (1968). *Massive Psychic Trauma*. International Universities Press.

Laub, D. (1992). Bearing witness or the vicissitudes of listening. In: S. Felman & D. Laub (Eds.), *Testimony: Crises of Witnessing in Literature, Psychoanalysis, and History* (pp. 57–74). New York: Routledge.

Levine, H. B. (2014). Psychoanalysis and trauma. *Psychoanalytic Inquiry, 34*(3), 214–224.

Lieberman, A. F., Chu, A., Van Horn, P., & Harris, W. W. (2011). Trauma in early childhood: Empirical evidence and clinical implications. *Development and Psychopathology, 23*(2), 397–410.

Lyons-Ruth, K., & Jacobvitz, D. (1999). Attachment disorganization: Unresolved loss, relational violence, and lapses in behavioral and attentional strategies. In: J. Cassidy & P. R. Shaver (Eds.), *Handbook of Attachment: Theory, Research, and Clinical Applications* (pp. 520–554). New York: The Guilford Press.

Mucci, C. (2013). *Beyond Individual and Collective Trauma: Intergenerational Transmission, Psychoanalytic Treatment, and the Dynamics of Forgiveness*. London: Karnac Books.

Osofsky, J. D. (2011). *Clinical Work with Traumatized Young Children*. New York, London: The Guilford Press.

Pisano, N. G. (2015). Ghosts in the mirror. A granddaughter of Holocaust survivors reflects the faces of history. In: M. O'Loughlin (Ed.), *The Ethics of Remembering and the Consequences of Forgetting. Essays on Trauma, History, and Memory* (pp. 143–160). Lanham, MD: Rowman & Littlefield.

Rachman, A. W. (2018). *Elizabeth Severn: The "Evil Genius" of Psychoanalysis.* New York: Routledge.

Read, J., Goodman, L., Morrison, A., Ross, C., & Aderhold, V. (2004). Childhood trauma, loss and stress. In: J. Read, L. Mosher, & R. Bentall (Eds.), *Models of Madness: Psychological, Social and Biological Approaches to Schizophrenia* (pp. 223–252). London: Brunner-Routledge.

Reik, T. (1948). *Listening with the Third Ear. The Inner Experience of a Psychoanalyst.* New York: Pyramid Books.

Schuengel, C., Van IJzendoorn, M. H., Bakermans-Kranenburg, M. J., & Blom, M. (1997). Frightening, frightened, and dissociated behavior, unresolved loss and infant disorganization. *Infant Behavior and Development, 19,* 729.

Silver, A. L. (2018). Psychoanalysis and Psychosis: Ferenczi's Influence at Chestnut Lodge. In: A. Dimitrijevic, G. Cassullo, & J. B. Frankel (Eds.), *Ferenczi's Influence on Contemporary Psychoanalytic Traditions. Lines of Development—Evolution of Theory and Practice over the Decades* (pp. 213–219). London: Routledge.

Valverde, C., & Martin-Cabrera, L. (2015). The silence of the grandchildren of the civil war. Transgenerational trauma in Spain. In: M. O'Loughlin (Ed.), *The Ethics of Remembering and the Consequences of Forgetting. Essays on Trauma, History, and Memory* (pp. 203–227). Lanham, MD: Rowman & Littlefield.

Varese, F., Smeets, F., Drukker, M., Lieverse, R., Lataster, T., Viechtbauer, W., Read, J., van Os, J., & Bentall, R. P. (2012). Childhood adversities increase the risk of psychosis: A meta-analysis of patient-control, prospective-and cross-sectional cohort studies. *Schizophrenia Bulletin, 38*(4), 661–671.

Volkan, V. D. (2018a). *Animal Killer: Transmission of War Trauma from One Generation to the Next.* London: Routledge.

Volkan, V. D. (2018b). *A Nazi Legacy: Depositing, Transgenerational Transmission, Dissociation, and Remembering through Action.* London: Routledge.

Part III

Research

Part III

Introduction to Part III
Researching silence in (therapeutic) conversation

Some philological flea cracking

Most clinical experts are not very familiar with the study of conversation, especially a type of study named "conversation analysis." Some of the papers in this section use conversation analysis in order to precisely research what function and form different types of silences, e.g. longer and shorter ones, have in the psychoanalytic treatment room. Conversation analysis has deep links to psychoanalytic thinking. In order to make these links visible we have written a longer introduction to this part than to the other two parts. We hope to show that research methods can inform and inspire clinical psychoanalysts in their practices. We start with a short episode in psychoanalytic history which is not well known, but was very influential in producing an unnecessary split between psychoanalysis and conversation analysis.

When Freud turned the attention of his listeners to slips of memory, forgetting of names or words, he pointed out how tiny details of a conversation convey deep and far-reaching meanings. One of his examples was welcoming an audience with the words, "I am happy to say goodbye – err – to welcome you all." He filled the pages of his most widely read book with many other cases. One of his examples is seldom quoted in English literature because it is difficult to translate. Freud writes about an instance when, in a salon society around the year 1910, the title of a book does not show up in a young lady's mind. She sees the cover of the book in front of her. However, she cannot manage to read the title. Even the young gentlemen present failed to come up with the right idea (Freud 1916/17, p. 90).

The title of the book is "Ben Hur," and the point is that the German word *"Hure"* means whore or prostitute. The translators of the Standard

Edition (vol. 6, p. 41) explain in a footnote: "The German words '*bin Hure*' sound not unlike 'Ben Hur.'" Freud explains why the young gentlemen failed to come up with the right title. He thinks that their unconscious might have understood the meaning of the young lady's failure to utter the title: because it might have compromised her. Freud writes (1901, pp. 41–42):

> We have reason for supposing that similarly unconscious processes had determined the young men's forgetting. Their unconscious understood the real significance of the girl's forgetting and, so to speak, interpreted it. The men's forgetting shows respect for this modest behaviour. … It is as if the girl who was talking with them had by her sudden lapse of memory given a clear sign, which the men had unconsciously understood well enough.

Now, we have to do some philological flea cracking, which will sharpen our eyes for the details of micro-analysis.

The first edition of Freud's book is from 1901, and the "Ben Hur example" is inserted in a later version. The example under scrutiny comes from Theodor Reik, which is announced by Freud. However, as the ellipsis (…) indicates, Freud does not quote Reik completely, he leaves something out. As we were not able to find an English translation of Reik's paper, here is the German version followed by our translation:

> Wir haben Grund zu der Annahme, daß ähnliche unbewußte Vorgänge das Vergessen der jungen Männer bedingt haben. Ihr Unbewußtes hat das Vergessen des Mädchens in seiner wirklichen Bedeutung erfaßt und es, *gestützt auf die eigene Kenntnis des Namens und die mimischen Zeichen,* gleichsam gedeutet; nun aber haben sie ihrerseits durch Vergessen reagiert. *Bedeutet das Vergessen jenes anrüchigen Titels auf seiten der Frau unbewußt die Vermeidung eines sexuellen Angebotes,* so stellt das Vergessen der Männer eine Rücksicht auf solches abweisende Verhalten dar und *zeigt das Zurückdrängen der eigenen sexuellen Begehrlichkeit, welche das Mädchen als Sexualobjekt nehmen will.* Es ist also, als hätte ihnen ihre Gesprächspartnerin durch ihre plötzliche Gedächtnisschwäche einen deutlichen Wink gegeben, den die Männer unbewußt wohl verstanden hätten.
>
> (Reik, 1920, 209f)

Here is our translation:

> We have reason to believe that similar unconscious processes have caused young men to forget. Their unconsciousness has grasped the forgetting of the girl in its real meaning and interpreted it, *so to speak, based on their knowledge of the name and the mimic signs*, but now they have reacted by forgetting. *If the oblivion of that infamous title on the part of the woman unconsciously means the avoidance of a sexual offer, then the oblivion of the men represents consideration for such rejecting behavior and shows the suppression of their sexual desire, which the girl wants to take as a sexual object* [!!!]. So it is as if their conversation partner had given them a clear hint through their sudden memory weakness, which the men unconsciously would have understood well.

We have set in italics those parts of Reik's text that were omitted in the Standard Edition. However, they are preserved in Reik's original text (in German) while in the German "*Gesammelte Werke*" three dots ("…") indicate the omission. We can see how Freud ignored what Reik clearly mentions, namely that the young men forgot the name "*based on their knowledge of the name and the mimic signs.*"

Reik described something, mimic signs, which were unconsciously visible for the men besides what was conveyed to them and alarmed them not to utter the title of the book. Reik had assumed something that Ferenczi later called "unconscious communication." We conclude that psychoanalysis that is interested in unconscious communication should not omit what is audible and visible, and by which such communication is performed. This ignorance refers strongly to small and tiny "sweet little nothings," as conversation analysts amusingly named it.

Five actions can be observed here, unrolling in a sequential line. First, there is a young lady who makes a slip: she cannot remember the title. Second, there are young men with a related, but second slip: the unconscious of the male party has understood that of the lady – a communication from unconscious to unconscious seems to be enacted, resulting in the inhibition of the male's utterance of the correct book title. Third, there is an observer (Reik) who presents us with the story as a document of something observable, mimic signs. Fourth, there is Freud, extinguishing what was center stage for Reik in favor of a theory of unconscious communication. Fifth, we conclude, in order to understand "unconscious communication" of the type discussed here, one must not ignore observables.

Let us stop our reasoning here for a moment and take up another thread. In psychoanalytic methodology, there is a long dispute between hermeneutics and so-called positivism or empiricism. In a nutshell, hermeneutics (which has a very long tradition) prefers to "interpret," and proclaims that the central psychoanalytic operation is "understanding." Empiricists, on the other side, draw on the methodology of physics and other hard sciences. They want to prove things, in particular the relationship between an independent and a dependent variable, between an "intervention" and an "effect" caused by the intervention.[1] Let us now pay attention to the self-description of the hermeneutic operation in the "Ben Hur" example: If the young men had "understood" why the lady's mind was blocked, they might have uttered a helpful remark about the objectionableness of the book title and then delivered the title. This conscious act is the traditional hermeneutic meaning of the verb "to understand" (Detel, 2011).

In Freud's description, what happened was that the young men's unconscious "understood"! We can learn that if this type of "understanding" were applied in a psychoanalytic session, it could lead to a stalemate. However, it was Reik, in his original case presentation, who revealed the title to the young lady, who was in analysis with him, and he insists that it was this information that opened the path for further analysis the results of which he then published.

The operation of "understanding" is more complex and best described by creating a series: psychoanalysts can learn that their type of "understanding" is an "understanding of understanding" (Detel, 2011). In every single act of understanding, this understanding can understand itself, an activity which requires a higher level of (self-)observation. Understanding evolves to understanding-understanding, and on higher levels in a recursive fashion. Applying the concept onto itself establishes a transient higher-order logic, which makes understanding translucent or transparent. It is as if, for a moment, we could look *through* the operation *into* its core procedure.

Observing "observables" deepens the understanding of understanding

What we have is an insight into one of the ways Freud conceptualized the process of making the unconscious conscious. There must be something like an event, something observable. The observable is indispensable. It serves as the empirical basis for conclusions, interpretations, and further theorizing. The process becomes transparent if and only if there is something that can be observed, and it changes by the process of understanding the "understanding" of "understanding."

This is not the only example of this kind in Freud's writings. There are many others in his case presentations, like the "Rat Man" or *Studies on Hysteria*. However, what Freud added is a new way of understanding what can be observed. Freud observed what a cultural tradition, even a scientific tradition, ignored. A slip is such an example, telling jokes is another, observing the details of dream-telling a third, and paying close attention to symptoms, the next. Freud started by scrutinizing the surface without interest to step *behind* the surface (Krejci, 2009; Levy & Inderbitzin, 1990; Paniagua, 1991; Poland, 1992; Smith, 1993). It is the analyst's theory (Spence, 1993) that makes steps behind the surface. If the surface-observables are addressed without criticism or diagnostic devaluation, then, Spence observed, a patient by him/herself will open up deeper dimensions of experience – and they show up on a new surface. Freud's early examples give hints of how the deep trench between the methodologies might be bridged. An unconscious that could not be observed would seduce every thinker into wild speculations; a methodology that would not apply its operations to itself could be accused of simplification. A science without some data would lose any recognition.

We are now prepared to understand how a close appreciation of surface in psychoanalysis coincides with that of conversation analysis. Conversation analysts persistently insist that it is not "language," produced in the philosopher's armchair, that should be studied, but how people really *speak*. Another shift from grammatical competence to "doing things with words" (Austin, 1962; Brown, 1958) which was accompanied by studying situated communicative events instead of painting the "big picture" of a whole language. Language was discovered to be a living system, used and changed by living people who create words and phrases and songs, rhythms, and rhymes, which could not be predicted. This "pragmatic turn" (Lepper, 2009) was welcomed in psychoanalysis. Freud had always seen treatment rooms as delivery rooms for all theory, and he maintained that nothing is going on there but "an exchange of words." This often-cited phrase was directed against the assumption of telepathic influence or even magnetism – not only words, and this did not mean that Freud in general would have excluded mimic, voice and gesture or the movement of hands and arms. Think of how he observed Dora's purse, which she permanently opened and closed. This "exchange of words including mimics, etc." he named "conversation." "One more thing before you start. What you tell me must differ in one respect from an ordinary conversation" (Freud, 1913, p. 134). (In German, he uses the word "*Konversation*" here, not "*Gespräch*" nor "*Dialog*").

In this way, in his paper on "lay analysis" he lets the anonymous listener know about the basic rule. He adds that the therapeutic conversation is different from ordinary conversation. However, it is conversation.

Many researchers have understood that social life is so deeply based on conversation and its various forms that there would be no social life without conversations. Harvey Sacks, the founder of "Conversation Analysis" (CA), quoted Freud often, thus demonstrating a consensual level of understanding (Sacks & Jefferson, 1992/1995). Another close connection between psychoanalysis and CA was delivered by the work of Gail Jefferson, published under the title *Repairing the Broken Surface* (2017). Jefferson is remembered as one of the most sensitive listeners in the history of social sciences: she could make the shadow of an utterance hearable and, thus, convince others that there were more levels of meaning observable in a conversation than was detectable by merely "applying" theory to the data. No wonder – her parents were psychoanalysts, Bess and Isador Zifferstein.

In the same fashion as Freud, who observed unconscious meaning where others overlooked what they saw and saw nothing, Jefferson could hear, as if she were a musician, the delicate subtleties of withdrawals, of list colligations, in the poetics of ordinary talk (Jefferson, 1996), which was her name for slips and many other topics.

What is it that Conversation Analysts do?

CA researchers believe that social life is structured by the details of linguistics, of speaking and understanding, of influential or failing talk, of the quarrels of complex or more simple conversations. This massive amount of knowledge will be referred to here partly in order to make some overlooked details of therapeutic conversations observable.

The most time-consuming aspect of the work of CA researchers is transcription: beginners need one hour to transcribe one minute precisely. After some practice, things go faster.

What follows is a list of diacritical signs used internationally. They serve the purpose of making observable what is mostly overheard: how people interrupt each other; how they pause or accelerate speech; how failures get corrected, and by whom; whose invitations are accepted or refused. In order to make the social connection of two speakers viewable, it is relevant to analyze the *sequence* of speech. If you answer a question, do it within 0.8 seconds – otherwise, trouble is likely to come. However, if one does not respond within this small time interval, what does one do? One responds with an explanation for this delay or an excuse: "wait a minute," prefaced very often by utterances like "oh, I do not have the word at hand." All these details are considered to be of utmost importance for the organization of the social encounter.

List of transcription symbols (diacritical signs)

Reading transcripts requires some practice, just like reading statistical tables or diagrams. However, the best comparison is to reading a musical score.

Transcription symbols

.	falling intonation
;	slightly falling intonation
,	level intonation
?	rising intonation
↑	rise in pitch
↓	fall in pitch
sp<u>ea</u>k	emphasis
>speak<	faster pace than in the surrounding talk
<…>	Angle brackets: <drawn-out slower> speech.
°speak°	quiet talk
sp-	word cut off
spea:k	sound lengthening (double colons :: show more time)
#speak#	creaky voice
£speak£	smiley voice
@speak@	other change in voice quality
.h	audible inhalation
h	audible exhalation

.speak	word spoken during inhalation
he he	laughter
sp(h)eak	laughter within talk
[	beginning of overlap
]	end of overlap
=	no gap between two adjacent items
(.)	micropause (less than 0.2 seconds)
(0.6)	pause in seconds
(speak)	item in doubt
( )	item not heard
(( ))	comment by transcriber (sometimes concerning gaze or embodied behavior)
*	point when still image is taken
↓	marked falling intonation
↑	marked rising intonation
Word	Underlined words or letters: spoken with emphasis.

WORDS in UPPER CASE are spoken loudly.
((sniffs)) audible non-speech sounds
(2.8)   silence measured in seconds

There is an extended debate about transcription rules (Bolden, 2015; Bucholtz, 2000; Hepburn, 2004; Hepburn & Bolden, 2013; Ochs, 2010) and practices. In this book, we use the simplified version of Jeffersonian transcription rules (Jefferson, 2004, p. 151; Muntigl & Horvath, 2016).

Pauses and silences – an overview

The contributions in this section show how CA researchers analyze pauses and silences.

This section opens a further view on silence, a view which is challenging for most clinically working psychoanalysts and psychotherapist who are not well acquainted with psychotherapeutic process research. However, one will quickly understand that this approach touches the central area of a clinician's daily work – although in an unfamiliar fashion.

Researchers and clinicians converge in viewing conversation as "the" central element of therapeutic action (Orange, Atwood, & Stolorow, 2015). The psychoanalytic tradition highlighted, in particular, "interpretation" as the unparalleled contribution of the analyst, and today we learned that there is more, much more. Creating an atmosphere of calmness and security, of listening to listening (Faimberg, 1996), enabling emotional resonance (Alvim, 2015; Hamburger, 2015; Watson & Greenberg, 2009), having a patient's mind in mind and letting the patient participate in this, is better achieved nonverbally. For instance, by a therapist's way of shaking hands, responding to a patient's gaze, mutually respecting each other's "face" while uttering a continuer-token and sometimes take a stance (Niemela, 2011), posing questions which indicate genuine interest, avoiding all kinds of blaming, remaining aloof while speaking words that touch (Quinodoz, 2003), and sometimes finding a humorous balance of respectless respect. Experienced clinicians develop some pride in learning these special abilities and competencies "beyond interpretation"; it is a contribution to personal growth and an increase of professional skills (Orlinsky & Ronnestad, 2005). We speak, and this is more than an "exchange of words" because a special kind of relationship is established by "something more" (Bruschweiler-Stern et al. 2010). This is the origin of all kinds of intersubjectivity and its theories. Intersubjectivity is done by talking plus glancing plus voice-modulation plus gesture plus ... plus ...

And also – by silence. We realize what a tremendously important element of talk and interaction silence is. It is not the patient who is silent; silence is created by both participants, in therapy as well as in everyday situations. Can silence be studied by methods used in psychotherapy process research? The answer is an unequivocal "Yes" as the contributions in this segment will show.

Heidi Levitt, a well-known psychotherapy researcher, has studied pauses longer than 3 seconds in psychotherapeutic dialogues. What she shows is that pauses can be classified on a scale from obstructive to thoughtful; the classification, then, is based on what happens before and after the pause, by context. A high number of obstructive pauses can be used to predict a negative outcome of therapy, a high number of contemplative pauses serves as a predictor of a positive outcome. Levitt's study is done with methodological rigor, which makes her results very convincing. Her results fit well into an overarching concept of silence as a threat or as deepening intersubjectivity. We come to understand better what contextual features this distinction is based on.

Buchholz studies pauses shorter than 3 seconds. Most often, they can be observed after slips. But not after all slips. Buchholz identifies that a specific pause length of 1.2 to 1.4 seconds after a slip is relevant for the relationship. His theory proposes to understand these pauses as composed from 0.6 seconds in which the speaker imagines how the slip might be heard in the ears of the listener and another 0.6 seconds in which the speaker projects a new start of speaking. If slips are evaluated as irrelevant for the ongoing relationship, pauses are much shorter. Characteristically, slips by therapists consume more pause-time. The theory proposed is that such slips have the potential to threaten the whole endeavor of continuing analysis. A scheme is developed for how these ruptures are repaired.

Florian Dreyer and Michael M. Franzen study pauses longer than 30 seconds. They show that what is said before those pauses has a typical structure of uncertainty markers and other conversational elements. If the following pause, then, is interrupted and the pause itself is made a salient element of conversation, thinking-while-pausing can be transformed into conversational objects. Joint attention, the base of all cooperation, emerges again, and pause and its thought content can be made to restart the therapeutic talk-in-interaction, which results in creating and sharing an image, a metaphor, or a scenario, for what was going on during the long pause. The schematic analysis is based on 53 examples of "long pauses."

Anna Vatanen, a linguist from Finland, starts her study of everyday interactional pauses with a new question: What is at stake? And how do participants shift from speaking to pause and vice versa? Her material comes from video-recordings. She discovers that participants do something during pauses; they change their position, look to a common point on a table or somewhere else. In short, a pause is in close connection to the situation and its environment, and is not just a mental or psychological phenomenon. To infer the meaning of a pause is a complex study – done by the interactants themselves. Her distinction between pause, gap, and lapse is useful for better understanding that in continuing the conversation after lapses means to take up nobody's responsibility and make it agentively one's own. She observes the rare event where, after a lapse, both participants begin to talk at precisely the same moment, which requires a "sharedness in orientation." Overall, she has under her conversation analytic microscope 130 lapses shorter than 2 seconds.

A final study presented here by Buchholz and his linguistic co-workers from the Freiburg Institute of Advanced Studies (FRIAS) focuses on another phenomenon: while we talk, it is always the case that many, many things remain unspoken. The simple fact of conversation silences them.

Conversation is a selection. This was the Freudian starting point for inventing the "basic rule": to tell everything that comes to mind. However, it is well known that this task cannot be fulfilled. What can be studied is what Harvey Sacks named "noticeable absence" – if you are greeted and do not respond, this absence of an expectable response is noticed. The material studied here is a video-recording of a couple in trouble looking for therapeutic help. A 10-minute segment is analyzed, and it is shown how both participants omit essential conversational requirements. This can be realized by scientific observers who, at the same time, observe what the participants do not. The study uses various theoretical approaches that became necessary as the phenomena under study could not be understood with one theoretical frame of reference only. However, to our knowledge, it is the first empirically transcribed and video-analyzed interactional sequence of what clinicians would call a "collusion" (Dicks, 1967).

All the conversation analytic studies presented here can conclusively show how rich such situations are. One could even say that they unfold an overwhelming richness in "information" – even if nothing is said. It is worth studying them in detail because only then do we learn *how* conversation is done, how conversation *analysis* is done and, for both, *for what purpose*. To answer the "*how*-something-is-done" points to the conversational "practices" in use; the next step is the analysis of conversational "functions." The other option is "sequentiality" – the description of how a sequential order between participants is established (e.g. an answer cannot be given at a first position, it must follow a question). Only after the analyses of sequentiality, practices, and functions are conducted with a sharp eye for details and the richness of "information," can we try to add an answer to the question of motivation.

We hope that these papers will help psychoanalysis develop a new interest in how strongly social human life is (Kirsch & Buchholz, 2020). It seems highly relevant that CA can contribute to psychoanalysis through its emphasis on listening to the surface and diving deep into the surface, which should be the required beginning of every interpretative process in psychoanalysis. Psychoanalysts can learn from CA not to look "behind" language before they have taken a careful look "onto" the conversation. Many hidden aspects can be discovered there, which would improve the understanding of clinical material, make analytic interpretations more relevant, and treatments more effective.

Note

1 That this meaning of "empirical" is much too narrow can be documented by a single quotation from empirical researchers: "Some of the confusion probably stems from the erroneous equation of "empirical" with "experimental" or "quantitative." Data derived from informal observations, such as non-quantified impressions collected during a psychotherapy session, are also empirical" (Lilienfeld et al., 2015, p. 11).

References

Alvim, A. (2015). From earthquakes to good vibes: Transformations through a resonance process. *International Forum of Psychoanalysis*, *25*(2), 143–148.
Austin, J. (1962). *How to Do Things with Words*. New York: Oxford University Press.
Bolden, G. B. (2015). Transcribing as research: "Manual" transcription and conversation analysis. *Research on Language and Social Interaction*, *48*(3), 276–280.
Brown, R. (1958). *Words and Things*. Glencoe, IL: The Free Press.
Bruschweiler-Stern, N., Lyons-Ruth, K., Morgan, A. C., Nahum, J. P., Sander, L. W., & Stern, D. N. (2010). *Change in Psychotherapy: A Unifying Paradigm*. New York: W.W. Norton & Co.
Bucholtz, M. (2000). The politics of transcription. *Journal of Pragmatics*, *32*(10), 1439–1465.
Chancer, L., & Andrews, J. (Eds.) (2014). *The Unhappy Divorce of Sociology and Psychoanalysis: Diverse Perspectives on the Psychosocial*. Basingstoke: Palgrave Macmillan.
Detel, W. (2011). *Geist und Verstehen. Historische Grundlagen Einer Modernen Hermeneutik*. Frankfurt am Main: Vittorio Klostermann.
Dicks, H. V. (1967). *Marital Tensions*. London: Routledge and Kegan Paul.
Faimberg, H. (1996). Listening to listening. *International Journal of Psycho-Analysis*, *77*(4), 667–677.
Freud, S. (1901). The psychopathology of everyday life: Forgetting, slips of the tongue, bungled actions, superstitions and errors. In: J. Strachey (Ed.), *The Standard Edition of the Complete Psychological Works of Sigmund Freud* (Vol. 6). London: Hogarth Press, 1960.
Freud, S. (1913). On beginning the treatment. Further Recommendations on the Technique of Psycho-Analysis I. In: J. Strachey (Ed.), *The Standard Edition of the Complete Psychological Works of Sigmund Freud* (Vol. 12, 1911–1913, pp. 121–144). London: Hogarth Press, 1958.
Freud, S. (1916–17). *Introductory Lectures on Psycho-analysis*. (Standard Edition 15, pp. 1–240). London: Hogarth Press.
Hamburger, A. (2015). Refracted attunement, affective resonance. Scenic-narrative microanalysis of entangled presence in a Holocaust survivor's testimony. *Contemporary Psychoanalysis*, *51*(2), 239–257.
Hepburn, A. (2004). Crying: Notes on description, transcription, and interaction. *Research on Language and Social Interaction*, *37*(3), 251–290.

Hepburn, A., & Bolden, G. B. (2013). The conversation analytic approach to transcription. In: J. Sidnell & T. Stivers (Eds.), *The Handbook of Conversation Analysis* (pp. 57–77). Chichester, West Sussex, UK: Wiley-Blackwell.
Jefferson, G. (1996). On the poetics of ordinary talk 1. *Text and Performance Quarterly*, *16*(1), 1–61.
Jefferson, G. (2004). "At first I thought"— A normalizing device for extraordinary events. In: G. H. Lerner (Ed.), *Conversation Analysis* (pp. 131–167). Amsterdam/Philadelphia, PA: John Benjamins Publishing Company.
Jefferson, G. (2017) *Repairing the Broken Surface of Talk: Managing Problems in Speaking, Hearing, and Understanding in Conversation* (J. R. Bergmann & P. Drew, Eds.). New York: Oxford University Press.
Kirsch, M., & Buchholz, M. B. (2020). On the nature of the mother-infant tie and its interaction with Freudian drives. *Frontiers in Psychology*, *11*, 317.
Krejci, E. (2009). Immersion in the surface. *International Journal of Psycho-Analysis*, *90*(4), 827–842.
Lepper, G. (2009). The pragmatics of therapeutic interaction: An empirical study. *The International Journal of Psycho-Analysis*, *90*(5), 1075–1094.
Levy, S. T., & Inderbitzin, L. B. (1990). The analytic surface and the theory of technique. *Journal of the American Psychoanalytic Association*, *38*(2), 371–391.
Lilienfeld, S. O., Sauvigné, K. C., Lynn, S. J., Cautin, R. L., Latzman, R. D., & Waldman, I. D. (2015). Fifty psychological and psychiatric terms to avoid: A list of inaccurate, misleading, misused, ambiguous, and logically confused words and phrases. *Frontiers in Psychology*, *6*, 1–15.
Muntigl, P., & Horvath, A. O. (2016). A conversation analytic study of building and repairing the alliance in family therapy. *Journal of Family Therapy*, *38*(1), 102–119.
Niemela, M. (2011). *Resonance in Storytelling: Verbal, Prosodic, and Embodied Practices of Stance Taking: Acta Universitatis Ouluensis. B, Humaniora* (Vol. 95). Oulu: University of Oulu.
Ochs, E. (2010). Transcription as theory. In: A. Jaworski & N. Coupland (Eds.), *The Discourse Reader* (2nd ed., pp. 166–178). London, New York: Routledge.
Orange, D. M., Atwood, G. E., & Stolorow, R. D. (2015). *Working Intersubjectively: Contextualism in Psychoanalytic Practice*. Psychoanalytic inquiry book series (Vol. 17). London, New York: Routledge.
Orlinsky, D. E., & Ronnestad, M. H. (2005). *How Psychotherapists Develop? A Study of Therapeutic Work and Professional Growth*. Washington, DC: American Psychological Association.
Paniagua, C. (1991). Patient's surface, clinical surface, and workable surface. *Journal of the American Psychoanalytic Association*, *39*(3), 669–685.
Poland, W. S. (1992). From analytic surface to analytic space. *Journal of the American Psychoanalytic Association*, *40*(2), 381–404.
Quinodoz, D. (2003). Words that touch. *International Journal of Psycho-Analysis*, *84*(6), 1469–1485.
Reik, T. (1920). Über kollektives Vergessen. *Internationale Zeitschrift für Psychoanalyse*, *6*(3), 202–215.
Sacks, H., & Jefferson, G. (1992/1995). *Lectures on Conversation*. Oxford: Basil Blackwell.

Smith, H. F. (1993). The analytic surface and the discovery of enactment. *The Annual of Psychoanalysis*, *21*, 243–255.
Spence, D. P. (1993). Beneath the analytic surface: The analysand's theory of mind. *International Journal of Psycho-Analysis*, *74*(4), 729–738.
Watson, J. C., & Greenberg, L. S. (2009). Empathic resonance: A neuroscience perspective. In: J. Decety & W. Ickes (Eds.), *The Social Neuroscience of Empathy* (pp. 125–138). Cambridge, London: MIT Press.

Chapter 13

Measuring silence
The pausing inventory categorization system and a review of findings

Heidi M. Levitt and Zenobia Morrill

Although clients' silences have long been thought to be of interest to psychotherapists, the theories on what they denote have been widely disparate. In-session pauses in dialogue seem significant because they indicate that a process is unfolding that demands attention to the point of halting the discourse. Something important is going on. These moments have been thought to indicate positive dynamics, such as emotional attunement (Gendlin, 1996), closeness (Ferber, 2004), and trust and intimacy (Trad, 1993), as well as problematic dynamics, such as transferential struggle (Fliess, 1949; Sabbadini, 1991), regression (Winnicott, 1965), rage (Zeligs, 1961), cognitive burden (Perfetti & Bertuccelli-Papi, 1985), and resistance (Freud, 1912; Reik, 1926). For clinicians, this means that it can be difficult to know how to respond to a client during a pause. For researchers, it can be difficult to know how to identify pauses and their function.

The initial approach to the study of silences in therapy was to tabulate the total number of seconds per session, creating one variable for examination. This practice led to the production of a contradictory body of literature with conflicting interpretations and results. For instance, both Wepfer (1996) and Cook (1964) found more silence in therapy to be associated with insight and therapeutic success, however, Brähler & Overbeck (1976) found that smaller proportions of silence led therapists and clients to agree that sessions were positive. While silence was associated with lower client anxiety (Siegman, 1978), it also was associated with greater anxiety (Mahl, 1956). Researchers interpreted findings regarding silence as evidence of various processes, such as empathy (Hargrove, 1974) and discomfort (Becker, Harrow, Astrachan, Etre, & Miller, 1968). It was this conflicted state of the literature that led the first author to develop a system to differentiate pauses (Levitt, 2001a), rather than to see them as homogeneous.

The generation and credibility of the Pausing Inventory Categorization System (PICS)

The PICS has high internal validity because it was derived from a qualitative research study (Levitt, 2001a). Because the literature was rooted in differing theoretical perspectives, it was thought to be important to learn how clients experience these, often poignant, therapeutic moments. Understanding the intrapsychic experience of silences can assist therapists, researchers, or interlocutors in gaining insight into how a dialogue is influencing its participants.

Measure development

Seven clients from four psychotherapy orientations (emotion-focused therapy, interpersonal therapy, cognitive therapy, and client-centered therapy) were interviewed about their experiences of silences. In these 1- to 2-hour interpersonal process recall (IPR) interviews (Elliott, 1986; Kagan, 1975), the clients reviewed recordings of their sessions and then described what was happening during silences lasting three seconds or more in duration; shorter silences were seen as dysfluencies. Segments of the videotaped therapy session that were replayed in each interview included pauses of at least 3 seconds in duration. A total of 168 pauses were explored, just over half of the pauses (52%) in the sessions. The main question posed after each pausing event was "Can you describe your experience during this moment?" Using a grounded theory method of analysis, their descriptions of each silence experience were examined and clustered together based upon commonalities therein, revealing seven forms of silences (for further details on this method, see Levitt, 2001a).

Types of silences

Of the seven types of pauses identified, three were classified as productive, two as neutral, and two as obstructive. Still, all may be helpful in the session if addressed properly by a therapist who is sensitive to their functions.

Measuring silence 235

Productive silences

There were three forms of silences that clients experienced as associated with progress in therapy: *emotional, expressive,* and *reflective pauses.* During these silences, clients developed new self-awareness and made gains.

Emotional pauses refer to the in-session pauses during which clients are accessing or experiencing their emotions. In these moments, emotional experiences range in valence and intensity and may include feelings such as fear, sadness, anger, and delight. Therapy discourse markers of emotional pauses include, but are not limited to, instances in which: clients expressed emotion words verbally (e.g., "I felt so sad. [Pause] I just feel so forlorn)"; emotion-laden context without accompaniment of emotion words (e.g., "I haven't seen my daughter for five years now [pause] it has just been so very long)"; and voice intonations that tend to signify emotional experiences (e.g., shaky voice, tearful voice, shouting voice).

Expressive pauses are silences in which clients are engaged in a process of searching for accurate words, phrases, or labels to describe their current experience. In these moments, clients seek to articulate or symbolize their feelings or ideas. These moments could range from a quick search process with the objective of locating the expression that felt "right," to a slower process that entailed a struggle to symbolize a complex or novel in-session experience.

Expressive pauses are associated with therapy discourse markers that include the awkward expression of experiences not previously articulated (e.g., "There's no good way to put it ... [Pause] I'm, I just not able to do that anymore"). In addition to this, when clients stutter or utter unusual or vague phrasing near an in-session pause, it could indicate that they are searching for a better, more accurate symbol of their experience (e.g., "I felt it had to do with all kinds of work things like ... [Pause] oh, not being ambitious").

During *reflective pauses,* clients are questioning ideas or generating connections and insights about an experience. Therapy session markers are mainly comprised of client expressions that indicate they are engaging in self-examination. The consideration of a new issue or idea could be initiated by the client or the therapist, and could result in client expressions of wondering, analyzing, judging, evaluating, or realizations of those behaviors. For instance, one client expressed: "Actually, it's playing out probably a big thing ... [Pause] now that I think about it. I was standing up to her." Or, in the following instance, a client considered how to answer her therapist's question about why she was being self-critical: "Well, just because [pause] I think I'm so used to being self-critical. It happens naturally." This example demonstrates a reflective pause in which the client is engaging in developing novel insights and meaning.

Later research using the PICS led to a differentiation in the reflective pauses, enabling more attuned coding of those silent processes (Levitt & Frankel, 2004). In this revision, *"low reflective"* pauses indicated self-reflection that was mundane and not requiring a depth of thought. For instance, a client who was thinking about what to do after the session might say, "Hmm. [Pause.] I wonder if I go to see a movie with my husband or if we should just get dinner?" This type of silence contrasts with *"high reflective"* pauses in which clients are engaging in therapeutic self-exploration. To give a counter example, a client might consider patterns in her history: "I wonder why I never felt like I could be successful [pause] and whether this was tied to my Father's hostility. [Pause.] I think he just chipped away at my self-esteem all the time." This second type of pausing indicates that the client is not only considering established preferences but is engaging in the process of making new connections.

Neutral silences

These pauses signaled moments in which clients' cognitive processing required some concentration. There are two forms of these silences. *Mnemonic pauses* are moments in which a client stops speaking in an attempt to recall an event or item. They also may entail remembering the order in which a happening unfolded, the use of a mnemonic phrase to stimulate memory, or a search for an event in a client's history. For instance, these would be coded as mnemonic pauses: "My father did not come home often for dinner [pause] probably about every other week for Shabbat but really not during the workweek at all." These pauses tended not to be associated with insights themselves, as they were accessing something that the clients already knew, but they could precede other productive pauses that were associated with moments of growth, for instance when remembering a childhood event, or could precede obstructive pauses if a resultant memory is too threatening.

Associational pauses indicate a style in which clients pause because they are switching from the description of one topic to another. Although these pauses are quite rare, some clients have a style of topic-switching and keeping the conversation at a more surface level, without any immediate threat that is causing them to veer the conversation away. Often, they seem to have a list of topics in their heads that they are wanting to review. An example of an associational pause is: "So, in the end we won the baseball game and all went to dinner. [Pause.] But, I wanted to tell you about what happened on my date last week." In the silence, clients seem to have a sense that one topic is concluded or have some internal association that moves them to switch to the next topic. Because these pauses are rare, researchers may choose not to code for them if they are not relevant to the data in question. However, it can be good for therapists to be aware of these types of pauses to inquire about them in order to learn more about associations at play and draw clients' attention to their topic-switching style, which might limit therapeutic activity.

Obstructive silences

Two forms of obstructive silences were identified as patterns in clients' experiences. These pauses were labeled "obstructive" because they stopped the clients' progress in the moment when they occurred. If the therapist was able to identify the process, however, and develop an attuned intervention to direct clients to consider these silences and how they influenced the exchange, these pauses could lead to central insights in the therapy.

Disengaged pauses signify clients' emotional avoidance during the discussion of a particular session topic. Clients often reported discomfort during these silences. Disengaged pauses function as a way to deflect the topic at hand, detract from the therapist's exploration of issues perceived as threatening, or simply withdraw from the interaction. Sometimes, client participants shared that this was a conscious process. In other instances, however, disengaged pauses represented an automatic response to heightened tension or emotional discomfort.

Disengaged pauses corresponded to numerous therapy session markers. They tend to occur alongside discussion of threatening emotions. Within such discussions, after pausing, clients typically signaled that they had stopped processing to the same depth as they had been prior to the pause.

This was done by engaging in jokes, summarizing, dismissing, or distracting from the prior topic or emotional state. Clients used methods such as reassuring themselves, distracting themselves, and coaching themselves to "swallow" or avoid feelings. In the following quote from an interview about a session, one client described what it was like to use techniques to compose herself and avoid feelings.

> C: I guess I feel it was like I was trying to choke something down, and I guess I was having a great deal of trouble with how I was doing at the time, how I was feeling. ... Like trying to swallow a bone ... Part of the problem is it's just the, I'm at the point where I'm so well practiced at that thing that it's very much an automatic process that kicks in, but I'm conscious of it happening. ... I get the feeling there would be some kind of negative consequence if I was to allow emotional side to get out, I feel as though, I've got this idea that there's some reason that I should be keeping it in like that ... A few seconds later I'd say that it's gone 'cause ... I successfully was able to contain it.

In addition to avoiding feelings by resisting them, clients described related disengaged strategies. These could unfold in the form of clients attempting to lighten the conversation, making a joke, or switching to topics that are not as threatening to discuss.

Also, some clients shut down or withdrew from the dialogue. Clients might find themselves forgetting what was being discussed, feeling tired or confused. They might feel disconnected from the words they are speaking, as though they are watching the conversation from afar and engage in self-soothing until they can re-engage again. These processes could occur automatically and disrupt explorations that could be fruitful if they were engaged safely.

The second type of obstructive silence was *interactional pauses*. In these moments, clients shifted away from focusing on personal exploration to a focus on the therapist or the therapy relationship. During sessions, clients continually monitored therapists' reactions and their own self-presentation. If clients felt negatively evaluated, confused by the therapist reaction or communication, or felt that they were not making a positive impression, they might engage in interactional pauses. In general, clients were invested in maintaining a positive alliance with the therapist and would stop to consider how to remedy any potential breech. Interactional pauses were found to be significantly longer in duration than the other types of silences (see Levitt 2001b) and they could feel awkward or stilted.

One client engaged in repeated interactional pauses during her session. While guiding her through a cognitive restructuring exercise, her therapist asked her what a friend might tell her about her negative thoughts. Although she knew that the therapist was seeking a response of affirmation, she paused and considered "all the disappointments I've had with friends not responding to my needs ... It wasn't really a good question for me." Reluctant to admit that the friend would say nothing encouraging, she remained silent, and then said she didn't know. The therapist then asked her what she might tell a friend who had these same thoughts, "but it just brought back [how] my friends let me down, and now I'm in a position where I have to tell *them* something that will be quite positive and I just wasn't able to do it." After a lengthy 34-second pause in which she wrestled with this dilemma, she replied to her therapist, "I suppose I'd tell a person in my shoes to have enough confidence in their proven ability to set limits" and then was quiet for another 16 seconds. When asked in the IPR interview about her experience of this last pause, she replied that it was due to feeling disbelief in what she had just said. Feeling as though she could not come up with an answer, she acted disingenuously to provide the correct response to the therapeutic task and hoped for time outside session to explore her true feelings. Throughout much of her session, this client engaged in a private evaluation of her interaction—none of which was shared with her therapist. She compared her experience of therapy to a game show, in which she was always waiting for a crowd to shout, "Good answer!" This example typifies the experience of interactional pauses as clients are trying to maintain their integrity and the alliance in the face of a potentially confusing or upsetting therapist reaction.

Although the last two categories of pauses are classified as obstructive, this characterizes their function if they are unaddressed. In contrast, these moments can lead to important insights when therapists notice these silences and invite clients to articulate their thoughts. By asking clients what is happening for them in the silence, they can initiate discussions about the therapy relationship and about the challenge of facing threatening topics that can be foundational.

As can be seen, the activities during these seven pauses are quite distinctive. The PICS can be useful in therapist training, as therapists can come to identify these processes by actively attending to the cues surrounding each silence. For instance, lengthy moments of awkward silence often are interactional pauses. Silences, when approaching threatening topics, may signal disengagement, especially if the client veers away from the issue. During moments of contemplation, clients may be reflecting. Therapists then can respond accordingly, to encourage clients to stay with or return to productive introspective pauses or to ask clients to put words to obstructive moments, increasing awareness of their in-session patterns.

For psychotherapy researchers or discourse analysts, the PICS allows for researchers to examine dynamics in dialogue that take into consideration the internal experiences that give meaning to these moments. The PICS manual (Levitt & Frankel, 2004) provides descriptions of cues using both transcripts and session recordings (available upon request from the first author). This categorization system provides an empirically based method for researchers to identify patterns that might otherwise go unnoticed.

Validity and credibility information

In addition to the strong internal validity based upon the qualitative analysis, there are a number of ways the rigor of the PICS has been established, including examinations of its reliability, cultural validations, and an empirically based sampling system.

Inter-rater and client-rater reliability

First, clients provided feedback upon the completion of their interview. They were encouraged to discuss anything that remained unsaid and to clarify experiences that may have been misinterpreted. In addition to this, the results of the study were mailed to clients for their review and any additional feedback. Most of the clients were no longer accessible, yet one client did respond. This client's response endorsed the model presented and they shared that they had experienced insight from partaking in the interview. As a third check, the PICS manual was developed to describe and exemplify the seven pausing processes based upon this analysis. An independent rater, guided by the PICS manual, categorized both pauses from the therapy sessions and descriptions of pauses from the IPR research interviews. The rater achieved a Cohen's kappa of .70 with the primary investigator on the rating of 40 randomly selected pauses from the session transcripts. When rating 35 randomly selected descriptions of pauses from the IPR interviews, their interrater agreement was .82. When rating recordings instead of transcripts, ratings were found to be higher. A recent study demonstrated a Kappa of .91 (Guzmán et al., 2018). The client-rater agreement was .83 when their descriptions of pauses in the IPR interviews were compared with the independent rater's ratings of in-session pauses. Client-rater reliability ratings tend to be rare in process measures research. In addition, the study did reach saturation. It seemed that new forms of silences were not forthcoming in the final interview, suggesting the analysis was comprehensive (Glaser & Strauss, 1967).

Empirically-based sampling system

Coding using process measures is time-intensive. It requires raters to locate and evaluate each instance of the phenomenon under consideration, and to obtain inter-rater reliability and/or engage in a method of consensus with other raters. To substantially reduce the time that this takes, a study was conducted to see the amount of text that would need to be coded to reliably represent the therapy dynamic (Frankel, Levitt, Murray, Greenberg & Angus, 2006). Across 90 sessions, 1,503 silences were coded. Three sampling strategies were compared with the complete census of silence data: one sampled the first three, middle three, and last three sessions, whereas the other two randomly sampled either a quarter or a half of every session. The one-half random sampling strategy provided results closest to the complete census. This finding means that researchers can randomly select and rate half of the silences and still have reliable results–considerably reducing the time and costs required for coding.

Cross-cultural validation

This measure has been used by researchers internationally. These have included projects in Austria (Innsbruk University); Canada (OISE); Germany (International Psychoanalytic University in Berlin; University of Ulm; University of Witten); Denmark (University of Copenhagen); Chile (Pontifical Catholic University); Greece (Aristotle University of Thessaloniki); the UK (Anna Freud Center/University College London); Israel (Bar Ilan University); and in the US (Gannon University, The University of Memphis). This international research has suggested that the PICS is useful across diverse languages and cultures (e.g., Avdi, Verdenhalven & Acheson, 2018; Daniel et al., 2018; Holtmann, Seybert, & Huber, 2018).

Researchers in Chile embarked on a cross-cultural validation study of the PICS. Guzmán et al. (2018) conducted an ambitious dissertation in which she engaged in retrospective interviews of therapists and clients about their experiences of in-session silences. The findings of that study endorsed the categories of the PICS, with the exception of the associational pauses, which were found to be quite rare in other research and had been theorized to be mostly applicable with patients with highly avoidant personality styles (Levitt, 2001a). This version of the PICS manual contains cues related to the Spanish language and can be helpful in that context (Guzmán et al., 2018). In addition, the Spanish version includes a coding system for therapist silences (see Ladany, Hill, Thompson & O'Brien, 2004 for an English language version of a measure to code therapists' pauses) and so offers the potential to consider the session from multiple perspectives. These findings support the use of the PICS for evaluating therapy in non-English languages. In contrast to most process measures that are developed theoretically, empirical evidence of the validity, reliability, sampling, and cultural use of the PICS has established it as unusually rigorous.

Findings

The PICS has been used in a number of research theses and dissertations, presentations, and published studies. It has been used in a variety of research designs, such as intensive case study, multi-case study, and randomized controlled trials comparing psychotherapy orientations.

Intensive case studies

In this section, two case studies are reviewed in which the PICS was used to examine the microprocesses that unfold within a therapy session.

Case study of client with learning disability

To better understand how silences function in successful therapy, Gindi (2002) examined 40 hour-long psychodynamic therapy sessions, with a young adult who had a learning disability, that were considered successful by both client and therapist. Out of every second session, a 15-minute excerpt was transcribed and analyzed according to the initial PICS manual (Levitt, 2001b). The results showed that the overall number of silences increased as the therapy progressed. Specifically, reflective silences were found to increase, thus supporting the hypothesis that increasing reflection is indicative of progress in therapy. *Feeling* silences also showed some evidence of an increasing trend. These findings suggested that, across their therapy, clients became more comfortable with therapeutic introspection or found it more valuable and so came to practice it more readily.

Case study of client recovery from trauma

In addition to the cross-cultural qualitative validation study, Guzmán et al. (2018) examined a three-year weekly psychodynamic psychotherapy that was 88 sessions in duration and focused on recovering from trauma related to family sexual abuse. Over this long-term therapy, they found the number of silences increased gradually during the therapy until about the midway point, when it gradually decreased, suggesting that long-term therapies might display a different trajectory. Clients engage first in concentrated work to gain insight and then shift toward integrating that insight. They examined 83 change episodes (Krause et al., 2007), indicating periods of new insight, and 79 rupture episodes (Safran & Muran, 1996), indicating relational problems from the same therapy. They coded 298 silences within those episodes. The evidence from this study confirmed the prior PICS findings, in that the numbers of reflective and expressive silences were significantly higher in the change events while the numbers of interactional and disengaged pauses were higher in the rupture events. Emotional pauses did not differ between these experiences, likely because strong emotions are characteristic of both change and relational rupture experiences. Together, these studies provide evidence that the amount of silence in therapy changes across its duration, supporting similar other findings (e.g., Frankel et al., 2006).

Comparisons of good and poor therapies

A question posed by the following research is whether differences exist in how silences function in therapies that are successful in comparison with ones in which change is minimal.

York Depression Project study

One of the first studies that used the PICS was a study of three good- and three poor-outcome emotion-focused psychotherapies from the York University Depression Project I (Frankel et al., 2006). In accordance with the hypotheses proposed by the PICS, the findings demonstrated that productive silences, namely reflective pauses, had a higher relative frequency in therapy sessions that resulted in positive outcomes. Conversely, obstructive silences, specifically disengaged pauses, were featured with a higher relative frequency than productive pauses in therapy dyads associated with poorer outcomes. In other words, the good-outcome dyads exhibited more emotional, expressive, and high-reflective silences and fewer disengaged and interactional silences than poor-outcome dyads.

Although power in this study was limited, large effect sizes that approached significance provided quantitative support for the PICS. The PICS demonstrated reliability in identifying pauses and subtly discerning their associated outcomes in psychotherapy. Frankel et al. (2006) also found that the frequency of silences changed across the duration of treatment. Emotional silences occurred earlier and more often in treatments associated with good outcomes. Poor outcome dyads were characterized by more emotional silences occurring later in treatment, possibly indicative of those clients taking longer to engage their feelings in psychotherapy.

Munich psychotherapy study

In Germany, Schlotheuber (2018) found similar findings using the PICS by looking at a good and a poor psychoanalytic therapy. She found significantly higher frequencies of productive pauses in the good-outcome case and significantly higher frequencies of obstructive pauses in the poor-outcome case. Although her coding reliability was only moderate, examining these data in conjunction with the other research supports prior findings. These data suggest clinicians should actively invite and sustain productive pauses in sessions but inquire directly about obstructive pauses to help clients work through blocks to their treatment.

Comparing silences across psychotherapy orientation

The following studies have examined the ways the silent processes of the PICS function across psychotherapies that were based in differing conceptual theories.

Psychoanalytic and CBT therapies for bulimia

A recent study examined the association of silences in session with client attachment, therapeutic alliance, and treatment outcome (Daniel,

Folke, Lunn, Gondan, & Poulsen, 2018). Clients were provided with either psychoanalytic psychotherapy or cognitive behavioral therapy (CBT) for bulimia nervosa. Their primary aim was to determine whether or not the quality and quantity of in-session silences accounted for the relationship between client attachment and therapeutic alliance. Using multilevel linear regression analyses, they found a significant relationship between client attachment and frequency of pauses in session. Sessions with dismissive-avoidant clients had the highest total frequency of pauses followed by secure clients and then preoccupied clients with the fewest pauses. A major finding was that better therapeutic alliance and treatment outcome was predicted by lower silence frequency and lower relative frequency of obstructive silences.

Daniel et al. (2018) also found that all types of pauses, except for obstructive pauses, occurred more frequently in the psychoanalytic psychotherapy sessions than in the CBT sessions. In the CBT sessions, obstructive pauses occurred more, particularly in the "working phase," the middle portion of treatment. During the working phase of CBT, not only did obstructive pauses increase but productive pauses decreased. This pattern was not observed in psychoanalytic psychotherapy. For CBT, frequent silences were thought to indicate that something is obstructing change whereas in psychoanalytic therapy, frequent silences were thought to be indicative of the therapy working. In concordance with the findings from other studies (e.g., Gindi, 2002; Guzmán et al., 2018), both types of therapy featured fewer silences initially than in the middle or late phases of treatment. Overall, this study suggested that attention to silence in session can aide therapists in tailoring to client attachment and bolster therapeutic relationship and treatment outcome.

Psychodynamic, psychoanalytic, and CBT therapies for depression

Using the PICS, Holtmann, Seybert, and Huber (2018) studied silences within a set of six therapies that were equally randomized between psychodynamic, psychoanalytic, and cognitive-behavioral therapy approaches. For each therapy, they examined a beginning, middle, and end session and coded, in total, 1,008 pauses of at least three seconds. Here, the findings from their fascinating research related to the comparison of therapies are summarized.

Across the therapies, CBT was found to show significantly fewer productive silences compared to the other treatments. For the psychodynamic therapy, there were significantly fewer obstructive pauses than for the psychoanalytic therapy. There were more obstructive pauses for the CBT approach, but this finding was not statistically significant. When examining high and low reflective pauses in the three treatments, the former were found to be significantly less frequent in CBT. These two studies together suggest that silences in CBT are more likely to be obstructive, while lengthy productive silences are more typical of insight-oriented therapies.

Examinations of silences and other processes

In addition to these studies, a number of innovative studies have examined silence processes in connection with other processes that unfold in psychotherapy to see how they relate.

Computer textual analysis of emotional tone and abstraction

To examine the ways in which these pauses related to emotional and reflective text, using a different coding system, the same six Process Experiential therapies from the York Depression Project were coded with both the PICS and the Therapeutic Cycle Model (Mergenthaler, 2008), that entails a computer analysis of verbal interactions. To examine the local context of each pause, the 75 words before and after pauses were classified for using this model. The sessions were rated as falling into one of the following four states which reflected different levels of affective experiencing (*emotional tone*: ET) and cognitive mastery (*abstraction*: AB): low ET and AB signaled a state of "Relaxing"; high ET and low AB indicated "Experiencing"; high AB and low ET suggested a process of "Reflecting"; and when both were high, the client was "Connecting." In that model, therapeutic change is attributed to states of "Connecting" as well as "Experiencing."

Findings from this study revealed a highly significant difference for types of reflective pauses. Connecting and Experiencing text was found to predict "high reflective pauses" and Relaxing and Reflecting text predicted "low" reflective pauses. This suggested that clients who were neither cognitively or emotionally engaged, or who were only cognitively engaged, produced more mundane reflective pauses. Emotional engagement was associated with high reflective pauses, indicating deeper connections, exploration, and insight. The findings were seen as mutual validation of two independent concepts (Mergenthaler & Levitt, 2005).

Adolescents in psychoanalytic therapy and therapists' interventions

At the Anna Freud Center, Evrinomy Avdi has directed the research of both Nia Verdenhalven and Rachel Acheson (2018) in which they used the PICS to study 18 sessions drawn from three short-term psychoanalytic psychotherapies of adolescents with depressive diagnoses. They used a process of consensus to agree on the coding of 1,248 silences, finding that approximately three quarters of the silences were 3 to 10 seconds in duration, a little under a quarter were 11 to 60 seconds, and only 3.37 percent exceeded a minute in length—the majority of these being obstructive silences (86% disengaged). Looking closer at these longer silences, they found that the therapists most frequently broke the silence using an interpretation (33%), followed by emotion reflections (16.7%) and questions (16.7%). They found that productive silences were most common in the middle phase of therapy, which they saw as coherent with the model of therapy in use that expects clients to be most engaged during this period. Notably, the patients all spontaneously raised the experience of silence as a notable and multi-dimensional aspect of their therapy during their interviews on this experience—speaking to the importance of these moments in therapy.

A closer look at disengaged silences in an effectiveness study

Early sessions (second or third sessions) of 52 clients (Stringer, Levitt, Berman & Mathews, 2010) from across many psychotherapy orientations were examined to shed light upon the role of disengaged silences in therapy. These silences indicate withdrawing or distancing from a threatening topic. The clients were seen in a counseling center and were seeking therapy for diverse reasons. Results indicated that disengagement predicted poorer proximal (third session typically) and distal outcome (end of therapy) as measured by a short form of the Beck Depression Inventory (BDI; Beck, Guth, Steer, & Ball, 1997) and poorer proximal outcome on the Symptom Checklist-5 (Tambs & Moum, 1993). Inter-item analyses revealed that disengagement had a significant proximal effect on depressive mood and negative self-evaluative items for the BDI-PC, but across time these effects were sustained for only the negative self-evaluative items. These findings suggest that disengaged silences are associated with negative mood in the short term and with longer-term negative self-evaluation.

Conclusion

Overwhelmingly, the PICS has been shown to identify patterns in how people create new understandings within therapy dialogue. The body of research reviewed in this chapter speaks to the importance of examining therapy not only as a verbal endeavor, but also as one in which the discourse reflects the rich internal world of its participants. By distinguishing types of pauses, the PICS has not only enabled researchers to differentiate clients' responses within their studies, but it has been helpful for developing therapists to act responsively to their clients' silences in session. Repeatedly, across the studies reviewed, it has been found that the internal experiences within silences matter. These are the moments in which clients are at the peak of introspection, connection making and emotional experience. They represent the heights of interpersonal tension and intrapsychic threat. This system holds utility for psychotherapy process researchers or discourse analysts that wish their research to reflect the meaningful internal experience of actors within dialogue.

References

Avdi, E., Verdenhalven, N., & Acheson, R. (2018). *Studying Silence in Psychoanalytic Psychotherapy with Adolescents with Depression* [Unpublished manuscript]. London: Anna Freud Center.

Brähler, E., & Overbeck, G. (1976). Therapist's and patient's speech-pause behavior and psychotherapy session. *Dynamische Psychiatrie*, 9(4), 275–286.

Beck, A. T., Guth, D., Steer, R. A., & Ball, R. (1997). Screening for major depression disorders in medical inpatients with the beck depression inventory for primary care. *Behaviour Research and Therapy*, 35(8), 785–791.

Becker, R. E., Harrow, M., Astrachan, B. M., Detre, T., & Miller, J. C. (1968). Influence of the leader on the activity level of therapy groups. *The Journal of Social Psychology*, 74(1), 39–51.

Cook, J. J. (1964). Silence in psychotherapy. *Journal of Counseling Psychology*, 11(1), 42–46.

Daniel, S. F., Folke, S., Lunn, S., Gondan, M., & Poulsen, S. (2018). Mind the gap: In-session silences are associated with client attachment insecurity, therapeutic alliance, and treatment outcome. *Psychotherapy Research*, 28(2), 203–216.

Elliott, R. (1986). Interpersonal Process Recall (IPR) as a process research method. In: L. Greenberg & W. Pinsoff (Eds.), *The Psychotherapeutic Process: A Research Handbook* (pp. 503–528). New York: Guilford Press.

Fliess, R. (1949). Silence and verbalization: A supplement to the theory of the analytic rule. *International Journal of Psycho-Analysis*, 30, 21–30.

Frankel, Z., Levitt, H. M., Murray, David, Greenberg, L. S., & Angus, L. (2006). Assessing silent processes in psychotherapy: An empirically derived

categorization system and sampling strategy. *Psychotherapy Research*, *16*(5), 627–638.
Freud, S. (1912). The dynamics of transference. In: J. Strachey (Ed.), *The Standard Edition of the Complete Psychological Works of Sigmund Freud* (Vol. 12, 1911–1913, pp. 99–108). London: Hogarth Press, 1958.
Ferber, S. G. (2004). Some development facets of silence: A case study of a struggle to have a proximity figure. *British Journal of Psychotherapy*, *20*(3), 315–332.
Gendlin, E. (1996). *Focusing-Oriented Psychotherapy: A Manual of the Experiential Method*. New York: Guilford Press.
Gindi, S. (2002). *Patterns of Silences: A Case Study of a Young Adult with Learning Disabilities* [Unpublished Master's Thesis]. Toronto, Canada: University of Toronto.
Glaser, B. G., & Strauss, A. L. (1967). *The Discovery of Grounded Theory: Strategies for Qualitative Theory*. New Brunswick: Aldine Transaction.
Guzmán, M., Vidal, J., Soto, M., Jaime, D., Tomicic, A., Martínez, C., & Levitt, H. M. (2018). *Coding System of Silences for Therapists and Patients (PICS-TP): A Manual for Training and Coding Silences of Therapists and Patients in Psychotherapy for a Spanish-Speaking Context*. Santiago, Chile: University of Chile.
Hargrove, D. S. (1974). Verbal interaction analysis of empathic and nonempathic responses of therapists. *Journal of Consulting and Clinical Psychology*, *42*(2), 305.
Holtmann, K. C., Seybert, C., & Huber, D. (2018). *Sprachliche Charakteristika der Depression. Eine vergleichende Empirische Studie zu Sprechverhalten und Sprechpausen in Psychotherapie*. [Verbal characteristics and speech-pause behavior in depressed patients. A compared process-analysis of psychoanalytic, psychodynamic and cognitive-behavioral therapy]. Berlin: International Psychoanalytic University.
Kagan, N. (1975). *Interpersonal Process Recall: A Method of Influencing Human Interaction*. Houston, TX: University of Houston.
Krause, M., De la Parra, G., Arístegui, R., Dagnino, P., Tomicic, A., & Valdés, N. (2007). The evolution of therapeutic change studied through generic change indicators. *Psychotherapy Research*, *17*(6), 673–689.
Ladany, N., Hill, C. E., Thompson, B. J., & O'Brien, K. M. (2004). Therapist perspectives on using silence in therapy: A qualitative study. *Counselling and Psychotherapy Research*, *4*(1), 80–89.
Levitt, H. M. (2001a). The sounds of silence in psychotherapy: The categorization of clients' pauses. *Psychotherapy Research*, *11*(3), 295–309.
Levitt, H. M. (2001b). Clients' experiences of obstructive silence: Integrating conscious reports and analytic theories. *Journal of Contemporary Psychotherapy*, *31*(4), 221–244.
Levitt, H. M. (2002). The unsaid in the psychotherapy narrative: Voicing the unvoiced. *Counselling Psychology Quarterly*, *15*(4), 333–350.
Levitt, H. M., & Frankel, Z. (2004). *Pausing Inventory Classification System (PICS) Manual, 2nd Revision*. [Unpublished Manuscript]. Memphis, TN: University of Memphis.
Mahl, G. F. (1956). Disturbances and silences in the patient's speech in psychotherapy. *Journal of Abnormal and Social Psychology*, *53*(1), 1–15.

Mergenthaler, E. (2008). Resonating minds: A school-independent theoretical conception and its empirical application to psychotherapeutic processes. *Psychotherapy Research*, *18*(2), 109–126.

Mergenthaler, E., & Levitt, H. M. (2005, June 24). Pausing experiences and the Therapeutic Cycles Model [Conference paper]. In: *Micro-Processes in Therapeutic Dialogue: How Do Patient and Therapist do the Work of Therapy? Conference Conducted at the 36th International Meeting of the Society for Psychotherapy Research*, Montreal, Canada.

Perfetti, C. C., & Bertuccelli-Papi, M. (1985). Towards a cognitive typology of pause phenomena. *Communication and Cognition*, *18*, 339–351.

Reik, T. (1926). The psychological meaning of silence. *Psychoanalytic Review*, *55*(2), 172–186.

Sabbadini, A. (1991). Listening to silence. *British Journal of Psychotherapy*, *7*(4), 406–415.

Safran, J. D., & Muran, J. C. (1996). The resolution of ruptures in the therapeutic alliance. *Journal of Consulting and Clinical Psychology*, *64*(3), 447–458.

Schlotheuber, R. E. (2018). *Pausing Processes in Psychoanalytic Therapies* [Unpublished Master's Thesis]. Herdecke, Witten: University of Witten.

Siegman, A. W. (1978). The meaning of silent pauses in the initial interview. *The Journal of Nervous and Mental Disease*, *166*(9), 642–654.

Stringer, J. V., Levitt, H. M., Berman, J. S., & Mathews, S. S. (2010). A study of silent disengagement and distressing emotion in psychotherapy. *Psychotherapy Research : Journal of the Society for Psychotherapy Research*, *20*(5), 495–510.

Tambs, K., & Moum, T. (1993). How well can a few questionnaire items indicate anxiety and depression? *Acta psychiatrica scandinavica*, *87*(5), 364–367.

Trad, P. V. (1993). Silence: The resounding experience. *American Journal of Psychotherapy*, *47*(2), 167–170.

Wepfer, R. (1996). Silence in psychotherapy: A quantitative analysis [Conference paper]. In: *Conference Conducted at the 27th International Meeting of the Society for Psychotherapy Research*, Amelia Island, FL.

Winnicott, D. W. (1965). *The Maturational Process and the Facilitating Environment*. London: Hogarth Press.

Zeligs, M. A. (1961). The psychology of silence. *Journal of the American Psychoanalytic Association*, *9*(1), 7–43.

Chapter 14

Pauses are conversations
What they tell us when we listen

Michael B. Buchholz

Clinical experience – our point of departure

German *belle lettres* distinguishes between pauses (*Pausen*), silence (*Schweigen*), and quiet (*Stille*). This distinction is not based on the dimension of duration. In music there are pauses which are very brief, but also pauses which last an entire bar, with a fermata marked above the final barline; the pause can and should be lengthened by feel, and not in accordance with the exact beat of the bar.[1] We would not call this silence. One difference might be that the type of pause tells us whether there is something to come, that the communicative figure has not ended.

This is reminiscent of the "phatic communication" postulated by Bronisław Malinowski (Ogden & Richards, 1923), sometimes called "phatic communion".[2] It refers to expressions inviting us to "hold the line" (as they used to say on telephone switchboards), that is, they are related exclusively to maintaining social contact. Remarks include "Nice weather today, isn't it?", greetings and final remarks such as "OK" or "Bye". From a psychoanalytical perspective, they formulate a compromise – between recognising the temporary end of a relationship and the prospect of swift continuation. Such phrases could be assigned to the psychopathology of everyday life, structured like compromises. Yet an assessment of "pathological" cannot be reasonably advanced.

Even in the case of the musical pause, the question of whether there is continuation, whether the "line is held" is just that – a question, and the answer provided by the immediate recognition that music does not end but goes on is always rather consoling.

In silence something has come to an end and firmly independent initiative is required to take it up again. Therapeutic practice locates silence between the poles of "repelling secrecy" and mutual, pensive silence. In the case of the latter, phatic communion is particularly clear. Herein lies the silent recognition of mutuality which is virtually broken by its antithesis, the act of repelling. Defence, although usually understood as intrapsychic, reveals its communicative informative function even in silence. Defence ensures that the "line is cut off".

Quiet is another case entirely. In psychoanalysis, the expression "reverie" has become established, in overt allusion to religious devotion. Conversation is quiet, the spiritual world can come to the fore in its realisation; an entirely different conversation opens up in the quiet of prayer. Quiet has connections with the holy, the sacred; it has certain designated places such as cathedrals, but it is by no means reserved to this sphere. The noise of everyday life barely allows it. Ultimately, silence can be intensified as falling silent; then the proximity of death can be felt, as in Mahler's symphonies for instance. What exactly is happening in longer silences, during phases of reverie or devotional quiet, largely remains a mystery to scholarship, but it can be studied by conversation analysis (CA) (see Dreyer & Franzen, this volume).

Let us turn to "brief pauses", since they allow something to be expressed which is not without significance for therapeutic practice. Experienced clinicians occasionally maintain that "which is essential" plays out in silence, while others (Cremerius, 1969) have regarded silence as an expression of regression (oral component) or resistance (with a rather anal component of refusal, truculence, or retention). In this understanding, silence articulates yearning for a return to the earliest childhood experience of wordless communication, expresses helplessness, or the desire for control. Classical drive theory offered a coherent frame of reference for this phenomenon too. Motivated by drives, silence was the *opposite* of conversation (see Chapter 8).

Lane et al. (2002) provide an extensive survey of the importance of silence as described by psychoanalytical authors from Balint and Bollas to Langs and Winnicott, drawing on Freud. Whereas Freud recognised in silence in particular a form of (anally retentive) resistance, the later authors clearly approached silence as a form of communication – of sadness, barely articulable feelings, yearning. Hence Lane et al. (2002) can honour silence as an "intrinsic element" of all conversations. Patients are said to be silent due to the abovementioned motivations, but the therapist's silence is examined as a "tool" (p. 1102), as part of interventionist practice; it is not recognised that this division may well do justice to silence, but not to pauses.

Relational psychoanalysis offered different frames of reference. Silence was seen not so much as a drive derivative but as an *element* of communication (Gale & Sanchez, 2005). This conceptual change from pauses as *opposites* to *elements* of conversation is where CA provides helpful insights for clinical conversations in the treatment room.

CA makes visible via empirical observation of therapeutic conversations something that psychoanalysis describes via more global concepts. In the best case, CA allows us to see which details of conversation constitute "intuition". Empathy is of course not something one has on tap; sometimes one can turn it on, sometimes one is deaf and dull – and CA with its love of details seeks to find possible reasons in the conversation. Speaking must take place so that "the case" can appear thematizable[3]; the receptive "organ" of hovering attention can be located in the communication's environment; we think of something while listening. The result of thinking and contemplating with ideas one has to that end, must be realised as contributions to the therapeutic conversation. Or we would know nothing of them and they would remain lost to it. If one observes a conversation very closely one can pleasingly recognise both the "dance of insight" (Buchholz & Reich, 2015) and fine grades of spoken rhythm (Buchholz & Dittmann, 2017; Buchholz, Spiekerman, & Kächele, 2015; Harrison, 2013).

Psychoanalysts combine music theory (Rose, 2004), descriptions of musical experience and concepts (Sand & Levin, 1992) or history (Cheshire, 1996) or of family relations (Feder, 1981). Thus, *receptive* aspects of experiencing music become subtly describable. However, there is the *productive* side: how and in what fashion music is *created* in the concert hall: how it comes about, how it is made. It is the productive side that makes countertransference a valuable tool. Experiencing (in) the therapeutic session could and should thus be complemented by investigation of the "score"; here, the score is the transcription. In conversation it follows the "performance". It allows a reader familiar with the few diacritic signs to "hear" or internally reconstruct conversational detail, to understand how receptive experience is produced. To a significant degree experiencing reacts to conversational events going unnoticed. The musical aesthetic of therapeutic dialogue ("dance", prosody, rhythm) can be made accessible by careful transcription (Buchholz, 2014). Pauses are a *part* of communicative practice, not its antithesis. Gale and Sanchez (2005) suggest demystifying silence by regarding it as an "essential ally of speech in the therapeutic process". As allies in the therapeutic process, I want to examine their significance by transcriptions of the CEMPP study.[4]

Slip: "fall out a questionnaire"

A fourth cognitive-behavioral session begins thus:

```
(10.00) (squeaking noises))
P: so these question::aires: (-) they are
always very difficult to fall out (1.2) a to fill
out h h h h ((nasal))
T: What err:: what [do you find =
P: =↑ [.hh ((laughing)) I FIND
IT SO SO SHTREN (.) SO ↑STRESSFUL because I
always think
I can't judge that.
```

The patient has to fill out a form she received in the previous sessions and begins the session by commenting on this task. A psychoanalytic ear perceives her slip ("to fall out") as a condensation of "to fill out" and "to fall out" and wonders how fitting such an interpretation might be. The small pause for 1.2 sec. following the slip might provide some indication. Compared with the abovementioned points on the organisation of turn taking, this pause is unusually long. Its significance is quite clear, since it is followed by a "self-initiated self-repair" (Schegloff, 2013). Unlike when self-repairs are initiated by others, here the patient has noticed her mistake independently and corrected herself.

The patient was able to correct herself because on the basis of "my mind is with you" (MMWY), as Harvey Sacks & Jefferson (1992/1995) named this presupposition of talk, she was listening to herself in the same way as the therapist might have listened to her. This process of listening to oneself (with the other's ears) would require the same neuronal processing time of 0.6 sec. as when one is listening to someone else who says something so unexpected that one *cannot* plan one's own speech. In this interpretation, the patient would be surprised by her own slip; she listens to herself and now has to plan a new turn, also around 0.6 sec. in length. Both temporal components add up to 1.2 sec. According to this hypothesis, the length of the pause (in third line) is no coincidence.

Thinking about how what one says oneself sounds to the ear of the listener motivates "repair" on the part of the speaker (Schegloff, 2013). The same author (Schegloff, 2000) analyses slips the way Freud taught (Freud, 1901), namely that a conscious and an unconscious intention to speak are in conflict with one another and the slip is the result of their interference. Furthermore, Schegloff adds that a slip that goes uncommented has the tendency to cause further slips for the following one and a half minutes.[5] This is exactly what happens here. The effect of these slips runs through the entire therapy session (Alder, Brakemeier et al., 2016).

"Suicide suspects" – thirtieth session of a psychodynamic psychotherapy

Here there is a different example of a small pause after a slip. The patient sought therapy due to several suicidal crises which he had managed to conceal from his family and work colleagues. He begins to sense that concealing is not the solution but part of his problem, and asks both himself and the therapist whether anyone could empathise with such a gloomy and discouraging situation:

```
P: Now [the question arises again
T:      [Mhmh;
P: in me .h (--) can you understand; because
you have certainly had to deal with a lot of eh
.hhh self murder suspects eh:: (1.2) candidates
in your life and and .h (-) can you actually
imagine yourself in in
in: that situation? .hh (1.1) HOW ONE
or °mh::° HOW IT (.) actually can happen to
someone
THAT he is capable of taking such a= step. (.)
T: Mhmh;
P: And you don't have to answer that now
```

The pause following the small, very original slip ("self murder suspects") lasting 1.2 sec. is what interests us here. It prolongs "*Selbstmord*" (suicide) with "*Mordverdächtigen*" (murder suspect) and plays with the possibility of portraying oneself as a "murderer" and the therapist somewhat ironically as leading a kind of "murder inquiry". But the speaker cannot know for sure how the therapist takes such a transformation of role and situation and hence has to pause to think how the formulation might sound to the ear of the listener (MMWY supposition) before selecting a correction: "-*Kandidaten*" (suicide-candidate). Hence the slip is of *relevance to the relationship* between listener and speaker, as was the case with "falling out" a questionnaire. In conclusion: it is due to this relevance that there is a need to correct oneself.

The second pause of 3.3 sec. is worth analysing in terms of MMWY. The patient had not only asked the therapist a question, which with conditional relevance makes a response within said timeframe of 0.8 sec. expectable. The question itself is "face-threatening"; asking a therapist who has clearly helped him through a difficult time if he could "understand" after 30 sessions, implies doubt and has the potential to put the past collaboration in an entirely new, unfavourable light. On the other hand, it is via the course of therapy hitherto that the patient has developed the courage to ask such a question. That the therapist hesitated to answer (except for an information receipt token) would be determined by this experience of being doubted and the accompanying assessment; the pause is motivated by countertransference. We can see how countertransference is "made". According to the MMWY supposition, the patient now reacts to the pause himself, takes the pause as a conversational element, and initiates continuation by offering to relieve the burden on the therapist by saying he does not have to answer his question just "now". He could certainly assume that the therapist's pause is determined by his doubting question – in psychoanalytical terms, we can recognise how an "attack on linking" (Bion) is followed by feelings of guilt.

Thus, conversation analysis and psychoanalysis can supplement their considerations. The relevance of the slip for the relationship with the listener consists in the fact that the speaker must ask her/himself whether and to what extent s/he might have injured the listener's interests or self-definitions. To want to let questionnaires "fall out" would be to contradict the therapist; to implicitly depict the therapist as an "investigator" is to insult his professional self-understanding; to doubt him in face-threatening fashion is to become wracked with guilt. In all these cases, the speaker cannot know for sure how the listener might react, be it to a slip or to doubts. And thus he corrects the slip with the same self-initiation as in the case of the longer pause. The self-initiation of repair, in the case of slips and doubting questions, would thus be psychologically motivated, assuming my argumentation is valid. My analysis combines conversational form with psychological motivation.

First session of an analysis: "how shall I put it?"

I would first like to consider a few more examples in order to demonstrate that the small pause regularly occurs in the case of such self-initiated self-repairs within the same turn:

```
P: because I always have the feeling
   that she's a completely
   (1.4)((clicks tongue)) well                    ←
   should I say .h
   such a controlled person who hmhm who is
   quite not ve:ry or quite quite hard (.) has
   hardly any feelings then I think that she
   wouldn't understand it .h that she would find
   it ridiculous .h

(1.0)                                              ←

T: hm

(10.3)                                             ←

P: an=well for it's always like that
   when I (-) .h have or sEE someone in my
   circle of friends when I notice he is a
   bit (1.2) hhh yes how should I               ←
   put it .hh wh=wh=who
   is a bit weaker (---) I trEAt them the same
   way (---) do you understand? .hh and then I
   think th=that they perhaps do exactly the
   same thing I don't want that

(2.7)                                              ←
```

In this excerpt from an initial analytical session, five pauses (marked with arrows) can be observed. The first and the fourth pause show an embodied conflict in the speaker's speech planning: the clicking of the tongue slightly prolongs the 1.2-second pause and in both cases the "hesitation marker" (Chafe, 1985; Lerner, 2013) of "how should I put it" can be interpreted as an indicator of this conflict. Such an interpretation is coherent with a Freudian perspective.

However, everyday phrases like "how should I put it?" are more than "fillers" or delay. Recently the proposal was made to view such remarks in analogy to the pointing gesture. There is not only an "origo", as Karl Bühler (2011/1934) termed what psychoanalysts would call the "ego"; pointing gestures do not only point to a demonstratum in a physical environment:

> In all but the simplest situations, the identification of the demonstratum among the objects in the pointing cone identified by a pointing gesture is a complex reasoning process involving consideration of a number of additional aspects of the Interaction Situation.
> (Ginzburg & Poesio, 2016, p. 10)

The term "complex reasoning process", introduced by these linguistic authors is helpful to understand the transcript in the following way. In a non-face-to-face situation, as in psychoanalysis with a patient lying on a couch, phrases like "how should I put it?" can be conceptualised as functional equivalents to gestural pointings to a process of complex reasoning. This complexity originates out of "additional aspects of the interaction situation". A speaker using such phrases can be conceptualised as someone pointing to elements of his or her own complex reasoning that is being processed at the very moment. We see a large number of such verbal pointing gestures:

a) "well should I say",
b) "person who hmhm who is quite not ve:ry or quite quite hard",
c) "she would find it ridiculous",
d) "someone in my circle of friends when I notice he is a bit (1.2) hhh yes how should I put it .hh wh=wh=who is a bit weaker (---)"
e) "and then I think"
f) "do you understand?"

These elements have different conversational features. They include self-interruptions and self-corrections (b and d), judgements of one's own's actions attributed to another agent (as in c), questions addressed to the speaker himself as if he were another speaker (in a and d) and poses questions to the actual listener (as in f) and they document some self-observation of one's own thinking and speech-production process (as in e).

Taken together, these elements point to complex reasoning a) about other persons outside the treatment room; b) how one's own reasoning can be communicated to the therapist; c) how to describe other persons in a way that the therapist gets a clear picture (or not too clear a picture); and d) about the patient's concern how other persons (including the therapist) would describe the patient if they had the chance to listen when present (the MMWY dimension). All these aspects have a two-directional perspective: How the patient evaluates these people and how he imagines he is evaluated ("that she would find it ridiculous"). Directed to the therapist, we hear the question "do you understand?" Such a phrase is not simply used for stalling, but a meaningful event as part of "complex reasoning".

Complex reasoning here means that the patient makes use of both his actual origo-perspective and, at least, one displaced one. "Displacement of origo" is a term used by Bühler (2011/1934, p. 150ff.) The patient presents questions, judgements, assertions, and a general sense of agency to other agents as if they would not originate from herself but from other agents. This is what Bühler called "displacement of origo" and psychoanalysts would term "projection".

Psychoanalysts typically hear "one speaker" pointing to real or imagined objects while taking a "one-origo perspective" including a "one-person agency". In *this* perspective, what the patient does here is not only an everyday displacement but a pathological compartmentalisation of one's own feelings whereby undesired ones are falsely attributed to other agents. However, this has to be determined considering many other factors. It is quite clear that displacements of this kind are normal and everyday occurrences in non-pathological conversation.

However, the speech segment analysed here indicates that the speaker deals not only with "pointing to" from a single-origo agency but that he expects a response from the objects pointed to – complex reasoning results. It is as if a rich social world with questions, answers, evaluations, and mutual corrections creates a compulsion to consider too many viewpoints with a confusing effect. This, then, prevents the speaker from unifying these heterogenous voices into a more coherent narrative perspective. This defines what the therapeutic task then is. In order to grasp the complex reasoning, Ginzburg and Poesio (2016) propose one has to proceed from a traditional sequential analysis as is standard in CA to a more complex view so as to get the whole picture. This contributes to a deeper understanding of such patients' communicative style as they try to let the therapist participate in a confused life.

Two pauses follow in the middle of that segment. After a pause of one second indicating a transition-relevant place, the therapist expresses a "go-ahead" token. It is well known (Peräkylä, 2004) that one of the characteristic features of therapists' speech habits is to drop a "hm" into a pause – *as if* someone had just said something. The isolated "hm" can only have the function of placing the therapist in a "second position". The therapist behaves *as if* he was coupled to the complex reasoning of the patient.

But the therapist's attempt to restart does not succeed here. What follows is a pause of more than 10 seconds and then another of 1.2, again with "how should I put it" articulating confused speech planning. This interpretation is compatible with the Freudian supposition of "complex reasoning" describing a current conflict between two speech intentions. According to the MMWY supposition, the question ("you understand?") implies precisely how the speaker realises that and how she feels being listened to. This detail is a plea for being understood and consecutive doubt: can one's own "complex reasoning" be understood at all? How does it sound in the listener's ear?

"Nett ausziehen"[6] – *the pause as a temporary refusal to converse*

A patient talks about having met coincidentally a former girlfriend and become "so nervous" and then the therapist asks him:

```
T: why is she not allowed to notice that you
   are nervous? (-) mh?
P: .h I don't know I would have h .h yes I
   would either have the feeling that I am
   showing her a weakness and I .h I somehow
   don't want her to know that (---) that the
   whole thing gets me so agitated
(1.3)
P: yes of course we [did]n't
```

```
T:    [hm::]
P:    just nice- (1.2) she didn't exactly move
      out ((n German another understanding is
      possible: "undress")) in nice circumstances
      (-) and and=yes (-) but in the end we didn't
      get on with each other at all anymore
```

The pause of 1.3 sec is a transition-relevant place (TRP), after which the patient self-selects himself as the next speaker. Because it is a TRP, it has its own line in the transcript; it is *not* a pause *within* the turn. The pause is co-produced by both. The "yes" with which the patient prefaces his next utterance is an element that could only be made in a "second position" again. He starts this turn *as if* responding to a remark from the therapist attributing the pause to the therapist.

The following pause *within* the turn of 1.2 sec is followed by an abrupt end of his speech start, followed by a self-initiated self-repair. The ambiguity of the German "*ausziehen*" (to get undressed or to move out) has motivated the slip which was broken off at the last minute. Again, the patient "repairs" his utterance as this is relevant for the relationship.

Derivative comments – the therapist makes a slip

What about when it is the therapist committing slips or mistakes? A host of recent publications have advocated a benevolent approach to therapists' "mistakes". There has been little examination of the effects specific therapists' mistakes have on therapeutic conversation and how mistakes can be defined. The mistakes analysed here are easy to define; they are mistaken therapeutic utterances (for instance in relation to names) or they are manifest slips. I compare two selected examples, with regard to their influence on pauses.

The same patient as in the previous section relates around 70 seconds later that he hadn't wanted to tell his then girlfriend that he had failed the exam, since her reaction would have been one of *schadenfreude*, and continues:

```
P:    (...) I alw↑ays get so nervous (-) I hate it
      (.) so (.) much.
(-)
```

```
T: hm. (.) .h (-) [mm]  °°just well°° when you
P:                [HH]
T: have Len[a.
P:         [°Lisa° ]
(-)
P: [yes: when I] meet someone or other who I
(2.2)
T: [please excuse me hmhm]
P: yes m hm:: who I somehow know from the past
   I haven't seen for a while=and, (--) and
   with whom I've (---) yes well=#rather fallen
   out, (-) well o- or somehow n:-there was
   something or other and it hasn't been sorted
   out (-).h
```

The patient fights his "nervousness" ("I hate it") because it is not pleasant to encounter someone with whom one has "fallen out" or when something has not been "sorted out". This is the narrative and self-explanatory context.

The therapist commits a slip and incorrectly uses the name of the patient's *current* girlfriend. This adds another contextual element with explanatory power for his nervousness, suggesting that he perhaps gets nervous because he has different ties now. In doing so, the therapist cannot recall the current girlfriend's name and is quietly corrected by the patient; Lena becomes "°Lisa°". This is an other-initiated repair which *very seldom* is observed to be performed within the same turn. Hence a small pause *must* follow, after around a third of a second – the correction must be thought through. Both speakers then start talking at the same moment. The patient begins by continuing his contribution about meeting "someone or other" – when he hears that the therapist has once again committed a second slip by addressing the patient with the familiar "*Du*" form (in German the therapist says: "*Bitte entschuldige*"). This irritation causes the pause of 2.2 sec. It *must* be longer than the type of pause following self-initiated repairs analysed hitherto, since there is more complex reasoning to be done. What is the relevance of the momentary use of "*Du*" for the status of the relationship? How can one proceed? Should one comment? Pass over it?

The patient takes the latter option with his "Yes hm:"; a certain hesitation serves to extend the "hm::"-token, indicating again "complex reasoning". The subject of determining relevance alluded to by the slip cannot be processed thus; with "who I", the patient repeats how he started and the short internal pause in "(-) well o- or somehow n:-there" is followed by a derivative comment: "there was something or other and it hasn't been sorted out (-) .h" (ll. 151ff.). This utterance can be interpreted in two ways: a) in relation to the *narrative* theme of the encounter with people who have "fallen out" or b) as a *conversational* pointing to the therapist's two slips.[7] The way such a micro-event is processed has a decisive impact on the treatment process.

An important feature is that the length of pauses changes; there are other moments in which the relationship is regulated however. They can be recognised if we consider the course of the conversation:

1. Slip on the part of the therapist
2. Other-initiated correction
3. Small pause of ca. 0.3 sec
4. Overlap (both begin speaking at the same time)
5. Attempted repair with another slip
6. Somewhat longer pause (2.2) that comes *after* the therapist's attempt at repair
7. Normalising sequence
8. Derivative comment ("allusion")

Such a sequence escapes self-observation by the participants during the session. It occurs between an utterance requiring other-correction and an attempt by both participants to resolve the trouble that has arisen by returning to a thematic continuation of the conversation as if nothing had happened. Despite all attempts to repair the first mistake, it is not possible to resolve the trouble; the derivative comment indicates a clandestine fashion. If we summarise Steps 2 to 6 as "face work" (Goffman, 1955; Peräkylä, 2015), we can see how both parties cooperate in attempting to undo what would be face-threatening, without full success. What is repressed returns (Schegloff 2000). A reduced version of this scheme would look like this:

1. Therapist's slip
2. Face-saving activities by both participants
3. Normalising sequence
    a) Continuation of conversation after successful repair or
    b) Derivative comment after unsuccessful repair

The conversation can proceed in different ways, depending on the result of the normalising sequence; if it fails, it must be followed by a derivative comment or way of noticing the suppressed topic. By way of comparison, I want to test this scheme with another example in which the therapist commits a slip.

The time of the session – the therapist makes a mistake

In her first therapy session after two initial interviews a patient thinks about how therapy can bring things to the fore that she had suppressed, about what might come up, and whether she will cry – and then adds:

```
P: and I was also sca:red somehow about the
   number of hours(--) now it's three times
   a week it's like, (--) well; how should I
   put it (-) a bit of purpose to my life (--)
   i=i=if not purpo=>yes how should I put it,<
   .hh well it=is not where I go three times a
   week now apart from dancing .hh that would
   then be roughly the (--) this room would be
   the place I ehm .hh whe=where I spend the
   third largest amount of time;
T: yeah:;
  (6.6)
T: where would the first two be?
P: yes the first is at home at my place?
T: At home mh[mh]
P: [and] the second dancing.
  (--)
T: ah not at your boyfriend's;
P: no=no he lives at mine doesn't he
T: Oh of course ((chair creaks)) (-) he=e lives
   °°at your place°° now
  (0.3)
T: [yes?]
P: [yes:;]
T: mhmh (.) .hhh ((swallowing sound))
```

```
      (13.8)
   P: it' quite funny when I (--) well now but
      when I leave the session here then I was
      totally .hh then I felt good and then=I
      was in a good mood (--) but that only ever
      lasted as=l=long as (--) .h as how shall I
      put it (--) as the next session was not very
      close in sight again (1.2) I mean before the
      next one I am always completely nervous; and
      when this is over then I'm gonna be totally
      psyched
```

In clinical terminology, one could say that the patient is probing her ambivalence to therapy or that she is beginning to sense and wrestle with her tendency for transference. Comparison of the two therapeutic slips allows us to make another observation. Again, complex reasoning can be concluded from utterances like "how should I put it?" – the patient realises how her analysis would occupy an important time-place in her life. Thus, she compares where in the future she will spent most of her time.

Here, I consider this as contextualisation and omit what happens before the therapist's failure (not knowing that she lives together with her boyfriend) from a detailed analysis. Turning attention to what happens after this forgetting a relevant detail of the patient's life, the other initiated repair, and the following face-work one immediately recognises the above four-level scheme. It is worth considering the details.

The therapist has forgotten that the patient's boyfriend lives with her. She acknowledges this error by "Oh of course", and so one can assume that she could have been expected to know this from previous sessions.

At the same time, the slip is something more; the utterance contains a hidden interpretative tendency. While in the previous case the point was to remind the patient that he was in a different relationship (with Lena/Lisa), here the "oh" expresses surprise that something is "not normal". The patient does indeed mention "at mine" as the first place in which she spends most of her time, then her engagement in dancing, followed in her logic by the therapy sessions, in which she spends the "third largest amount of time". In the therapist's logic however, the boyfriend is missing, which would reduce therapy's demands on her time somewhat. At the same time, the patient is reminded of her boyfriend. Being reminded of something implies that one should have done or said it; not having thought about it makes such "forgetfulness" *look* like a slip on the part of the patient. The remark "he lives at mine" reverts this very relationship; the other-initiated repair is now face-threatening for the therapist – it is she who is mistaken. She readily admits that and repeats the utterance, becoming quieter as she does so.

Following the "time-to-think pause" of 0.3 sec, both start again with their speech overlapping, as in the previous example. Some interesting turn-taking follows: The therapist's "yes?" is morpho-syntactically a question, has the intonation of a question and demands – like a delayed "tag" – for consent, and the patient's "yes" has a falling, confirming intonation. The therapist quickly asks if her understanding that the boyfriend was living with the patient is correct. She receives confirmation, and then utters a brief "mhmh", breathes deeply, and swallows. This sequence of three turns is followed by a comparatively long pause of 13.8 seconds. The three turns can be read as an activity in which it seems like the therapist is looking for confirmation for her previous question "he lives at your place now" with "yes?" as an almost demanding "tag question".[8] Hence it *seems* that the therapist was not wrong at all. Because the therapist has now been "right", the patient cannot withhold her agreement, but she is placed under subtle pressure to confirm what the therapist has said. The patient has to take a stance on this manoeuvre and the long pause of 13.8 seconds is an example of complex reasoning about the preliminary interaction described here. Her subsequent remark that she feels good after leaving the session can be read as a derivative comment ("allusion") on this manoeuvre. Again, we have the schema of therapist's slip, face-saving activities, normalising sequence, and derivative comment; the last step indicating that the conflict is not solved. What happens after the pause can be understood again as allusive commentary to the preliminary interaction. The patient tells the therapist that she feels good leaving a session – which can be heard as double meaning: confirming the work done in the session with relief *and* as a relief to leave the session. This second, rather critical, meaning of her statement is then continued with the statement that she has difficulties when the time of the next meeting approaches. She presents this more critical attitude in a kind of "symptomatic" speech, again prefaced by her "how shall I put it?" phrase of complex reasoning. In psychoanalytic terms this indicates her actual conflict at the beginning analysis. However, the conversation analytic approach presented here points to the relational dimension; the therapist provides his current contribution which should not be overlooked (Thomä, 1984).

Conclusion

I analysed various examples of pauses in therapeutic dialogues; the focus was on pauses induced by slips followed by self-initiated repair after a characteristic length of pause of 1.2 seconds. People listen to how they might be heard. In case of slips with relevance to the ongoing relationship correcting activities follow in order to "re-pair" the relationship with their interlocutor. The conversationalist's "pairing", affiliation, and common ground, is restored. However, such "re-pairing" would be just one potential activity.

Slips by therapists receive different treatment by each participant. They are quickly followed by face-saving activities and normalising tendencies. This, then, determines whether these activities have brought the conversation back on track or whether further derivative comments and longer pauses indicate that it cannot proceed yet. Patients' and therapists' slips produce different pauses; they are different in terms of length and of contextualisation and what follows the pause.

Pauses before self-initiated self-repairs in case of patients' slips pose no threat. They are part of conversational objects that can be pointed at and they are treated as being motivated. Motivations are to articulate a protest, produce witty turns of phrase, play with a transformed self- and object definition, point to conflict, or serve as euphemisms. The pauses virtually prove that the patient continues work.

Therapists' failures, however, have a more serious effect. They have a long-term negative impact on the patient's faith in the analytic endeavour if he discovers that the therapist was unable to remember relevant information, forgets for example names and hence the therapist's failure feeds serious doubts as to whether or to what extent the therapist really is "with me". This doubt, I propose, motivates repair activities transitioning into swift normalising – by both parties. For if doubts continued to be fed, the entire project of therapy would be called into question. Complex reasoning as a kind of cost-benefit calculation (is it worth continuing with the sessions?) might motivate the much longer pauses in such moments.

Appendix – original German transcripts

Slip – "fall out a questionnaire" ("Fragebogen ausfallen / ausfüllen)

```
(10.00) ((quietschende Geräusche))

P: also diese Fragebö::gen; (-) die sind schon
   immer sehr schwierig auszufalln (1.2) a
   auszufülln h h h h ((nasal))
T: was ä:: was [empfinden Sie als =
P: =↑[.hh ((lachend)) ICH FIND
DES SO SO ANSCH (.) SO ↑STRESSIG Weil ich mir
immer denk
ich kann das gar net so beurteilen.
```

"Suicide suspects" – "Selbst-Mord-Verdächtige"

```
P: da [taucht jetzt gleich wieder die Frage in
T:     [Mhmh;
P: mir auf .h (--) können Sie das begreifen;
   weil Sie ham's sicher mit sehr vielen äh
   .hhh Selbstmordverdächtigen äh:: (1.2)
   Kandidaten zu tun gehabt in Ihrem Leben
   und und .h (-) könn Sie sich in in in:
   die Situation tatsächlich reinversetzen?
   .hh (1.1) WIE MAN oder °mh::° WAS ES (.)
   tatsächlich in einem Menschen passieren
   kann dass er zu so=m Schritt fähig ist. (.)
T: Mhmh;
(3.3)
P: Und das brauch jetzt gar nicht beantwortet
   sein
```

First session of an analysis: "how should I put it?"

```
P: weil ich immer das Gefühl hab dass sie n
   total (1.4)                              ←
   ((Zungenschnalzen)) nu soll ich sagen .h
```

so n beherrschter Mensch ist die hmhm die
ziemlich weni:g oder ziemlich hart ist (.)
fast keine Gefühle hat dann denk ich mir
dass sie das .h nicht verstehen würde dass
sie das lächerlich fände .h

(1.0) ←

T: hm

(10.3) ←

P: un=na mir geht's immer so wenn ich wenn ich
   jemanden (-)
.h sEH oder jemanden in meinem Freundeskreis
hab wo ich
merke der is n bisschen **(1.2)** ←
hhh ja wie soll ich sagen
.hh d=d=der is n bisschen schwächer (---) den
beHAndel ich
auch so (---) verstehen Sie? .hh und dann denk
ich mir
d=dass die das vielleicht dann genauso machen
das will ich nich.

(2.7) ←

"Nett ausziehen" – the pause as a temporary refusal to converse

T: warum darf die das nicht merken dass Sie
   nervös sind? (-) mh?
P: .h weiß nich ich hätt da h .h ja ich hätte
   entweder das Gefühl dass ich ihr da ne
   Schwäche zeig und ich .h ich will dis
   irgendwie nicht dass sie weiß dass (---)
   dass mich das Ganze so aufregt
40 (1.3)
41 P: ja wir [ham] uns ja nich
42 T: [hm::]
43 P: gerade pleas- (1.2) Sie is ja nich
gerade unter netten Umständen ausgezogen (-)

und und=ja (-) sondern wir ham uns am Schluss
überhaupt nicht mehr verstanden,

Derivative comments – the therapist makes a slip

P: (…)ich werd da imm↑er so nervös (-) dis hass
(.) ich (.) so.
(-)
T: hm. (-) .h (-)[mm] °°nur mal so°° wenn Sie
die
P: [HH
T: Len[a haben
P: [°Lisa.°]
(-)
P: [ja: wenn ich] irgendjemand treff den ich
(2.2)
T: [bitte entschuldige hmhm]
P: ja m hm: den ich irgendwie von früher kenne
oder ich den länger nicht gesehn hab=und,
(--) und mit dem hab ich mich irgendwie (---
) ja so=#eher zerstritten, (-) also o- oder
irgendwie n:- da war irgendwas und dis wurde
nicht geklärt (-) .h

The time of the analysis – the therapist makes a mistake

P: und auch irgendwie vor der Anzahl der
Stunden hab ich auch n bisschen Schi:ss
(--) jetzt so dreimal die Woche dis is
dann so, (--) so; wie soll ich sagen (-)
so'ne Art Lebensinhalt (--) we=ne=nee nicht
Lebensi=>ja wie soll ich sagen,< .hh also
das=is kein wo ich dreimal die Woche hingehe
jetzt ausser Tanzen .hh das wär ja dann
ungefähr der (--)dieses Zimmer wär dann der
Ort ich am .hh wo=wo ich die drittmeiste
Zeit verbringe;

```
T: ja:;
(6.6)
T: wo steht die ersten beiden Male?
P: ja das erste Mal is bei mir Zuhause?
T: Zuhause mh[mh]
P:            [und] das zweite Mal beim Tanzen.
(--)
T: ach nicht beim Freund;
P: nein=nein der wohn ja bei mir
T: Ach stimmt ((Stuhlknatschen)) (-) d=der
   wohnt inzwischen °°bei Ihnen°°
(.)
T: [ja?]
P: [ja:;]
T: mhmh (.) .hhh ((Schluckgeräusch))
(13.8)
P: is ganz komisch wenn ich (--) also
   jetzt aber wenn ich aus der Stunde hier
   rausgegangen bin dann war ich total .hh
   dann gings mir gut und dann=war ich gut
   drauf (--)aber das hatt immer nur so=l=lange
   angehalten wie (--) .h wie soll ich sagen
   (--) wie nicht die nächste Stunde schon
   wieder ganz nah in Sicht war (1.2) also
   vor der nächsten bin ich dann immer total
   nervös; und wenn das dann wieder vorbei ist
   bin ich wieder total gut drauf,
```

Notes

1 I am indebted to Florian Dreyer for drawing my attention to a piece of music by John Cage that lasted 29 minutes at its premiere; it contained the composer's direction to play "as slow as possible". In Halberstadt, its duration was extended to 639 years and begun with a pause of one and a half years, from 5 September 2001 to 5 February 2003. Staging this temporal length as a "pause" allows the connection to be held for a small eternity; this is the essence of this particular performance. See http://www.aslsp.org/de/klangwechsel.html
2 Roman Jakobson (2010) considered the phatic function to be so essential that he expanded Bühler's Organon model (Bühler 2011/1934) accordingly.

3   The extent to which a case's construction depends on social-communicative practices (in court, in surgery, in adolescent welfare, in psychotherapy) preceding the respective theories that then arise is demonstrated by a volume (Bergmann, Dausendschön-Gay, and Oberzaucher, 2014) describing said practices in detail. Without such analysis, these practices remain part of the social unconsciousness.
4   CEMPP = Conversation analysis of empathy in the psychotherapy process. The project was managed by Horst Kächele and myself and with the generous support of the Köhlerstiftung. For full details cf. Buchholz (2016).
5   Two psychoanalysts (Kazanskaya & Kächele, 2000) commented on Schegloff's paper.
6   The German "*ausziehen*" can have two translations: to" undress somebody" or to "move out". Both meanings are appealed to here.
7   This double connection of analytical listening – to the conversational or to the narrative scenario – was identified as "derivative comment" in an earlier theory of psychotherapy technique. Others speak of "Hidden Conversation" (Langs, 2004; Smith, 1991), and the third ear (Theodor Reik) is rendered methodologically alert to derivative comments. In CA the term "allusion" or "allusive comments" is used (Alder 2016; Schegloff 1996).
8   "Tags" are those small utterances tagged on to a remark such as "isn't it", "eh?" etc. which seek the listener's agreement.

References

Alder, M.L. (2016). Dream-telling differences in psychotherapy: The dream as an allusion. *Language and Psychoanalysis*, 5(2), 19–26.

Alder, M.-L., Brakemeier, E.-L., Dittmann, M., Dreyer, F., & Buchholz, M. B. (2016). Fehlleistungen als Empathie-Chance – Die Gegenläufigkeit von "Projekten" der Patientin und der Therapeutin. *Psychotherapie Forum*, 21(1), 2–10.

Bergmann, J. R., Dausendschön-Gay, U., & Oberzaucher, F. (Eds.) (2014). *"Der fall". Studien zur epistemischen Praxis professionellen Handelns*. Bielefeld: Transcript-Verlag.

Buchholz, M. B. (2014). Patterns of empathy as embodied practice in clinical conversation — A musical dimension. *Frontiers in Psychology*, 5, 349.

Buchholz, M. B. (2016). Conversational errors and common ground activities in psychotherapy — Insights from conversation analysis. *International Journal of Psychological Studies*, 8(3), 134–153.

Buchholz, M. B., & Dittmann, M. M. (2017, June). Rhythm and Groove — Observing evenly hovering attention [Conference paper]. In: *Psychoanalytic Process Research Strategies IV* (M. B. Buchholz & H. Kächele, Organizers). Berlin: International Psychoanalytic University.

Buchholz, M. B., & Reich, U. (2015). Dancing insight. How a psychotherapist uses change of positioning in order to complement split-off areas of experience. *Chaos and Complexity Letters*, 8(2–3), 121–146.

Buchholz, M. B., Spiekermann, J., & Kächele, H. (2015). Rhythm and Blues — Amalie's 152nd session. From psychoanalysis to conversation and metaphor

analysis — And back again. *International Journal of Psycho-Analysis*, *96*(3), 877–910.
Bühler, K. (2011). *Theory of Language. The Representational Function of Language* (A. Eschbach Ed.,D. F. Goodwin, Trans.). Amsterdam, Philadelphia, PA: John Benjamins. (Original work published 1934).
Chafe, W. (1985). Some reasons for hesitating. In: D. Tannen & M. Saville-Troike (Eds.), *Perspectives on Silence* (pp. 77–89). Norwood, NJ: Ablex Publishing Corp.
Cheshire, N. M. (1996). The empire of the ear: Freud's problem with music. *International Journal of Psycho-Analysis*, *77*(6), 1127–1168.
Cremerius, J. (1969). Schweigen als Problem der psychoanalytischen Technik. *Jahrbuch der Psychoanalyse*, *6*, 69–103.
Feder, S. (1981). Gustav Mahler: The music of fratricide. *International Review of Psycho-Analysis*, *8*, 257–284.
Freud, S. (1901). The psychopathology of everyday life: Forgetting, slips of the tongue, bungled actions, superstitions and errors. In: J. Strachey (Ed.), *The Standard Edition of the Complete Psychological Works of Sigmund Freud* (Vol. 6). London: Hogarth Press, 1960.
Gale, J., & Sanchez, B. (2005). The meaning and function of silence in psychotherapy — With particular reference to a therapeutic community treatment programme. *Psychoanalytic Psychotherapy*, *19*(3), 205–220.
Ginzburg, J., & Poesio, M. (2016). Grammar is a system that characterizes talk in interaction. *Frontiers in Psychology*, *7*, 1–22.
Goffman, E. (1955). On face work. *Psychiatry*, *18*(3), 213–231.
Harrison, A. M. (2013). The sandwich model: The 'music and dance' of therapeutic action. *International Journal of Psycho-Analysis*, *95*(2), 313–340.
Jakobson, R. (2010). Linguistics and poetics. In: A. Jaworski & N. Coupland (Eds.), *The Discourse Reader* (2nd ed., pp. 48–54). London, New York: Routledge.
Kazanskaya, A., & Kächele, H. (2000). Kommentar Zu E. Schegloff: Das Wiederauftauchen des unterdrückten. *Psychotherapie & Sozialwissenschaft*, *2*(1), 30–33.
Lane, R. C., Koetting, M. G., & Bishop, J. (2002). Silence as communication in psychodynamic psychotherapy. *Clinical Psychology Review*, *22*(7), 1091–1104.
Langs, R. (2004). *Fundamentals of Adaptive Psychotherapy and Counselling*. Hampshire, New York: Palgrave Macmillan.
Lerner, G. H. (2013). On the place of hesitating in delicate formulations: A turn-constructional infrastructure for collaborative indiscretion. In: M. Hayashi, G. Raymond, & J. Sidnell (Eds.), *Studies in Interactional Sociolinguistics: Conversational Repair and Human Understanding* (Vol. 30, pp. 95–134). Cambridge, UK, New York: Cambridge University Press.
Ogden, D. K., & Richards, J. A. (1923). *Die Bedeutung der Bedeutung*. Frankfurt: Suhrkamp.
Peräkylä, A. (2004). Making links in psychoanalytic interpretations: A conversation analytical perspective. *Psychotherapy Research*, *14*(3), 289–307.
Peräkylä, A. (2015). From narcissism to face work: Two views on the self in social interaction. *AJS; American Journal of Sociology*, *121*(2), 445–474.

Rose, G. J. (2004). *Between Couch and Piano. Psychoanalysis, Music, Art and Neuroscience*. Hove/New York: Brunner-Routledge.

Sacks, H., & Jefferson, G. (1992/1995). *Lectures on Conversation*. Oxford: Basil Blackwell.

Sand, S., & Levin, R. (1992). Music and its relationship to dreams and the self. *Psychoanalysis and Contemporary Thought, 15*(2), 161–197.

Schegloff, E. A. (1996). Confirming allusions: Toward an empirical account of action. *American Journal of Sociology, 102*(1), 161–116.

Schegloff, E. A. (2000). Das Wiederauftauchen Des unterdrückten. *Psychotherapie & Sozialwissenschaft, 2*(1), 3–29.

Schegloff, E. A. (2013). Ten operations in self-initiated, same-turn repair. In: M. Hayashi, G. Raymond, & J. Sidnell (Eds.), *Studies in Interactional Sociolinguistics: Conversational Repair and Human Understanding* (Vol. 30, pp. 41–70). Cambridge, UK, New York: Cambridge University Press.

Smith, D. L. (1991). *Hidden Conversations. An Introduction to Communicative Psychoanalysis*. London/New York: Tavistock/Routledge.

Thomä, H. (1984). Der Beitrag des Psychoanalytikers zur Übertragung. *Psyche, 38*(1), 29–62.

Chapter 15

How to move on after silences
Addressing thought processes to restart conversation

Florian Dreyer and Michael M. Franzen[1]

Introduction[2]

A major aim of psychotherapy is to jointly find the right words for the patient's problems. Such a concept of therapy-as-communication has been formulated as "talking cure" (Freud & Breuer, 1895d). High levels of attentiveness to what has been said is one of the foundations of therapeutic interaction and "Conversation Analysis, as the study of talk-in-interaction, should therefore have much to say about psychotherapy" (Peräkylä, 2013, p. 551). CA findings can easily be implemented in clinical practice (Peräkylä, 2008). CA also directs the focus on material-bound analysis (Buchholz & Kächele, 2013) of what really happens in the consulting room.

The process of finding the right words in social interaction can be observed in speech (Brouwer, 2003; Oelschlaeger, 1999; Oelschlaeger & Damico, 2000; Rae, 2008) as well as bodily activities (Beattie & Coughlan, 1999; Hauser, 2014; Hayashi, 2003; Radford, 2009, 2010). Additionally, interlocutors need silences in conversation to process the co-constructed meaning of what has been said and to plan what they are saying next (Bögels, Magyari, & Levinson, 2015; Levinson & Torreira, 2015). CA points out different functions of silence in talk-in-interaction and draws a distinction between pauses, gaps and lapses on the basis of their position in turn taking (Hoey, 2015, 2017, 2018; Jefferson, 1988; Sacks, Schegloff, & Jefferson, 1974). Pauses occur before a turn is completed, gaps are described as silences at a transition-relevance place (TRP), the moment when the right to speak can be handed over. Sacks, Schegloff and Jefferson also point to lapses as a third function of silence in interaction:

"Discontinuities occur when, at some transition-relevance place, a current speaker has stopped, no speaker starts (or continues), and the ensuing space of non-talk constitutes itself as more than a gap – not a gap, but a lapse" (Sacks et al., 1974, p. 714).

Since our data only consists of transcribed audio recordings, we are unable to refer to multimodal displays of understanding of the participants (mutual gaze, gestures and movement or posture (Bowleg, Valera, Teti, & Tschann, 2010; Goodwin, 1980; Mondada, 2011, 2014; Müller, 2019; Rossano, 2013)). Nevertheless, we will show how interlocutors address aspects of lapses in following utterances. Following Acheson's proposal, we decided to treat lapses as conversational turns:

> If we are to understand silences in all their complexity, not simply as a field for speech, and not merely as a zero-signifier when the speech object is missing from that field, the study of silences as events, like speech, like action, must become the rule.
> (Acheson, 2008, p. 551)

In psychotherapy lapses occur quite regularly and are not only treated as events but are part of clinical theory itself (Buchholz, 2016b, 2018; Hill et al., 2018; Levitt, 2001b; Levitt, 2001a; Sharpley, Munro, & Elly, 2005). In our chapter we will apply the aforementioned material-bound analysis to lapses that occur after a patient reports a personal problem.

Data

The transcripts of therapeutic interactions are part of the CEMPP project (Conversation Analysis of Empathy in Psychotherapy Process Research) which is conducted at the International Psychoanalytic University (IPU) in Berlin. All 45 sessions stem from the Munich psychotherapy study (Huber & Klug, 2016), were transcribed in GAT 2 (Selting et al., 2009, 2011) and subsequently analyzed using Atlas.ti (ATLAS.ti Scientific Software Development GmbH, 2017).

We employed a GREP search (Global search for a Regular Expression and Print out matched lines) in Atlas.ti to search our data corpus for adequate silences and subsequently rechecked whether the transcribed silence is indeed found in the original audio file of the session. Our search was limited to silences longer than 30 seconds. Afterwards we checked in the transcripts whether the silence was indeed a lapse. This left us with 53 lapses longer than 30 seconds, out of which we chose 5 examples to illustrate our RLRI model.

All examples were translated and simplified.[3] In the appendix we provide a fine-grained German transcript adhering to the aforementioned GAT 2-conventions. We hope this helps readers to better understand our analysis.

Method

In one of his first "Lectures on conversation" (fall 1964) Harvey Sacks introduces the notion of "rules of conversational sequence" (Sacks, 1995, p. 4) which govern the succession of different turns in talk. Using transcripts he starts to make "objects that get used to make up ranges of activities" (Sacks, 1995, p. 11) visible. This idea, heavily inspired by the ethnomethodology of Harold Garfinkel (Bergmann, 1981; Garfinkel, 1967), was the foundation of CA. Conversation analysts first try to describe a "distinctive bit of behavior in social interaction" (Sidnell, 2013, p. 78) in its conversational context. While searching for similar instances of such bits of interaction the researcher starts to form a system, suitable to explain the sequences of talk. A detailed description of single examples is combined with an analysis of the reoccurring patterns. The analysis of the conversation thereby follows what Sacks, Schegloff and Jefferson describe as the "central methodological resource" (Sacks et al., 1974, p. 728) of CA, namely that a speaker not only reacts to a prior utterance, but simultaneously displays his or her understanding of this prior utterance. These mutual displays of understanding form the basis for further analysis. CA therefore turns to what has been said after an utterance, in order to understand the utterance in its sequential context.

Analysis

Even though we developed our model in the process of analyzing the ensuing examples, here we will briefly describe it in advance. This enables our readers to conduct the material-bound analysis for themselves while following our line of thoughts.

Our excerpts start with a problem report by the patients containing communicative cues for uncertainty like small pauses, self-interruptions, hesitation markers or word searches. Following this report and potential

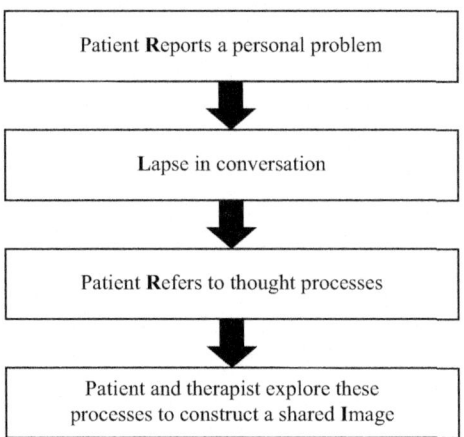

Figure 15.1 RLRI model.

primary interjections (Norrick, 2009) a lapse in conversation occurs. After the lapse the patients refer to thought processes during the lapse to restart the conversation. Conversational cues would be: "I wonder", "I just think about", "I ponder on", etc. The last step in our model involves the joint expansion of the thought processes that have been made accountable for the therapist. Both patient and therapist jointly evaluate the consequences of the thought processes and construct a shared image (see Figure 15.1).

Results

Excerpt 1[4]

Our first example is taken from a forty-ninth psychoanalytic session with a male therapist and a female patient. The patient speaks about her current problems, being in a long-distance relationship and simultaneously having a demanding job, therefore not being able to have a conversation about her relationship with her partner. The therapist takes up this tension and shifts it toward the notion of different parties pulling and dragging the patient in different directions. Additionally he brings in the patient's parents, who supposedly weren't able to have such conversations.

```
01    P:    Well it surely isn't enough,
02    T:    Mhmh
03    P:    to conduct such a conversation as we
```

04		did yesterday during the car journey, or so.
05	T:	Mhmh, aha
06	P:	Well that, that doesn't work. There are, well I
07		realize it for myself, I (--) try to make an effort but I
08		do not manage to do it. (--) Well I (1.0) I somehow
09		appease it, (-) because the topic on the phone,
10	T:	Aha (--)
11	P:	Mm! (9.5) so this contact with him per se (.)
12		well that, that (.) I would need that (--).
13	T:	Mhmh
14		(17.4)
15	P:	Yes, the danger, you are absolutely right about
16		that. It really was back then like that here now
17		again. (1.0) Everybody again (.) dives into his/her
18		own life and that this emotional and what has (--)
19		been there (---) is again being pushed away for
20		now.
21	T:	Mhmh
22		(96.5)

The patient starts with a clear statement (l. 01–04) about a current style of conversation with her partner while evaluating it negatively (Günthner, 2002). She thereby projects a difficulty which is elaborated further in lines 06–09. The therapist utters continuers which can be understood as "actions displaying [the] recipient's understanding that an extended turn at talk is in progress but not yet complete" (Goodwin, 1986, p. 207). He appears to expect the formerly mentioned explanation of the difficulty. The patient tries to restart her utterance several times, which can either be due to internal difficulties of the speaker, or, as Goodwin hypothesized, can also function interactively and demonstrate the competence of the speaker to construct sentences that are oriented to appropriately by a recipient" (Goodwin, 1980, p. 294). Since the patient speaks about her efforts to start a conversation, her struggling to pursue her own line of talk, the stumbling form of what has been said, mirrors its content. After a pause of 17.4 seconds the patient starts to shift between tenses. She mentions a `danger` (l. 15), links it to a former utterance of the therapist, and continues with a short insertion in past tense (`was`, l. 16) combined with `back then`, only to abruptly shift back into present tense with `here now again` (l. 16–17). She concludes her sentence by telling that two things are `being pushed away`, something `emotional` and something else that `has been there` (l. 18–19), which is not elaborated any further and a long lapse of 96.5 seconds occurs. Uncertainty is being displayed through:

- turn restarts and stumbling (l. 06–09)
- ellipsis (l. 08)
- tense shifting (l. 15–20)

After the lapse the conversation proceeds as follows:

```
-> 23  P:   Strangely I have to think about it
            again right
   24       now, because you just brought up my
            parents,
   25       when we children had to gather
            together when
   26       (1.7) they first (.) disclosed that
            (1.2) well they
   27       somehow would have separated bedrooms
            right
   28       now.
   29  T:   Mhmh
   30       (1.3)
   31  P:   And ehm (2.1) that this year we would
            simply
```

```
32              go on vacation separately.
33      T:      Mhmh (3.2) is this picture for you (-)
34      P:      Yes, it it it just now came somehow,
                the
35              whole time in fact.
36      T:      Yes, ah yes
```

In her first utterance after the long lapse the patient starts to speak about her thoughts, thereby converting her mental processes to a "conversational object" (Buchholz, 2016a, p. 135), thus making it observable. The evaluative Strangely (l. 23) and the reference to the recency (right now, l. 23–24) of the following utterance qualifies the reuptake of the conversation as a pre-announcement projecting the patient's understanding of what will be said next. In addition to this well-known projective feature of pre-announcements, we want to propose that both the evaluative and the temporal components obtain additional characteristics, when occurring after long lapses. They act as pivotal elements in the talk, being on the one hand clearly connected to and shaping what follows next. On the other hand they retrospectively attribute meaning to the lapse. Attributing meaning to the lapse is done in a second way – by punctuation (Bateson & Jackson, 1964). The patient addresses the therapist as cause of her thoughts and therefore as cause of a segment that starts way before the lapse (I have to think about (l. 23) and because you just brought up l. 24).

Since the evaluative Strangely (l. 23) not only acts as an indicator for a following announcement, but also displays the patient's understanding of the lapse as anomalous and potentially problematic, her following narration also opens up a space for a possible repair of the lapse. The therapist continues with an elliptical is this picture for you (l. 33), to which the patient responds with the utterance: yes, it it it just now came somehow, the whole time in fact (l. 34–35). She agrees to the notion picture. The subsequent self-correction (Schegloff, Jefferson, & Sacks, 1977) specifies what the patient means by now (l. 24), namely the whole time (l. 35).

Keeping RLRI in mind, we first find the report of a personal problem with uncertainty markers before a long lapse occurs. The lapse is subsequently resolved by the transformation of the thought process into a conversational object and the belated expansion of this thought process over the whole lapse. From here on they jointly explore the image brought up after the long lapse.

Excerpt 2[5]

The second example is taken from the one-hundred-and-fifty-sixth session of a psychoanalytic psychotherapy with a male therapist and a female patient. The patient has her first session after two weeks of holidays and is late. She starts to speak about her fear of being dismissed by the therapist after she "left him alone" for two weeks and how she is afraid to take something for herself (e.g. two weeks off). She subsequently connects this anxiety to her difficulties with "reconnecting" to people (therapist, boyfriend) after not having seen them for a while and to her own feelings and fears of being abandoned. The following sequence then takes place:

```
      01  P:  In situations in which I felt pushed
              away or
      02      abandoned, it was rather that I
              somehow
      03      so, not always have said that I'm
              simply
      04      estranged so. Somehow so you've left me
      05      alone, now you have to regain my favor
      06      first, so to say.
      07  T:  Mhmh
      08          (21.4)
      09  P:  Hm
      10          (33.4)
->    11      I'm wondering right now why, whatever
      12      situation, why this reconnection is
              always
      13      that hard for me. But I assume that
              (1.2)
      14      uhm (2.0) simply has to do with me.
              Uhm
      15      (6.6) well that there is a feeling of
              (1.0)
      16      woundedness presumably. So (---)
              where I
```

```
17        (-) somehow this (.) where I somehow
18        retreat (1.2) and simply (---) like
          from a,
19        well (1.1) peeking out of a snail
          shell and say,
20        well now I have to check the situation
          first.
21        (1.8)
```

The patient starts her turn with the description of past situations (l. 01). She isn't pointing to one or more single events but rather generalizing over different instances. While describing her handling of such situations she addresses an unnamed other, who is to blame for leaving her alone. The first part of the segment is full of elements which downgrade the relevance of what just has been said (somehow (l. 02 and l. 04), simply (l. 03), so to say (l. 06)), leaving the impression that something difficult has just been projected. As in our first example, uncertainty is displayed. The therapist utters a continuer (l. 07) after which a first lapse of 21.4 seconds occurs. At this point the second example differs from the first. Even though we have a first lapse, the patient isn't taking up the next turn. Instead she utters a single hm (l. 09) after which another lapse of 33.4 seconds takes place. Norrick states that interjections, such as hm, "can stand alone as complete utterances, generally meant to index an internal state of the speaker" (Norrick, 2009, p. 876). In our excerpt the hm seems rather to index thought processes happening during the lapse. This is supported by the patient's reuptake with the words I'm wondering right now (l. 11). Again there is a pivotal pre-announcement, which is on the one hand linked to the lapse and on the other hand projecting an explanation of what the patient is wondering about.

She continues to refer to her difficulties in reconnecting, which she already mentioned in the beginning of the session. Whereas she earlier spoke about reconnecting to different people, in this segment the notion of reconnection (l. 12) isn't tied to a person anymore. This utterance may be heard as a comment on what is going on in the therapy right now, a lapse after which one has to "reconnect" to the conversation. Following this line of thought, the patient is wondering why it is so hard to reconnect to what has been said before. Alder (2016) describes this mixture of conversational and narrative level as allusive talk. The patient further elaborates this difficulty and her reactions to it, finally arriving at the image of "peeking out of a snail shell" (l. 19) which is shared by the therapist:

```
22   T:    So, in case you've been abandoned?
23   P:    Yes
24   T:    Mhmh
25         (3.4)
26         And maybe you also think (1.1) that the other
27         one, in this case me, might feel the same.
28   P:    Yes, mhmh.
29         (1.7)
30   T:    That I, so to speak, am sitting injured in the
31         snail shell and
32   P:    Mhmh
33         (3.3)
34   T:    Maybe I'm thinking, now you have to really
35         make an effort.
```

He reassures himself as to whether he understood the patient correctly (l. 22), to which she agrees (l. 23). After a pause (l. 25), he starts to add another understanding to the patient's former elaborations. He not only widens the scope of possible interpretations, but also adds another train of thought to what might have happened during the lapse. Thus, patient and therapist are retroactively co-constructing the thought processes during the lapse. Starting from line 26 the therapist starts to take over the patient's picture of peeking out of a snail shell (l. 19) and transforms it to sitting injured in the snail shell (l. 30–31), thereby bringing the patient's problems outside the therapy into the consulting room.

Excerpt 3[6]

After analyzing the first two excerpts quite extensively we briefly want two introduce a third transcript, to demonstrate another occurrence of RLRI. The example is taken from the one-hundred-and-fiftieth session of a psychoanalytic psychotherapy with a female therapist and a male patient. The patient explains how he had an encounter with his ex-girlfriend (Klara) some days before the session, during which she told him of her new love affair. In addition his application for a geriatric nurse training program was rejected.

```
      01  P:  I also think that the (-) so (2.1) it
                somehow
      02        already was clear to me, but not so
                (--) so err
      03        (-)so fast, that that that that I had
                this (1.1)
      04        erm (-) this idea that I could start
                this
      05        training. (1.0) I had high hopes that
                haven't
      06        had anything to do with this training,
                (.)
      07        so(-) so with this.
      08  T:  Hm
      09  P:  So, (-) of course these hopes had
                somehow a
      10        connection to Klara.
      11  T:  Mhmh, yes
      12  P:  And (.) I think that this, (.) well
                now it's just
      13        so (-) err (-) much clearer that, (-)
                heh (1.1)
      14        that this was tied together.
      15        (1.0)
      16  T:  Yes
      17        (106.6)
->    18  P:  In the moment I just ponder,
      19  T:  Mh
      20        (1.6)
      21  P:  What I told you in the beginning of
                the session,
      22        (1.6)
      23        with (---) my fear that I once more
                really get
```

```
24          on your nerves.
25    T:    Mhmh
26          (1.1)
27    P:    And (--) I just think about whether I,
            (-) or (-)
28          in this case I would just bring it up
            again. (.)
29          Whether I should have left it with
            that, so not
30          to mention it again.
```

(12 lines omitted)

```
43    T:    Yes, that's all right.
44    P:    Good!
45          (1.7)
46    T:    Hehe what is the problem,
47          (3.4)
48    T:    for you?
49    P:    Hm
50          (3.9)
51    T:    That was, that is in fact our task
            here.
52          That your fears or imaginations (1.0)
53          can be brought up together.
```

The patient starts by telling about two seemingly independent problems – the rejection by Klara and the rejection of his application, which are subsequently linked. Once more we find displays of uncertainty in his narration, namely turn restarts (l. 01 and l. 12), hesitation markers (l. 02 and l. 13), speech pauses or self-interruptions (l. 01–07, l. 12–14), word repetitions or stammering (l. 02, 1.0 3, l. 07, l. 13–14), downgrading in relevance (l. 01) and tense shifting (l. 01-07, l. 12–14). He tells a problematic story with a clear display of uncertainty to which the therapist responds with a simple yes (l. 16) before the long lapse occurs. In this example we find a lapse of nearly two minutes before the patient restarts the conversation with the described transformation of his thought processes to a conversational object. The point of reference, as in Excerpt 1, is an utterance made before the pause, this time by the patient himself. Toward the end of this example the therapist starts to explore the patient's `fear` (l. 23) and reassures the patient by re-evoking the image of jointly bringing up his `fears or imaginations` (l. 52).

Contrast I – lapse without preceding markers of uncertainty[7]

This excerpt is taken from the sixty-fifth session of a psychodynamic psychotherapy with a male therapist and a female patient. The patient talks about memories of her mother sharing potentially delicate information they had exchanged, with others. The patient links these aversive experiences, to past behavior where she kept experiences to herself or carefully examined others, before becoming talkative. Based on this experience, it was harmful to the patient when a friend, Sarah, behaved similarly (to the patient's mother), and told Carola (another friend) something the patient did not want Carola to know. This led the patient to doubt her friendship with the Sarah and made her an "alone fighter".

```
01    P:    And for that reason, I assume that
            this just
02          well, (1.1) this betrayal was,
03    T:    Yes
04    P:    Hurt me immensely.
05    T:    Yes
06    P:    Because I (2.1) didnt really expect it
            from sarah.
07    T:    Yes Mhmh.
08    P:    Because everyone else, doesn't matter
09          who they are, but not from Sarah.
10    T:    Yes
11    P:    Mhmh (1.9) mm yes
12          (74.3)
```

The patient formulates the problem (`hurt me immensely`, l. 05), this time without displaying uncertainty, as seen in Excerpts 1, 2 and 3. Instead the problem is presented with a judgmental evaluation of the other's action (`didnt really expect it from sarah`, l. 06). In terms of RLRI, we find one presupposition met (problem report), but not the other (uncertainty). The topic is mutually closed (`T: yes – P: mhmh (1.9) mm` yes, l. 10–11), as described in the minimal scheme of closings (Schegloff & Sacks, 1973), before the long lapse (l. 12) occurs.

```
       13   P:    (clears her throat)
       14         (8.1)
  ->   15         Mm yes apart from that nothing else
                  comes
       16         to my mind.
       17         (clears her throat)
       18         Hm
```

In lines 15–16 the patient actively rejects the continuation strategy proposed by RLRI. For her, there are no thought processes ready to be transformed into conversational objects (apart from that nothing else comes to my mind). She hands the task to restart the conversation over to the therapist. He accepts it and continues as such:

```
  19     T:    Yes (---) I just had to [think] about
               if you say,
  20     P:                             [mhmh  ]
  21           (1.6)
  22     T:    Betrayal, mistrust,
  23     P:    Mhmh,
  24     T:    Towards everyone, not towards Sarah,
               (1.7) how
  25           you actually feel about me. (2.6) I
               should be
  26           included in ‚everyone' 1.4)
```

After the patient's rejection of providing a transformed thought process, the therapist himself refers to a thought process (I just had to think about, l. 19). Additionally, his punctuation strategy links this lapse with an earlier utterance by the patient (if you say (1.6) Betrayal, mistrust, l. 19 and l. 22). He demonstrates potential consequences of the patient's utterance (I should be included in ‚everyone', l. 25–26), which transforms a personal problem into an interactional problem. At this moment RLRI starts anew, with the patient producing an utterance filled with uncertainty markers.

```
27  P:  Naw, (2.0) you are the third group.
        You are
28      standing on your own. No, (2.8) no I
        can
29      can't say it that way.
30  T:  Yes
31      (1.0)
32  P:  Naw, (1.2) mm.
33  T:  Mhmh
34      (5.6)
-> 35  P:  No, even here I think, m- as it was in
        the
36      beginning, when when I said somehow,
        (1.3) hm
37      I have difficulties talking.
38  T:  Yes
```

As RLRI assumes, the patient produces uncertainty by placing pauses-in-speech (l. 27–28) and stammering (no I can can't say, l. 28–29). After closing the topic mutually (l. 32–33), a lapse of 5.6 seconds follows (l. 34). Once more the patient refers to thought processes (I think, l. 35) but arrives at a punctuation (in the beginning, l. 35–36) instead of a shared image.

Contrast 2 – Transforming bodily sensations to conversational objects[8]

The first four examples demonstrate only one of the resources used by interactants in psychotherapy to restart their conversation. Another possible solution to do so, namely introducing bodily sensations, is presented in the following example. It is taken from a seventeenth session of a psychodynamic therapy with a male therapist and a male patient.

```
01  P:  Then the question how, (.) how could,
        (.) how
02      did it (--) end up like this? How (--)
        can a
03      life, (3.0) that started out so
        wonderful, how
```

04		can a life end like this somehow or continue
05		or go on. I consciously do not say end because,
06	T:	Mhmh
07	P:	Because I do not want that.
08	T:	Mhmh
09	P:	But (2.3) how did it end up like this? (3.6)
10		And I try to extract everything from our long
11		talks. (1.6) And and and (1.3) somehow I think
12		you⁹ should somehow figure it out why, (1.4)
13		why. (4.6) Nothing, no cases in the family
14		no (--) situations to deduce from. (1.2) That
15		there were severe depressions, which somehow
16		were hereditary or so
17	T:	Mhmh, mhmh, no [explanations.]
18	P:	............[Nothing,] no explanations
19	T:	No explanations (-) yes. Mhmh
20		(91.4)
-> 21	P:	Everything in me trembles
22	T:	Mhmh
23		(29.6)
24	P:	And nevertheless, the ride the ride to you
25		today, (2.3) somehow the whole day. (1.0) Counted
26		the hours till it was three o'clock, till I
27		could start driving and [°hh] could drive to you.
28	T:	..................................[Mhmh]

```
29            (12.1)
30   P:       Somehow in the (--) hope of driving to
              the doctor
31            who, [who ] heals the wound.
32   T:            [Mhmh]
33            (1.0)
34   T:       Who has thread and needle (1.6) and
              who can
35            close the wound. (1.6) Mhmh, such a
              picture I can
36            understand, I think.
```

After the long lapse (91.4 seconds) in line 20, the patient refers to a current, bodily sensation as a means to restart the talk, Everything in me trembles (l. 21). The therapist utters a minimal response (Mhmh, l. 22) and another lapse of 29.6 (l. 23) seconds occurs.

Semantically, this utterance is radically different from our previous examples where thought processes were mentioned. However, taking into consideration the notion: "The mind is inherently embodied" (Lakoff & Johnson, 1999, p. 3), using the body as a reference shows similarities to referring to thought processes. As the patient utters Everything in me trembles, she transforms an inner sensation to a conversational object, just as the patients in our first three examples did. Please note that we once more find speech pauses and self-interruptions (l. 01–05 and 09–16), word repetitions and stammering (l. 01–03, l. 11), downgrading in relevance (l. 04, l. 12, l. 15) before the lapse as well as the joint production of an image afterwards (the image of a doctor who, [who] heals the wound. (l. 30–31) and Who has thread and needle (l. 34)). Including embodied processes as potential point of reference enables the RLRI to function as a broader description of the processes around lapses. Due to limitations in chapter length we can only show one of these embodied examples. For our discussion we put "embodied" in brackets, to include the hypothesis that referring to bodily sensations might function on the same level as referring to thought processes, since it is ultimately a communicative display of externalization.

Discussion

In our chapter we have demonstrated a prototypical sequence in psychotherapeutic interaction in which lapses may be found. After (1) the patient reports a problem, (2) a lapse occurs. The patient (3) subsequently refers to (embodied) thought processes to restart the conversation. Eventually, (4) the participants jointly elaborate on these verbalized thought processes and construct a shared image.

Referring to these (embodied) thought processes to reestablish talk-in-interaction might function on two different levels. Buchholz (2016a) describes how mutually perceived objects around interlocutors find their way into the conversation while directing the joint attention (Scaife & Bruner, 1975; Tomasello & Todd, 1983) of both participants. This leads to the building of a common ground (Stalnaker, 2002) from which further conversation can be started. In contrast to this observation the patients in our examples do something else after the long lapses. They direct the joint attention to an entity only perceivable by themselves, their inner processes (thoughts or bodily sensations). This "epistemic imbalance" (Heritage, 2012, p. 32) leads to a further elaboration of a topic or a sequence. Or, as Heritage puts it, it "is sufficient to motivate and warrant a sequence of interaction that will be closed when the imbalance is acknowledged as equalized for all practical purposes" (Heritage, 2012, p. 32); the joint construction of an image aids in the compensation of this imbalance. We further propose that lapses can contribute to this imbalance, especially considering a classical psychoanalytic setting (patient lying on the couch, therapist sitting behind him) where the acquisition of mutual gaze is heavily impaired. Tomasello and Carpenter link gaze-following and joint attention to the concept of "shared intentionality". They propose that one of the reasons for its development is "for sharing psychological states with others, which seems to be present in nascent form from very early in human ontogeny as infants share emotional states with others in turn-taking sequences" (Tomasello & Carpenter, 2007, p. 124).

Speaking about one's (embodied) thought processes not only resolves the lapse but furthermore displays that the speaker was still involved in the therapeutic process, even though he or she didn't communicate it directly. As a consequence, addressing (embodied) thought processes after lapses is a means to retrospectively ensure shared intentionality.

Appendix

Transcript I – Excerpt I

```
01     P:      also es REICHT `auf jeden fall nicht-
02     T:      <<pp>hm_hm,>=
```

```
03    P:    =so_n geSPRÄCH zu ´führen wie wir_s
            gestern auf der <<p>Autofahrt
            getan haben <<creaky>[oder so-]>>
04    T:                   [hm_hm, ] a_ha,
06          (---)
07    P:    <<p><<all>also> KLAPPT nicht;> (--)
08          dass i? also Ich merk des auch bei
            MI:R,
09          ich °hh versUch mir ganz <<creaky>doll
            ´MÜhe zu geben;> (--)
10          aber es geLINGT mir dann auch nie;
            (--)
11          also <<creaky>ICH:->
12          (1.2)
13          ich WIEgel_s dann <<creaky>ab
            Irgendwie->
14          weil die theMA:tik am tEle[fon,]
15    T:                                [hm; ]
16    P:    <<p>?hm?hm;>
17          (9.5)
18          so diese beGEGnung an sIch mit I:hm;
19          <<p>also dass_dass->(.) das BRÄUCHT
            ich schOn;
20    T:    a_ha,
21          (17.4)
22    P:    ja die geFAHR dass;
23          da ham sie komPLETT recht-
24          <<creaky>des WAR auch wirklich damals
            so dass da nich jeder;>
            (1.0)
25          <<f>wIeder jEder in sein LEben>
            eintaucht;
26          un_dass dieses emotioNA:le-
27          das was (--) DA: war- (---)
28          ERSTmal ´wieder (---) wEggeschoben
            wird.
29    T:    hm_hm,
30          (96.5)
```

```
31    P:    <<all>ich muss jetzt kOmischerweise
            die gAnze zeit dran DENken;>
32          weil sie jetzt grAde meine ELtern
            angesprochen haben-
33          wo: (---) ↑wir kInder uns damals da
            verSAMmeln mussten als;
34          (1.7)
35          sie uns Erst <<creaky>offenBART haben
            dass->
36          (1.2)
37          dass sie jetz <<all>irgendwie
            getrennte> SCHLAFzimmer ha? hÄtten,
38    T:    hm_hm,
39          (1.3)
40    P:    UN:D_ähm;
41          (2.1)
42          <<p>dass wir dieses jahr auch einfach
            mal geTRENNT in urlaub
            fahren->
43    T:    hm_hm,
44          (3.2)
45          is `ihnen s_BILD,
46    P:    ja s_s_es KAM jetz grad.
47          <<all>bei mir die gAnze zeit
            EIgentlich schon,>=
48    T:    =ja:, (-) ah_ja;
```

Transcript 2 – Excerpt 2

```
01    P:    <<creaky>äh i_i> in sItuationen wo
            ICH-
02          mir `ABgeschoben oder;
03          verlAssen: `VORgekommen bin-
04          °h dA: war des schon Eher so dass ich:
            irgendwie so:-
05          wie ich immer gesagt hab FREMD `bin
            <<creaky>einfach->
```

```
06            also IRgendwie so:-
07            jetzt hast mich alLEIN gelassen,=
08            =jetzt musst du dir <<len>meine GUNST
              erst amal wieder (---)
09            äh:: (--) `erARbeiten
              <<creaky>sozusAgen->
10    T:      hm_hm,
11            (21.4)
12    P:      hm;
13            (33.4)
14            ich überlEge gerade waRUM,
15            in welcher situatIon auch IMmer,=
16            =mir dieses ANknüpfen immer wieder so
              schwEr fällt;
17            aber ich nehm AN des,
18            (1.2)
19    P:      äh::m-
20            (2.0)
21            hat EINfach, (---)
22            was (.) DAmit zu tun dass ich, (---)
23            äh:::-
24            (6.6)
25            `ja: dass dann ein geFÜHL von:-
26            (1.0)
27            verLETZTheit (.) wohl dA is:
              <<p>also->(---)
28            WO ich (.) In:s; (-)
29            <<all>wo ich mich irgendwie>
              zuRÜCKzieh;
30            (1.2)
31            und EINfach::, (--)
32            WIE so aus so_m:;
33            (1.1)
34            so_m `schnEckenhaus erstmal
              RAUSkucke;=
35            =und sag äh <<all>jetzt muss ich
              erstmal sehn wie hier so die>
              LAge ist;
```

```
36              (1.8)
37      T:      also für den ´fAll dass SIE verlassen
                worden sind.
38      P:      ja:,
39      T:      <<p>hm_hm,>
40              (3.4)
41              und vielleicht DENken sie ja auch,
42              (1.1)
43              dass es dem ANderen,=
44              =in dE:m fall MI:R, (-)
45              AUCH so ge[hen könnte.]
46      P:                 [´ja: ] (--) hm_hm,
47              (1.7)
48      T:      dass ich AUCH sozusagen; (-)
49              verLETZT im schnEckenhaus
                ´sit[ze und-]
50      P:          [hm_hm, ]
51              (3.3)
52      T:      <<p>jetz: vielleicht erstmal DENke->=
53              =<<pp>jetzt müssen sie Erstmal sich
                zIemlich ANstrengen.>
54      P:      hm_hm,
```

Transcript 3 – Excerpt 3

```
01      P:      ich: DENK_auch dass ich dIe: (--)
                also;
02              (2.1)
03              es war mir schOn n ↑BISschen ↓klar-=
04              =<<all>aber nich SO:,> (---)
05              <<creaky>so:> (--) so SCHNELL,
06              <<p><<all>dass dass dass> dass ich
                DIEse:-
07              (1.1)
08              hm- (--) vOrstellung <<stimmlos> dass
                ich diese> Ausbildung
                ANfangen könnte;
```

```
09            (1.0)
10            des hab ich mit_n mit_n (--) <<f>mit
              hOffnung beSETZT,>=
11            =die mit dieser AUSbildung gar nichts
              zu tUn haben; (---)
12            <<p>also (.) also mit diese:r->
13     T:     hm;
14     P:     also: (.) natÜrlich hOffnung die: in
              irgend nem zusammenhang noch
              mit der KLAra [standen;]
15     T:                   [hm_hm, ]
16     P:     [un:d] ich GLAUB dass des:- (-)
17     T:     [ja:;]
18     P:     also JETZT bin ich mir <<all>nur so;>
              (--)
19            ähm (--) viel Eher klar darüber dass:-
20            (1.0)
21            ((lacht kurz auf))
22            dass das damit zuSAMmenhängt;
23            (1.0)
24     T:     ja-
25            (115.7)
26     P:     ich überLEG jetzt grA:d-
27            (2.8)
28            das was ich Ihnen am (.) ANfang der
              stunde erzählt hAbe-
29            (1.7)
30            <<p>mit> (---) meiner befÜrCHtung dass
              ich Ihnen dann mal wieder
              doch sehr auf die NER[ven ge]hen
              könnte,
31     T:                          [˅hm    ]
32            (1.1)
33     P:     un::d (1.1) ich: (.) DENK jetzt grad
              drüber nach ob ich-
34            oder (-) in DEM fall,
35            <<p>würd ichs jetzt einfach
              An:sprechen nochmAl,> °hhh
```

```
36            ob ich's hätte lieber dabei
              <<f>beLASsen sollen;>
37            <<p>also nich nochmal des erWÄHnen;
              (12 lines ommited)
50      T:    <<f>`JA> <<p>des is schon in Ordnung;>
51      P:    <<p>gut>
52            (1.1)
53      T:    <<:-)>ha> °h was is da des `proBLEM
              dabei,
54            (3.4)
55            <<p>FÜR sie;>
56            (1.1)
57            <<p>hm;>
58            (4.1)
59            <<p>des war des is doch unsere>
              AUFgabe hier;
60            <<pp>dass wir> (---) ÄNGSte oder
              vOrstellungen von Ihnen,
61            (1.0)
62            äh: (-) zur SPRAche bringen;
```

Transcript 4 – Contrast I

```
01      P:    <<p>°h und aus DIEsem grund nehm ich
              an,=
02            dass mich DES jetzt eben so->
03            (1.1)
04            dieser <<lachend>verRat->
05      T:    <<f>ja->
06      P:    mich ´so: massIv geTROFfen [hat;=]
07      T:                               [ja:, ]
08      P:    =weil (-) ich den auch (2.1)
              eigentlich von sArah NICHT erwartet
              hät[te.  ]
09      T:       [ja:-] (-) [hm_hm,]
10      P:                  [in ] in meinem ´gAnzen
              Umfeld von JEdem Andern.
```

```
11            egal wie sie `hEißen von jedem;
12            aber NICHT von sArah.
13     T:     ja:;
14     P:     <<p>hm_hm,>
15            (1.9)
16            <<p>mja:,>
17            (74.3)
18            ((räuspert sich))
19            (8.1)
20            `mja: sonst fällt mir zu dem thema NIX
              mehr ein-
21            ((räuspert sich))
22            <<lachend>hm->
23     T:     ja- (---)
24            ich MUSste `grade drüber nAchden[ken ]
              wenn sie sagen-
25     P:                                    [<<p>hm_hm,>]
26            (1.6)
27     T:     verRAT,
28            MISStrauen-
29     P:     hm_hm,=
30     T:     =gegenüber JEdem.
31            <<p>SArah gegenüber,> (--)
32            NICHT.
33            (1.7)
34            wIe: (--) sIe das eigentlich MIR
              gegenüber empfInden.
35            (2.6)
36            ich müsste ja zu dem JEden-
37            AUCH dazugehÖren.
38            (1.4)
39     P:     ne:,
40            (2.0)
41            sie sind die DRITte gruppe;
42            sie <<lachend>STEHN für sich> allEine.
43            NEI:N,
44            (2.8)
```

```
45            NEI:N kann ´ich kann ich so nich
              sAgen;
46     T:     ja:?
47            (1.0)
48     P:     ne:,
49            (1.2)
50            ?hm?hm
51     T:     hm_hm,
52            (5.6)
53     P:     nEin ich glaube auch DA:,
54            so: so wie's auch am ANfang war-
55            wo? wo ich auch gesagt hab IRgendwie-
56            (1.3)
57            hm- h°
58            fällts mir auch SCHWE:R,
59            das REden;
60     T:     JA.
```

Transcript 5 – Contrast 2

```
01     P:     dann die frAge WIE,
02            wIe konnte` (.) wIe konnte es so (--)
              KOMmen;
03            wIe (--) wie kann ein LEben,
04            (3.0)
05            des: (.) sO ´TOLL (---) begOnnen hat-=
06            =wie kann ein leben <<creaky>so: (.)
              so:> (.) ENden irgendwo,=
07            =<<creaky>oder so WEIterlaufen oder-
              >°h
08            daHINlaufen- °hh
09            ich sag jetzt beWUSST nicht Enden;
10            [weil] des WILL ich <<stimmlos>auch
              nicht>
11     T:     [hm:,]
12            hm;
13     P:     Aber,
14            (2.3)
```

```
15          wie konnte es <<creaky>SO> kOmmen;
16          (3.6)
17          und aus unseren GANzen lAngen
            gesprÄchen-
18          (1.6)
19          versUch ich Alles RAUSzuziehen und_und
            und;
20          (1.3)
21          denk mir IrgendwO mÜsstest du doch
            <<creaky>da mal DRAUFkommen;>=
22          =waRUM-
23          (1.4)
24          wesHALB;
25          (4.6)
26          <<p>NICHTS>
27          keine FÄLle in der famIlie;
28          keine °hh (--) situaTIOnen die
            rÜckschließen könnten;
29          (1.2)
30          <<t>da GAB es stArke depressIonen;=
31          =und des: hat sich <<creaky>irgendwo
            verERBT oder so->
32    T:    ´hm_hm hm_hm,
33          keine erKLÄ[rungen,]
34    P:               [NICHTS ] <<creaky>keine
            erklÄrung->=
35    T:    =keine erKLÄrung.
36          <<stimmlos>ja> hm_hm,
37          (91.4)
38    P:    °hh <<p>alles in mir BE:BT->
39    T:    hm_hm-
40          (29.6)
41    P:    °hh und trOtzdem die FAHRT,
42          die ´FAHRT hEute zu Ihnen hIer-
43          (2.3)
44    P:       hhh° irgendwO: den gAnzen TA:G,
45          (1.0)
46          die stUnden gezÄhlt bis es: DREI Uhr war-
```

```
47            bis ich von zuhAuse LOSfahren konte,=
48            =und [°hh ] (--) und zu IHnen fahren
              konnte,
49    T:            [hm_hm,]
50            (12.1)
51    P:      irgendwO in der (1.1) in der HOFFnung,
52            zum ARZT zu fAhren de:r-
53            [der ] die WUNde heilt;
54    T:      [hm_hm,]
55            (1.0)
56            der NAdel und fAden hat,
57            (1.6)
58            <<p><<all>und der die ´wUnde wieder
              ZUmachen kann;>>
59            (1.6)
60            hm_hm,
61            so_n bIld_des °hh ich gut verSTEhen
              <<dim>kann dEnk ich.>
```

Notes

1 These authors contributed equally to this work.
2 We would like to thank Dennis Didinger for his comments to an earlier draft of this article.
3 In the data extracts a simplified version of the GAT 2 notation is used.

(.)	: micro pause, estimated, up to 0.2 sec. duration
(-), (--), (---)	: short (0.2-0.5 sec.), intermediary (0.5-0.8 sec.) and longer (0.8-1.0 sec.) pause
(2.4)	: measured pause of approximately 2.4 sec. duration
[ ] [ ]	: overlap and simultaneous talk

4 For a fine-grained German transcript, please go to the appendix, section "Transcript 1 – Excerpt 1."
5 For a fine-grained German transcript, please go to the appendix, section "Transcript 2 – Excerpt 2."
6 For a fine-grained German transcript, please go to the appendix, section "Transcript 3 – Excerpt 3."
7 For a fine-grained German transcript, please go to the appendix, section "Transcript 4 – Contrast 1."
8 For a fine-grained German transcript, please go to the appendix, section "Transcript 5 – Contrast 2."
9 This *you* is referring to the patient himself.

References

Acheson, K. (2008). Silence as Gesture: Rethinking the Nature of Communicative Silences. *Communication Theory*, *18*(4), 535–555. doi:10.1111/j.1468-2885.2008.00333.x.

Alder, M.-L. (2016). Dream-Telling Differences in Psychotherapy: The Dream as an Allusion. *Language and Psychoanalysis*, *5*(2), 19–26. doi:10.7565/landp.v5i2.1558.

ATLAS.ti Scientific Software Development GmbH. (2017). Atlas.Ti.

Bateson, G., & Jackson, D. (1964). Social Factors and Disorders of Communication. Some Varieties of Pathogenic Organization. *Research Publications - Association for Research in Nervous and Mental Disease*, *42*, 270–290.

Beattie, G., & Coughlan, J. (1999). An Experimental Investigation of the Role of Iconic Gestures in Lexical Access Using the Tip-of-the-Tongue Phenomenon. *British Journal of Psychology* (London, England: 1953), *90*(Pt 1), 35–56. https://doi.org/10.1348/000712699161251.

Bergmann, J. (1981). Ethnomethodologische Konversationsanalyse. In: P. Schröder & H. Steger (Eds.), *Jahrbuch des Instituts für Deutsche Sprache*: Vol. 1980. Dialogforschung (1st ed., pp. 9–52). Düsseldorf: Schwann.

Bogels, S., Magyari, L., & Levinson, S. C. (2015). Neural Signatures of Response Planning Occur Midway through an Incoming Question in Conversation. *Scientific Reports*, *5*, 1–11. doi:10.1038/srep12881.

Bowleg, L., Valera, P., Teti, M., & Tschann, J. M. (2010). Silences, Gestures, and Words: Nonverbal and Verbal Communication about HIV/AIDS and Condom Use in Black Heterosexual Relationships. *Health Communication*, *25*(1), 80–90. https://doi.org/10.1080/10410230903474019.

Brouwer, C. E. (2003). Word Searches in NNS-NS Interaction: Opportunities for Language Learning? *The Modern Language Journal*, *87*(4), 534–545. https://doi.org/10.1111/1540-4781.00206.

Buchholz, M. B., & Kächele, H. (2013). Conversation Analysis: A Powerful Tool for Psychoanalytic Practice and Psychotherapy Research. *Language and Psychoanalysis*, *2*(2), 4–30.

Buchholz, M. B. (2016a). Psychotherapy – Analyzing Conversation of Typical Problematic Situations (TPS). *Language and Psychoanalysis*, *5*(2), 11–18. doi:10.7565/landp.v5i2.1557.

Buchholz, M. B. (2016b). Conversational Errors and Common Ground Activities in Psychotherapy: Insights from Conversation Analysis. *International Journal of Psychological Studies*, *8*(3), 134–153. doi:10.5539/ijps.v8n3p134.

Buchholz, M. B. (2018). Kleine Theorie der Pause. *PSYCHE*, *72*(02), 91–121. https://doi.org/10.21706/ps-72-2-91

Freud, S., & Breuer, J. (Eds.) (1895d). *Studien über Hysterie. GW I.*

Garfinkel, H. (1967). *Studies in Ethnomethodology*. Englewood Cliffs, NJ: Prentice-Hall, Inc.

Goodwin, C. (1980). Restarts, Pauses, and the Achievement of a State of Mutual Gaze at Turn-Beginning. *Sociological Inquiry*, *50*(3–4), 272–302. doi:10.1111/j.1475-682X.1980.tb00023.x.

Goodwin, C. (1986). Between and within: Alternative Sequential Treatments of Continuers and Assessments. *Human Studies*, *9*(2–3), 205–217. doi:10.1007/BF00148127.

Günthner, S. (2002). Perspectivity in Reported Dialogues: The Contextualization of Evaluative Stances in Reconstructing Speech. In: C. F. Graumann (Ed.), *Human Cognitive Processing: Vol. 9. Perspective and Perspectivation in Discourse* (pp. 347–374). Amsterdamm, NY: Benjamins.

Hauser, E. (2014). Solution Strokes. *Gesture, 14*(3), 297–319.

Hayashi, M. (2003). Language and the Body as Resources for Collaborative Action: A Study of Word Searches in Japanese Conversation. *Research on Language & Social Interaction, 36*(2), 109–141. https://doi.org/10.1207/S15327973RLSI3602_2.

Heritage, J. (2012). The Epistemic Engine: Sequence Organization and Territories of Knowledge. *Research on Language and Social Interaction, 45*(1), 30–52. doi:10.1080/08351813.2012.646685.

Hill, C. E., Kline, K. V., O'Connor, S., Morales, K., Li, X., Kivlighan, D. M., & Hillman, J. (2018). Silence is Golden: A Mixed Methods Investigation of Silence in One Case of Psychodynamic Psychotherapy. Psychotherapy (Chicago, IL). Advance online publication; https://doi.org/10.1037/pst0000196.

Hoey, E. M. (2015). Lapses: How People Arrive at, and Deal With, Discontinuities in Talk. *Research on Language & Social Interaction, 48*(4), 430–453. https://doi.org/10.1080/08351813.2015.1090116.

Hoey, E. M. (2017). Lapse organization in interaction (Dissertation). Radboud University, Nijmegen.

Hoey, E. M. (2018). How Speakers Continue with Talk After a Lapse in Conversation. *Research on Language & Social Interaction, 51*(3), 329–346. https://doi.org/10.1080/08351813.2018.1485234.

Huber, D., & Klug, G. (2016). Münchner Psychotherapiestudie. *Psychotherapeut, 61*(6), 462–467. doi:10.1007/s00278-016-0139-7.

Jefferson, G. (1988). Preliminary Notes on a Possible Metric Which Provides for a 'Standard Maximum' Silence of Approximately One Second in Conversation. In: D. Roger & P. Bull (Eds.), *Conversation: An Interdisciplinary Perspective* (pp. 166–196). Clevedon, UK: Multilingual Matters.

Lakoff, G., & Johnson, M. (1999). *Philosophy in the Flesh: The Embodied Mind and Its Challenge to Western Thought*. New York, NY: Basic Books.

Levinson, S. C., & Torreira, F. (2015). Timing in Turn-Taking and Its Implications for Processing Models of Language. *Frontiers in Psychology, 6*. doi:10.3389/fpsyg.2015.00731.

Levitt, H. M. (2001a). Sounds of Silence in Psychotherapy: The Categorization of Clients' Pauses. *Psychotherapy Research : Journal of the Society for Psychotherapy Research, 11*(3), 295–309. doi:10.1080/713663985.

Levitt, H. M. (2001b). Clients' Experiences of Obstructive Silence: Integrating Conscious Reports and Analytic Theories. *Journal of Contemporary Psychotherapy, 31*(4), 221–244.

Mondada, L. (2011). Understanding as an Embodied, Situated and Sequential Achievement in Interaction. *Journal of Pragmatics, 43*(2), 542–552.

Mondada, L. (2014). Pointing, Talk, and the Bodies: Reference and Joint Attention as Embodied Interactional Achievements. In M. Seyfeddinipur & M. Gullberg (Eds.), *From Gesture in Conversation to Visible Action as Utterance: Essays in honor of Adam Kendon* (pp. 95–124). Amsterdam/Philadelphia: John Benjamins Publishing Company.

Müller, C. (2019). Metaphorizing as Embodied Interactivity: What Gesturing and Film Viewing Can Tell Us About an Ecological View on Metaphor. *Metaphor and Symbol, 34*(1), 61–79. https://doi.org/10.1080/10926488.2019.1591723.
Norrick, N. R. (2009). Interjections as Pragmatic Markers. *Journal of Pragmatics, 41*(5), 866–891. doi:10.1016/j.pragma.2008.08.005.
Oelschlaeger, M. L. (1999). Participation of a Conversation Partner in the Word Searches of a Person with Aphasia. *American Journal of Speech-Language Pathology, 8*(1), 62–71. https://doi.org/10.1044/1058-0360.0801.62.
Oelschlaeger, M. L., & Damico, J. S. (2000). Partnership in Conversation. *Journal of Communication Disorders, 33*(3), 205–225. https://doi.org/10.1016/S0021-9924(00)00019-8.
Peräkylä, A. (Ed.) (2008). *Conversation Analysis and Psychotherapy*. Cambridge, New York: Cambridge University Press.
Peräkylä, A. (2013). Conversation Analysis in Psychotherapy. In: J. Sidnell & T. Stivers (Eds.), *Blackwell Handbooks in Linguistics. The Handbook of Conversation Analysis* (1st ed., pp. 551–574). Malden, MA: Wiley-Blackwell.
Radford, J. (2009). Word Searches: On the Use of Verbal and Non-Verbal Resources during Classroom Talk. *Clinical Linguistics & Phonetics, 23*(8), 598–610. https://doi.org/10.1080/02699200902997491.
Radford, J. (2010). Adult Participation in Children's Word Searches: On the Use of Prompting, Hinting, and Supplying a Model. *Clinical Linguistics & Phonetics, 24*(2), 83–100. https://doi.org/10.3109/02699200903407149.
Rae, J. (2008). Lexical Substitution as a Therapeutic Resource. In: A. Peräkylä, C. Antaki, S. Vehviläinen, & I. Leudar (Eds.), *Conversation Analysis and Psychotherapy* (1st ed., pp. 62–79). Cambridge: Cambridge University Press.
Rossano, F. (2013). Gaze in Conversation. In: J. Sidnell & T. Stivers (Eds.), *Blackwell Handbooks in Linguistics. The Handbook of Conversation Analysis* (1st ed., pp. 308–329). Malden, MA: Wiley-Blackwell.
Sacks, H., & Jefferson, G. (Eds.). (1995). *Lectures on Conversation: Volume I* (1. published in one paperback vol). Oxford: Blackwell.
Sacks, H., Schegloff, E. A., & Jefferson, G. (1974). A Simplest Systematics for the Organization of Turn-Taking for Conversation. *Language, 50*(4), 696–735. doi:10.2307/412243.
Scaife, M., & Bruner, J. S. (1975). The Capacity for Joint Visual Attention in the Infant. *Nature, 253*(5489), 265–266.
Schegloff, E. A., Jefferson, G., & Sacks, H. (1977). The Preference for Self-Correction in the Organization of Repair in Conversation. *Language, 53*(2), 361–382. doi:10.2307/413107.
Schegloff, E. A., & Sacks, H. (1973). Opening up Closings. *Semiotica, 8*(4), 289–327.
Selting, M., Auer, P., Barth-Weingarten, D., Bergmann, J., Bergmann, P., Birkner, K., . . . Uhmann, S. (2009). Gesprächsanalytisches Transkriptionssystem 2 (GAT 2). *Gesprächsforschung : Online-Zeitschrift zur verbalen Interaktion, 10*(2009), 353–402.
Selting, M., Auer, P., Barth-Weingarten, D., Bergmann, J., Bergmann, P., & Birkner, K., Uhmann, S. (2011). A System for Transcribing Talk-In-Interaction: GAT 2 Translated and Adapted for English by Elizabeth Couper-Kuhlen and

Dagmar Barth-Weingarten. *Gesprächsforschung - Online-Zeitschrift zur Verbalen Interaktion, 12,* 1–51.

Sharpley, C. F., Munro, D. M., & Elly, M. J. (2005). Silence and Rapport during Initial Interviews. *Counselling Psychology Quarterly, 18*(2), 149–159. https://doi.org/10.1080/09515070500142189

Sidnell, J. (2013). Basic Conversation Analytic Methods. In: J. Sidnell & T. Stivers (Eds.), *Blackwell Handbooks in Linguistics. The Handbook of Conversation Analysis* (1st ed., pp. 77–98). Malden, MA: Wiley-Blackwell.

Stalnaker, R. (2002). Common Ground. *Linguistics and Philosophy, 25*(5/6), 701–721. doi:10.1023/A:1020867916902.

Tomasello, M., & Carpenter, M. (2007). Shared Intentionality. *Developmental Science, 10*(1), 121–125. doi:10.1111/j.1467-7687.2007.00573.x.

Tomasello, M., & Todd, J. (1983). Joint Attention and Lexical Acquisition Style. *First Language, 4*(12), 197–212. doi:10.1177/014272378300401202.

Chapter 16

The interaction order of silent moments in everyday life
Lapses as joint embodied achievements[1]

Anna Vatanen

Introduction

"Silence" can be defined and understood in countless ways. For instance, an individual can be described as silent – that is, not talkative; a situation can be characterized as silent – that is, not involving much talk; and a place or a space, such as a forest, can be thought of as being silent, and so forth. In contrast, "silence" is sometimes used to denote a moment of non-talk in an otherwise continuous conversation. Caution is thus needed as to what is actually meant when the words "silence" and "silent" are used. Even when referring to a silent moment in an interactional situation, precaution is essential, as there is considerable variation in the kinds of situations that exist. What is the focal activity in the situation, and what role does talking have in it? Who are the people involved, what are their relationships? (For an overview of different approaches to silence, see Hoey 2017, chap. 1.) These and many other issues are crucial in analyzing silences in interaction.

Another focal question is how to interpret the silence. What does it convey, what meaning is it given? Furthermore, it is also important to consider whether the interpretation of the silence is supplied by the participants themselves or by outsider analysts, as these may differ. In studies of psychoanalytic encounters, silence has been given many types of meanings and interpretations (see, e.g., Ronningstam, this volume), as Part II of the present volume shows – for instance, silence as resistance (Dimitrijević, this volume). Long silences can indeed be related to professional practice; for example, in psychotherapy sessions they may retroactively be construed as "contemplation" (Peräkylä et al. 2008). On occasions such as these, the institutional context is used to account for what is going on in the silence, and the absence of talk is understood in relation to that institutional activity (Levinson 1992).

The chosen research approach and methodology also have a crucial role in the kinds of phenomena that can be studied and the results the investigation may engender. Studying interactive situations with a method that allows for detailed and precise analyses of actual interaction – such as conversation analysis – affords fine-grained interpretations of when and how silent moments emerge as well as the ways in which they are used. When conversation analysis is used – as in the current study – the primary focus is on the participants' actual behavior, both vocal and embodied, in a given situation. The analysis aims to uncover the methods that the participants themselves use for making sense of what happens, and the meanings they ascribe to any given phenomenon. This kind of analysis may (or may not) engender discussions of issues such as identity, emotion, power, culture, and the like – issues that may be essential in psychoanalytic sessions, for instance.

In the current chapter, the issue of silence is approached from the viewpoint of interaction order in the context of casual conversations between friends and family members. Attention is paid to what the participants themselves publicly orient to and how they make sense of one another's behavior. The analysis is solely based on publicly observable vocal and visible behavior: the participants' talk, activities, movements, gestures, facial expressions, use of the environment, and so forth. Hence, the internal thought processes of the participants are beyond the scope of the analysis. The essential questions are: What is at stake at the moments of silence? What is the central activity in the overall situation? More specifically, how do participants shift from one phase or activity to the next – from talking to being silent, and from silence back again to talking?

Let us take an initial look at one of the examples of this study. Here Jaana (on the right) is telling a story to her sister Tuula (on the left), both of them sitting in Tuula's kitchen after finishing a meal. Once Jaana's story is potentially complete (l. 5), a silence emerges (l. 7). What happens during the silence is captured in stills from the video. (This extract will be analyzed in more detail below as Example 6. The later analysis, which contains more frames, uses the same numbering system. All data extracts comprise English translations of the data; original transcripts in Finnish are in the Appendix. Transcription symbols can be found in the Introduction to Part III in this volume.)

Figure 16.1 Frames of Example 1

Example 1 (Figure 16.1)
Sg 437, 57:35

```
01 Jaana: so that (she) then was able to put the little
02        sister in clean clo- ↑clothes, (0.4)
03        to day [care and, (.) [and, (.) all canvas shoes=
04 Tuula:        [mm           [yeah
05 Jaana: =and [all such #things#,
06 Tuula:      [°yeah°
07        (0.1) * (0.2) * (6.5) * (0.2) ((=7.0))
              *fr3    *fr4    *fr5
08 Jaana: .mth but it is (as you know) like they have that ((telling continues))
```

The above example shows how, at the beginning of the silent moment, which is to last for 7 seconds, Jaana gazes at Tuula (see Frame 3). Finding Tuula not gazing at her, Jaana quickly brings her gaze down (Fr. 4) and continues to gaze at the table for the duration of the silence, as does her sister (see Fr. 5). After the 7 seconds of joint being-together without talking, Jaana breaks the silence by continuing her telling (l. 8). Here the silence thus ends as one of the participants simply continues talking; there are no changes in the participants' bodily behavior prior to that. In other cases, on the other hand, the continuation of talk is preceded by certain embodied behaviors. (For a more detailed analysis of this and other instances of silent moments, see below.)

Understanding the ongoing activity is a central concern of the analyses described in the current chapter. Hence, even though they focus on mundane interactions between familiars, the chapter also has relevance for scholars interested in psychological phenomena and psychotherapy sessions, for instance. The analyses show that silent moments are closely connected to the actual situation and how it unfolds; they are not merely psychological phenomena or mental experiences of the individuals. Furthermore, it will be shown that the meaning and interpretation of each silence is created moment by moment in interaction, in collaboration between the participants. It is thus not possible to infer the meaning of a silence for instance by solely looking at its measurable characteristics such as length, as is sometimes done in certain research traditions. Instead, what any given moment of silence "means" is always a complex phenomenon, sensitive to local contingencies, with varied characteristics and interpretations.

What is also at issue in the present analysis is the question of the central activity of each situation. There are moments when talk may not have an important role, for instance some moments when family members are casually together. During these, the central activity may be watching television, petting a dog, having coffee, and so forth – it may even be mere co-presence. Thus the present analysis does not take talking itself as its starting point; instead, each occasion is analyzed individually to determine its unique characteristics as oriented to by the participants. The aim is to provide an empirical account of how the participants collaboratively create and transform the silent moments into recognizable social objects – the kinds of things they are for them.

Even in situations where people with familiar or intimate relationships have gathered together, the meaning of each silence may vary greatly. One of the most crucial factors is the exact position of the silent moment in the flow of conversation. These positions will be discussed next, and the precise focus of the present study will be described.

Background

In conversation analytic literature, silent moments that occur in conversations have been divided into three categories based on the specific point in a turn and sequence at which they occur (Sacks, Schegloff & Jefferson 1974). *Pause* is a silent moment within one speaker's turn before its projected completion, i.e., an intra-turn silence. *Gap*, on the other hand, occurs between two turns within a sequence. It is silence at a moment when a certain turn-at-talk is expected to occur, for instance, when a second pair-part (such as an answer) is expected after a first pair-part (such as a question) – i.e., it is an inter-turn silence. There is an extensive body of literature on gaps and the impact and meaning they may carry in conversation (e.g.,

Jefferson 1989, Kendrick & Torreira 2015, Mushin & Gardner 2009, Stivers et al. 2009). Lapses, in contrast, have been investigated much less. *Lapse* is a silent moment that may occur at a sequence ending when no specific turn is being expected and no one takes up the option to speak (Sacks et al. 1974). These silences do not "belong" to anyone: no one has been selected as the next speaker and no one has self-selected. It is thus everyone's and no one's responsibility to end the silence and resume talking again. At these moments, the turn-taking machinery (Sacks et al. 1974) provides no next speaker or next thing-to-do; the previous sequence has been completed, and often the topic has been exhausted. A silence emerging at the end of some course of action may be treated as constituting the completion of that sequence (Schegloff 2007: 137). It has also been noted that after these moments, the topic typically changes (Maynard 1980). The current study focuses on silent moments classified as lapses.

When faced with a lapse, the participants may have various orientations to the emerging silence – they may deal with it in three different ways, as shown by Hoey (2015). The participants may treat the silence as (1) "now relevant" and begin engaging with an activity that precludes simultaneous talking. They may also treat the silence as (2) "allowable", whereupon they orient to an alternative engagement such as watching television or eating. In this type of situation, talking is not even expected, as the focus is elsewhere and the lapse is occupied by another activity.[2] Participants may also orient to the lapse as (3) potentially problematic or awkward – in Hoey's (2015) words, as "the conspicuous absence of talk". This orientation is typically visible in the participants' embodied and/or vocal behavior during the lapse: they utilize behaviors such as bodily disengagement, certain embodied practices, or lexical resources such as particles to manage the lapse (see, e.g., Goffman 1963, 1967, Goodwin 1981, 1986, Hoey 2017). These devices show that participants may orient to the lapse as possibly problematic. Hence, whether the emerging silence is "allowable" or "awkward" is not predetermined by the analyst; instead, the interpretation is based on the participants' observable behavior during that silence.

When participants have a clearly available common activity at hand, they frequently transition between talking and being engaged in that activity. The local devices for achieving such transitions have been described for several activities such as students doing group work in classrooms (Szymanski 1999), friends playing video games (Mondada 2012), and family members watching television (Ergül 2016). Also, so-called "multiactivity" settings (see Haddington et al. 2014) often involve situations where participants "fill" silent moments by engaging in relevant non-talk activities, which are thus used to account for the silence. Furthermore, as is evident based on many of the chapters in the present volume, in the psychoanalytic therapy tradition, as well, silent moments are seen as having a specific function in themselves, and they do not necessarily need to be "filled" in with talk.

What have been studied much less are situations where the central activity is (ostensibly) talking, such as situations where a person visits a friend and they sit around a table, perhaps having a drink – such as the situations in the present study. The participants' roles and social relationships affect the expectations in the situation and how the participants deal with what may happen – and this can be analyzed based on their observable behavior. Most often in social situations continuous talk is normatively expected. What do participants then do when a lapse emerges? Three possible ways to orient to the silent moment were described above, based on Hoey's (2015) studies. The present chapter aims to provide a more detailed analysis of the participants' bodily behavior at the moment when a lapse emerges, and at the moment when talking is resumed again. As will be shown, in both instances, the participants' embodied orientation to the emerging lapse and the relevance of talking at that moment may be more or less shared; it may be reciprocated or not. An interesting question is how sharedness of orientation is achieved among the participants. And what happens if the embodied orientation is not shared at all but it remains unilateral throughout? In addition to analyzing bodily behavior, we will also observe the linguistic details of the participants' post-lapse talk, as it is indicative of the meaning they give to the silent moment.

Aligned with Acheson's (2008) exhortation "to study silences as situated, embodied practices", the present study thus investigates the ways in which silence is *created*, as a result of the participants' active behavior, and the kind of bodily behavior that leads to *being in silence* – and leads the way out of it. Silence is seen as a way of being in a social situation, not just as lack of talk (see also Vatanen, submitted). It will be shown that the different ways of being silent are jointly constructed by the participants in the actual situation.

Data and method

The data for this study consist of three hours of video-recorded, naturally occurring, everyday interactions between speakers of Finnish. While there is a rather widespread stereotype of Finns favoring silence in certain situations where speakers of other languages may favor talking (as described by, e.g., Lehtonen & Sajavaara 1985 and Sajavaara & Lehtonen 1997), the current study steps back from this generalized view of culture and interactional situations and examines specific types of silent moments as they actually occur in authentic spontaneous interaction.

Each recording in the data corpus involves two participants who know each other well. The data are naturalistic, which means that the events that were recorded – visits by a friend or a family member – would have taken place irrespective of the current study. In the videos, the participants are seated around a table in a kitchen or in adjacent armchairs in a living room. These participant configurations may have been influenced by the recording layout; however, such spatial organization is nevertheless natural in the given settings. At least seemingly, the situations are thus organized for sustained talk. At these moments, the participants are together mainly for the sake of interaction, and initially there seems to be a joint, normative commitment to socialize.

In the data, 130 lapses (no less than 2 seconds long) were identified. At these moments, the previous sequence of talk has been completed, and no specific turn is expected next. No one has been selected as the next speaker, and no one self-selects themselves. Instead, both participants remain silent. The data is analyzed using multimodal conversation analysis (Sidnell & Stivers 2013, Mondada 2016a; for conversation analysis in psychotherapy, see Peräkylä 2013). The sections below present close moment-by-moment sequential analyses of lapses, focusing on the participants' verbal and embodied conduct in the situated, material environment. The data fragments have been transcribed according to conversation analytic standards (Jefferson 2004). As regards embodied conduct, I follow the conventions developed by Mondada (2016b). For the most part, for ease of reading, still images taken from the videos have been inserted into the transcripts with a specification of their exact placement in the flow of interaction.

Let us now examine in more detail the ways in which participants enter into and navigate out of the emerging lapse, with their bodily behavior displaying their orientation to the lapse and the relevance of talk.

Entering into a lapse

How do participants in interaction enter into a lapse? What does "falling silent" actually look like? This section presents an analysis of the participants' embodiment and the multimodal resources they use in achieving the state of being in a lapse. As mentioned above, the participants' orientations, the gradual and sometimes even stepwise moving into and out of a lapse, are observable in their visible behavior – their gaze, face, body, and physical activities. It will be shown that entering into (and also moving out of) a lapse is a collaborative, joint interactional achievement. Sometimes, however, it may be unilateral. The data of the present study suggest that it is most common to enter the lapse jointly and to move out of it unilaterally, whereas unilateral entering and joint moving out are rare.

In his work on lapses in interaction, Hoey (2015) showed how participants may be misaligned with regard to whether the now-relevant thing is talking or being silent (and doing something else). His examples are from situations where participants have another activity with which they can engage (e.g., doing school assignments), instead of talking together. In my data, on the contrary, this is not the case. Instead, the main activity in the situation is the joint conversation. However, when faced with silence, participants may also utilize the local environment in order to create some other, ad hoc activities to turn to. Crucial questions for participants are thus: What do we do now? What is the relevant activity? In the following, I propose a detailed account of the participants' orientations to the now-relevant activity, especially as regards their embodied behavior.

Shared orientation

Most often, participants enter a lapse jointly, as was discussed above. Their embodied behavior shows a similar orientation to the situation: the preceding sequence is complete, and it is possible and allowable to lapse for a moment. The following fragment is an example of this. Here friends Aino (on the left) and Bea (on the right), sitting in Bea's kitchen having tea and snacks, are talking about a TV show they both have seen and jointly discuss what has happened in it. In lines 1 and 3, Bea reenacts the behavior of an actress in a certain scene (see Figure 16.2):

Example 2
Sg 377, 09:35

01 Bea: £so she [looks (then),£
02 Aino: [he heh

03 Bea: £this ended up l(h)ooking really good£ .hhh*
                                                 *fr1
04 Aino: °it is good. .nfff* oh my°
                      *fr2
05   (0.1) * (0.6) * (1.4) * (3.2) * (0.2) ((=5.5))
             *fr3   *fr4   *fr5   *fr6

When Bea finishes her reenactment of the scene (ll. 1, 3), both Aino and Bea smile and sustain mutual gaze (see Fr. 1). Aino then assesses Bea's telling of the TV show positively (l. 4), successfully ending the sequence. At the end of the assessment, she averts her gaze to her right, and her smile begins to fade away (Fr. 2). She then utters *oi oi* (translated here as "oh my"; l. 4), reduplicating the rare Finnish interjection *oi* which tends to occur in exclamations (ISK 2004, §856). *Oi oi* seems similar in function to the English *oh dear*, which, when occurring at post-sequence transitions, treats the prior sequence as finished and shows preparedness to move on (Hoey 2017: 58). After *oi oi*, Aino brings her teacup to her mouth and tilts it, preparing to

Figure 16.2 Frames of Example 2

drink (Fr. 3). Slightly over half a second of silence after Aino's *oi oi*, Bea has lowered her gaze to the cat in her lap (which she strokes throughout the fragment) and her smile has disappeared; Aino is drinking (Fr. 4). Both participants lower their heads exactly at the same time (cp. Fr. 3 and 4) and reset their faces (cp. Fr. 1 and 4), showing that their orientation shifts from being in a conversation to being in a lapse. In addition, they both look away from their co-participant at the possible sequence ending (see Fr. 2–4) and thus treat the sequence as effectively complete (Rossano 2012). After having taken the sip, Aino keeps the cup in her hand, gazing towards the table, whereas Bea continues to stroke the cat in her lap, looking at it (Fr. 5–6). In other words, entering into the lapse is achieved here jointly, with reciprocal orientations by the participants. This is the most common way in which silences emerge in everyday interactions. In the next section, we will examine cases where the participants' orientations are more unilateral.

Unilateral orientation

Participants' orientations to what to do now in interaction – to talk or not to talk, to be engaged or not – are not necessarily shared: one may be oriented to sustaining mutual orientation and engagement but the other withdraws bodily and orients to something else instead. However, this is relatively rare. Moreover, if the participants' orientations are not shared in the very beginning of the lapse, most often they will soon realign. This happens when one participant withdraws gaze and perhaps engages in another activity when one sequence ends and no talk follows. At this moment, the other participant – who, after talking has ceased, is still looking at her co-participant – soon adjusts to the co-participant's behavior by withdrawing gaze as well. In this way, the orientation to the lapse becomes shared. This is visible in the participants' gaze behavior and sometimes in their other embodiment as well.

Let us examine an example where the participants' orientations are unilateral at first but then become shared. In this data fragment, middle-aged sisters Tuula (on the left) and Jaana (on the right) spend time together in Tuula's kitchen, sitting at the table, Tuula holding her cat in her lap. Jaana is about to finish her telling about how things are nowadays in her profession (customer service). In line 1, she provides a generalized statement, gazing at Tuula, who gazes at the table (Fr. 1). Tuula provides a mildly affiliating response to Jaana's telling (l. 2), and a short lapse follows (l. 3) (see Figure 16.3):

Silent moments in everyday life 317

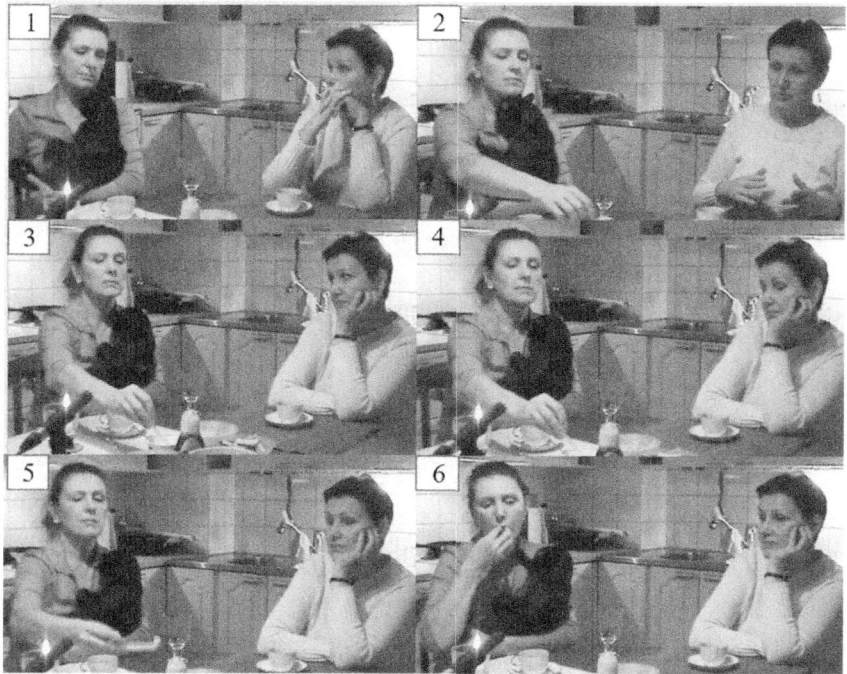

Figure 16.3 Frames of Example 3

Example 3
Sg 437, 1:08:59

```
01 Jaana: this is the present #t[ime (so)#.]
02 Tuula:                     [  i n d e ]ed;*
                                           *fr1

03        (1.2)
04 Jaana: so it is,* (0.2) such that:
              *fr2
05 Jaana: from this end in (and) from the [other end out,]*
06 Tuula:                                 [ mhm          ]*
                                                          *fr3
07        (0.2) * (0.5) * (5.6) * (1.0) ((=7.3))
               *fr4    *fr5    *fr6
```

During the short lapse in line 3, Tuula begins to take a slice of bell pepper, showing an interpretation of the prior sequence/topic as finished. She reaches for the pepper as Jaana continues her telling (l. 4, Fr. 2) by providing an additional (yet generalized) detail about the situation she has described. Jaana is about to complete her utterance (l. 5) as Tuula, in terminal overlap, acknowledges it minimally with the particle *mm* (l. 6; see Gardner 1997, Siitonen & Wahlberg 2015), again showing her orientation to the sequence/topic as complete. At this moment, Tuula is dipping the pepper, looking at it, while Jaana gazes at Tuula (Fr. 3). In other words, at the very beginning of the ensuing lapse, Jaana shows her engagement to continue the conversation (see Rossano 2012). However, after a micro pause (0.2 sec), Jaana withdraws by closing her eyes for a brief moment (0.5 sec; Fr. 4), after which she gazes at the table for several seconds (Fr. 5–6), until resuming talking again (data not shown here; how this lapse ends will be analyzed below in Ex. 5). For the duration of the lapse, Tuula dips and bites the pepper, gazing towards the table. That is, here the participants' orientations regarding whether to enter into a lapse or not are not immediately reciprocated but then one participant – here, Jaana – adjusts to the co-participant's behavior and embraces a similar orientation by withdrawing, too. In addition to the wholly shared orientation examined in Example 2, this maneuver too is a common way to enter into a lapse in everyday interaction.

In the next fragment, the participants' orientations to the lapse, as displayed by their embodied behavior, are non-reciprocated throughout the silence. In this case, friends Aino and Bea are talking about Bea's cat, who is in the kitchen with them. Bea has just told that for a period of time the cat was quieter than normally, after which Aino asks a question that implies some knowledge of the cat (l. 1). After a brief gap (l. 2), Bea responds (ll. 3–4) (see Figure 16.4):

Example 4
Sg 377, 21:00

```
01 Aino:  >hasn't he< ↑always been quite a growler.
02        (0.3)
03 Bea:   yeah I mean or I mean h(h)e is l(h)ik(h)e, .hh
04        £tells* about his things£?=
                *fr1
05 Aino:  =mm*
             *fr2
06        (2.1) * (1.6) * (0.2) ((=3.9))
                *fr3    *fr4
07 Bea:   but it really is tiring/annoying that …
```

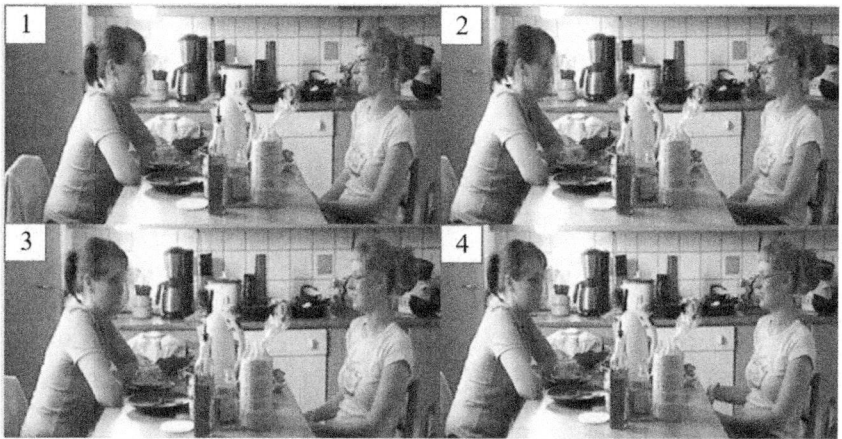

Figure 16.4 Frames of Example 4

At the end of Bea's response (l. 4), the participants hold mutual gaze (Fr. 1). While producing the weak acknowledgment token *mm* to Bea's response (l. 5; see Gardner 1997, Siitonen & Wahlberg 2015), Aino lowers her gaze, showing her orientation to the sequence as complete (Fr. 2; see Rossano 2012). A lapse follows, during which Aino keeps her gaze on the table while Bea keeps gazing at Aino (Fr. 3–4). Thus the participants' bodily orientation to the emerging lapse is non-reciprocated throughout its duration – even though they both remain silent and in that sense orient to that moment in a similar manner. After nearly 4 seconds of silence, Bea resumes talking by returning to the pre-lapse topic, indicating this with the connector *mut* "but". The sequence thus gets expanded, which, according to Rossano (2012: 239, 258–266), typically happens in situations where one participant shows an orientation to the sequence as not yet over by continuing to look at the co-participant.

This section showed different ways in which participants may create a silent moment. Let us now examine how they end the silence and resume the state of talking again.

Navigating out of a lapse

In terms of how to continue after a lapse, participants have three alternatives: they may move to end the interaction, continue with prior talk, or start something new (Hoey 2018). But how do they practically achieve the state of talking again? The current study focuses on the role and significance of the participants' embodied behavior *before* they resume talking. Here, again, the participants' orientations may be unilateral or shared. Let us first examine the former.

Unilateral orientation

Most often moving out of a lapse – that is, resuming talking – is performed by one of the participants only. There are two principal ways this happens. One is where one participant produces some embodied behavior during the lapse, and at the moment when that behavior's trajectory is about to reach its projectable completion, one of the participants (either the embodiment-producer or the co-participant) resumes talking. The second way is that the embodied orientation of the participants does not change at all – for instance, the participants remain not gazing at one another, staying still – and the lapse ends as one participant simply starts to talk. Let us first have a look at a case where there is a change in the embodiment first and talking comes only after it. Example 5 below features the same fragment as Example 3; the lapse (l. 7) has emerged after Tuula acknowledged Jaana's prior telling (not shown here; see Ex. 3 above). During the lapse, Jaana gazes at the table and remains still, while Tuula dips a slice of bell pepper and bites it, holding a cat in her lap (Fr. 5–6) (see Figure 16.5):

Example 5 (continuation of Example 3)
Sg 437, 1:08:59

```
07       (0.2) * (0.5) * (5.6) * (1.0) ((=7.3))
              *fr4    *fr5    *fr6
08 Jaana: *.mthh (0.2) so like before;* (.) um, (.) #w-# (it) was just
         *fr7                        *fr8
09       such #that#, (0.8) the staff knew each other and …
```

During the lapse in this fragment, Tuula dips the pepper and bites it twice (Fr. 5–6). When she has put the final piece of pepper in her mouth (Fr. 6) and places her hand again around the cat (Fr. 7–8), Jaana resumes talking. During the lapse Jaana gazes at the table, slightly towards Tuula, and is thus able to monitor Tuula's bodily conduct – at least with peripheral vision – and to project the end of Tuula's embodied activity's trajectory. Jaana then strategically positions the onset of further talk at the moment when the visible bodily behavior of her co-participant ends (for a more

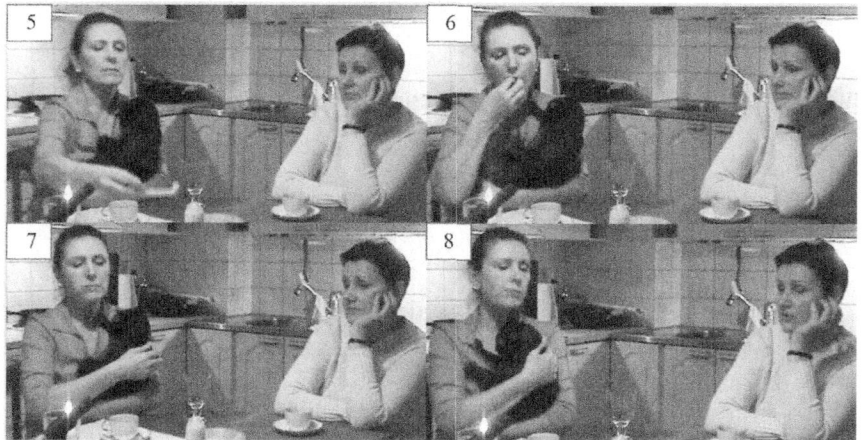

Figure 16.5 Frames of Example 5

detailed analysis of this phenomenon, see Vatanen 2018). However, when she begins to talk, Jaana is still looking at the table and does not change her bodily behavior at that point yet (Fr. 7–8). As regards linguistic detail, she ties her utterance to the pre-lapse topic using the conjunction *et* "so", thus in a way sequentially deleting the lapse.

In the next case, the unilateral moving out of the lapse is accomplished just with talk; embodiment plays no role here. Sometimes this happens when the silence is occupied by some activity that does not have a projectable ending, such as stroking a cat (see Ex. 2). However, the same may happen also during silences where there is no activity going on at all. This is what we observe in the next example (which was briefly introduced above as Ex. 1). Here Jaana is telling her sister Tuula about an incident in the past. Tuula responds to Jaana's telling (ll. 1–3, 5) solely with the acknowledgment tokens *mm*, *nii* (l. 4; *nii* translated here as "yeah") and the inhaled *joo* ("yeah"; l. 6) which implicates closure (Sorjonen 2001). Then, a lapse follows (l. 7) (see Figure 16.6):

Example 6
Sg 437, 57:35

01 Jaana: so that (she) then was able to put the little
02   sister in clean clo- *↑clothes, (0.4)
              *fr1

Figure 16.6 Frames of Example 6

```
03            to day* [care and, (.) [and, (.) all* canvas shoes=
              *T gaze down              *fr2
04 Tuula:           [mm           [yeah
05 Jaana: =and [all such #things#,
06 Tuula:         [°yeah°
07         (0.1) * (0.2) * (6.5) * (0.2) ((=7.0))
                 *fr3   *fr4   *fr5
08 Jaana: .mth but it is (as you know) like they have that (.)
09         .hhhhhh Tommi as well* so #he:# he is also such,
                              *fr6
10         .hh (0.4) @he is a very #sensible# pe*rson?@
                                              *fr7
```

Having gazed at Jaana during the telling (Fr. 1), Tuula brings her gaze down at a moment that is close to a possible end of the story (l. 3, Fr. 2) and does not look up for a while. Jaana finishes her telling, and for a couple tenths of a second, still gazes at Tuula (Fr. 3, l. 7), bodily orienting to continuing the conversation. She then brings her gaze down (Fr. 4), after which both participants look at the table for almost 7 seconds (see Fr. 5 which has no visible differences compared to Fr. 4; see Vatanen, submitted, for a closer analysis of cases like this). Both sisters still gazing down, Jaana starts another telling. Embodiment plays no role here, as the lapse ends when Jaana simply starts talking, keeping her gaze down at that moment. She looks up at Tuula only when saying the name of the main-character-to-be of the current telling (l. 9, Fr. 6), and her sister looks at her only at the end of line 10, at the end of Tuula's animated reported speech (see Fr. 7). Jaana's post-lapse turn begins with the conjunction *mut* "but", by which she ties her turn back to what went on before the lapse, bringing in a contrastive view to the topic.

After these unilateral endings of lapses, let us now examine a case where the participants start talking simultaneously after a lapse and their orientation is thus shared.

Shared orientation

As shown above, most often moving out of a lapse is performed by one of the participants only: the participant resumes talking, sometimes positioning the onset of talk at the projectable ending of some embodied activity. Occasionally it happens, though, that both participants do the same thing simultaneously, even after lengthy silences. Let us examine one such example. Here again friends Aino and Bea talk about cats. Aino, stroking one of Bea's cats, enquires about the duration of time that Bea housed a cat called Mirre (l. 1). Bea responds (ll. 2–3, 5) and Aino acknowledges the response with the particle *nii* (l. 4). Then, a lapse follows (l. 6) (see Figure 16.7):

Example 7
Sg 377, 19:00

```
01 Aino:  for ↑how long did you have Mirre then.*
                                                *fr1
02 Bea:   for ↑quite long (he was).=he was probably
03        (-) (1.0) a bit over a month at lea[st.
04 Aino:                                     [yeah
05 Bea:   about one and a half months* or something?
                                     *fr2
```

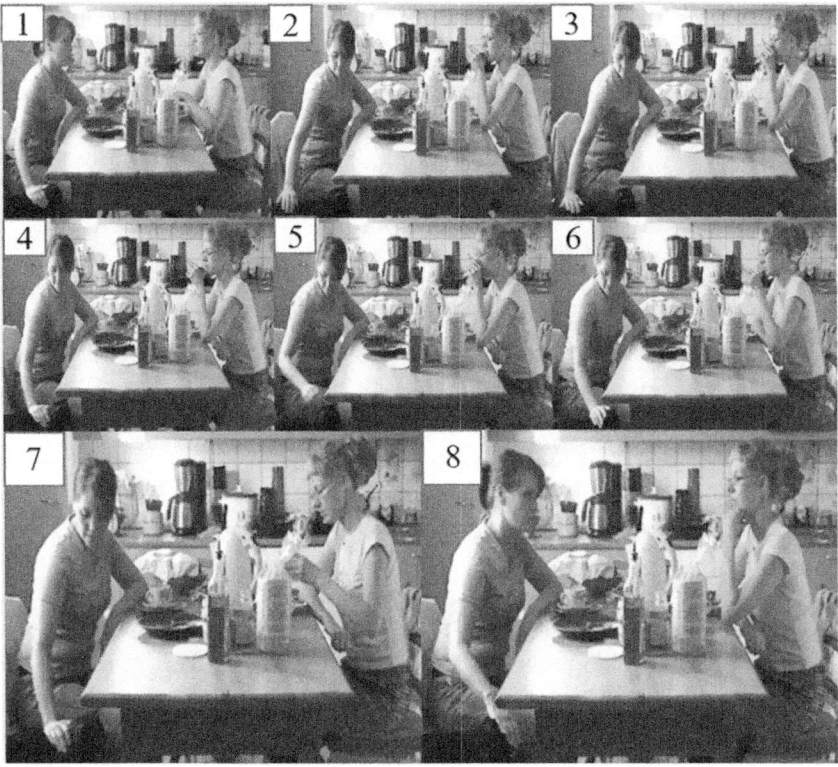

Figure 16.7 Frames of Example 7

```
06        (2.0) * (1.5) * (2.4) * (0.5) * (0.1) ((=6.5))
               *fr3    *fr4    *fr5    *fr6
07 Bea:   *a[nd also otherwise;]
          *fr7
08 Aino:   [our Viljo has      b]ecome old because
09         he has started to sleep secretly* on the couch,
                                           *fr8
10 Bea:   ↑a↓ww::.
```

At the end of Aino's initial question (l. 1), the participants have mutual gaze (Fr. 1). After Bea has started her response, Aino shifts her gaze to the cat she is stroking, while Bea sustains her gaze direction towards Aino (Fr. 2). During the ensuing lapse, which lasts for 6.5 seconds (l. 6), Aino continuously strokes the cat, looking at it, while Bea takes two sips from her teacup, resting her elbows on the table and gazing towards Aino (or the window behind her; Fr. 3–5). After Bea has taken the second sip, she removes her elbow from the table and begins to put her teacup on the table, gazing down at the cup (Fr. 6–7). When she is about to complete that movement, both participants start talking virtually simultaneously (ll. 7–8), Bea continuing the prior topic (using the conjunction *ja* "and" and the clitic particle *ki* "also" to tie back to the previous talk) and Aino starting a new one (using full clauses with full referential elements such as *meiän Viljo* "our Viljo"). Bea soon discontinues her talk while Aino goes on to complete the announcement about her dog. At the end of Aino's turn, the participants reach mutual gaze again (l. 9, Fr. 8).

The remarkable simultaneous start is temporally related to the moment when Bea's embodied activity is about to reach its completion. As I have already mentioned and as we saw in a previous case (Ex. 5; see also Vatanen 2018), this is quite common: even though the participants do not seem to look at each other, they can use their peripheral vision to monitor one another's activities and time the beginning of their talk to coincide with the projected end of the trajectory of an ongoing embodied activity. In the case above, then, both the participant producing the embodiment and her co-participant use the same moment to resume talking again, which attests to the strategic use of that particular moment. Even though the participants move out of the lapse individually, both starting to talk at the same time about different topics – and thus the ending of the lapse is not, strictly speaking, accomplished collaboratively – their individual orientations to that particular moment is shared in the instant. The relationship between unilateral and shared orientations appears thus more like a continuum, not a dichotomy.

Conclusions and discussion

By using conversation analytic methodology, the present study has aimed to uncover some of the mechanisms of lapses – silent moments after a possible sequence ending – in everyday interactions between familiars. Examining how the participants themselves create and organize such moments with their bodily behavior revealed that both entering into a lapse and moving out of it can be accomplished either by both participants together via a shared orientation to (and understanding of) that moment, or by one of the participants only, in which situation their orientations are unilateral. As regards the participants' vocal behavior, however, their orientations are naturally shared, as neither of them talks at that moment. Furthermore, the participants' embodied orientations during the lapse may be unilateral in the beginning and become shared only later. Based on the data, it was claimed that the most common way to enter into a lapse is via shared bodily orientations, whereas moving out of a lapse is most often accomplished by one of the participants only. The analysis above also showed how the sharedness of orientation is practically achieved moment by moment among the participants.

I also hope to have demonstrated that in order to understand what actually happens in interaction, it is essential to use video recordings. As is clear from the analyses above, the participants' embodiment – their gaze, body posture, bodily activities, etc. – has a crucial role in understanding and interpreting silences. Conversation analysts would also insist that claims on what a silence "tells" or "means" should be grounded in what the participants themselves publicly orient to, in order to avoid discrepancies in analysts' and participants' perspectives. If not supported by direct evidence in the data, conversation analysts would not argue that a silence indicates things like disinterest in the co-participant, for instance (but compare Bonacchi, this volume).

This study has not primarily dealt with what the silences would possibly mean for the participants or tell about their inner thinking. As the conversation analytic method is strictly based on what can be observed from the video recording, it provides relatively little insight into what the participants think or feel during the interaction – unless they explicitly speak about their internal experiences, or their orientation becomes otherwise visible in the interaction. To reach a more thorough understanding of the meaning and interpretation of, for instance, silent moments in interaction, it would be useful to combine conversation analysis with other types of qualitative methods. One possibility is to exploit the Interpersonal Process Recall method (IPR) (for an example of how to combine these two methods, see Janusz, Józefik & Peräkylä 2018). IPR is a qualitative research method that is used to investigate participants' internal experiences (Elliott 1986, Larsen, Flesaker & Stege 2008). When IPR is used, the focused-on interactional situation, such as a therapy session, is video-recorded. Very soon after the session, the video recording is shown to the participants, who are then individually interviewed concerning their inner thoughts and feelings during specific moments in the session. What is achieved with this procedure are not facts but rather the participant's discursively created reconstruction of what is thought and felt, as the participant remembers it.

As has been shown in the present chapter, conversation analytic investigation reveals the particularities of how interaction is structured and how, for instance, silent moments emerge and are created in collaboration between participants. To combine the methods of CA and IPR for studying silences, there seem to be at least two opportunities. One is to first identify certain silent moments using CA, after which the IPR methods could be used to investigate the meanings that the participants themselves give to those moments, how they felt and what they thought during them. Or, alternatively, certain types of meaningful silent moments could first be identified with the IPR interviews, and CA could then be used to analyze how those moments were co-created and co-organized in interaction moment by moment, possibly comparing them to other types of silences. In whichever way the two methods were combined, I see their joint use to be potentially highly beneficial for understanding the structures and characteristics of silent moments in interaction – and perhaps many other kinds of interactional phenomena as well. Hence it could be explored how the actual interactions, such as therapy sessions, realize (or do not realize) the concepts and ideas expressed in clinical and professional theories (Peräkylä & Vehviläinen 2003) – for instance, concerning silence.

The present study suggests that entering and exiting lapses are joint, negotiable, and gradual embodied achievements. This finding most likely pertains not only to everyday conversations but to other interactive situations as well, including psychoanalytic and other psychotherapy sessions: the silent moments that occur in them, regardless of the kind of meaning they are given by the participants, are likewise collaboratively created by the participants then and there. Additional factors that may and most probably will come into play when making sense of the silent moments in therapy sessions are the institutional context and related practices. However, also, these factors should and will emerge in the interaction itself. Conversation analytic research thus has great potential to deepen our understanding of how those moments are jointly achieved in interaction *in situ*.

Appendix: Original transcripts

Example 1
01 Jaana: sillai että sai sitten siisteissä va̲a̲st-
02   a ↑vaatteis pikkusisko ni, (0.4)
03   päiväko[tii ja, (.) [ja, (.) kaikki ka̲ngaskengät=
04 Tuula: [mm.   [nii?
05 Jaana: =ja [kaikki tämmöset #näi#,
06 Tuula: [°.tjoo°
07   (0.1) * (0.2) * (6.5) * (0.2) ((=7.0))
            *fr3   *fr4   *fr5
08 Jaana: .mth mut ohan niinku niil justiin ni toi, ...

Example 2
01 Bea: £ni se [kattoo (sit),£
02 Aino: [he heh
03 Bea: £to̲si hyvä t(h)uli£ .hhh*
                           *fr1
04 Aino: °se on hy̲vä. .nfff* oi oi°
                   *fr2
05   (0.1) * (0.6) * (1.4) * (3.2) * (0.2) ((=5.5))
            *fr3   *fr4   *fr5   *fr6

Example 3
01 Jaana: tää on tät nyky#ai[kaa että#.]
02 Tuula: [n i i m]päh;*
                                     *fr1
03   (1.2)
04 Jaana: et se on,* (0.2) se̲mmosta että: #ä#
           *fr2
05 Jaana: ta̲stä päästä sisään (ja) toisest [pääst u̲los,]*
06 Tuula: [↑m↓m?]*
                                             *fr3
07   (0.2) * (0.5) * (5.6) * (1.0) ((=7.3))
            *fr4   *fr5   *fr6

Example 4
01 Aino: >eiks se oo< ↑a̲ina ollu aika kova mo̲u̲ruamaa.
02   (0.3)

03 Bea: nii siis tai siis s(h)e onh s(h)ill(h)ee, .hh
04   £kertoo* asioistaan£?=
                *fr1
05 Aino: =mm;*
              *fr2
06   (2.1) * (1.6) * (0.2) ((=3.9))
        *fr3   *fr4
07 Bea: mut se on kyl just rasittavaa ku, ...

Example 5 (continuation of Example 3)
07   (0.2) * (0.5) * (5.6) * (1.0) ((=7.3))
        *fr4   *fr5   *fr6
08 Jaana: *.mthh (0.2) et niinku ennempää;* (.) öh, (.) #o-# oli just
          *fr7   *fr8
09   semmos#ta että#, (0.8) henkilökunta tuns toisensa ja ...

Example 6
01 Jaana: sillai että sai sitten siisteissä vaast-
02   a *↑vaatteis pikkusisko ni, (0.4)
            *fr1
03   päiväk*o[tii ja, (.) [ja, (.) kaikki* kangaskengät=
                *T gaze down   *fr2
04 Tuula: [mm.   [nii?
05 Jaana: =ja [kaikki tämmöset #näi#,
06 Tuula: [°.tjoo°
07   (0.1) * (0.2) * (6.5) * (0.2) ((=7.0))
        *fr3   *fr4   *fr5
08 Jaana: .mth mut ohan niinku niil justiin ni toi, (.)
09   .hhhhhh Tommiki* ni #se:# se on kans semmone,
                         *fr6
10   .hh (0.4) @hän on hyvin #järkevä# ih*minen?@
                                              *fr7

Example 7
01 Aino: ni ↑kauanko Mirre sit oli teil.*
                                        *fr1
02 Bea: ↑kyl se aika pitkään.=oli se varmaa
03   m- (1.0) jotain yli kuukauden aina[ki.
04 Aino: [nii;

05 Bea: varmaan p<u>uo</u>ltoist kuukautta* tai j<u>o</u>tain?
            *fr2
06   (2.0) * (1.5) * (2.4) * (0.5) * (0.1) ((=6.5))
           *fr3   *fr4   *fr5   *fr6
07 Bea: *j[a muutenki;   ]
         *fr7
08 Aino: [meiän V<u>i</u>ljo on t]ullu v<u>a</u>nhaks ku
09   se on ruvennu nukkumaan s<u>a</u>laa* s<u>o</u>hvalla,
                                          *fr8
10 Bea: ↑o↓:::h.

Notes

1 This study was supported by a grant from the Finnish Cultural Foundation. I have worked on this topic in three universities: at the University of Helsinki, where I received the abovementioned grant; as a visiting scholar at the University of Sydney, where I presented my work at the events organized by the School of Literature, Art and Media; and at the University of Oulu, where I wrote this chapter and received comments on it at the Grassroots Writing Group. In addition, I have given talks and data sessions on the topic also at the University of Queensland, University of Melbourne, and Monash University, as well as in the Intersubjectivity in Action conference (Helsinki, May 2017), and have benefited from the discussion in all these events. I would also like to express my gratitude to Anssi Peräkylä and the editors of this volume for their valuable comments on earlier versions of this chapter.
2 These types of moments are sometimes also called "continuing states of incipient talk" (see Schegloff & Sacks 1973: 324–326, Berger et al. 2016).

References

Acheson, K. (2008). Silence as gesture. Rethinking the nature of communicative silences. *Communication Theory 18*(4), 535–555.

Berger, I., Viney, R., & Rae, J. P. (2016). Do continuing states of incipient talk exist? *Journal of Pragmatics 91*, 29–44.

Elliott, R. (1986). Interpersonal Process Recall (IPR) as a psychotherapy process research method. In: L. S. Greenberg & W. M. Pinsof (Eds.), *The Psychotherapeutic Process: A Research Handbook*, pp. 503–527. New York: Guilford Press.

Ergül, H. (2016). Adjournments during TV watching: A closer look into the organization of continuing states of incipient talk. *Discourse Studies 18*(2), 144–164.

Gardner, R. (1997). The conversation object *mm*: A weak and variable acknowledging token. *Research on Language and Social Interaction 30*(2), 131–156.

Goffman, E. (1963). *Behavior in Public Places*. New York: Free Press.
Goffman, E. (1967). *Interaction Ritual: Essays in Face to Face Behavior*. Garden City, NY: Doubleday.
Goodwin, C. (1981). *Conversational Organization: Interaction between Speakers and Hearers*. New York: Academic Press.
Goodwin, C. (1986). Gesture as a resource for the organization of mutual orientation. *Semiotica 62*(1–2), 29–49.
Haddington, P., Kcisanen, T., Mondada, L., & Nevile, M. (2014). Towards multiactivity as a social and interactional phenomenon. In: P. Haddington, T. Keisanen, L. Mondada & M. Nevile (Eds.), *Beyond Multitasking: Multiactivity in Social Interaction*, pp. 3–32. Amsterdam: John Benjamins Publishing.
Hoey, E. (2015). Lapses: How people arrive at, and deal with, discontinuities in talk. *Research on Language and Social Interaction 48*(4), 430–453.
Hoey, E. (2017). Lapse Organization in Interaction. Unpublished doctoral dissertation. Radboud University Nijmegen.
Hoey, E. M. (2018). How speakers continue with talk after a lapse in conversation. *Research on Language and Social Interaction 51*(3), 329–346.
ISK = A. Hakulinen, M. Vilkuna, R. Korhonen, V Koivisto, T. R. Heinonen & I. Alho (Eds.) (2004). *Iso suomen kielioppi* [Descriptive Grammar of Finnish]. Helsinki: Suomalaisen Kirjallisuuden Seura.
Janusz, B., Józefik, B., & Peräkylä, A. (2018). Gender-related issues in couple therapists' internal voices and interactional practices. *Australian and New Zealand Journal of Family Therapy 39*(4), 436–449.
Jefferson, G. (1989). Preliminary notes on a possible metric which provides for a 'standard maximum' silence of approximately one second in conversation. In: D. Roger & P. Bull (Eds.), *Conversation: An Interdisciplinary Perspective*, pp. 166–196. Clevedon: Multilingual Matters.
Jefferson, G. (2004). Glossary of transcript symbols with an introduction. In: G. Lerner (Ed.), *Conversation Analysis: Studies from the First Generation*, pp. 13–31. Amsterdam: Benjamins.
Kendrick, K. H. & Torreira, F. (2015). The timing and construction of preference: A quantitative study. *Discourse Processes 52*(4), 255–289.
Larsen, D., Flesaker, K., & Stege, R. (2008). Qualitative interviewing using interpersonal process recall: Investigating internal experiences during professional-client conversations. *International Journal of Qualitative Methods 7*(1), 18–37.
Lehtonen, J. & Sajavaara, K. (1985). The silent Finn. In: D. Tannen & M. Saville-Troike (Eds.), *Perspectives on Silence*, pp. 193–201. Norwood: Ablex.
Levinson, S. C. (1992). Activity types and language. In: P. Drew & J. Heritage (Eds.), *Talk at Work: Interaction in Institutional Settings*, pp. 66–100. Cambridge: Cambridge University Press.
Maynard, D. W. (1980). Placement of topic changes in conversation. *Semiotica 30*(3–4), 263–290.
Mondada, L. (2012). Coordinating action and talk-in-interaction in and out of video games. In: R. Ayaß & C. Gerhardt (Eds.), *The Appropriation of Media in Everyday Life*, pp. 231–270. Amsterdam: John Benjamins Publishing.
Mondada, L. (2016a). Challenges of multimodality: Language and the body in social interaction. *Journal of Sociolinguistics 20*(3), 336–366.

Mondada, L. (2016b). Conventions for multimodal transcription. Retrieved from https://franzoesistik.philhist.unibas.ch/fileadmin/user_upload/franzoesistik/mondada_multimodal_conventions.pdf.
Mushin, I. & Gardner, R. (2009). Silence is talk: Conversational silence in Australian Aboriginal talk-in interaction. *Journal of Pragmatics 41*(10), 2033–2052.
Peräkylä, A. (2013). Conversation analysis in psychotherapy. In: J. Sidnell & T. Stivers (Eds.), *The Handbook of Conversation Analysis*, pp. 551–574. Chichester: Wiley-Blackwell.
Peräkylä, A., Antaki, C., Vehviläinen, S., & Leudar, I. (Eds.) (2008). *Conversation Analysis and Psychotherapy*. Cambridge: Cambridge University Press.
Peräkylä, A. & Vehviläinen, S. (2003). Conversation analysis and the professional stocks of interactional knowledge. *Discourse and Society 14*(6), 727–750.
Rossano, F. (2012). *Gaze Behavior in Face-To-Face Interaction*. PhD Thesis. MPI Series 71. Nijmegen: Radboud University Nijmegen.
Sacks, H., Schegloff, E., & Jefferson, G. (1974). A simplest systematics for the organization of turn-taking for conversation. *Language 50*(4), 696–735.
Sajavaara, K. & Lehtonen, J. (1997). The silent Finn revisited. In: A. Jaworski (Ed.), *Silence. Interdisciplinary Perspectives*, pp. 263–284. Berlin: Mouton de Gruyter.
Schegloff, E. A. (2007). *Sequence Organization in Interaction: A Primer in Conversation Analysis*. Cambridge: Cambridge University Press.
Schegloff, E. A. & Sacks, H. (1973). Opening up closings. *Semiotica 8*(4), 289–327.
Sidnell, J. & Stivers, T. (Eds.) (2013). *The Handbook of Conversation Analysis*. Oxford: Wiley-Blackwell.
Siitonen, P. & Wahlberg, K.-E. (2015). Finnish particles *mm, jaa* and *joo* as responses to a proposal in negotiation activity. *Journal of Pragmatics 75*, 73–88.
Sorjonen, M.-L. (2001). *Responding in Conversation. A Study of Response Particles in Finnish*. Amsterdam: Benjamins.
Stivers, T., Enfield, N. J., Brown, P., Englert, C., Hayashi, M., Heinemann, T., Hoymann, G., Rossano, F., De Ruiter, J. P., Yoon, K.-E.,. & Levinson, S. C. (2009). Universals and cultural variation in turn-taking in conversation. *Proceedings of the National Academy of Sciences of the United States of America 106*(26), 10587–10592.
Szymanski, M. H. (1999). Re-engaging and dis-engaging talk in activity. *Language in Society 28*(1), 1–23.
Vatanen, A. (2018). Trajectories of embodied activities and the management of lapses. Paper Presented at *The 5th International Conference on Conversation Analysis (ICCA2018)*, Loughborough, UK, 11–15 July.
Vatanen, A. (Submitted). Exploring co-presence (in Finnish everyday interaction): Transitioning from an encounter to a gathering, and inhabiting the silent moment. Submitted to J. Lindström, R. Laury, A. Peräkylä & M.-L. Sorjonen (Eds.), *Intersubjectivity in Action*.

Chapter 17

Speaking that silences
A single case multi-method analysis of a couple's interview

Michael B. Buchholz, Oliver Ehmer, Christopher Mahlstedt, Stefan Pfänder, and Elke Schumann

Introduction

Social scientists, linguists, psychologists gather a lot of private experience of their own and other people's behavior. Sometimes you observe others talking together and you can't help it, there is this strong feeling that they are talking together and many topics relevant at the time of their talking are being omitted. You have no proof for it, it's just a feeling. You know this is a public place and people observe that they are observed, what Goffman termed "mutual monitoring" (Goffman 1963). This is a relatively simple case of "communicative absence". A certain topic is not talked about in the presence of foreigners.

Goffman described another type of "communicative absence" under the heading "Treatment of the absence":

> individuals are treated relatively well to their faces and relatively badly behind their backs. This seems to be one of the basic generalizations that can be made about interaction, but we should not seek in our all-too-human nature an explanation of it. As previously suggested, backstage derogation of the audience serves to maintain the morale of the team.
>
> (Goffman, 1959/2008, p. 111)

People wear their public masks and even in narrow friendships, Goffman muses, friends hold certain opinions about each other back in most circumstances. And in others they utter them freely.

There are further types of communicative absence. When therapists see a patient for the first time, they expect moments of silence to happen, the process will bring things to light. The situation changes again when therapists interview a couple. Here one is in a different observer position; you can observe them talking (in front of you). More often than not there is this pervasive feeling that they talk and in the same move they silence the most relevant things; although they seem to know what they silence and share this knowledge. That they cannot address it is one of the reasons they seek support.

It is this type of situation that we want to study. Our material is a video record of a couple demanding therapy. They were given the task to talk in front of a camera about "what are our most relevant problems at the time". They had to fulfill the task before, and again after, treatment.[1] Here we analyze the first tape only.

We will proceed in the following way: first, we will give a short reminder of how "noticeable absences" are theorized in the tradition of conversation analysis (CA) in order to contextualize the following analysis; second, we will analyze some scenarios directed to the couple's verbal level; third, a more fine-grained linguistic analysis is directed (a) to the vocal level by using a new method of musicalization of how relevant aspects are spoken and (b) to the embodied aspects of the couple's conversation; fourth, we will present an integration of these views; and fifth, we will propose some theoretical conclusions and types of silence and silencing.

Noticeable absence as silenced talk

Viewing the tape several times we were initially touched by an undefinable impression that this couple was not really in touch with each other. It took some time until we could define the problem methodologically. The work of Pietikäinen (2018) shows, in subtly detailed study of a couple's interactions, that there are silences that speak. Is it possible to turn this around? Is there talk that silences? And how could it be detected?

We will start with some thoughts about membership categorization. Harvey Sacks in his second lecture discusses the smallest narrative: "The baby cried. The mother picked it up", and shows how nearly every listener assumes that mother and baby are members of one category "family". But, then, he makes a serious thought experiment:

> Were it the case that you had to decide in some way like going up and asking these persons whether they were the proper set of people to be

> doing whatever it is they're doing, then the world might become much more complicated than it is. And I will call, in principle, such things as people 'passing' under such rules, 'subversion.' When a woman walks away from a supermarket with the baby carriage filled with a baby that's not hers, that's the sort of thing I'm talking about with 'subversion.' It's not seeable.
>
> (Sacks & Jefferson, 1992/1995, p. 254)

Membership categorization might be erroneous and you cannot distinguish both cases – if the woman is a mother that is entitled to take the baby or not – easily from one another. The correction of *membership categorization* makes the event, absences become noticed.

Furthermore, Sacks is deeply engaged in the topic of "seeing lies" (p. 114). We take another example how Sacks described how people deal with everyday lies:

> It may seem artificial to talk about a 'monitoring operation' except that it seems that the subset counts, so that it wouldn't be obviously wrong to say that a person first selects a subset, as compared to, e.g. merely just picking a term. And consider, for example, that people don't go about saying "You are lying. It's not true that you're feeling 'rotten', you are feeling 'lousy'," or "It's not true that you're feeling 'great', you're feeling 'wonderful'." But they might well say "You are not feeling 'great', you're feeling 'lousy'." That is, what happens when you announce the term is that it's handled by virtue of subset membership.
>
> (Sacks & Jefferson, 1992/1995, p. 556)

So the special correction of the *subset membership* makes the lie an event.

In order to focus on activities which are not going to happen, we draw on the term "noticeable absence". This term refers to the fact that in a given sequential context some kind of next action is *expected* but not realized. Due to the participants' expectations, this creates a recognizable absence of the not-realized action. An observer can notice that something relevant is absent. The examples Sacks delivers are as follows:

> One of the nice things about greetings is that while greetings sometimes do not occur in actual conversations, at least sometimes when

they do not occur their absence is noticeable. For example, people say about somebody they talked to, "He didn't even say hello." That the absence of greetings is at least sometimes noticeable suggests that they have a relevance beyond their actual use. That is to say, they are used in some corpus of conversations but beyond that corpus they have a relevance for other conversations in which they are noticeably absent.
(Sacks & Jefferson, 1992/1995, vol 1, p. 31)

The analytical advantage of "noticable absence" is thus to deal with phenomena that are "not present" or "not realized" in an interaction. The tricky methodological problem is designed by Sacks in the following way:

The 'noticeably absent' thing is very, very important and it will come up again and again. If you're going to make a statement which proposes that something is absent, then you can't in any serious way propose that X is absent unless you have some way of discriminating the absence of X from the assertable absence of millions of things, or ten things that anybody could name. In order to make a non-trivial assertion that X is absent, you have to have some way of showing that a statement, 'X is absent,' is different from some statement, 'Y is absent,' where Y may also be absent. For example, I might say 'There is no greeting in this conversation' and somebody else might say 'Well, there is no suicide threat, either, so what is it that makes your statement that there was no greeting something other than just something you're saying?' Now one way to go about dealing with making non-trivial statements about absences is to have some way to say that the absence is also an event. That is to say, for only some class of things will it be the case that you can say that X is absent by virtue of the fact that the absence of X is a noticeable feature of what happened. And one criterion for its noticeable status is that people say about it, 'X is absent.'
(Sacks & Jefferson, 1992/1995, p. 35)

Another type of noticeable absence may appear in the context of quoting (Pomerantz 1984), e.g. two working colleagues talk about their boss. Fred tells Paul how the boss recently told Fred how incompetent Fred is. Quoting self-directed foreign critical remarks of somebody else is a risky endeavor; the risk is that the listener – Paul – might silently agree. In order to avoid this impression Paul is expected to take a stance. If not, Paul's silence is interpreted as agreement to the boss's opinion. A similar type is enacted when Fred reports a negative statement of the boss about Paul. Then, Fred is expected to discredit the boss and his opinion of Paul. If Fred however produces a noticeable absence or "silence", however, the relationship is at risk. Imagine now a couple, Peter and Mary, quoting a third party's opinion about their relationship – without taking a stance. This is the type of silencing we want to deal with.

How are noticeable absences made noticeable events? First, they might be recognized and addressed by participants themselves. Second, they have "relevance for other conversations" (as Sacks wrote, above). Third, they indicate relevance for the relational status participants assign to each other. Fourth, they exert a devastating impact, followed by utterances of emotional disturbance or further silence.

The accuse-and-defense scenario

From the first 90 seconds of the video with Peter and Mary we learn that they have lived together for 16 years without having talked very much about relevant things. Peter feels too controlled by Mary. Contributing to the task to talk about "most relevant" problems he tells an example of the "lemon pie" he lately ate, telling Mary that he liked it. She is "sour" about this. She often baked a lemon pie and Peter never liked it, because the lemon pie tastes sour. This recent lemon pie was baked by Sabine, no, by Jacob, he corrects himself. Mary complains that Peter often obeys what others advise him to do or how things are; it is she who wishes to be his "counselor". She mocks him, quoting what his father or his mother have said to him, introducing his objections – in her quotation – by the generic "yes-but-no" phrase-introduction. She suffers from feeling without influence, but her attacks make him build up stronger walls of defense, which stirs up her attacks. Thus, both are caught in a circular pattern. Here is a transcript segment following the first 90 seconds:

Segment (1)

32	**Mary:**	*I don't want to control you*
33		*what I what I always (2.1)*

34		what I always intend is ehm (0.7)
35		just that you take me as someone giving you advice for once
36		and that is a feeling I do not have
37	(1.0)	
38		I have the feeling that uhm
39		that you listen more (0.7) to uhm (.) the advice of other people
40		when you eventually make a decision
41		whether or not to do something (0.5)
42		you listen more to the decisions of those other people
43		than to the advice I gave you
44		because after all it is exactly the same as what I told you but
45		in the thir\ n_n when you inform me saying
46		yes but Felix has suggested that (0.4)
47		no but my daddy has said that
48		no mom has suggested ←
49	Peter:	*I don't listen to my dad* ←
50	Mary:	okay well your mother
51	Peter:	<<*exhaling loudly*>h°> *laughing*> hehe>> (0.7) °hh eh ←
52	(2.6)	

Accuse by list-colligation...

In lines 44–48 we observe Mary projecting a "list-in-progress" (Jefferson, 2017, p. 333). As Jefferson observed, three-part lists are generally considered to be sufficient in order to convey generality. Mary does not list objects or names; she lists quotations with the common denominator that Peter lent his ears to these speakers. Felix, Daddy, and Mama must not necessarily be members of the same *class* of persons; their belonging together on this list is simply due to the fact that it is Peter who *makes* them (in Mary's view) "belong together". Jefferson termed this phenomenon "colligation":

> Again, then, CO-*CLASS MEMBERSHIP,* this 'belonging together', is not necessary inherent in THE ITEMS, BUT CAN BE IMPARTED TO THEM BY THEIR CO-*LIST* MEMBERSHIP.

It is this feature that I mean to be invoking with the term 'colligation'.
(Jefferson 2017, p. 333, capitals and italics by Jefferson)

Mary's list has, as Selting (2004) described, a three-part structure. In lines 38–45 Mary projects her list, then the single list elements follow (lines 46–48); the closure component is lacking as Peter repairs the last element. What follows is a pause and a change to another focus.

The function of this listing is to prove that Peter's bonds to these figures in his life are more influential on his conduct than is Mary's influence. The list appears sequentially after the formulation of a claim ("you listen more to the decisions of these other persons than to pieces of advice I gave you"); the list has the status of presenting evidence for her claim by quoting Peter's own words (Selting 2004, 2007). As has been observed, quotations are used when a higher degree of genuineness or authenticity is warranted (Bergmann 1987).

However, the quotations (lines 46–48) are incomplete. It is relevant that Peter is quoted as quoting Felix, Daddy, or Mama; but what these persons said need not to be mentioned. It is silenced. But one can assume that both know the unspoken quotes.

... *defense by disassembly*

Peter behaves like a good lawyer who dismembers the list. By showing that at least one list-item has no justified place on the list, a shadow falls on the other items; the whole list might collapse. Mary rapidly replaces the removed list-item "father" by "okay well your mother". Peter can doubt single list-items just because they are not members of a *class*, but they are colligated on one list. The colligation makes the list an object of the couple's common negotiations.

Why negotiations here at all? One speculative answer might be that Mary and Peter perform a court-scenario: Mary in the role of prosecutor, Peter in the role of defendant and lawyer. Who might be the judge? The answer could be: the jury-audience represented by the camera which takes the role of a *silent* member. The "judge" should not speak, because if he does, then one of them would be declared "guilty" and the relationship is at risk. This little speculation throws some light on the enormous burdens on a therapist's shoulders when working with such a couple.

Jefferson describes that lists are often closed by what she terms a "General List Completer" (GLC). GLCs indicate that many more items could be found but that they need not be specified here. Thus, lists-in-progress are often closed by fragments like "or whatever" or similar phrases. Selting (2007, p. 504) observed,

> in all closed lists, whether formatted as one or as more than one prosodic units, final falling pitch is used to complete the list proper; with some other TCU [turn constructional unit] following to close the superordinated activity, by either the speaker him/herself or the interlocutor. In those cases in which the number of list items is not projected, especially if formulated within single syntactic clauses or sentences, downstep of the successive list items is deployed to make the list recognizable as a closed list.

However, Pietikäinen (2018) found that in quarreling couples, things often run differently; questions are not responded to in due time, silence arises, and then a counter-question follows, but no response. Listing completion here takes another prosody, as analyzed by Selting (2007).

Musicalization – Mary's voice in producing and closing the list

We used a new method of "musicalization" invented by Christopher Mahlstedt who is a fully trained musician. This method aims to make visible how the couple mutually adjusts to each other in terms of pitch and rhythm (Gregory, Webster & Huang, 1993; Jaffe, Beebe, Feldstein et al., 2001). The method unfolds in four steps: first, writing down, like a composer, the melody and rhythm of a spoken utterance; second, playing the documented notation with an instrument, like, for example, a saxophone; third, parallel playing of the original spoken audio sound *and* saxophone accompaniment; fourth, presenting the record in the group of analysts for correction or confirmation.

In this way, listening to the prosody of each of Mary's list elements we hear a repeating sequence of pitches slightly variated. The following handmade transcription[2] can make it hearable again, in a certain sense: "However, who tries to adopt music by reading a score reads something into it by sounding it out" (de La Motte-Haber, 1985, p. 14) (see Figure 17.1).

First of all, we look at the three quotations-without-quoting by Mary (bars 1–3). They are spoken with a loud voice in a sixteenth-note rhythm,

Speaking that silences 341

Figure 17.1 "Yes, but Felix".

beginning with a stretched, slightly rising pitch (c#'–d') in the beginning and ending harshly with two accented eight notes one octave lower (d). The wide ambitus of the first two phrases (d'–d) as well as the inner structure of the intervals provide attention and tension: Mary, imitating Peter when pointing to the persons Peter is referring to, does this by an upwards directed chromatic (B♭–c') – within the given pitches this can be heard as a minor seventh. Both phrases end by a tritone (g#–d), a very dissonant sounding interval. The third phrase, starting a half note lower on a c'–c#' is shorter, the ambitus is reduced to a sixth and it ends by a fourth from b–e.

Since our hearing is primed by musical and linguistic experience we compare endings with cadences – a formal gestalt that typically appears at the end of a piece of music or a sentence. But Mary's tensed and raised voice repeats the melodic citation; she rather seems to cry. The pauses between the musical gestalts "quote" by silent insertion what Peter's loyalties (Felix, Daddy, Mother) are quoted to have said, making them "noticeable absent"; the repetitive gestalt suggests continuation. One hears the dissonance in her voice and the pauses are framed as "noticeable absence". In this sense the reduced contour of the third list-item with the non-dissonant ending is alluding and can be heard as a "musical" GLC. Thus, a *paradoxon* is created – the musical gestalt of the contours is "closed, conclusive, assertive, reinforcing on the other" (Papoušek, Papoušek, & Symmes, 1991, p. 435) but the syntactic ending, the relative clause, is left open. Does Peter fill the gaps Mary produced? And if so, will *he* now take a stance instead?

With a slight laid-back feel, Peter joins in, changing the rhythmic pattern by slowing down to eighth-note triplets and intonating the pitches c#, d#, g#, and c#, as if picking up Mary's "riff" and displaying it now very simply, as a cadence movement from I to V to I. Regarding this rhythmic shift and the artificial sound of his voice, saying "(auf) mein PApa hör_ch nich" (I don't listen to my dad), his alterations must be heard as disaffiliative (cf. Couper-Kuhlen & Selting, 2018, p. 33). Further analyses indicate confirmation.

We conclude that this is a noticeable absence, again. Further analyses confirm this conclusion: Whereas the beginning of his phrase (the tone c#) is in line with the starting pitch of the third list-item, indicating a "tuning-in" (Gregory, Webster, & Huang, 1993, p. 200) with the musical gestalt of that part of the list, the d# sets a contrast to the prior dominance of the ds, and the upward motion of a fourth (d#–g#) sounding like an exaggeration to the described tonal pointing devices confirm the impression that Peter hardly takes serious what Mary is saying.

Mary grasping up the sixteenth-note pattern again and confirming Peter's other-repair "na gut deine MUTter" (okay well your mother) intonates now a f# that is a fourth higher than Peter's c# – a reversed fourth and now *within* the turn-taking. Thus, Mary's uptake of Peter's repair sounds clearly downgraded in relevance (Couper-Kuhlen & Selting, 2018, p. 163); the melodic frame of an octave has flattened almost to a prime, the volume of her voice is *mezzo piano*. The two words "na gut" (okay well) confirm the prosodic impression of making irrelevant relevance: that it doesn't matter who Peter is listening to; the musical gestalt shows little differences in terms of rhythm and tonality. Peter laughs out loud, celebrating a triumph over his father, while Mary with resignation points to his mother. Then, in a lower volume but a higher pitch, he grindingly hits a d'; adding harmonies to a passage where a *false cadence* in f# is hearable. Peter suddenly hesitates and forms an "äh", tonally shaped in a downward movement of a minor third and not sounding amused anymore. All three – Mary, Peter's now absent mother, and Peter – pause from being in silence with each other.

What can be concluded from this? The observation of a paradox can be confirmed when we refer this analysis to a recent CA-theory of intersubjectivity (Stevanovic & Koski, 2018). Accepting a pre-announcement of a quotation which does not follow can be understood as *epistemic* reference to a common knowledge store. Things must not be spoken out loud as both know what is meant. However, the *affective* order as documented in the musical analysis of prosody does not confirm a co-construction of utterances. And, more: Casually, Peter joins in, changing the rhythmic pattern by slowing down to eighth-note triplets and intonating the pitches c#, d#, g# and c#, as picking up Mary's "riff" and displaying it now very simply, as a cadence movement from I to V to I. Regarding this rhythmic shift and the artificial sound of his voice, saying "(auf) mein PApa hör_ch nich" (I don't listen to my dad), his repairs must be heard as disaffiliative (cf. Couper-Kuhlen & Selting, 2018, p. 33). Peter is the one who decides – a *deontic* order without taking a stance. The three orders of intersubjectivity Stevanovic & Koski (2018) described are not well aligned; they are in disharmony.

Invisible loyalties

By analyzing list colligation and list disassembly practices in this couple's conflict we detect practices of silencing. One element of the list is disassembled and the others get out of sight. In what follows we see other practices of silence and silencing.

In a "token-as-a-type" format the couple chooses the lemon pie in order to perform the therapeutic task to talk about their actual problems. The lemon-pie episode is presented as "typical" for the kind of conflicts this couple discusses. Some background is explored in the couple's conversation which we want to analyze now.

Mary's baking of a lemon pie is hardly positively responded to by Peter, but Mary accuses Peter of liking the lemon pie made by Sabine. Mary argues about why she mentioned Sabine, because Peter had formerly quoted her opinion about Mary's and Peter's relationship:

Segment (2)

90	**Mary:**	*and besides it was Sabine,*
91	**(3.6)**	
92		*because you know Sabine said that we should better split up*
93	**(0.5)**	
94	**Peter:**	*no that is not what Sabine said*
95		*Sabine said that I uhm (1.2)*
96		*that that (1.0) it uhm (2.6)*
97		*yes well alright maybe <<aspirated>> she did say it*
98	**Mary:**	*it's what you said to me*
99	**Peter:**	*uhm she did not say that we should split up=*
100		*=that perhaps another kind of woman would be better for me*
101	**(3.4)**	

((*Mary forcefully pushing the backs of her hands down onto her knees and then openingher palms upwards, as if saying: "That's what I said"*))

102	**Mary:**	*that's hurting me*
103	**(0.6)**	
104		*yeah as close as Sabine is to you*
105		*because for such a long time*
106	**Peter:**	*[((clearing throat))]*
107	**Mary:**	*she took care of you when you were a child*
108	**Peter:**	*[((clearing throat))]*
109	**(0.9)**	
110	**Mary:**	*and and you do very much value her like a mother*
111	**Peter:**	*uhm_uhm*

Undoubtedly, Sabine's recommendation to separate or that another woman "would be better" for Peter have high relevance for the relationship. This recommendation comes as indirect quotation, a format which increases the relevance (in the sense that "Sabine says…") *and* decreases the relevance (in the sense that "it's only Sabine saying such things…"). Peter retells these quotations with self-interruptions, hesitation markers, pauses and word-repetitions, and changes in speech rate. With fast speech-rate he admits Sabine's words that "perhaps another kind of woman would be better for me".

Figure 17.2 The brooding thinker.

His speaking slowly is suddenly accelerated when he corrects what Mary reported he had told her (line 94) about Sabine's utterance. His left hand rubs the top of his nose between his eyes during the pause of 2.5 sec (line 94), a gesture displaying the brooding thinker (see Figure 17.2).

Gesture, self-interruptions and pauses, rapid changes of speech rate, and rapid changes of turning voice up–down give the impression that he is making a confession. The whole configuration of Mary's first quotation of what Sabine had said is quickly corrected; his hesitations while brooding on what Sabine had "really said" while Mary reminds him that he himself has told this to her; his fast repair; and finally, what Sabine had said, reminds us of a well-described pattern:

> It is important that one considers when and where in the interview sequence a subject might lie, as an additional factor in determining how long a subject has to concoct his or her lie. This period of time should be as long as the amount of time a truthteller has to mull over the issue that he or she will truthfully describe. Each of these issues is affected by the cognitive complexity of the lie (i.e. simple denial

versus fabricating an opinion) which, based on most models of how lies are betrayed, will affect the behavioral information that follows.

(Frank 2005, p. 353)

We do not say that Peter is lying. It is the consumption of time, a high degree of cognitive complexity in Peter's utterance indicated by self-repair and hesitation, and there is the gestural quotation of the brooding thinker. Format and content of his utterance and gesture present a lot of cognitive and emotional complexity for Mary which contributes to the pause of 3.4 sec (line 103) now following. It is a pause in words, not in gesturing.

In this pause she makes a gesture with both hands. These are held in her lap, then taken up while the head nods, turned outside, and then allowed to fall back in her lap. We show the sequence in Figures 17.3, 17.4, and 17.5.

Figure 17.3 Start of the gesture, hands on the left knee, gaze into emptiness, strike of a gesture uprising and outside.

Figure 17.4 The apex of the gesture, hands open, head bowed, and gaze downwards. Depressed face.

When we try to translate this gesture into words it seemed to be equivalent to "This is what I said". Mary receives a negative message from Peter's quotations from Sabine and she has the paradoxical satisfaction of having understood everything in the right way. However, this satisfaction cannot and does not please her.

There is more than epistemic complexity to cope with. The affective complexity is expressed in Mary's response that she feels hurt. Then follows a remark acknowledging Peter's loyalty bonds to Sabine who cared for him when he was a child and who seems to have taken a place in his emotional household like a mother, as Mary, uncontradicted, formulates. He agrees. What comes into sight here has been termed "invisible loyalties" (Boszormenyi-Nagy 1973) by couple therapists. Peter is seen to be loyal to Sabine like a son to a mother. This loyalty bond is in conflict with his loyalty to Mary. Via quotations Sabine is presented as a "counselor" in Peter's

Figure 17.5 The refraction phase of the gesture: return to start.

relationship to Mary, while Mary herself has claimed to be respected as "counselor" by Peter. To enjoy Sabine's lemon pie might be heard by Mary as Peter downgrading his loyalty bonds to her as compared to those with Sabine. The lemon pie seems to symbolize this loyalty conflict.

We want to describe some of the cognitive, affective, and loyalty complexities this couple has to deal with. We assume that high-complexity events in conversation have a potential to cause pauses. These pauses grant some time to think over what has been said and what has been going on. And, what has not been said.

Using quotations as conversational tools (Ehmer 2011) adds an animating dimension to symbolic talk. Direct quotations (Bergmann 1987) make a higher claim of authenticity, they come with a subtext like "this is what was *really* said". They are part of a technique of information management aiming to ensure the content and source of the information given. This is part of Peter's enactment when searching for the "true version" of what Sabine had really said. Search for the truth is in itself considered to be a valuable activity; the actor can claim that his efforts make him a respectable person. Frank (2005) points out that just this positive side-effect of struggling for the "true quotation" can be used to cover other topics of relevance. In this segment the quotations are spelled out, efforts are made to quote correctly, but Peter does not take a stance to the quotations of Sabine. This is what makes a noticeable absence a noticeable event. We refer to two theoretical offers taken from CA-traditions to make this more understandable.

The analysis of the couple's conversation can be sharpened by our "ability to see in tandem with the expansion of our theories", as we quoted Collins at the beginning of this chapter. Thus, this is a reminder of Goffman (1981).

A *speaker* is a term for a *social* role complemented by a *listener*. But *speaker* can be differentiated by three *analytical roles* which are described by Goffman in the following way:

> It is necessary now to look at the remaining element of the conversational paradigm, the notion of *speaker*.
>
> In canonical talk, one of the two participants moves his lips up and down to the accompaniment of his own facial (and somewhat bodily) gesticulations; and words can be heard issuing from the locus of his mouth. He is the **sounding box** in use ... He is functioning as an **'animator'**. Animator and recipient are part of the same level and mode of analysis, two terms cut from the same cloth, not social roles in the full sense so much as functional nodes in a communication system.
>
> But, of course, when one uses the term 'speaker', one very often beclouds the issue, having additional things in mind, this being one reason why 'animator' cannot comfortably be termed a social role, merely an analytic one.
>
> Sometimes one has in mind that there is an **'author'** of the words that are heard, that is, someone who has selected the sentiments that are being expressed and the words in which they are encoded.
>
> Sometimes one has in mind that a **'principal'** (in the legislative sense) is involved, that is, someone whose position is established by the words that are spoken, someone whose beliefs have been told, someone who is committed to what the words say.
>
> (Goffman, 1981, p. 144)

With these preparations we can return to the couple's conversation.

Using the distinction of animator, author, and principal we can see in the following segment what is covered by Peter's intensified search for the truth of Sabine's quotations. He does not commit himself as a principal "to what the words say". What is silenced is his positioning to Sabine's words quoted in full truth.

In many comparable cases of non-committing in everyday talk, we are accustomed to assume that the listener is sure of the prior speaker's commitment. However, this is not the case in our example. Mary nowhere makes an explicit attempt to find out Peter's position towards Sabine's so-directly presented opinion. Peter silences by not taking a stance; Mary silences by not challenging Peter's stance. Both silence while talking.

Musicalization – what hurts Mary?

We answer this question by starting with Mary's words in line 102: "°that's hurting me". Here is the prosody of Mary's part after the pause in line 101 (see Figure 17.6).

Figure 17.6 Musicalization of Mary's complaint: "and that is hurting me".

Mary reacts slowly, pointing out without clear time, in chromatically ascending triplets "and that's" – she rushes, finishing in a descending E-minor–shaped melodic contour, saying "hurting me." The emotional content gets audibly transferred in a sad-sounding gestalt. In a "creaky voice" with unclear tonal location (Dreyer, 2018), she affirms herself by saying "yes" while Peter remains silent. She continues, accelerating the tempo up to 116 beats per minute and phrasing mechanically, sounding eighth-note triplets on just one tone (b) – her understanding of Peter being close to Sabine is semantically *and* musically articulated in a rational manner. Again, we hear a rising chromatic line, now at the end of the phrase. This time Peter joins in, continuing Mary's prosodic line with two rising tones (d# and e) by short hesitations twice. Being onomatopoetically very "close" to Sabine, he is far from taking a stance.

"Stance", following recent definitions (Couper-Kuhlen & Selting, 2018; Goodwin, 2012; Goodwin et al., 2012; Heritage, 2012), can be combined with the theory of Stevanovic and Peräkylä (2014). First of all, "epistemic stance" is at stake, when participants make and negotiate a claim about *who knows what*. In this perspective, speakers can position themselves as having a greater epistemic authority than their co-interlocutor. Second, "deontic stance" is taken by participants when they label an action as necessary or desirable. This type of stance is mostly expected in contexts of requests and offers, invitations, and advice-giving. Finally, "affective stance" refers to attitudes or feelings publicly displayed. Instances of affective stance can either be *laminated* onto turns at talk or constitute a turn themselves. As Couper-Kuhlen and Selting state, affect in interaction "is seldom made explicit through words; rather it is indexed through verbal and non-verbal means, meaning that sequence-sensitive interpretation is required" (2018: 44).

Mary meanwhile concludes repetitively in eighth-note triplets "because for such a long time she took care of you when you were a child", ending her statement again with intervals sounding like E minor. After a short pause, distinctively a tritone higher, Mary, hesitating in "broken" eighth-note triplets and finishing fluently in an F#-minor–like triad, says that he values her very much like a mother. That sounds brighter than before and Peter joins in, this time articulating a recipient token "uhm uhm". By intonating the pitches d and f# the gestalt of the minor-sounding "mother" gets retrospectively contextualized in a D major sound. By these musical means Peter seems to make an optimistic jump away from Mary's "sad" prosody in E minor at the beginning.

What we conclude is, first, that we have here an example where not only the *affective* order can be considered as somehow "disordered" but the *epistemic* order, too. Second, we find again that Peter seems to be the one who decides *deontic* imbalances; Mary does not challenge his not taking a stance with respect to the question of relevance for the couple's definition of their relationship. She lets him talk as *animator* of Sabine's quotation; however, his not taking the analytical role as *principal* makes a further *noticeable absence* recognizable. So, sometimes, to speak by quotations can mix other voices with one's own. The extreme possibility is to silence one's own voice, although one continues speaking (Günthner, 1997). Third, we feel this paradox requires a further frame of reference.

The displacement of origo

Thus, we continue to ask what she might mean by "that" (in line 102). It is a *verbal deixis*, she points to something – but to what? What is it that hurts her? Is it Sabine's opinion, quoted by Peter, that she considers Mary to be the wrong woman for Peter? Is it that Peter does not take a stance? Is it that she gets to hear this in front of the camera representing an anonymous audience? Is it that Peter does not defend her? We will try an answer in turning to another author.

Karl Bühler, German psychologist, in his famous "theory of language" (Bühler, 1934/2011) describes the *deictic gesture* as the beginning of communication and language: Pointing to something and controlling if the other's gaze follows. The *deictic* gesture is soon followed by *deictic words* ("*Zeigwörter*"), of which *here* and *now* are the most important:

> My claim is that if this arrangement is to represent the deictic field of human language, three deictic words must be placed where the 0 is, namely the deictic words *here, now* and *I*. ... There is nothing conspicuous about the phonetic form, about the phonematic impress of the words *now, here, I;* all that is peculiar about them is what each of them demands: the first demands, look at me, an acoustic phenomenon, and take me as a mark of the moment; as a mark of the place, says the second; and the third, as a mark of the sender (or characteristic of the sender).
>
> (Bühler, 1934/2011, p. 117f)

The deictic field (of I, time, and space) is constituted in a fully subjective orientation which Bühler calls *"origo"*. The *origo*-perspective can now be transferred into a field of phantasmatic (or "imaginative") deixis. Bühler (p. 151) mentions examples, e.g. if you think of a friend it may happen that you hear his voice directly left or right of you. The absent person can be pointed to. And the *I* can be displaced to another locality, imaginatively. My wife doesn't find an instrument in the kitchen, she calls me by phone and I displace myself from my reality into the phantasmatic situation to be in our kitchen and guide her gaze where I think she can see the missing instrument.

Such displacement into a phantasma of another person regularly takes place when someone quotes another person directly, using the pronoun *I* and the recipient immediately understands that another speaker is copied. So, we can understand how we can follow another *"origo"* into another phantasma, which we enter with flexibility and thus can follow the deictic operations within this phantasmatic world. However, there is a psychological problem Bühler did not address. We enter phantasmatic worlds, but how do we leave them and find our way back to what we think is shared reality? What if someone quotes another person using *I* and constructs the utterances in a way that it remains unclear where the quotation ended? Or did it end at all? What if there is no exit?

Gallagher (2015) has dedicated a paper to this situation. We all read novels, go to movies, or to the theater, and, when the evening ends, leave the movie or theater, finding ourselves again sharing "our world". But sometimes one can observe young people who jump out of their seats when Hamlet approaches Polonius behind the curtain and the person cries out a warning. Such a person cannot make a distinction between the world of theater and "our world". Following Alfred Schütz, Gallagher proposes a "multiple-reality" theory, thinking of children's pretend play, affordances that motivate various actions and change self-concepts (e.g. when a child sees a banana and plays with it as a telephone). The cognitive requirement is to see something *as* something and, at the same time know that it *is not* the thing; the banana remains a banana.

Mary's and Peter's world consists of two components: Peter's loyalty bonds to his "counselors" (like Sabine) and Mary's attempts to be accepted as a "counselor", too. In this world Peter would be guided by his counselors; no necessity emerges to create his own voice. Entering this world, Mary positions herself in rivalry to other "counselors" and utters empathic understanding for Peter's life-long bonds with Sabine. She does not directly challenge that Peter takes a stance. However, this would be an exit-option for Peter to leave the world shared with Sabine and reenter a world shared with Mary. Couple's therapists call this sharing a phantasmatic world a "collusion" (Dicks 1967; Willi 1984). Thus, the *noticeable absence* observed here is of relevance for the therapeutic endeavor in couple's therapy and we propose a linguistic version of what is described as "collusion". Therapy is an endeavor that tries to build pathways out of a one-world-phantasma in order to find a reentry into a multiple-reality world that can be shared. The therapeutic activity has been described precisely:

> In an interpretation, the therapist points out something that (in reference to therapeutic expertise) may be heard as implicit in what the patient has just been talking about (cf. Bercelli et al., 2008; Peräkylä, 2015; Vehviläinen, 2003). By pointing out this 'something else' than what the patient said, the interpretations inherently also take some distance from the patient's own description of her experience.
> (Voutilainen et al., 2010, p. 92)

Now follows a moment where the lemon pie *is* a lemon pie *and* is "*something else*" (Voutilainen et al., 2010) or "something more" (Stern, 2004).

The lemon pie is sour

In the following segment Mary speaks about having earned a living for the couple while Peter was still studying. But some friends, again *quoted* by Peter, had described her as something like a career-addict. Being assessed from such a critical perspective enrages Mary; she finds it unjust. And a source of her complaint is that she did not know that others have been speaking so negatively about her. She tries to correct this view:

Segment (3)

```
180 Mary:    I (.) I'd like to have a family
181   (1.2)
182          I'd like to relax in someone (0.3)
183          to relax  with someone
184   (1.5)
```

185		*and that is what I didn't have in the last years*
186	(0.8)	
187	Peter:	*yes, but you didn't actively ask for it either and neither*
188	Mary:	*because I wasn't quite aware of it*
189		*but only now I do know it*
190		*but if I (0.4) had had the opportunity °h ((sniffling)) with*
191		*one of these people that are now saying*
192		*I want to build a career and the like (0.7)*
193		*(if they) ever would have brought it up with me (1.3)*
194		*I would have talked to them and then <<pp> uhm>*
195		*I'd be definitely eh eh the\ my\ I would have made my point of view better*
196	(2.0)	
197		*or more clearly*
198	(0.7)	
199		*yeah (0.3) could have said*
200	(2.7)	
201		*((sniffling))*
202	(4.7)	
203		*the lemon pie is so:: sour*
204	(0.8)	
205	Peter:	*what do you say*
206	Mary:	*((laughing))*
207	(1.7)	
208	Peter:	*<<laughing>what>*
209		*it was really sweet it barely tastes like lemon*
210	Mary:	*[(xxx xxx xxx)]*
211	Peter:	*<<laughing> it's alright to eat it>*
212	Mary:	*<< laughing> ah barely>*
213		*((sniffling))*
214	Peter:	*((laughing))*
215	(0.8)	
216	Peter:	*yeah*
217	(1.2)	
218	Peter:	*but I just find (.) we::ll eh eh eh that \I just still find (some_how) that you shouldn't (1.0)*
219		*well y_is\ it is difficult to say*
220		*I'd like you not to take it so personally /*

In line 203 Mary speaks with a low voice: "The lemon pie is so sour" – an utterance out of a pause and followed by extensive laughter on her part. Peter responds contagiously, but it seems that he did not understand what Mary said or, more, that he understood the words but not the meaning of her words or that he doesn't understand why Mary laughs.

We make a proposal to understand this utterance and the following laughter by taking the sequential position into account. Mary repeatedly has used the word "sour" for the lemon pie's taste and as colloquial denominator for her own emotional state; to be "sour" means to be in a rage, to be angry. This was what she talked about. Again, she had had to realize that Peter had quoted the utterances of friends ("career-addict"), which increased her being "sour". In lines 200–202 there is a pause of almost 8 seconds, interrupted by her sniffing. Out of this silence comes her sentence, which is not only a repetition, but is slightly changed: "so:: sour". We assume that in this pause something important happened of which this sentence is the result, with a leap into relieved laughter. Here is how Mary and Peter interact at line 200 (see Figure 17.7).

She fights back her tears, he leans his head back and tackles his fingers. He looks at her, she directs her gaze inwardly (see Figure 17.8).

With protruded lips she utters "The lemon pie is so:: sour". And then it looks like as if she is surprised by her own words, she seems to try to take back what she has said, but she explodes into laughter (see Figure 17.9).

And laughter begins on her face, followed by her covering her face with her hands, feet pointing upwards (see Figure 17.10).

Figure 17.7 The pause before Mary's saying "the lemon pie is so:: sour".

Speaking that silences 357

Figure 17.8 Mary fighting with her tears, Peter tackling with fingers.

Figure 17.9 Mary: "The lemon pie is so:: sour" – her face lightened and fresh.

This analysis focuses on the utterance from line 200 onward. One irregular thing is that Peter does not understand; in lines 205–208 he twice asks "What?". The basic CA rule that the meaning of an utterance is generated in the ear of the hearer does not apply here – unless we assume that she responds (with laughter) to her own utterance. She listens to her own

Figure 17.10 Mary surprised by her own discovering how sour the lemon pie is, face in hands, feet in tension upwards, Peter having stopped tackling his fingers, looking down bored.

words that seem to come "out of the blue" and they represent a "something else". A new definition of the common "token-as-type" format seems to emerge; not only is the lemon pie sour. It is she herself who is sour and the tacit equation that she meant by "lemon pie" is like a new discovery for her. She is a lemon pie and, of course, she is not a lemon pie. She seems to ponder the idea that to talk about lemon pie was a metaphor for her. What happens here is a "now moment" as described in the clinical literature (Stern 2004).

Our conclusion is, first, to expand the basic CA rule so that speakers can be considered self-listeners and that sometimes they respond to their own utterances. This is, for example, the case in the many studies on self-repair (Corrin 2010; Forrester 2008; Kitzinger 2013). Mary responds to her utterance with a delay, she seems to need time to understand, herself, what she has uttered here. Something seems to happen that could not have been predicted from the previous turns. Then, Mary points out something implicit, her formulation not only says "I am sour" or "lemon pies are sour", both of which would be trivial; she combines both formulations in a way that "something else" is created. Applying the linguistic analysis of metaphor (Lakoff 1987) we can write in a formal way:

a) Lemon pie = (attribute) "sour"
b) Mary = (attribute) "sour" (summarizing many of her utterances in such a formula)
   From what follows the abductive conclusion
c) (talk about) Lemon pie = (talk about) Mary

Which means, the flash of that moment throws a new light on the couple's common talk, retrospectively. Talking about lemon pie acquires a new meaning, it appears as talk about being "sour" oneself, she and Peter. Talking about lemon pie silences a relevant emotional meaning of the couple's talk. The cognitive dimension of this affordance cannot be overlooked. It requires a style of cognitive fluidity, it frees her from the anger she has uttered. She explodes in laughter about her self-surprising formulation; Peter cannot follow the curvilinearity of this change. A surplus of meaning emerges which can be read as "I am the lemon pie (we have been talking about)".

Daniel Stern: "now moments"

Mary laughs because she listens to how she produced a "now moment" (Stern 2004). Her formulation could open a playground in the same way as a child discovers a banana as a telephone and another person steps in by taking a second banana and so a funny telephone play could start. However, now moments require a special kind of answer that changes them to "moments of meetings" – a meeting not within the limits of rules and institutionalized forms, but existential encounter. Stern describes how "now moments" have a time of 8 to 10 seconds to wait for a response. Here it is Peter who does not grasp the chance to evolve the now moment into a moment-of-meeting.

It is a pity that Daniel Stern's theory has been developed without an exchange with CA traditions. But these traditions can easily be recalled. In a shortened version one could say that people's conversation under normal circumstances is guided by standard rules of conduct. This is even the case in psychotherapy. However, sometimes it happens that this role-guided conversation ends and a new, more existential, deeper level of conversation is opened (the now moment) and during 8 to 10 seconds one can wait to see if a response is found, that the other conversationalist has understood that "something more" (Stern 2004) happens (Voutilainen et al. spoke of "something else"). Viewed in a social science framework this is not as surprising as one might think:

> Joint spontaneous involvement is a *unio mystico*[3](!), a socialized trance. We must also see that a conversation has a life of its own and makes demands on its own behalf.
>
> (Goffman, 1967, p. 113)

Goffman views role-bound interaction as unavoidable in order to protect each other's face, mutually. As well as *unio mystico* having a slight spiritual overtone, he considers the individual self as "ceremonial", even as "sacred":

> It is therefore important to see that the self is in part a ceremonial thing, a sacred object which must be treated with proper ritual care and in turn must be presented in a proper light to others. As a means through which this self is established, the individual acts with proper demeanor while in contact with others and is treated by others with deference. It is just as important to see that if the individual is to play this kind of sacred game, then the field must be suited to it. The environment must assure that the individual will not pay too high a price with good demeanor and the deference will be accorded to him. Deference and demeanor practices must be institutionalized so that the individual will be able to project a viable, sacred self and stay in the game on a proper ritual basis.
>
> (Goffman, 1967, p. 91)

Ritual and ritual care, "game", field, institutionalized practice (and we could add "rules" and "norms") – Goffman uses all these terms in order to analyze how individuals mutually protect each other from malicious behavior. He knows that conversation and interaction always run this risk of derailment. However, he sees more than such destructive ends if rule-governed behavior were to be given up. In rare "moments and their men" (p. 3) a kind of higher deference might be enacted. We add, that these moments might include a realization that we live not only in one world, but in many. This is a step out of a couple's collusion (in clinical terms), out of only one "phantasma" (in Bühler's terms) into a multifaceted world with various (epistemic, affective, deontic) "orders" (in terms of intersubjectivity theory) and all this is done by talk-in-interaction of which we have described the power of silencing-while-speaking.

Conclusion – toward a typology of interactive silencing

As to the topic of silence and silencing, we found the analysis of this couple's conversation extremely fruitful. Social theorists and conversation analysts take intense interest in processes of silence and silencing. Keywords for their theoretical interests in silencing are communicative absence, noticeable absence, the developing of analytical role conceptions, and we could show the usefulness of linguistic metaphor analysis demonstrating that something like a "lemon pie" is an object of reality and then can jump into another cognitive context. We want to inspire a further study of such "hybrid objects" (Gallagher 2015).

We saw how Mary accuses Peter with list-colligations, how he defends himself by disassembly, and how Peter managed not to take a stance, and how, for one moment, Mary could allow herself to formulate an utterance which could have had the potential to change things deeply; unfortunately, Peter could not respond. Although this couple speaks a lot, one gets a detailed impression of what it is that is unsaid. Relevant theories were brought in, in order to make some things visible.

One gets an idea why talking with couples in a therapeutic context is so often difficult. We were informed that this couple finished a two-year therapy, and today, a katamnestic interview revealed, they live happily together, with children.

Why, we want to ask at the end, is it so difficult for a couple to break through the walls of silence? Are there general reasons that might make it difficult to perform or demand a personal stance? We think, there are some general reasons why this is a risky endeavor. To conclude, we will try to address these reasons or motivations as different types of silence and/or silencing.

We described how Goffman had a fine sensitivity for the "sacred game" of interaction and conversation. Skillfully, many people manage to correct errors and this is, often enough, an interactional resource. Not to address difficult things in an interaction often enough keeps things going. We call this first type "Silence or Silencing as not addressing the obvious".

We could learn (Jefferson 1974) that people often do this in such a way that they do not seem to realize at all how they denied that a noteworthy difficulty appeared. However, such denial is, then, soon established as a next rule for the continuing conversation and once you have committed yourself to this rule of denial you begin to feel how difficult it would be to break it. One reason can be assumed in circumstances thus produced. If you deny the denial you risk being accused of having committed yourself to the rule. Thus, to overcome this second type, "Silence as denial of denial", is a complex conversational operation; whoever tries to overcome this in a long-established relationship runs the risk of being treated as a traitor or a scapegoat. To understand this conversational process more deeply will be a task for applied conversation analysis in psychotherapy.

We made use of the concept of "stance" as developed in Conversation Analysis and Interactional Linguistics. Drawing on the systematics outlined in Couper-Kuhlen and Selting (2018: chap. C, 1–68), we interpreted moments of silence and/or silencing as public displays of epistemic, deontic, or affective stance.

We continue our simple systematics of silencing by including, but going beyond, noticeable absences as advocated from the early days of CA onwards by Sacks and colleagues by the following types.

In moments of *epistemic stance*, we found that after a long pause, Mary displays a broader or, if you will, deeper understanding of the couple's complex situation by uttering "the lemon pie is so:: sour". Peter displays no understanding here and does not make any attempt to question or sustain her epistemic stance. Third, we call this "Silence as passing over an initiative (without further comment")".

Fourth, he positions himself as someone who can give his wife good advice, telling her what she has to do in order to cope with her difficult relationship to the people surrounding the couple who do not appreciate her pursuing a serious carreer: "I'd like you not to take it so personally /" (line 220). We call this type "Silencing as repression of a disturbance or worry". We could argue that this *deontic stance* is, in a way, silencing his wife's attempt to achieve a better understanding via self-irony and thus to see their collusional curse from a bird's-eye perspective.

Fifth, in displays of affective stance we saw that a silence can reign as a sign of something missing. After having reported that his "second mother Sabine" actually said that he would be better off with "another type of woman" instead of Mary, Mary waits for him to take an affective stance, which he does not. We call this "Silencing as non-delivery". As Couper-Kuhlen and Selting have it:

Since speakers are interacting with others and these others can be expected to have stances too, a speaker's stance will align, or not, with that of the co-interlocutor.

(2018, p. 1; cf. also Du Bois 2007)

But, sixth, Peter does not take this affective stance. This noticeable absence is followed by a stance by Mary, affective in nature, claiming to be hurt. This is yet again another type of silencing, because Mary only does her husband's job, so to speak. Instead, she could have requested the delivery of the missing stance, by insisting that Peter utter it. Thus, Mary practices what we call a "Silence as non-challenging."

In a nutshell then, the communicative task the participants in our single case study attributed to themselves and quite thoroughly pursuit could be phrased as

- either keeping silence, i.e. not wording what the other expects in sequentially defined moments of talk-in-interaction (cf. the noticeable absences due to the expectation of (dis)alignment with stance above)
- or to take a stance without being invited to do so in order to silence certain affects as in the case of the deontic stance "you should not take things too personally".

This simplest of systematics, so we hope, could inspire further investigation for a classification of silencing in conversation.

Appendix – German transcript versions

Segment (1)

```
32 Mary: ich wIll dich nicht kontrolLIEren.
33       w:as ich\ was ich IMmer, (2.1)
34       was ich immer MEIne is ähm:- (0.7)
35       einfach dass du mich auch mal so als beRA-
         terin siehst.
36       und das gefÜhl HAB ich nIcht;
37       (1.0)
38       ich hab das geFÜHL dass: ähm-
39       dass du meh:r (0.7) auf ähm: (.) auf den rat
         anderer MENschen hörst?
```

```
40   wenn du (den\ letztendlich) ne entSCHEIdung
     triffst-
41   was zu machen oder NICH zu machen? (0.5)
42   mEhr auf die entscheidung dieser anderen per-
     SOnen hörst-
43   als dass was ich dir (0.6) gerRAten hab;
44   <<all> weil letzendlich is genau dasSELbe was
     ich dir gesAgt hab> nur- °hh
45   im dritt\ n_n: wenn du mir was MITteilst
     sagst-
46   jA aber FElix hat gemeint dass; (0.4)
47   nEin aber mein PApa hat gesagt dass;
48   nee MAma hat gemeint;=
49 Peter: =<<:->(auf) mein PApa hör_ch nich;>=
50 Mary: =na gut deine MUTter;
  51 Peter: <<schnaufend>h° <lachend>hehe>> (0.7)
°hh äh::;
    52   (2.6)
```

Segment (2)

```
90 Mary: und AUßerdem weil es saBIne war.
91   (3.6)
92   weil saBIne ja gesagt hat dass wir uns lieber
     TRENnen sollten.
93   (0.5)                                    ←
94 Peter: nEin das hat sabIne NICH gesagt.
95   saBIne hatte gesagt dass ich äh: (1.2)
96   DASS: dass (1.0) es::: äh:::(2.6)
97   ja doch vielleicht hat sie_s <<behaucht>DOCH
     gesagt->
98 Mary: hast du mir doch geS[AGT,]
99 Peter: [äh ] sie hat nIch gesagt
   dass wir uns TRENnen sollen.=
100 =(dass) vielleicht für mich ne andere Art
    FRAU besser wäre;
101 (3.4)
102 Mary: n_das_is: verLETzend für mich.
```

103 (0.6)
104 <<creaky, p> ja> so sehr die sabIne dir
     NAheliegt,
105 [weil sie] ja solange
106 Peter: [((räuspern))]
107 Mary: [auf dich] Aufgepasst hat als du KIND
     warst.
108 Peter: [((räuspern))]
109 (0.9)
110 Mary: und und du sie schOn: sehr wie eine
     MUTter (wert)schätzt;
111 Peter: hm_hm,

Segment (3)

180 Mary ich (.) ich hÄtte gern faMIlie.
181 (1.2)
182 ich wÜrde mich gerne auch AUSruhen in
     jEmandem; (0.3)
183 bei jemandem AUSruhen;
184 (1.5)
185 und das is das: was ich in den letzten jAh-
     ren nich HATte;
186 (0.8)
187 Peter: ja aber du hast es auch nich EINge-
     fordert oder auch nich-
188 Mary: wEil es mir nich ganz beWUSST war.
189 aber jetzt WEISS ich es auch.
190 aber hätte ich (0.4) die möglichkeit geHABT
     mit °h ((schnieft)) mit- (0.5)
191 EIner von diesen leuten die jetzt sAgen;
192 ich will karRIEre oder sowas. (0.7)
193 JEmals drauf Angesprochen HÄTten; (1.3)
194 hätte ich mit denen geREdet und dann
     <<pp>ähm>-
195 wäre ich sicherlich auch äh_äh den\ mein\
     hätte ich denen meinen
  STANDpunkt besser (xxx xxx) machen können.

196 (2.0)
197 oder KLArer.
198 (0.7)
199 <<p>ja (0.3) SAgen können;>
200 (2.7)
201 ((schnieft))
202 (4.7)
203 <<p> der zitrOnenkuchen is so: SAUer;
204 (0.8)
205 Peter: <<all> WAS sagst du;>
206 Mary: ((lacht))
207 (1.7)
208 Peter: <<lachend> WAS,>
209 [der war ganz] süß der schmeckt ganz wenig nur nach ziTROne.
210 Mary: [(xxx xxx xxx)] lachend ⬅——————
211 Peter: [<<lachend>(ka_ma schon ESsen;)>]
212 Mary: [<<>(ah ganz WEnig;)>]
213 ((schnieft))
214 Peter: ((lacht))
215 (0.8)
216 Peter °h ja
217 (1.2)
218 Peter aber ich find halt (.) also äh_äh_äh: dass-\ ich find halt
 trOtzdem (irg_wie) dass du das NICH so- (1.0)
219 <<p> na j_is\ es_is so schwer zu SAgen;>
220 ich hätte gerne dass du_s wEniger perSÖNlich nimmst.

Notes

1 Thanks to Professor Dr. Christian Roesler, Freiburg (Germany) for handing over the videotapes to our research group; the couple signed an informed consent sheet and was assured anonymity in all publications.
2 The transcriptions have been made by ear and with the help of the Software *Overtone Analyser*. Special thanks to Maruan Sakas for lending his correcting ears. The number eight beneath Peter's stave indicates that his voice sounds one octave lower. Music notes are transcribed to the German words; notes and syllables are not synchronous in the English version.
3 The correct Latin version should be *unio mystica*.

References

Bercelli, F., Rossano, F., & Viaro, M. (2008). Clients' responses to therapists' reinterpretations. In: A. Peräkylä, C. Antaki, S. Vehviläinen, & I. Leudar (Eds.), *Conversation Analysis and Psychotherapy* (pp. 43–61). Cambridge: Cambridge University Press.
Bergmann, J. R. (1987). *Klatsch. Zur Sozialform der diskreten Indiskretion.* Berlin/New York: de Gruyter.
Boszormenyi-Nagy, I. (1973). *Invisible Loyalties.* Hagerstown, MD: Medical Department Harper & Row.
Bühler, K. (2011). *Theory of Language. The Representational Function of Language* (A. Eschbach &.,D. F. Goodwin, Trans.). Amsterdam, Philadelphia, PA: John Benjamins. (Original work published 1934).
Collins, R. (2008). *Violence — A Micro-Sociological Theory.* Princeton, NJ, Oxford: Princeton University Press.
Corrin, J. (2010). Hm? What? Maternal repair and early child talk. In: H. Gardner & M. A. Forrester (Eds.), *Analysing Interactions in Childhood. Insights from Conversation Analysis* (pp. 23–42). Chichester, UK: Wiley-Blackwell.
Couper-Kuhlen, E., & Selting, M. (2018). *Interactional Linguistics.* Cambridge: Cambridge University Press.
Dicks, H. V. (1967). *Marital Tensions.* London: Routledge and Kegan Paul.
Dreyer, F. (2018). "Und ich bin der Räuber" – Erwartungsstrukturen in der alternativen Realität des Spiels. In: G. Brandstetter, M. B. Buchholz, A. Hamburger, & C. Wulf (Eds.), *Balance – Rhythmus – Resonanz – Sonderheft der Zeitschrift Paragrana, Internationale Zeitschrift für Historische Anthropologie, Band 27, Heft 1* (pp. 237–252). Berlin: Walter de Gruyter.
Ehmer, O. (2011). *Imagination und Animation. Die Herstellung mentaler Räume durch Animierte Rede.* Berlin, New York: de Gruyter.
Forrester, M. A. (2008). The emergence of self-repair: A case study of one child during the early preschool years. *Research on Language and Social Interaction, 41*(1), 99–128.
Frank, M. G. (2005). Research methods in detecting deception research. In: J. A. Harrigan, R. Rosenthal, & K. R. Scherer (Eds.), *The New Handbook of Methods in Nonverbal Behavior Research* (pp. 341–368). New York: Oxford University Press.
Gallagher, S. (2015). Why we are not all novelists. In: P. F. Bundgaard & F. Stjernfelt (Eds.), *Investigations into the Phenomenology and the Ontology of the Work of Art* (pp. 129–143). Cham: Springer International Publishing.
Goffman, E. (1963). *Behavior in Public Places. Notes on the Social Organization of Gatherings.* New York: The Free Press.
Goffman, E. (1967). *Interaction Ritual: Essays on Face-To-Face Behavior.* Garden City, NY: Doubleday.
Goffman, E. (1981). *Forms of Talk.* Philadelphia, PA: University of Pennsylvania Press.
Goffman, E. (2008). *The Presentation of Self in Everyday Life.* New York: Anchor Books. (Original work published 1959).
Goodwin, M. H. (2012). Interaktion, Sprachpraxis und die Konstruktion sozialer Universen. In: R. Ayaß & C. Meyer (Eds.), *Sozialität in slow motion. Theoretische und Empirische Perspektiven; Festschrift für Jörg Bergmann* (pp. 269–299). Wiesbaden: Springer VS.

Goodwin, M. H., Cekaite, A., & Goodwin, C. (2012). Emotion as stance. In: A. Peräkylä & M.-L. Sorjonen (Eds.), *Emotion in Interaction* (pp. 16–41). New York: Oxford University Press.

Gregory, S., Webster, S., & Huang, G. (1993). Voice pitch and amplitude convergence as a metric of quality in dyadic interviews. *Language and Communication, 13*(3), 195–217.

Günthner, S. (1997). The contextualization of affect in reported dialogues. In: S. Niemeier & R. Dirven (Eds.), *The Language of Emotions* (pp. 247–277). Amsterdam/Philadelphia, PA: John Benjamins.

Heritage, J. (2012). The epistemic engine: Sequence organization and territories of knowledge. *Research on Language and Social Interaction, 45*(1), 30–52.

Jaffe, J., Beebe, B., Feldstein, S., Crown, C. L., & Jasnow, M. D. (2001). Rhythms of dialogue in infancy: Coordinated timing in development. *Monographs of the Society for Research in Child Development, 66*(2), 1–132.

Jefferson, G. (1974). Error correction as an interactional resource. *Language in Society, 3*(2), 181–199.

Jefferson, G. (2017) *Repairing the Broken Surface of Talk. Managing Problems in Speaking, Hearing, and Understanding in Conversation* (J. R. Bergmann & P. Drew, Eds.). New York: Oxford University Press.

Kitzinger, C. (2013). Repair. In: J. Sidnell & T. Stivers (Eds.), *The Handbook of Conversation Analysis* (pp. 229–257). Chichester, West Sussex, UK: Wiley-Blackwell.

Lakoff, G. (1987). *Women, Fire, and Dangerous Things. What Categories Reveal about the Mind*. Chicago, IL/London: The University of Chicago Press.

De la Motte-Haber, H. (1985). *Handbuch der Musikpsychologie* [A handbook of music psychology]. Laaber, Germany: Laaber-Verlag.

Papoušek, M., Papoušek, H., & Symmes, D. (1991). The meanings of melodies in motherese in tone and stress languages. *Infant Behavior and Development, 14*(4), 415–440.

Peräkylä, A. (2015). From narcissism to face work: Two views on the self in social interaction. *American Journal of Sociology, 121*(2), 445–474.

Pietikäinen, K. S. (2018). Silence that speaks. The local inferences of withholding a response in intercultural couples' conflicts. *Journal of Pragmatics, 129*, 76–89.

Pomerantz, A. (1984). Pursuing a response. In: J. M. Atkinson & J. Heritage (Eds.), *Structures of Social Action* (pp. 152–166). New York: Cambridge University Press.

Sacks, H., & Jefferson, G. (1992/1995). *Lectures on Conversation*. Oxford: Basil Blackwell.

Selting, M. (2004). Listen: Sequenzielle und prosodische Struktur einer kommunikativen Praktik – Eine Untersuchung im Rahmen der Interaktionalen Linguistik. *Zeitschrift für Sprachwissenschaft, 23*(1), 1–46.

Selting, M. (2007). Lists as embedded structures and the prosody of list construction as an interactional resource. *Journal of Pragmatics, 39*(3), 483–526.

Stevanovic, M., & Koski, S. E. (2018). Intersubjectivity and the domains of social interaction: Proposal of a cross-sectional approach. *Psychology of Language and Communication, 22*(1), 39–70.

Stevanovic, M., & Peräkylä, A. (2014). Three orders in the organization of human action: On the interface between knowledge, power, and emotion in interaction and social relations. *Language in Society, 43*(2), 185–207.
Stern, D. N. (2004). *The Present Moment in Psychotherapy and Everyday Life.* New York/London: W.W. Norton & Company.
Vehviläinen, S. (2003). Preparing and delivering interpretations in psychoanalytic interaction. *Textile, 23*(4), 573–606.
Voutilainen, L., Peräkylä, A., & Ruusuvuori, J. (2010). Recognition and interpretation: Responding to emotional experience in psychotherapy. *Research on Language and Social Interaction, 43*(1), 85–107.
Willi, J. (1984). The concept of collusion: A combined systemic-psychodynamic approach to marital therapy. *Family Process, 23*, 177–185.

Index

Note: Page numbers in *italics* indicate figures and page numbers in **bold** indicate tables.

4'33" (Cage) 77, 81–84

Abhishiktananda, S. 29
Abraham, K. 145
abstraction: aesthetic thinking and 68; Feldman and 77–80; Mondrian and 79; music and 68, 73–74, 77–79; visual arts and 68, 79–80; Xenakis and 73–74
Acheson, K. 276, 312
Acheson, Rachel 247
acoustic silence 88
active developmental process 110
active silencing 3
Adelung, Johann Christoph 64
adolescent therapy 247
Adorno, Theodor W. 70–71
aesthetics 64–66, 68, 80
affective stance 351–352, 362–363
affect regulation 111
African music 77
afterwards silence 10
Akhtar, Salman 101
Alder, M.-L. 283
Allais, Alphonse 62
allusive talk 283
ambient sounds 81–82, 84
American Psychoanalytic Association 109
Améry, Jean 18
Ames, Van Meter 82
anacoluthons 46
anal eroticism 134
analytic listening: analyst silence and 187, 190, 192–193; derivative comment and 272n7; silence and 102; traumatic silence and 208
analytic site 187–189
analytic state of consciousness 161–162
Analyzing Situation, The (Donnet) 187
anechoic chambers 94–95
Anna Freud Center 247
Anthropometrien 66
anticipatory silence 10
area of creation 128–129, 161
Arlow, J. A. 132–133
articulated speech (*exophasia*) 43, 94
associational pauses 237
attachment trauma: acknowledgment and 200; children and 199–200, 202; disorganized attachment patterns and 199; silencing and 102, 199–200, 202–203, 209
attention: analyst silence and 187; as commodity 92; contemplative silence and 136; continuous speech and 88; demands on 92–93, 95;

distractions and 93, 96; free-floating 149, 209; maintaining 66; musical silences and xxiii, 66–67, 76; shared intentionality and 292; silence and 7, 43, 74, 148; verbal signals for 50
Aurobindo, Sri 29
Avdi, Evrinomy 247

Bach, Johann Sebastian 67
Bagatellen für Streichquartett (Webern) 68
Baker, R. 117
Balint, Michael 4, 57n4, 159–161, 165, 168, 252
Baudelaire, Charles 71
Beck, Aron 211
Beck Depression Inventory (BDI) 247
Beebe, Beatrice 163
Beethoven, Ludwig van 22, 68, 80
benign regression 157, 160, 165
Bergson, Henri 78
Bern, Eric 211
Bertman, Stephen 93
Bertrand, Aloysius 72
Bion, W. 102, 129, 148, 193
Black Lives Matter protests 11
black silence 108
blank silence 138
Bollas, Christopher 252
Bonacchi, Silvia 4
Bose, Girindrasekhar 38
Bowlby, John 17
Boyle Spelman, Margaret 102
Brähler, E. 233
Breuer, Josef 142
brief pauses 252
Bromberg, P. M. 23n9
Bucci, Wilma 165
Buchholtz, Michael B. 227–228, 292
Buddhism 30–31, 38
Bühler, Karl 258, 259, 352–353
bulimia nervosa treatment 244–245
burdening silence 46
Burke, Edmund 16

Bush administration 16, 19
Busoni, Ferruccio 65

Cage, John: *4'33"* 77, 81–84; on absence of silence 88–89; ambient sounds and 84; influence of Buddhism on 82–83; musical silences and 77, 81–82; pauses in music 271n1; silence as awakening and 88; silence as collaborator 90
Cain, Susan 88
Carpenter, M. 292
CEMPP-Project (Conversation analysis of Empathy-Psychotherapy Process) 272n4
CEMPP project transcriptions: complex reasoning and 258–260; lapses in 276–291; Munich psychotherapy study 276; original German transcripts 268–271, 292–302; patient slips and 254–258; pauses in 254–263, 266–267; pointing gestures and 258–259; RLRI model and 277–278, 284, 287–289, 291; self-repairs and 254–258, 261–263, 267; silence in 276–277; therapist slips in 261–267
Chaudhuri, H. 29
childhood trauma: acknowledgment and 200–201, 203; attachment trauma and 199–200, 202–203, 209; consequences of 199–200; helpful adults and 200–201; lack of empathic understanding for 201, 210; mental disorders and 200–203, 212n1; silencing and 200–203, 209; *see also* trauma
chordal signals 50
Christianity 31–35, 37
classical drive theory 252
Clinical Diary (Ferenczi) 162, 209
Clinical Notes on Disorders of Childhood (Winnicott) 173
co-construction 49–50, 343

cocoon transference 114
cognitive behavioral therapy (CBT) 244–246
Collines d'Anacapri, Les (Debussy) 70
Collins, R. 349
collusion 153–154, 165, 229, 354, 360
Coltart, N. 109, 144
common ground 50, 57n9, 107, 267, 292
communication: nonverbal 42, 56n2, 106; Other-referential 42, 47; pauses in 254; phatic 251; self-referential 42; silence and 110; silence in dialogical situations (DS) 42, 44–50; silence in non-dialogical situations (NDS) 42–44; silencing in 53–54; *see also* conversations; social interactions
Communicational Structure (Scheflen) 56n2
communicative absence 333–334
competitive overlapping 49
complex reasoning 258–260
Compositions (Young) 77
computer textual analysis 246
conspiracy of silence 102–103, 206–207
contemplative silence 135–136
conversation analysis (CA): central methodological resource of 277; clinical practice and 275; computer textual analysis and 246; feeling silences 243; gaps in 310; General List Completer (GLC) and 339–340; information in 229; Interpersonal Process Recall method (IPR) and 326–327; intersubjectivity and 343; intuition and 253; lapses in 10, 310–311, 325–326; linguistics and 45, 224–225; meaning of an utterance in 357–358; neutral silences 236–237; noticeable absences in 334–337; obstructive silences 237–240; patient silence and 55, 233–240; patient slips and 254–258; pauses and silences in 226–229, 252, 275, 310, 326–327; PICS and 234–248; pointing gesture and 258–259; productive silences 235–236; psychoanalysis and 55, 219, 224; RLRI model 277–278, **278**, 284, 287–289, 291; rules of conversational sequence in 277; sequential analysis and 45, 229, 260; social life and 224; speakers as self-listeners 358; speech and 223; stance in 351–352, 362; transcription and 224–226; transcription symbols 225–226; *see also* lapses; pauses
conversations: affect in 351; central activities and 310, 314; common activities and 311–312; deictic gesture and 352; embodied behaviors in 309, *309*; finding the right words in 275; gaps in 310; interaction order in 308; interpreting silence in 307–310; lapses in 310–311; listeners in 349; noticeable absences in 334–337; pauses as elements of 253–254; pauses in 275, 310; quiet and 252; rules of sequence in 277; silence and 252, 275; social roles in 349; speaker in 349; transition-relevant place (TRP) and 275–276; *see also* social interactions
Cook, J. J. 233
cooperative overlapping 49–50
countertransference: analyst silence and 188, 256; negative 149; psychoanalysts and 111; silence as resistance to 146–150, 155n6; *see also* transference-countertransference
Couper-Kuhlen, E. 351, 362
couple's interview: accuse-and-defense scenario in 337–339; accuse

by list-colligation 338–339, 361; brooding thinking and 345, *345*, 346; cognitive fluidity and 359; communicative absence and 334; critical assessment and 354–356; defense by disassembly in 339–340, 361; displacement of *origo* 352–354; embodied behaviors in *345*, 346, *346*, 347, *347*, 348, *348*, 356, *356*, 357, *357*, 358, *358*; German transcripts of 363–366; interactive silencing in 361; invisible loyalties and 343–348; musicalization and 340–343, 350, *350*, 351–352; noticeable absences in 342, 352, 354; "now moment" in 359–360; paradoxon in 342–343; producing and closing the list 340–343; role-bound interaction 360–361; sequential analysis and 356; silence in 361–362; silencing and 343, 350, 361–363; stance in 351–352, 361–362; token-as-type format in 343, 358; use of quotations 348–350, 352, 354
Crafoord, C. 107
creative silence 108
creativity 184, 210–211
Cremerius, J. 148
cultural contexts: idealized silence in 106; nonverbal communication and 106; psychoanalysis and 108–109; psychotherapeutic interactions and 108–109; silence in 4–5, 105–108, 118
Cushman, Philip 15–22

Dadaism 62–63
Dalai Lama 35–36
Daniel, S. F. 245
Dauenhauer, Bernard 10
Davies, O. 30
Davoine, F. 14
Debussy, Claude 69–72

deep listening 76
deep silence 10
defensive silence 130–132
deictic gesture 352
deictic words 352–353
De la Motte-Haber, H. 4
Delic, Amra 206–207
De Mauro, T. 43
Denhoff, Michael 63
deontic stance 351–352, 362–363
depression 245–247
developmental arrest 110
dialogical situations (DS): burdening silence in 46; chordal signals and 50; co-construction and 49–50; common ground in 50, 57n9; competitive overlapping in 49; conditional access and 50; cooperative overlapping in 49–50; eloquent silence in 53; interpreting silence in 51–53; interruptions in 49; length of silence in 47–49; Listener silence in 44–50; Other-referential 42, 47; overlapping in 49–50; prolonged gaps and 49; responce latency 51–52; silence as off-record act in 51–52; silence in 42; Speaker silence in 44–50; TRPs in 44, 48–49; turn-taking in 48–50
Dimitrijević, Aleksandar 101–102
direct quotations 348
disengaged pauses 237, 247
Distracted (Jackson) 93
Donnet, Jean-Luc 187
Dorsky, Nathaniel 90
doublethinking 16
Dreyer, Florian 4, 228, 271n1
drive theory 134, 139n3, 252

early identity formation 110
Eckart, Meister 64, 82
ego psychology 139n3, 258
Egypt 28
Ehrenberg, Darlene 148

Ekelöf, Gunnar 105
Eliot, George 27
eloquent silence 43, 53
embodied silence 43
emotional pauses 235
empathy 179, 201, 210, 233, 253
empiricism 222, 230n1
enactive silence 132–134
Endo, Shusaku 37
endophasia (inner speech) 43
epistemic stance 351–352, 362
Erikson, Erik 17
ethical ambiguity 17
ethical speaking 14
exophasia (articulated speech) 43
expressive pauses 235

Faimberg, H. 192
Fanon, Frantz 11
Fast Runner 106
feeling silences 243
Feldman, Morton 77–81
Ferenczi, Sándor: on countertransference 149; on hypocrisy in psychoanalysis 209; ostracism of 14, 213n11; on personal analysis 155n8; on psychoanalysis 208; on regressed patients 158; on silence in patients 145, 149; therapeutic silence and 102; traumatic silence and 14; on traumatized children 201; on unconscious communication 162–163
film 89–90
Finland 107, 228, 312–313
folk rituals 27–28
Fonagy, P. 129
For Philip Guston (Feldman) 78
forsaken silence 37–38
Fragmente – Stille, an Diotima (Nono) 74–75
Frank, A. 129
Frank, M. G. 348

Frankel, Jay 102, 153, 162
Frankel, Z. 244
Frankfurt School 208
Franzen, Michael M. 4, 228
Freedman, Norbert 102, 165–169
Freiburg Institute of Advanced Studies (FRIAS) 228
French métamusique 69–72
Freud, Sigmund: analysis of slips 255; on analyst silence 146; conversation and 223–224; infant development and 172, 179; on memory lapses 219–222; on object absence 190, 195; on perceptual identity 194; psychoanalysis and xxiii, 102; on silence as resistance 57n11, 145, 252; talking cure and 142, 171, 208; on unconscious communication 221–224; unconscious motivation and 16
Fromm, Erich 17, 208
Fromm-Reichman, Frieda 211

Gadamer, Hans-Georg 10
Gale, J. 254
Gallagher, S. 353
Gandhi, Mahatma 29
gaps 49, 56, 275, 310
Garfinkel, Harold 277
Gaspard de la nuit (Ravel) 72
Gaudillière, J.-M. 14
gender 139
General List Completer (GLC) 339–340
Gill, Merton 148
Gindi, S. 242
Ginzburg, J. 260
Glass, Philip 77
Glover, E. 168
Goethe, Johann Wolfgang 68
Goffman, E. 333, 349, 360, 361
Goldberg, J. A. 49
Goldman, D. 172
Goodwin, C. 280

Greece 28, 32
Green, A. 102, 189, 192–195
Greene, Graham 18
Greenson, R. R. 145
Gregory Palamas, Saint 32
Gröning, Philip 34, 90
Grosz, George 62
Guzmán, M. 242, 243

Hadda, J. 109
Hall, Tom 78
Hallelujah (Händel) 67
Händel, Georg Friedrich 67
Handford, Michael 88
Hart, Onno van der 23n8
Haydn, Joseph 66
Hegel, G. W. F. 10
Heidegger, Martin 10
Heimann, P. 191
Henry, Pierre 66
Heritage, J. 292
Herma (Xenakis) 73
hermeneutics 222
heroism of silence 8–9
Heschel, Abraham 15
Hirsbrunner, Theo 72
history 20–22
Hoey, E. 311–312, 314
Hoffman, Irwin 16, 19–20
Holocaust 12, 204, 206
Holtmann, K. C. 245
Huber, D. 245
human dignity 13–14
human experience: distractions and 93–95; dizzying disorientation and 92–93, 95–96; noise and 90–92; silence and 87, 90, 106; technology and 91
Huxley, Aldous 91, 94
Hyperculture (Bertman) 93

immigrants 208
India 28–29
Indian music 77

"Indirect Language and the Voices of Silence" (Merleau-Ponty) 9
ineffable, the 26–27, 37–38, 64
inner speech 94
inner speech (*endophasia*) 43, 94
inner transformation 106
Inori (Stockhausen) 65
In Pursuit of Silence 4, 94
In Silence (Merton) 36
interactional linguistics 362
interactional pauses 238
inter-affectivity 191
Intermission 6 (Feldman) 77–78
International Psychoanalytic Association 210
Interpersonal Process Recall method (IPR) 326–327
interpersonal relationships 106, 109–110; *see also* couple's interview
interruptions 46–47, 49–50; *see also* self-interruptions
interruption science 93
intersubjective silence 152–154, 158, 162–165
intersubjective systems theory 14
intersubjectivity 191, 343
intervening silence 10
Into Great Silence (*Die Grosse Stille*) 34, 90
intrapsychic conflict 157, 161
invisible loyalties 343–348
Ironien (*Ironies*) (Schulhoff) 63
Isaac, Bishop of Ninevah 32
Ives, Charles 65
Iyer, Pico 90, 95

Jackson, Maggie 93
Jacobs, T. 111
James, William 82–84
Jefferson, Gail 48, 224, 254, 275, 277, 339
Jesu, meine Freude (Bach) 67
John of the Cross 33, 37

Judaism 29–30
Jung, Carl 38
Just Mercy (Stevenson) 21

Kahn, M. 110
Kakar, Sudhir 38
Kandahar 106
Kandinsky, Wassily 68
Kant, Immanuel 22
Kavanagh, K. 33–34
Kenny, Colum 3
Khan, M. 137, 175
Kierkegaard, Søren 79
Kinderman, William 80
Kitarō, Nishida 83
Klein, Melanie 183, 211
Klein, Yves 66
Kleinberg-Levin, David 7–8
Kohut, Heinz 161, 210
Koski, S. E. 343
Krauss, Rosalind E. 79
Kurz, S. 109

Lachenmann, Helmut 75
Lacueva 28
Lane, R. C. 252
Langs, R. 252
language: cinematic 89; conversation analysis (CA) and 229; deictic gesture and 352; immigrant silencing and 208; impact of childhood trauma on 199, 204; the ineffable and 26; infant development and 172, 174; as living system 223; minority silencing and 212n7; music as 64, 71; in psychoanalysis 57n4; silent communication and 183
Lanzmann, Claude 12
Laplanche, J. 188
lapses: attributing meaning to 281; co-construction and 284; conversational objects and 281, 286, 288–289; as conversational turns 276; pre-announcements and 281; in social interactions 275–281; thought processes and 278, 281, 283–284, 286, 288–289, 291–292; uncertainty and 280–281, 283, 286
lapses in social interactions: common activities and 311–312; embodied behaviors in 312–314, 316, 318–320, 322–327; falling silent in 313–314; gaps and 310; interpreting silence in 307–309, *309*, 310; navigating out of 319–323; original Finnish transcripts 328–330; pauses and silences in 310; shared orientation of 314–315, *315*, 316, 323–326; treatment of 311; turn-taking in 311; unilateral orientation of 316–317, *317*, 318–321, *321*, 322, *322*, 323
L'art incohérent 62
learning disability case study 242–243
Leira, T. 111, 144
Levi, Primo 14
Levinas, Emmanuel 8, 12–15
Levine, Howard 102
Levitt, Heidi 227
Liebling, A. J. 9
Lifton, Robert Jay 16
Ligeti, György 64
linguistics: conversation analysis and 45, 224–225; *endophasia* (inner speech) and 43; *exophasia* (articulated speech) and 43; interactional 362; silence and 4, 41; silence in dialogical situations (DS) 42, 44–53; silence in non-dialogical situations (NDS) 42–44; silencing and 41; *Sprachnot* 54
listening: analyst silence and 181, 187, 190–193; analytic 102, 208, 272n7; attentive 46–47, 70; auditory comprehension and 73; conversation analysis (CA) and 229; deep 76; self-repairs and 254–255; traumatic memories and 204, 208, 212

Loewald, Hans 17
Lowen, Alexander 211
Lyotard, Jean-François 64

Maeterlinck, Maurice 71
Mahlstedt, Christopher 340
Maier, Thomas M. 81
malignant regressions 160, 165
Malinowski, B. 251
Mallarmé, Stéphane 71
Mannheimer Walze (Mannheim roller) 68
Marche funèbre composée pour les funérailles d'un grand homme sourd (Allais) 62
Maslow, Abraham 211
Mauclair, Camille 69, 71
Mazis, G. 9–10
meditation/contemplation 34–37
membership categorization 335
mental disorders: silencing and 198, 201–203; talking cure and 142; traumatic experience and 101–103, 201, 203
mental noise 91, 95–96
Merleau-Ponty, Maurice 8–12, 22, 37
Merleau-Ponty and the Face of the World (Mazis) 9
Merton, Thomas 35–36
Mesopotamia 28
Messiaen, Olivier 71–72
Metamusik Festivals 77
Middlemarch (Eliot) 27
Milarepa 31
mimic signs 221
minimal music 77
minority silencing 212n7
Mitchell, S. A. 162
Mit innigster Empfindung (Beethoven) 80
MMWY principle 50, 56, 254, 256, 260
mnemonic pauses 236
Modell, A. 109, 114

Molinos, Miguel de 88
Mondada, L. 313
Mondrian, Piet 79
Morrison, A. P. 109
Morrison, Jim xxiii
mother-infant interactions: empathy and 179; essential silence and 181–182; infant sense of self and 173, 182; integration and 175; me/not me divide in 176–177; personalization and 175; realization and 175; silence as transitional object 176–177; silence in 174; silent holding in 177–180; silent integration in 178; silent subjective communication and 183–184; unconscious communication and 163; Winnicott on 172–179, 181–184
movement 64
Mozart, Wolfgang Amadeus 69
Mudge, P. J. P. 30
Munich psychotherapy study 244, 276
music: abstraction and 68, 74; aesthetic thinking and 64–66; African 77; Dadaism and 62–63; forms of silence in 62–66; grid structures in 78–79; Indian 77; as language 64, 71; long-duration 77; metaphysics and 71–72; minimal 77; non-sounding elements in 65; pauses in 251; pragmatism and 82–83; production of 253; receptive aspects of 253
musicalization: couple's interview and 340–343, 350, *350*, 351–352; example of *341*; method of 340
musical silences: abstraction and 77–80; ambient sounds and 81–82, 84; attention and xxiii, 66–67, 76; Cage and 77, 81–84; Debussy and 69–71; deep listening and 76; fading elements in 65, 74–80; Feldman and 77–81; French métamusique and

69–72; importance of xxiii; Ives and 65; mathematical methods and 73–74; metaphysics and 84–85; minimal music and 77; new forms of silence in 76–77; Nono and 74–76; open closing cadences in 80; pure experience and 82–84; Ravel and 72; religious notions and 4, 84; rests in 66–70, 72–73, 84; sieve theory and 73; silence as collaborator 90; symbolist thought and 71–72, 84; twelve-tone music and 67–68; unsaid and 69; Webern and 67–68; Xenakis and 73–74
music theory 253
Musique de Silence, La (Mauclair) 69
mutual monitoring 333
my-mind-is-with-you (MMWY) *see* MMWY principle
mysticism xxiii, 38, 66

narcissism 109–110, 161
nature 9–10
neutral silences 236
New England Bound (Warren) 20
Newman, Barnett 80
Nhat Hanh, Thích 35
noise 90–92, 95–96
noise pollution 91
non-dialogical situations (NDS) 42–44
Nono, Luigi 74–76
nonverbal communication: body resources and 42; mother-infant interactions 163, 183–184; psychotherapeutic interactions and 56n2, 163; silence and 106; therapeutic transitions and 110–111; unconscious communication and 162–163
noticeable absences: collusion and 354; in conversation analysis 334–337; couple's interview and 342, 352, 354; as noticeable events 337; in quoting 336–337, 349

Nouwen, Henri 89
"now moments" 359–360

object relations: analyst presence and 117, 124; early trauma and 158, 160; projective identifications and 111; regressed patients and 158–160; renegotiating internalized 102, 157, 168; therapeutic silence and 158–161
object relations psychology 139n3
observables 222–223
obstructive silences 237–240
Ogden, Thomas 181
Oliver, Mary 90
Orange, Donna 3
Orfield Labs 94
origo 352–353
Ouspenskii, Pyotr Demianovich 68
Overbeck, G. 233
overlapping 49–50

Pappenheim, Bertha (Anna O.) 142
paradoxon 342–343
Parks, Tim 94
Parmenides 74
Part, Arvo 90
passionate silence 107
patient silence: associational pauses 237; conversation analysis and 55, 233–239; disengaged pauses 237–238, 247; emotional pauses 235; expressive pauses 235; in-session pauses and 233–234; interactional pauses 238–239; mnemonic pauses 236; neutral silences 236–237; obstructive silences 237–240; productive silences 235–236, 247; reflective pauses 235–236, 246; regressed patients and 158–162; as resistance 143–146, 152, 154, 154n1; silent holding and 177–178
patient slips 254–258, 267

pauses: associational 237; brief 252; communication and 254; in conversation analysis 226–229, 252; countertransference and 256; defining 310; disengaged 237–238, 247; as elements of conversation 253–254; emotional 235; expressive 235; in-session 233–234; interactional 238–239; mnemonic 236; musical 251; patient slips and 254–258; reflective 235–236, 246; self-repairs in 254–255, 257–258, 261; as temporary refusal to converse 260–261; transition-relevant place (TRP) and 275
Pausing Inventory Categorization System (PICS): across psychotherapy orientations 244–246; cross-cultural validation 241; examinations of silences and other processes 246–247; findings 242–246; intensive case studies and 242–243; interpersonal process recall (IPR) interviews 234; measure development 234; Munich psychotherapy study 244; therapist training and 239–240; therapy dialogue and 248; types of pauses 236–240; types of silences 234–240; validity and credibility 240–242; York University Depression Project I 243–244
Pavane pour une infante défunte (Ravel) 72
pediatrician-psychoanalysts 102
Pelléas et Mélisande (Debussy) 69
Peräkylä, A. 351
Perelberg, R. 193
phantasmatic worlds 353–354
phatic communion 251–252
phenomenology of silence: ambiguity and 7; ethical speaking and 14; Levinas and 13–14; Merleau-Ponty and 9–11, 22, 23n4; pregnant silence and 8–11; Sartre and 8–9; silence as complicity 15–22; technical rationality and 10; threatening silences and 11; trauma-frozen silences in 11–12
Picard, Max 90
PICS *see* Pausing Inventory Categorization System (PICS)
Pietikäinen, K. S. 334, 340
Pine, F. 139n3
Pizer, S. A. 162
Pluralistic Universe, A (James) 84
Poesio, M. 260
pointing gesture 258–259
Poland, Warren 17
pondering silence 107
pop music 77
positivism 222
power interruptions 49
pragmatism 82–83
pre-announcements 281
Prélude à l'après-midi d'un faune (Debussy) 69
Pressman, M. D. 146, 150
primal repression 129
process control interruptions 49
Process Experiential therapies 246
productive silences 235–236, 247
progressional overlap 50
prolonged gaps 49
Prophets, The (Heschel) 15
protection 106, 111
psychoanalysis: bulimia nervosa treatment and 244–245; burdening silence in 46; conversation analysis and 224; cultural significance of silence in 108–109; depression treatment and 245–247; empiricism/positivism in 222, 230n1; hermeneutics and 222; religious/spiritual silence and 38; research methods in 219; shame and 15; silence as complicity and 15–20; silence in xxi, xxii, xxiii, xxiv, xxv,

42, 101–102, 105–106, 138–139; silencing in 42, 54, 56, 103, 207–210; speaking the unspeakable in 14; as the talking cure 14, 108, 142; undoing silence in 14–15
psychoanalysts: countertransference and 111, 146–150, 191; ethical ambiguity and 17; ethical failures of 15–20; ethical responsibility and 21–22; fight against trauma 208–209; figurability and 195n2; intersubjectivity and 191; negative transference and 190–191; peer-supervision and 151; self-reflection and 150, 168; slips by 261–267; social trauma victims and 200–201
psychoanalyst silence: as action or thing 192; as analytic listening 187, 190, 192–193; analytic site and 188; attention and 187; as a behavior 187; countertransference and 188, 256; framing structure of 193; as impediment to analytic process 190; interpersonal negotiation and 162–163; as intersubjective resistance 152–154; metapsychological 187; neurotic patients and 189–190; patient interpretation of 192, 194; as potential space 192–195; presence/absence and 190, 193–195, 196n9; as resistance 111, 146–154; speech and 192, 195; transference and 188–189; Winnicott on 180
psychoanalytic institutions 210–211
psychodynamic therapy 245
psychotherapeutic interactions: attentiveness to communication in 275; blank silence and 138; complex reasoning in 258–260; contemplative silence and 135–136; cultural significance of silence in 108–109, 125; defensive silence and 130–132; desymbolizing silence and 167; enactive silence and 132–134; experiencing in 253; exploratory strategy and 119–123; forms of silence in 57n11; interpersonal negotiation and 157; interpreting silence in 54–56; intersubjective silence and 162–165; language in 57n4; lapses in 276, 291–292; micro-failures in 190; MMWY principle in 50, 56; narcissistic function of silence 164; negative transference and 190–191; nonverbal communication and 56n2, 163; patient slips and 254–258; pauses and silences in 254–267; pointing gestures and 258–259; regenerative silence and 137; regressed patients and 158–159; resistant silence and 143–154, 157, 161; silence and patient symbolizing 166–169; silence as benign regression in 157; silence as consolidation in 166; silence in 109–111, 180–181, 233; silencing in 54, 56; silent holding in 177–178; structural silence and 128–129; symbolic silence and 134–135; therapist slips in 261–267; transference-countertransference 116–119, 122–123; transformative silence and 167; transition-relevant place (TRP) and 261, 275; unconscious communication in 162–163; unmentalised silence and 129–130; verbal therapy in 55
Pythagoras 28

quiet 252
Quiet (Cain) 88
quotations 336–337, 348–349

Racker, H. 191
Rank, Otto 211
rape 206–207
Rauschenberg, Robert 89

Ravel, Maurice 72
recognitional overlap 50
reflective pauses 235–236, 246
regenerative silence 137
regressed patients 158–162
Reich, Steve 77
Reich, Wilhelm 208
Reik, Theodore xxi, xxii, 146, 220–222
Reinhardt, Ad 89
relational psychoanalysis 14, 162–163, 253
relational trauma 14
Religion de la Musique, La (Mauclair) 71
religious/spiritual silence: in Buddhism 30–31, 38; in Christianity 31–35; divine communication and 26; Egyptian 28; folk rituals and 27–28; forsaken silence and 37–38; Greek 28, 32; historical 3–4; in India 28–29, 38; the ineffable and 26–27; Jesus and 31–32; in Judaism 29–30; meditation/contemplation and 34–37; psychoanalysis and 38; receptivity and 26; relaxation and 26
Repairing the Broken Surface (Jefferson) 224
Repetition (Kierkegaard) 79
Requiem (Verdi) 76
resistance: analyst silence as 146–154; to countertransference 146–150, 155n6; intersubjective silence and 152–154, 158; intrapsychic conflict and 157, 161; meanings of 144–146; patient silence as 143–146, 152–154, 154n1; silence as 102, 109–111, 142, 157, 168, 252
responce latency 51–52
reverie 252
Revue Francaise de Psychanalyse 187
Ricoeur, Paul 13

Riley, Terry 77
Rilke, Rainer Maria 36, 90
ritual/taboo-motivated silence 44
Rizzuto, A. M. 110, 114
RLRI model 277–278, **278**, 281, 284, 287–289, 291
Rodriguez, O. 33–34
Roger, Frère 36–37
Rogers, Carl 211
role-bound interaction 360
Ronningstam, Elsa 101
Rossano, F. 319
Rothko, Mark 80

Sacks, Harvey 224, 229, 254, 275, 277, 334–336, 362
Sampson, H. 163
Sanchez, B. 254
Sandler, J. 190
Sartre, Jean-Paul 8–9, 12
Scelsi, Giacinto 76–77
scenic presentation 190
Scheflen, A. E. 56n2
Schegloff, E. A. 255, 275, 277
Schelling, Friedrich Wilhelm 9
Schlotheuber, R. E. 244
Schoenberg, Arnold 68
Schulhoff, Ervin 62–63
Schütz, Alfred 353
Schütz, Roger 35, 37
Scott, Raymond 62
searching silence 107
Sechaud, Evelyne 187
selective silence 109
self-esteem 109
selfhood 17, 23n9, 23n10
self-interruptions 258, 277, 286, 291, 344–345
self psychology 139n3
self-reflection 102, 150, 158, 168
self-repairs: in CEMPP project transcriptions 254–258, 261–263, 267; cognitive complexity and 346;

communicative discomfort and 46; competitive overlapping and 49; self-initiated 254, 267; self-listeners and 358
self states 14, 17, 23n8
Selting, M. 339–340, 351, 362
Severn, Elizabeth 149
Seybert, C. 245
Shakespeare, William 11, 46
shame 15, 109–110
Sharpe, E. F. 134–135
Shen, Patrick 4
Shoah 12
Shostakovich, Dmitrii xxiii
sieve theory 73
Sifianou, M. 107
silence: absence and 88; as benign regression 157, 160–162, 165; blank 138; as collaborator 90; communicative function of 110; containing function of 107; contemplative 135–136; cross-cultural meanings of 106–109, 118; defensive 130–131; defining 41, 63–64, 87, 307; effectiveness of actions and 43; embodied practices of 312; enactive 132–134; importance of xxi; interpersonal negotiation and 157, 162; interpreting 307–308; linguistic approach to 4, 41–53; movement and 64; in music xxiii, 4; mysticism and xxiii; narcissistic function of 109–110; phenomenological approaches to 3, 7–12, 22; protection of inner space and 106, 111; psychoanalysis and 42, 101–102, 105–106, 109–111; regenerative 137; as resistance 102, 109–111, 142–154, 157–158, 168, 252; ritual/taboo-motivated silence 44; self-reflection and 102; structural 128–129; symbolic 134–135; as transitional object 176–177;

unmentalised 129–130; words and 89; *see also* musical silences; patient silence; psychoanalyst silence; religious/spiritual silence
Silence (Endo) 37
silence as complicity 15–20
silence of the mind 88
silence of the mouth 88
silence of the will 88
silencing: affective stance and 362–363; attachment trauma and 102, 199–200, 202–203, 209; childhood trauma and 200–203, 209; as communicative violence 54; conspiracy of 102–103; of creativity 210–211; interactive 361; latent forms of 53; linguistic approach to 41; mental disorders and 198, 201–203; as non-delivery 362–363; open forms of 53; power relations and 53; in psychoanalysis 42, 54, 56, 103, 207–210; in psychoanalytic institutions 210–211; social trauma and 203–207; systematic war rape and 206–207; trauma and 211–212
silent holding 177–178
silent integration 178
Silent Music (Scott) 62
Silva, Ann-Louise 211
Simons, Jonathan 95–96
Sixth Congress of Aesthetics 82
Sketch of a New Aesthetic of Music (Busoni) 65
social interactions: affect in 351; central activities and 310, 314; finding the right words in 275; lapses in 275–276, 312–315, *315*, 316–317, *317*, 318–319, *319*, 320–324, *324*, 325–326; pauses in 275; rules of conversational sequence in 277; silence in 275, 307–308; transition-relevant place (TRP) and 275–276; *see also* conversations

social trauma: defining 203; silencing and 203–207; systematic war rape and 206–207; transgenerational transmission of 205–206, 213n8; *see also* trauma
Socrates 94
speakers 349
speech: articulated (*exophasia*) 43, 94; attention to continuous 88; awkward silence in 88; Buddhism and 'right' 31; conversation analysis and 223; discharge of affect and 145; finding the right words in 275; inner 94; inner (*endophasia*) 43, 94; non-dialogical situations (NDS) and 42; obfuscation and 12; pauses in 87; planning for 258, 260; presence/absence and 41; progressional overlap and 50; religious silence and 33, 38; self-repairs and 254, 261; sequence of 225; silence as abstention of 9, 41, 45, 69; silencing and 53
Spence, D. P. 223
Sprachnot 54
stance 351–352, 362
Stern, Daniel 359
Stern, Donnel 150
Stevanovic, M. 343, 351
Stevenson, Bryan 21
Stockhausen, Karlheinz 64
structural silence 128–129
Studies on Hysteria (Freud) 223
sublime 80
Sublime Is Now, The (Newman) 80
Suite Bergamasque (Debussy) 69
Susan (case study): childhood/adult history and 112–114; cocoon transference and 114; exploratory strategy and 119–123; family functions of silence 112–113; identifying feelings and 123–124; long-term treatment and 114–115; narcissism and 113, 116; silence phase 115–118, 123–125; suicidal ideations 115–116; suicide attempt by 114; transference-countertransference and 116–119, 122–124
Suzuki, Daisetz Teitaro 82–83
Swedenborg, Emanuel 68
symbolic silence 134–135
symbolism 71–72, 84, 348
Symphonie Monotone-Silence (Klein) 66
systematic war rape 206–207

talking cure xxiv, 14, 101, 108, 142, 208, 275
Tao Te Ching 26
Target, M. 129
technical rationality 10
technology 91, 95
Teresa of Avila 33
terminal overlaps 50
Theater of Eternal Music, The 77
Therapeutic Cycle Model 246
therapeutic transitions 110
Thoreau, Henry David 90
thought processes: co-construction and 284; embodied 291–292; joint evaluation of 278, 292; lapses and 86, 278, 281, 283–284, 288–289, 291–292; RLRI model and **278**, 281
threatening silences 11, 108
Toffler, Alvin 91
token-as-type format 343, 358
Tomasello, M. 292
Tombeau de Couperin, Le (Ravel) 72
Toop, David 63
torture: admission of 18–19; Bush administration and 16, 19; heroic silence and 7–8; listening to the unspeakable 14; psychoanalyst involvement in 16–17, 19; silence as complicity and 15–16

transcription 224–226
transcription symbols 225–226
transference-countertransference: affect regulation and 111; analysts and 191; cocoon transference 114; exploratory strategy and 119–123; negative transference and 190–191; silence and 111, 116–120, 124, 139; *see also* countertransference
transformative silence 167
transitional objects 158, 176–177
transitional overlaps 50
transitional space 158
Transition Relevant Points (TRPs) 45, 48–49, 56, 261
trauma: clinical fight against 208–209; intersubjective systems theory and 14; mental disorders and 103, 201–203; multiple self-states and 23n8; overcoming 103; relational psychoanalysis and 14; silencing and 102–103, 198, 200–207, 211–212; systematic war rape and 206–207; transgenerational transmission of 205–206, 213n8; undoing silence in 14–15, 208–209; *see also* childhood trauma; social trauma
trauma recovery case study 243
traumatic silence 11–15
TRPs *see* Transition Relevant Points (TRPs)
true self 128
Tudor, David 81
Turn Construction Units (TCU) 45
Tzu, Chuang 4

Über das Geistige in der Kunst (Kandinsky) 68
Unanswered Question, The (Ives) 65
unconscious communication 162–163, 221–224
understanding 222–223
unmentalised silence 129–130

Van der Heide, C. 138
Varieties of Religious Experience (James) 83
Vatanen, Anna 228
verbal therapy 55
Verdenhalven, Nia 247
Verdi, Giuseppe 76
Verlaine, Paul 71
Vingt Regards sur l'enfant-Jésus (Messiaen) 71–72
violent silencing 8
Visible and the Invisible (Merleau-Ponty) 22
visual arts 64, 68, 79–80, 89
Voegelin, Salomé 63
Volkan, Vamik 213n8

Ware, K. 33
Warren, Wendy 20
Watts, R. J. 48
Way of the Heart, The (Nouwen) 89
Webern, Anton 67–68
Weinberger, J. L. 109–110
Weiss, J. 163
Weizsäcker, Viktor von 38
Wepfer, R. 233
white gaze 11
Williams, James 95
Winnicott, D. W.: on analyst silence 180; concept of the true self 128, 137, 174; developmental theory and 102, 158–159, 172–180; on mother-infant interactions 172–184; on non-communicating 182; on nonverbal communication 110; on regenerative silence 137; on silence in analysis 177–178, 252; on silence in development 158, 171, 174, 188; on silent integration 178–179; on the silent self 183–184; silent subjective

communication and 183–185; therapeutic breakdowns and 180, 190; on therapeutic silence 159, 185; on transitional objects 158, 176–177; on transitional space 158, 165
Wittgenstein, Ludwig 8, 11, 22
words 89
World Community for Christian Meditation 35
Wurmser, L. 135

Xenakis, Iannis 73–74

York University Depression Project I 243–244, 246
Young, La Monte 77

Zeligs, M. A. 146
Zen Buddhism 82–83
Zifferstein, Bess 224
Zifferstein, Isador 224

Printed in Great Britain
by Amazon